D1713614

ADVANCES IN PSYCHOANALYTIC SOCIOLOGY

ADVANCES IN PSYCHOANALYTIC SOCIOLOGY

by
Jerome Rabow, Ph.D.
Gerald M. Platt, Ph.D.
and
Marion S. Goldman, Ph.D.

Robert E. Krieger Publishing Company
Malabar, Florida
1987

Original edition 1987

Printed and Published by
ROBERT E. KRIEGER PUBLISHING COMPANY, INC.
KRIEGER DRIVE
MALABAR, FL 32950

Printed in the United States of America

Library of Congress Cataloging in Publication Data
Main entry under title:

Psychoanalytic sociology.

   1. Sociology—Addresses, essays, lectures.
   2. Psychoanalysis—Addresses, essays, lec-
tures. I. Rabow, Jerome. II. Platt, Gerald M.
III. Goldman, Marion S.
HM51.P79   1987   301   83-86
ISBN 0-89874-608-6

10 9 8 7 6 5 4 3 2

To our families:

Roslyn Rabow, Lynne Berman, Joshua Rabow, Steven Berman, David Rabow, and Tricia Berman

Lucas and Genevieve Platt

Paul, Michael, and Henry Goldman.

TABLE OF CONTENTS

PREFACE

This book is designed to introduce readers to the ideas and works in an old, but new and emerging field of psychoanalytic sociology. A lengthy tradition exists for this area of sociology, since the foundations of sociology in the works of Durkheim, Simmel, and Weber are laced with references to subjective realities and to nonrational social mechanisms similar to Freud's conception of the unconscious. Indeed, one of the major discoveries of sociology is that rationality in human affairs is limited and only arises under certain selective conditions (Collins, 1982). There has also been a considerable amount of recent and more sophisticated sociological work that is strongly influenced and guided by Freudian theory and is beginning to emerge as a more coherent field. This "new" field of work is emerging as sociologists look to other disciplines to develop better social theory; theory that can describe and analyze social life in all its complexity and multidimensionality. This book represents an effort to delineate the main themes in this developing field. The field is so new and so amorphous that while we cannot presume to offer a detailed map to it, we can provide a compass to chart the main directions of the psychoanalytic and sociological disciplines as they are brought to bear on problems of social structure, process, and change. Specifically, the substantive areas of gender, deviance, collective behavior, science, and society are focused upon in the chapters that follow. These five substantive chapters are preceded by Chapter 1, which introduces the field of psychoanalytic sociology, and Chapter 2, which addresses questions of integration between these disciplines. Chapter 7 summarizes the efforts and progress in the field of psychoanalytic sociology.

Psychoanalytic sociology is defined as the relationship between the existence and character of unconscious mental processes and the organization of conscious social life. This book is designed to introduce readers to the scope and range of this field and to encourage the growth of psychoanalytic sociology as a distinctive arena of research and thought.

We invite comments from our readers and manuscripts from our colleagues so that we may continue to push forward.

Collins, R.
  1982 Sociological Insight: An Introduction to Nonobvious Sociology. New York: Oxford Univ. Press.

ACKNOWLEDGMENTS

A number of students read articles in this book and evaluated them from the perspective of those in the classroom. Their efforts and candor are acknowledged and appreciated. Sheree Carl, Matthew J. Dalton, Ida M. Ipjian, Kelly McFadden, Carlotta Miraflor, Marlene Sakakibara Petronovich, Mickley Siegel, and Katherine Wurtz all participated in this evaluation. Students in Prof. Rabow's fall 1985 class in psychoanalytic sociology, who served as group discussion leaders and who also evaluated the article, included Elizabeth Chandler, Tracy J. Groper, Gayle Jackson, Dine LaVigne, Karen Laukka, Jaime Medvene, and Lynn A. Sappington. Loretta Amaro, Yvone Sohn and Simon Kuo helped Professor Rabow meet final proofing deadlines. Steve Cleamons, Neal Donovan, and Andrea Feldman read an earlier version of the text and were valuable critics. Roxanne Copeland and Leah Mintz did an outstanding job with the final editing and reading. The subject and author index were facilitated by the work of Leah Mintz, Susan Moriarty, Lynn A. Sappington, and Yvonne Sohn.

The support of the Center for the Study of Women in Society at the University of Oregon is also gratefully acknowledged. The Center provided funds to facilitate communication among the editors and authors through long distance telephone and travel grants.

The Word Processing Center at the University of California, Los Angeles, under Jane Bitar, labored dilligently and responsibly. Special efforts by Betty Baker, Margaret Brownlie, and Peggy Johnson are gratefully appreciated. Typing by the U.C.L.A. Sociology Department, under Ceil Mirsky, also contributed to the completion of this text.

I
AN INTRODUCTION TO THE FIELD OF PSYCHOANALYTIC SOCIOLOGY

Introduction

In this first chapter, written by Professor Jerome Rabow, some of the fundamental assumptions in psychoanalysis are defined, and two different models of psychoanalytic theory are presented. A brief biography of Freud is then offered along with some of his major concepts. After the biography, a more developed view of psychoanalysis is presented by developing and elaborating three basic principles of psychoanalysis. Finally, to round out the section under psychoanalysis, comments on the Freudian movement, Freud the person, and psychoanalytic therapy are presented. After stating some assumptions of sociology, Professor Rabow shows how psychoanalysis and sociology may be integrated. First he explores the concept of identification. Then he argues that the language and concepts that Freud used made Freud unacceptable to sociologists. By focusing on a "later" Freud and by "rewriting" Freud, Professor Rabow argues for an integrative approach. Such an approach arises from the current problems within sociology and is thus a "cure" for these problems.

The Field of Psychoanalytic Sociology

JEROME RABOW

THE FIELD OF PSYCHOANALYSIS: AN INTRODUCTION

In 1923 Sigmund Freud published two encyclopedic articles in which he summarized the cornerstones of psychoanalytic theory. He wrote:

> The assumption that there are unconscious mental processes, the recognition of the theory of resistance and repression, the appreciation of the importance of sexuality and of the Oedipus complex—these constitute the principal subject-matter of psychoanalysis and the foundation of its theory. No one who cannot accept them all should count himself a psycho-analyst (Freud, 1923, 247).

While this quotation from Freud captures or distills the essence of psychoanalytic theory and thought, enough interpretations and modifications in psychoanalytic theory have been made so that various paradigms or models exist within psychoanalysis. I shall discuss what I believe to be the two major schools or models in Freudian or psychoanalytic theory.

On one hand, there are those social scientists and psychoanalysts who recognize the significance of the unconscious with its implication that the search for meaning is the *major* task of a psychoanalytically oriented social science. For these adherents, meanings—revealed in the psychology of persons who dream, make mistakes, have symptoms, perform slips of the tongue, of hearing, and of seeing—can be determined mainly by the unconscious aspects that accompany such behavior. We call this Freud's *psychological* model.

Another model or paradigm of Freudian and psychoanalytic thought talks of energies, forces, cathexes, systems, and layers and stresses mechanical and physical analogues when explicating human behavior. Adherents believe that such forces may ultimately be found in our biological or neurological systems: cell endings, nerve centers, and the like. This orientation—often called Lamarckian, metapsychology, or reductionist—still has some influence in modern psychoanalytic theory, and we call this Freud's *neurophysiological* model. While Freud argued for both a biological and a psychological model, it is my belief that at the end of his career he took his biology less seriously than his psychology. His theories, which were continually being revised, moved away from their roots in neurology and physiology toward psychology. It is the *psychological model*, the belief in the significance of meaning in human endeavor, that we emphasize in this text.[1] What is this psychological model? A number of efforts summarize and distill the corpus of concepts from Freud's psychological model, and these shall be reviewed.

In what is considered a classical rendition of psychoanalysis, *An Elementary Text Book of Psychoanalysis*, Charles Brenner, an M.D. and a psychoanalyst, states what he calls the two fundamental hypotheses of psychoanalysis. Noting that psychoanalytic theory is part of general psychology and is concerned with *normal* and *pathological* mental functioning, Brenner asserts:

Two such fundamental hypotheses which have been abundantly confirmed are the principle of psychic determinism or causality and the proposition that consciousness is an exceptional rather than a regular attribute of psychic processes (Brenner, 1974, 2).

The careful reader may note that three words, *hypothesis*, *principle*, and *proposition*, are being used to describe what are not, in fact, hypotheses but are really in Brenner's view, and in ours, scientific *laws* of the mind.

Psychic determinism specifies that all our minded processes, unuttered thoughts, fantasies, and wishes as well as our verbalized, conscious, and rational expressions are all connected to and interdependent with each other. These connections are not random or chance occurrences. The connections are causal. All activities of the mind thus have *logical* connections. No accidents exist. Nothing "just happens." No one "just wonders." No slips of the tongue are "just slips." Verbal and nonverbal thoughts and affects influence each other and are causally related to each other. Whether such causes are immediately recognizable to us or to those with whom we interact is another question. Psychoanalysis, in practice and theory, proceeds with this law of psychic determinism in mind. Freud demonstrated in his analysis of dreams how each image in the dream and the dream as a whole were related and caused by *both* daily events *and* the prior history of persons. Here is a contemporary illustration from the experience of the authors. A close friend announced to her husband that she had finally decided to enter psychoanalysis. The husband, a doctor himself, and a believer in psychoanalysis, became immediately enthusiastic about his wife's decision. Right after they completed their discussion about the costs, the time involved, and the need to do some financial juggling, the husband got up from his chair and walked to his study. As he left the room, he started whistling a tune. The lyrics resonated in the wife's mind. "Tonight you're mine completely, but will you love me tomorrow?" That tune could not be explained as an old favorite song (it was not a favorite) or as recent exposure (he had not recently heard it). The unexpressed feeling was one of fear of losing his wife. This was confirmed later by the wife who raised the incident with her husband. The example also brings us to the second law proposed by Brenner: the existence and significance of the unconscious in our mental functioning. Unconscious processes are not directly observable. They are, thus, not comparable to viruses, sound waves, or microbes. While unconscious processes must be inferred, they have real impact on every aspect of our lives. How can I dispose you to believe this? Although we can occasionally infer such processes in ourselves and others, more often our deeper unconscious thoughts and unconscious determinants of behavior can be determined best through the techniques invented by Freud. How can I move you, with your training in science, objectivity, and positivism to believe that the unconscious is real? For the moment, let me describe how Freud convinced others.

Just as the telescope allowed us to make progress in astronomy and as the modern computer allows us to make progress in logic, math, and science, Freud's development of techniques in psychoanalysis allowed him first to see, understand, and then establish the significance of the unconscious in mental life and the importance of sexuality and repression in human development. The idea of an unconscious certainly predated Freud. He did not invent or discover the idea. It was Freud's *methodology* that helped contribute to an intellectual revolution as well as the *prominence* that the unconscious played in his theories and the massive *evidence* he presented in favor of the idea of an unconscious. What was this method? Freud had patients "talk" about whatever came to mind! No matter how bizzare, silly, or seemingly trivial, patients were encouraged to *talk* to the doctor. This method, known as free association, requires the patient to show the way. The method throws the burden upon patients to remember. While seemingly simple, the suggestion was quite radical, for it took some power away from Viennese doctors, who were often eager to prescribe electric shock, hydrotherapy, rest cures, exercise, and exhortation for their patients. Now a doctor was being asked to wait patiently and to *trust* the patients to provide the clues and answers to their problems. The patient is unaware of what is being repressed. Yet, it is only the patient who can lead the therapist to the hidden meanings. But *both* patient and doctor must search. In a very real sense, Freud's method contributed to a democratization of the doctor-patient relationship, a fact of some significance both for medical history and the medical model of disease. Such an effort might even be considered a forerunner in current developments to involve patients in their own cures, even with diseases such as cancer. Freud's methodology helped establish the validity and power of the unconscious in social life and brought a "person" into the medical office, not a patient. But to appreciate more fully the revolutionary aspects of the methodology that Freud developed and show how the unconscious was discovered, a brief biographical background of Freud is necessary.

FREUD'S BACKGROUND

Freud was born in 1851 in Freiburg, Moravia, which is today in Czechoslovakia but was then part of the Austro-Hungarian Empire. His father was a successful merchant, and Freud was the first child and the favorite of his mother. When he was four, his family moved to Vienna, which was Roman Catholic and anti-Semitic. Vienna was a cultural and philosophical center, but the empire was in deep economic trouble. Indeed, Adolph Hitler was one of the many starving in the Vienna of 1902-12. Despite his Jewish ancestry and his training in the Talmud in Hebrew School, Freud was an atheist. The study of medicine for a nonreligious Jew was Freud's way to pursue his interest in basic science. While in medical school at the University of Vienna, Freud studied with Ernst Brucke, an eminent physiologist and the founder of "mechanism," which stressed the experimental methods of chemistry and physics. Freud was very interested in a research career connected with academia, and he trained as a research physiologist and neuroanatomist. When he could not gain an appointment due to anti-Semitic practices in the university, he became discouraged. Because his research and scientific career could barely support his family, and under the advice of Brucke, whose laboratory Freud had worked in, he moved toward private practice with its promise of greater financial reward. Besides, his father's finances were destroyed by the economic crash of 1873, and Freud had fallen in love and wanted to marry.

He had already distinguished himself as someone of considerable research promise in the field of neurophysiology with work on nerve cells and studies in the uses of cocaine.[2] Yet Freud felt it necessary to further prepare himself to deal with nervous diseases. He spent a winter in Paris in 1885 studying with Charcot, who was using hypnosis for the treatment of nervous diseases, particularly hysteria. Hysteria was thought to be "imaginings" caused by physiological conditions, especially irritations of the female sexual organs. Charcot was breaking new ground in trying to explore not the physiological causes but the possible *psychological* causes of hysteria. Freud noticed, for example, that a "hysterical" paralysis of the arm ended precisely and abruptly, whereas a genuine or physiologically induced paralysis faded gently and gradually. When Freud returned to Vienna, he made presentations to the medical community in which he advocated hypnosis as a way to get at the roots and causes of hysteria. He argued that the *experiences* of his patients were causal factors. He was not well received. A paper read to the Vienna Medical Society in 1896, in which he said that he found hysteria in a male (remember, at that time it was only considered a woman's disease) and that he could produce hysterical "symptoms" by suggestion, did not convince his medical and scientific colleagues in Vienna. The suggestion that hysteria was caused by *ideas* or *feelings*, and hence was psychological in origin, received a very hostile reception from his physiologically oriented medical colleagues who believed in a different paradigm. Although Freud withdrew into his private practice, he remained undaunted in pursuit of his ideas.

One local Viennese physician who was receptive to Freud's new ideas was Josef Breuer, who himself had used hypnosis in the treatment of hysteria, an idea that Charcot had rejected. Freud had met Breuer prior to his study in Paris with Charcot. Upon Freud's return to Vienna, he turned to Breuer to begin exploring a particular case that involved a young women who had developed paralysis while nursing her aging father. Breuer noted that the woman's symptoms—coughing, squinting, paralysis of the arm and neck—lessened after she *talked* about her emotions. Moreover, under hypnosis the woman remembered and associated experiences with her father, experiences that were connected to the paralysis and her other symptoms. The technique of Breuer was to have Anna, the patient, trace the symptom to its first occasion. The symptoms stopped after the recall. Anna seemed cured by Breuer's cathartic method. But one night a new symptom appeared. Anna was convinced that she was pregnant and was carrying Breuer's child. Despite Breuer's knowledge of hallucinations, he was shocked by this new symptom, and he left Vienna the next day, apparently in fear.

In retrospect, this case was the key to "invention" of the psychoanalytic model of treatment. Freud felt that Anna's falling in love with Breuer should not have frightened Breuer but should have been seen as another symptom—a substitute for what was unknown or *unconscious* to Anna.[3] Freud split with Breuer over this idea and began to press forward. *As he used hypnosis to get patients to talk, their troubles diminished.* As time wore on, Freud grew dissatisfied with the use of hypnosis. He was particularly upset about "demanding" that the patient talk, and he did not enjoy the dependence on the physician that the technique required. Over time, through error and stumbling, Freud discovered that if he continued to encourage patients to relax and report whatever ideas, thoughts, and feelings were in their heads, no matter how silly, bizarre, frightening, or unflattering, *what would be expressed by the patient could be linked to their symptoms or problems.* This method, known as free association, is the cornerstone of the psychoanalytic method. It was also the basis for his theories of human development, human sexuality, and civilization, itself. So Freud adapted Breuer's cathartic method to his own technique of free association, and the term "psychoanalysis" was used in 1896 for the first time.

Modern sources for validating the significance of the unconscious in our daily lives can be derived from hypnosis, by analyzing the content of dreams, and by the study of parapraxes. Now even solid experimental evidence exists for these phenomena (Masling, 1983).

In 1896, Freud's father died, and he began writing the two-volume work, *The Interpretation of Dreams* (1900). Through some self-analysis and the use of his own dreams, this great work marks off a new period of intellectual and psychoanalytic discovery. With the idea that all dreams represent the fulfillment of wishes and that dreams provide the clearest basis and evidence for the unconscious, Freud further examined questions of sexual repression; the nature and consequences of psychosexual stages and their influence on character and personality; and the Oedipal complex, all of which firmly established a psychology of the unconscious. In the next years, he produced *The Psychopathology of Everyday Life* (1901), *Three essays on the Theory of Sexuality* (1905), *Jokes and Their Relation to the Unconscious* (1905), the famous cases of Little Hans—or *Analysis of a Phobia in a Five-Year-Old Boy* (1909), the *Rat Man* or *Notes Upon a Case of Obsessional Neurosis* (1909), and *Totem and Taboo* (1913). He had become an international figure, and in 1910 came to America at Stanley Hall's invitation to lecture at Clark University. He then returned to Austria, where his work continued and his fame spread. Political events, however, were to affect his last years. Fascism threatened most independent thinkers, and Freudian thought would have been especially threatening to totalitarian regimes. Freud stated that we should question *who* we are so we might shed certain restraints and inhibitions; that we should adopt a set of values that supports individual self-examination, freedom, and social responsibility; and that increased acceptance of the self might lead to understanding and acceptance of others. This was, and still is, threatening to many individuals and political regimes. Freud was forced to leave Austria in 1938 when the Nazis took over. For his sisters, it was too late. They were killed in German death camps. Freud emigrated to London, where he died of cancer on September 23, 1939, leaving a legacy for all of us. At minimum, this legacy includes: the idea of the unconscious; the concept of infant sexuality; the role of the family in character formation or imprinting; the logic of dreams and slips; and the ambivalent relationships between civilization and sexuality.

THE FIELD OF PSYCHOANALYSIS: ANOTHER ADVANCED VIEW

Many have tried to summarize the essence of Freud's twenty-four volumes of work. Forty years after Freud wrote his encyclopedic article, Jane Loevinger, focusing on the ideas of psychological and clinical theory, suggested *three* basic principles of psychoanalysis derived from Freud's more general assumptions:

(1) . . . the principle of the *dynamic unconscious* and the effects of behavior alter only its conscious (and preconscious), not its unconscious sources; (2) the *principle of the plasticity of the interpersonal drives*, that sex and aggression are psychically elaborated because they can and must be socialized; (3) the *principle of mastery through reversal of voice*, that one must do what one has suffered. . .account for major aspects of normal development, pathology and therapy according to classical psychoanalytic writings (1966 432-433).

Since these principles are not self explanatory, I shall provide some limited elaboration.

The principle of a *dynamic unconscious* rests on the assumption that both conscious and unconscious ideas influence behavior and that the unconsious mind is at least as important, if not a more important, determinant of behavior than the conscious mind. More notably, the principle of a dynamic unconscious implies that the consequences of behavior, the rewards and punishments that we know can influence our conscious behavior, do not affect the unconscious. Only conscious sources of behavior are influenced by sanctions. Urging and exhorting an anorexic to eat, a recalcitrant child to clean up a room, or a student to study harder, and providing rewards for these behaviors will not always eliminate the behavior, especially if it has unconscious sources. Exhortations and rewards may influence and shape behavior under some conditions, but when the sources and structure of the behavior are unconscious, rational efforts will fail.

Another way of understanding this principle is to illustrate the difference between the unconscious when it is used in only a descriptive sense in contrast to the dynamic manner described above. That people have always forgotten appointments, dates, names, and made slips of the tongue, or are later able to remember and correct their errors, is of no great significance for psychoanalytic theory. That experience exists outside of our conscious awareness is a fact known and appreciated by the Greeks, Shakespeare, and in our day, almost everyone. A dynamic unconscious, however, implies something much more significant. It implies that the powerful forces that shape our mental life (ideas, feelings, dreams, wishes, memories) are *beyond* our daily awareness. These forces are especially revealed to us through our dreams or parapraxes and in mental illness. A dynamic unconscious thus pervades our mental life or "minded activities."

This focus stands in sharp contrast to a behaviorist psychology which would exclude "mind" as a scientific term. Behaviorists see "mind" as a construction invoked by those of us who are not willing to understand behavior. The concept of meaning, a cornerstone of a psychoanalytic enterprise, is alien to the behaviorist approach.

A counterpart to the idea of dynamic unconscious is psychic determinism. Our everyday behavior, as well as our dreams, slips, and forgetting, is determined or can be explained by tracing its origin to unconscious facts. This is not to say that all behavior is *totally* determined by a dynamic unconscious. A dynamic unconscious along with consciousness is implicated in all our mental activities, thoughts, cognitions, perceptions, fantasies, wishes, rationality, and intellectual theorizing. Psychoanalysis turned to the inner life and to meanings when Freud realized that the stories told by his patients about their childhood traumas were not true! Since he had published these reports believing their veracity and tracing adult neurosis to childhood sexual traumas, he was faced with a dilemma. Should he retract his assertion? Had he made an error, as he had done earlier with his research on cocaine, when he had not waited long enough to determine the addicting qualities of cocaine? Should he lie and conceal or should he try to reinterpret the data? Freud chose the latter course.[4]

Freud decided that the false reports of his patients were even more interesting than the truth he originally thought he had uncovered. Freud's discovery that the adult memories of seduction and molestation were fabricated led him to want to know more about his patients' childhood, their imaginations, wishes, longings and fears. The false reports were a clue to the sexual life of children. This again helped transfer the then psychiatric practice of Freud's contemporaries from a search for neurological damages of the body and brain to a focus on the inner experiences, meanings, memories of adults, and the significance of these events in their childhood.

Current research in psychoanalytic sociology has demonstrated how a child's experiences are influenced not merely by the *presence or absence* of an event, its duration or intensity, but by the developmental stage the child was in, the symbolic elaboration performed by the child and adult, and a host of other factors. Contemporary social scientists may no longer assume that a "yes" or "no" response to questions regarding parental discipline or parental absence can be comprehensive, adequate, predictor variables. These variables occur in a context of individual development and family relationships and have conscious and unconscious meanings (Swanson, 1961b). A newborn sibling is quite a different order of event for a younger child of three as compared with an older child of eight. It will not mean the same thing to each child's mental life and later behavior. While this sounds like common sense nowadays, much of *early social science* proceeded without emphasizing the aspects of conscious and unconscious meanings and development stressed by Freud. Thus, early studies of delinquents focused on broken and intact homes without trying to determine the meaning of such events to the participants. Some current work has found that parental absence can be beneficial to children (Rabow, 1985) as well as detrimental.

The second principle, *the plasticity of interpersonal drives*, suggests that sexual and aggressive drives can be satisfied by a *variety of acts* with a variety of *objects* and with a variety of *persons*. A drive for oxygen, or the thirst drive, cannot be greatly delayed and does not permit wide substitution—sex and aggression *do* permit such substitutes. While one can eat or drink alone, sex and aggression are *interpersonal*—they require and demand socialization. The *plasticity of these drives* allows for such socialization. When socialization pressures are in the form of taboos, we usually need to deny those feelings, wishes, and actions. The feelings and actions that are most often unconscious in our culture are the sexual and aggressive feelings. Freud's writings, concerned with dreams, slips, and suppressed wishes, were efforts to show how behavior often has *sexual* and *aggressive* roots that are unknown to the actor, for they are unconscious.

The third principle, *mastery through reversal of voice*, states that experience is mastered by repeating in an active manner what one has previously experienced in a passive manner. What alter has done to ego, ego must then do to alter. One need not do exactly to others what has been done, nor need the other be the same person. Substitutions of people, animals, or animate and inanimate objects are possible, especially in childhood. We all begin life in a relatively helpless and passive position. We all suffer from this original helplessness, and each new experience to be mastered must involve a transformation of our passivity, our suffering due to loss or pain. A visit to a doctor who pokes and injects us is mastered when we subjugate friends, dolls, toys, and the like. These are substitutes for the indignities we suffered. Freud describes how a child of one and one-half continually threw away his toys under his bed and made a great to-do about looking for and finding them. The child would repeat this act over and over. It was a game that the child had invented himself. The only use of his toys was to play this game of "gone."

In throwing away his toys playing gone with them, the child mastered by repeating in an active part what he had experienced passively when his mother left him periodically (Freud, 1920, 16-17).

Freud saw in this simple repetitive act a cultural achievement of mankind . . . namely, instinctual renunciation. The child does not protest violently or too vehemently. He has sublimated his frustration, anger, loss, rage, hurt, and pain into a harmless repetitive act. This single act of a child is repeated by all of us . . . with an important consequence. Since we are restrained in our effort to become actively aggressive, and since efforts to communicate anger are frightening in their real or fantasized implications, and since many of these experiences occur before we have developed language and can even express ourselves, let alone understand—we, as children, often take such revenge on ourselves. *We turn anger inward.* We produce internalized authority. The child recreates, in his mind, the former *external* authority—and there is now obedience to new *internal* authority relationships. Such obedience in later adult life situations may be a way to achieve mastery of a potentially dangerous or frustrating situation, but it also may be the ancient repetition involved with fear of losing love or fear of retaliation. This internalized authority, now called the superego, watches over the ego as the parent, or caretaker, once watched over the child. Through the active repetition of what one has passively and painfully experienced, one can overcome the reexperiencing of the painful affects and can now successfully cope with reality. Excessive loss and excessive trauma and pain severely damage the person. But appropriate levels can be mastered successfully. This principle, because of its relation to reality, is the core of ego functioning. When we say that someone is functioning neurotically, we imply that the person is out of touch with current reality. Efforts to master current reality are invoking old patterns of dealing with trauma, pain, loss, anguish, or anxiety, and the current responses are inappropriate. They are repetitions of older patterns and are not appropriate to current realities. One then can successfully master current reality by actively repeating in the present what one has passively experienced in the past. The successful mastering of reality depends on the recreation of the passive experience with its affects and meaning and a new conscious awareness of how this older adaptation is not appropriate.

Before I move to a discussion of sociology, I wish to mention some other aspects of Freudian theory. The first concerns the psychoanalytic movement, the second concerns Freud the person, the third concerns psychoanalytic therapy. Finally, I shall address you and your personal disbeliefs and/or curiosity about the unconscious.

THE MOVEMENT

Many adherents and disciples of Freud helped carry the message and teachings of psychoanalysis. Karl Abraham, Alfred Adler, Sandor Ferenczi, Max Eitinjong, Ernest Jones, Carl C. Jung, Otto Rank, Hanns Sachs, and Wilhelm Stekel were its first practitioners and formed the Vienna Psychoanalytic Society, which held its first International Congress in 1908. Freud seemed especially receptive to women and nonmedical persons as colleagues. Though he was an international figure, stature and fame had their costs. Freud struggled and fought with many of his disciples and many friendships ended bitterly. Adler, Jung, and Rank broke with Freud, and although many say that Freud was a tyrant and was dogmatic, his own firm beliefs in the significance of *sexuality* and the *unconscious* were the cornerstones of his theory. He *refused* to budge on those principles. Psychoanalysis as a movement and psychoanalysis as a theory should not be confused.

To survive, the psychoanalytic movement, like any professional group, must seek and gain adherents concerned with the development of new knowledge as well as training, licensing, malpractice issues, and quack representatives. Psychoanalysis has survived much more successfully in Europe than in America. In Europe, it tends to be part of the intellectual discourse of university training. Psychoanalysts are recruited and trained and need not be M.D.'s. Whether it *will* survive in America is problematic. Evidence for continued rejection of nonmedical applicants in America by the psychoanalytic movement can be well documented along with some evidence for increased acceptance of nonmedical people. Interest in drug therapy, radio talk shows, pop psychology, and quick treatment all tend to discredit psychoanalysis and diminish interest in both the theory and the practice. That psychoanalysts have sought to exclude nonmedical persons from psychoanalytic training, and in so doing have excluded literary, artistic, and scientifically trained persons, has undoubtedly also contributed to the decline of the movement's reputation and stature in the United States (Turkle, 1980; Rabow, 1981).

FREUD: THE PERSON

Freud, himself, was probably not as rigid as many of his European and American counterparts and disciples. He genuinely believed that his theories were theories—to be *revised* on the basis of evidence. He genuinely believed that good analysts could be trained regardless of their background and/or disciplinary specialty. He genuinely believed that what he had to say about women and feminity was incomplete. He encouraged and supported women analysts, and many of the early analysts were women. Anna Freud (his daughter), Marie Bonaparte, Helen Deutsch, and Lou Andrews-Salome were just a few.

Because many college students never get to read Freud, they often parrot their instructors, and words like "sexist," "prude," "Victorian," and "elitist" emanate from the mouths of innocents who have not read Freud's work. This book will argue that aspects of Freud's theories can be perceived as useful to radicals and conservatives, feminists and Schafley adherents alike. In the final analysis, Freud was concerned with making the intersubjective situation—the analytic process and dialogue—the subject of scientific inquiry. His break with a natural science methodology was a key step in his own evolution, a break that many social scientists still find difficult to embrace. But Freud would probably agree with an evaluation about his own work, and that of the work of Karl Marx, made by Joel Kovel. "Unable to finally free themselves, they took critique as far as it would go, then turned it over to the future" (Kovel, 1980). In sum, Freud, being a true genius, was a figure greatly moved by the pursuit of truth, and he continually tried to recognize his own limitations and the limitations of his work.

PSYCHOANALYSIS: THE PRACTICE

I recently used *August* (Rossner, 1981) in my psychoanalytic sociology class. It's a novel about a young, sensitive woman who enters college and psychoanalysis at the same time. My students were amazed that psychoanalysis could uncover and understand so much. They were amazed that the daily realities of this young woman's existence—her classes, grades, boyfriends, dates—dimmed and faded into the background as she examined herself. They were amazed how the analyst would not *advise* or make *suggestions*. The notion that silences meant something, that answers were the beginning of new questions, that childhood traumas were given expression in repetitive behaviors and patterns and in the artistic expression of this young woman, were all new revelations to the students as they were exposed to a psychoanalytic exploration of character. On the other hand, to say "you see" is not to prove. Establishing the power, value, and validity of psychoanalysis has remained an elusive, obstinate, and difficult problem for both scientifically oriented positivists and subjectivists. The positivists decry the lack of control groups and belittle the personal testimony. Those who complete psychoanalysis (analysands) testify with different degrees of support and testimony. When outcome issues are reduced to more manageable issues, such as recurrent themes that patients discuss and their diminishing and changing with interpretations (Luborsky, 1978, 1977), psychoanalysis seems to work. But so do other therapies. Indeed I do not wish to suggest that psychoanalyses is a "better" form of treatment. Psychoanalysis produces benefits that are similar to those of other therapies because there are common therapeutic factors in well-conducted therapy. Frank has delineated the components that underlie all approaches. These include (1) a relationship with another person designed to help to arouse emotions; (2) a rationale for suffering and its relief; (3) new information about the person and the world; and (4) experiences that lead to success, mastery, independence, and competence (Frank, 1974). How can psychoanalysis be for everyone? Isn't it expensive? Yes! Doesn't it take a long time? Yes! Is it for rich and poor, black and white? Is it for feminists? Yes. Good psychoanalysis, be it with poor or rich—black, brown, or white—man or woman, can be done. It is not a question of which therapy is better! The answer is to see psychoanalysis as a situation that makes *different demands* on *patient* and *doctor* than other therapies do. The psychoanalytic situation, like all other therapies, is a learning and educational experience in which *reality* and *psychodynamics* are dealt with. In psychoanalysis, however, at least in its ideal, persons and dynamics are the raisons d'être and not issues of reality. Reality problems like poverty can interfere with psychoanalysis when they entail *countertransference* on the part of the psychoanalyst and elicit responses that are not therapeutic. Thus, therapists from a poor background might see a poor patient as a failure because of feelings related to their own struggles. "If I can do it so can you" may get translated into an attitude and an interpretation by the analyst that would not be empathic. Therapists with an upper-class background should avoid romanticizing poverty. When they respond out of guilt because poverty, racism, or sexism was not a part of their own background, this is not therapeutic and presents countertransference problems. These are difficult and troublesome issues. But each person must not be in *awe* of the other. Each person must not devalue the other. Each person must not be afraid to criticize and confront the other. If a patient or therapist starts out in awe or is frightened to confront or criticize, then these conditions must be confronted and comprehended by the therapist and the patient. What this means, in terms of our hypothetical poor patient, is that the questions of mobility, of adaptation to poverty, or of escape from poverty are not therapeutic questions. But psychoanalysis can help clients evaluate alternatives, and the clients can then act in whatever fashion they choose. They may choose to escape, to adapt, or whatever seems appropriate for their life circumstances, but the key word here is (awareness of) choice. The decision is made by the clients. Such a decision should not be influenced by a psychoanalyst. To assume that a psychoanalyst should direct or suggest to patients what they should do is to return to the Vienna that Freud struggled so hard to relegate to the annals of the past, a struggle in which he was only partly successful. The quick "fixes," easy cures, simple remedies—these are still available (Rabow, 1979; Rabow and Manos, 1980) in simplistic "how to" books, call-in talk shows, and with directive therapies. It is the task of a psychoanalyst to help persons become fully responsible for their own choices and decisions. These choices by the patient, or client, are subjected to inspection and psychoanalysis so that the influences of society, parents, teachers, and friends are diminished. One becomes more responsible for one's own life.

Now, for our last problem. How might I convince you of the existence of the unconscious? I can but try out these few exercises, thoughts, or questions on you. Have you ever wondered why you continue to repeat a certain pattern of behavior that you have vowed to stop? Don't you, as you again face your final exams, promise yourself once again to change your study habits? And what about the reoccurring romances? Haven't you said to yourself that you're going to change your pattern of interpersonal relations? Do people you know continue to repeat behavior that they say they want to change? Have you ever realized that someone was repeating a pattern even when talking about changing it? Have you ever been shocked to hear perceptions and evaluations about yourself that are new and incomprehensible to you? If your answer is "yes" to *any* of the questions posed, then you have been in touch with the effects and power of your unconscious. To paraphrase and repeat an old saying: "to be in touch with is not to prove." It is, however, a start. This book is also a start. It is an effort to introduce a psychology of the unconscious to sociology students. It is an effort to move across boundaries and disciplines in order to develop a more comprehensive theory of social behavior. It will introduce you to the importance of the unconscious and irrational in scientific affairs, in studies of gender, deviance, and collective behavior. It is a beginning that could not have occurred without Sigmund Freud.

THE FIELD OF SOCIOLOGY

Identifying basic sociological principles is somewhat more difficult than a comparable effort in psychoanalytic theory. There was no single founder of sociology similar to Freud for psychoanalysis. Early contributors to the discipline often disagreed about such basic issues as whether values, ideas and culture, or economic interests were most important in shaping social organization, and what unit of analysis—individual, collective, or institutional—was most critical to the study of society. We offer no biographies about Durkheim, Weber, Marx, or Simmel, as interesting as each of them would be. The founders all agreed, and modern sociologists concur that social phenomena have structure and functions greater than their mere individual constituents. After this basic agreement, however, there are wide divergences concerning fundamental principles of sociology and levels of theoretical and empirical analysis. The first psychoanalysts could agree that the individual's emotions were *most* important, but sociologists did and do dispute whether the foundations of society were or are ideas or material culture, and whether the basic unit of social order was or is the individual, the primary group, the community, the nation-state, or the world system.

Our delineation of those principles is even more arbitrary than our discussion of fundamental elements of psychoanalytic theory. However, I do not wish the reader to infer that because sociology has diverse sources and many contemporary schools that it is less solid theoretically or that psychoanalysis is more fundamental to our understanding of human behavior. I have assumed that most readers have some sociological background and are less informed about psychoanalysis, and have in this introduction tried to fill an assumed lacuna. To study social organization, we first must make several assumptions about human nature. These are:

1. Individuals are social, i.e., they are not human because of their biological makeup but become human only through interactions with other people. They must learn to be human within the framework of their particular cultures; that is, they become human through socialization. (This is a view now shared by many psychoanalysts and one we elaborated earlier.)

2. Socialization processes have a major effect on individual personality or the sense of self. The particular norms, values, and roles to which an individual is socialized have profound effects on the individual's self-image and ways of being in the world. This view is also implied in the psychosexual stages of Freud and the developmental stages of Erikson.

3. Individuals are capable of symbolization and symbolic communication enabling them to relate to and to take account of each other's thoughts as well as overt behaviors, and thus, to interact on a social as opposed to a purely behavioral level. This is akin to discarding the psychic energy view discussed earlier and reaffirming a psychological level of functioning.

4. Individuals view themselves not as isolated persons but as members of groups. Although the particular groups that individuals see themselves belonging to may depend on age, sex, class, ethnic group, and many other variables, each person will tend to conform to the norms of his particular membership or reference groups (Rabow and Pincus, 1971). This is also an elaboration of the point made regarding the power and significance of particular relationships.

Human nature is embedded in social structure, and sociologists must also be concerned with the characteristics of social organization itself. Social organizations as a whole display the following attributes:

1. Social organization reflects a complex interplay of belief systems and material conditions affecting the day-to-day lives of its members. Material conditions, however, determine to a large extent both social priorities and also individual aspirations and capacities.

2. Any instance of social order involves positions and roles which will in turn give rise to and become infused with at least some distinctive *cultural* elements. The norms, values, beliefs, and other cultural components which emerge from the social order contribute to its maintenance and perpetuation and give meaning to social life. This generic social process may assume many specific forms—from families and friendship groups to urban metropolises, from complex formal bureaucracies to total societies. Wherever we have social organization, these fundamental properties of patterned and recurrent behaviors infused with cultural meaning are the same.

Exploring Some General Integrations Between Psychoanalysis and Sociology

Upon some reflection, the reader may become aware of how these two disciplines often presented as opposing and conflicting can be integrated. Exploring the possibilities and demonstrating the power of integration is the major goal of this book. Indeed, the recognition of the reality of society—its institutions, its social classes, its formal and informal organization, and its values—provides us with the blueprints for understanding the psychological assumptions laid out by psychoanalysis. Since social classes are real and are governed by conflict and oppression, it would follow that the psychology of oppressed and oppressor is formed in those human relationships which have already well-developed and formed psychologies. In a society where class struggle is fairly clear, the *ideologies* of the contestants are not random *beliefs*. Sentiments about luck, laziness, hard work, exploitation, and minimum wage are not distributed randomly. The position of the family in a class and prestige structure is especially important since it is in the family that major beliefs, values, and attitudes are developed. The development and socialization of gender, of deviants; the processes of revolution and change; the myths and fantasies of individuals and collectives are neither random or chance.

THE IMPORTANCE OF IDENTIFICATION

A description of the process of identification may clarify the independent and mutual influences of persons, families, class, culture, and institutions involved in our psychoanalytic sociology.

The discussion of identification as utilized by Freud is intricate, especially as Freud's own thinking changed so much over time. He often used the same terms to refer to different processes. Much of this discussion is influenced by the modern work of social scientists who have tried to study identification and its significance in social life.

At an introductory level, identification involves an emotional tie or feeling with or toward an object. The first object, the parent, is augmented by subsequent ties to siblings, peers, teachers, heroes, books, hobbies, cultural myths, clothes, proverbs, philosophies, and ideologies. Ties to various objects are positive and negative in varying degrees. Freud first used attachment in a sexual sense in his discussion of the Oedipal complex, noting that the first sexual impulses are toward the mother, while the first impulses of hatred and violence are toward the father (Freud, 1900, *Interpretation of Dreams*). This initial sense of identification involving sexual feelings was changed in a later essay, "On Narcissism" (1914). Here Freud described a *pre-sexual* object choice that was based on the needs of dependency, e.g., upon feeding, care, and protection. This object choice, pre-sexual in character, was called anaclitic by Freud. Thinking and feeling the need for food, care, and protection given by a real person, and their possible loss are the basis for anaclitic identification. A second form of identification is based upon fear of the aggressor and identification with the aggressor or simply put, aggressive identification (the phrase coined by Anna Freud). The establishment of object choices or the identification with persons is not just an interpersonal process for Freud but is also an intrapsychic process. The ego and the object(s), (person and other(s)) are represented internally in the individual's conscious and unconscious. These internal representations form the basis for his cognitive and emotional makeup. Internal representations or early object relations (called introjects) are associated with a whole set of affects involving anaclitic and aggressive identifications. The article by Marion Goldman (Chapter 4), for example, argues that particular experiences of prostitutes are linked to an internalized conscious and unconscious vision and model of particular family experiences with fathers and mothers during the Oedipal and pre-Oedipal period and that the exchange of affection or sexual favors for material considerations plays a dynamic role in future adult activities. While there is no simple jump from such childhood experiences to prostitution, Goldman illustrates how economic, cultural, and psychological factors may enter into the prostitutes' and clients' activity.

To return to our general discussion of identification, then, we may ask what happens to our sexual and affectional impulses and our impulses of hatred and violence? These feelings are the precursors of the superego. How so? This occurs when parental criticism and reactions are brought to bear upon such impulses. Intense love and hatred cannot be tolerated, but because of the child's dependency, a special institution in the mind performs the task of seeing that gratification is secured from the superego and the ego ideal. This arises because children, who are preverbal and dependent, cannot develop just and realistic standards. The superego constantly watches the real ego and measures it by the ego ideal. What happens is that both an ego ideal and conscience or superego are developed.

As Freud saw it then, the conscience or superego was the embodiment first of parental criticism, and then of society. In a later essay *Group Psychology and the Analyses of the Ego* (1921), Freud gives us a more precise formulation of identification.

It is easy to state in a formula the distinction between an identification with the father and the choice of the father as an object. In the first case, one's father is what one would like to be, and in the second he is what one would like to have. The distinction, that is, depends upon whether the tie attaches to the subject or the object of the ego. The former is therefore already possible before any sexual object choice has been made. It is much more difficult to give a clear metapsychological representation of the distinction. We can only see that identification endeavors to mold a person's own ego after the fashion of one that has been taken as a "model" (106).

The balance of forces which affect anaclitic and aggressive identification is not equal in Freud's thinking. As time went by, Freud gave more and more weight to the punitive, castrating father in bringing about identification. Indeed, in "The Dissolution of the Oedipus Complex" (1924) and "Some Psychological Consequences of the Anatomical Distinction Between the Sexes" (1925), Freud develops the theory of identification in such a way that the theory is a differential one for boys and girls. Although boys and girls have the opportunity in the Oedipus phase to resolve it by *actively* replacing the father or by *passively* replacing the mother, the fact that the girl recognizes she has already been castrated puts an end to two possibilities. The male child usually elects not to attach to his mother and murder the father because of the threat to his penis.

The male child chooses to save his body and turns away from interest in replacing the father. Thus the Oedipus complex "succumbs to the threat of castration."

But what about girls? Although, as you shall read later in Nancy Chodorow's essay, this theory is no longer accepted, it deserves attention and understanding. This excerpt comes from "Some Psychological Consequences of the Anatomical Distinction Between the Sexes."

In girls the motive for the destruction of the Oedipus complex is lacking. Castration had already had its effect, which was to force the child into the situation of the Oedipus complex. Thus the Oedipus complex escapes the fate which it meets with in boys; . . . I cannot escape the notion (though I hesitate to give it expression) that for women what is ethically normal is different from what is in men. Their superego is never so inexorable, so impersonal, so independent of its emotional origins as we require it to be in men. Character traits which critics of every epoch have up against women-that they show less sense of justice than men, that they are less ready to submit to the great necessities of life, that they are more often influenced in their judgments by feelings of affection and hostility-all these would be amply accounted for by the modification in the formation of their superego which we have already inferred. We must not allow ourselves to be deflected from such conclusions by the denials of feminists, who are anxious to force us to regard the two sexes as completely equal in position and worth; but we shall, of course, willingly agree that the majority of men are also far behind the masculine ideal (1925: 257).

So while Freud is somewhat apologetic about these different developmental outcomes in the superego for boys and girls and men and women, here at least we can put his argument to some empirical tests.

What is the evidence for sex differences in personality? Early work of Terman and Miles (1936) found such differences. Females were found to have compassion and sympathy motivated less by principle than by active sympathy. Modern work by Carole Gilligan further corroborates differing orientations to persons and the world in the two sexes (Gilligan, 1980). Many essays in our text elaborate and explore these differences.

Bronfenbrenner (1960) asked where the feelings of compassion and sympathy in the female come from. He noted that Freud turned to anaclitic identification or the loss of a loved object. Thus the fear of castration (as in the case of men) is not the motive for repression with women. Women do not have fear of castration, they fear the loss of love.

Later work in a learning theory framework by Sears, Maccoby, and Levin (1957) found that "withdrawal of love" was a discipline technique more used with girls than boys, while physical punishment and threats of deprivation of property more often were used with boys. The anaclitic threats were more effective than the aggressive threats for *both* sexes in achieving socialization and eliminating alien aggression from children.

This is confirmed later by Miller and Swanson (1968). In *Inner Conflict and Defense*, they found that boys whose mothers used psychological punishment (appeals to guilt, reasoning, acting hurt) showed greater evidence of guilt (in projective test) than boys who were punished directly through physical means. The latter were aggressive, both in their behavior and in their projective test scores. So, the two major mechanisms of identification are shown to have relevance for *both* boys and girls and affect personality types between and within the sexes. While Sears and his colleagues' and Miller and Swanson's findings are consistent with some aspects of Freud's ideas of identification, they also have extended aspects of Freud's work. The use of defense mechanisms and the linkages of these defenses to types of childrearing practices and to families in different class positions have been hypothesized by Swanson (1961b).

Making Freud Useful for Sociologists

Identification is one of the key Freudian concepts that has been modified in a way that makes it researchable and testable. In a sense, all modern social scientists, if they wish to utilize and develop Freud, have to cope with certain tensions and conflict within Freud's own work. Such conflicts have to do with the varying paradigms, discussed earlier, that Freud utilized and the limitations that existed with respect to the states of knowledge in psychology, anthropology, and sociology at the time he wrote. Scholars develop and extend parts of other scholars' work as new research techniques and new research findings are made public. While much of Freud is considered untestable or outdated, a number of scholars have worked to deepen and extend, as well as modify, Freudian theory. It is, perhaps, necessary to interpret Freud before we utilize him. The two models I described earlier give us a clue to the conflicts, and while his work is conflicting, resolving some of these conflicts can facilitate our appreciation. By understanding the conflicts and tensions within the work itself and resolving them, we can hope to make psychoanalysis more legitimate for future students of sociology.

Freud felt conflict and ambivalence regarding his observations and discoveries on a clinical level. These discoveries showed him, and now us, how feelings of rage, terror, shame, guilt, and sexual desire are implicated in neurotic symptoms. Yet his efforts to conform to a scientific and materialist basis for these discoveries encouraged him to use concepts like *energy, cathexis, stimulation* and *counter-cathexis*, and *discharge*. These ultimately proved too narrow for many of his disciples and for Freud, himself. For example, he discusses, a "quota of affect" and a "sum of excitations," "spread over the memory traces of ideas somewhat as electric charge is spread over the surface of a body." But what do we feel and experience when we have a "quota of affect"? We certainly experience something real, something that influences us. These *affects* and *feelings* often guide us. These need not be confused with "discharge" or "cathexis" and other mechanistic concepts. Schaefer has helped us to see this clearly in his effort to rewrite the language and vocabulary of psychoanalysis. *A New Language for Psychoanalysis* (1976), Schaefer uses "anger" as illustrative of his argument about affects in general. He asks: Is anger anywhere? Where does it go when it is discharged or expressed? What is left in its place? A vacuum? A clear inside? (p. 165). These questions are completely unanswerable, for anger is not the kind of word about which such questions can be asked. Of course, if anger is thought of in terms of the physical concepts of energy and discharge then such questions seem reasonable. But arousal and activity and discharge are not the *affect* of "anger." We have obscured what anger *is* by using Freud's spatial *metaphors*. There is an important difference when I say: "I was angry" or "I behaved angrily." The former emphasizes a concrete state. To say "I was angry" is not to invoke a psychological description. Schaefer argues that we need to give up the "illusion" that anger is a concrete noun. If we refashion our language to say that "people" or "John" or "Mary" act angrily, we are describing *action*. This is a subtle but important difference. Schaefer says this well when he explains what we mean by calling someone an "angry woman. . ."

Her acting angrily may be or may not be done consciously. She may imagine herself to be filled with some quantity of anger. She may try to avoid acting angrily or to avoid being aware that she is so acting, and she may succeed entirely or intermittently. She may act angrily in different ways at different times. She may put on a show of behaving angrily (p. 168).

If this woman behaves in such a way that she feels a sense of adequate revenge or that she can adequately express herself with respect to her grievance, she will see her situation as having improved and will no longer act angrily:

Concurrently her physiological arousal for vigorous action will subside, and she may begin to think of other, perhaps more pleasant matters. She will then be said to be "feeling better." This is nonspatial, nonquantitative, nonsubstantial. . . . Nothing has gotten *into or out of anyone's system except in fantasy*. Objectively there has been no anal event (p. 168).

Schaefer's conceptualization encourages us to *stress* the part of Freud's work that focuses upon his psychology of *meanings*, *affects*, and *relation-*

ships, and to ignore the theoretical apparatus involving mechanistic and physicalistic parts. Although he is not the first to argue for dispensing with the hypothesis of psychic energy he, perhaps more eloquently and forcefully than others, allows us to see the ways in which Freud's work is relevant to the social behavior of concern to sociology.

Helen Lewis likewise argues that if Freud had been totally comfortable with a theory of affects (his psychology), he would have pursued further his most important scientific discovery: the power of "human emotional connectedness." Lewis argues that Freud's formulation of the sexual instinct was fundamentally a social argument. The sexual instincts had more to do with the individual's personal development than with the preservation of the species. But Freud cast it in more intrapersonal and species terms, not in interpersonal and social terms. Lewis recasts it for us when she notes:

the sex drive is the only drive which involves (although it does not always literally require) union with another individual for its consummation" (Lewis, p. 8). Freud's concentration on sex turned out to be more productive than he foresaw for it led to the concept that *psychosocial* and *psychosexual* development are inter-related. "Human personality incorporates 'transforms' significant beloved figures into the self (1980: 8).

The connections that Freud dimly perceived between the psychosexual, psychosocial, and society were limited by his personal history, his intellectual background, and by the state of knowledge in anthropology and sociology a century ago. Systematic observations among nonliterate people were just beginning, and the idea that all societies have cultural rules governing all interactions was not viable in Freud's time. Much of Freud's work, then, on society and its institutions lacks precision and is more often metaphorical than an accurate description of actual processes of mutual influence. Sometimes for Freud social institutions are merely the individual personalities writ large. While he was aware of the social nature of men and woman, he could not complete his only partial vision of the power and significance of "affects," "emotions," and "experiences" upon human behavior. The connection(s) of a person to the social and society is complicated, dynamic, interdependent, and independent. We all develop and exist in relationships. It is this vision that underlies our belief in the value of a psychoanalytic sociology—a level or discourse that recognizes *both* the independent *realities* of a psychology of persons with an emphasis upon the unconscious, and also the reality of social life—rules, relationships, and social institutions. These two levels of re-ality—the reality that the human organism is psychological and the reality that this psychological being is inconceivable outside of society—are the parameters of our psychoanalytic sociology. These two realities cannot and do not operate independently of one another, nor can one be reduced to the essential components of the other. Social phenomena are not merely the unconscious motives of the individual or the species. Nor is the individual the carbon copy of cultural prescriptions or prohibitions. How do these ideas fit into our conception of sociology? I would like now to respecify the principles of psychoanalysis that are utilized in our understanding of the sociological enterprise. These principles guide our understanding of psychoanalysis as Freud understood it but include some significant revisions of Freud based upon modern work in psychology and in sociology. These revisions help push us toward a clearer conception of psychoanalytic sociology.

George S. Klein and Louis Breger's observations schematize basic psychoanalytic principles that draw upon our current knowledge of social life. Breger (1981) elaborates on Klein in the following seven principles, and we have added sociological dimensions to the first of these three principles.

1. The personality (or 'psychic structure') both in normal and pathological development, results from the resolution of conflict. Psychological growth occurs in response to the confrontation of incompatible needs and aims, and developmental crisis. The theory assumes both a dialectical process of change and also, the inevitability—indeed, the necessity—of conflict. Sociologically, we recognize that such conflict may occur between the individual and his family, the family and other institutions, and the individual and institutions. Conflicts may involve *values, needs,* or *resources*.

2. There is a striving for integration—for the resolution of conflicting trends into wholes—and this striving is experienced as the need for a coherent *self*. This principle relates to, but is also quite different from, what is known to many psychoanalysts as 'ego-psychology'. Cultural rules allow for interpretation so that individual and group differences may occur but there are some limits to how different any person may be within a culture.

3 and 4. Experiences of *pleasure*, on one hand, and *anxiety*, on the other, are crucial determinants in the development of the personality and the structuring of motives. Pleasure is associated with states of well-being, desirability, love, and connection; anxiety is associated with estrangement, threat, and conflict. Such experience can occur in a variety of situations and experiences throughout the life cycle and between persons of different cultures, groups, and classes.

5. Developmental crises and conflicts, especially those heavily laden with anxiety, are repressed, disassociated, or split off from the con-

scious self. This is the well-known principle of *repression and the unconscious*: its effects are seen in the many forms of defense, resistance, neurotic character structure, and the like. Sociologically, societies vary in what they emphasize and, thus, in what they repress. Socialiation practices can influence the content and the degree of repression without ever reducing all repression.

6. The integrated ego developes through a process of *active mastery* in which passively endured experiences and traumas are actively repeated and become part of the self, via identification. The process described in 5 and 6 is connected to the second and third principles: experiences imbued with great anxiety lead to repression and disassociative splitting. Experiences imbued with *pleasure* lead to *active mastery*.

7. Conflicts in adult life reactivate earlier prototypes of conflict resolution of both the disassociative and mastery type. This is the principle of *regressive repetition*. Such repetition is a necessary explanation for interpersonal phenomena, object relations, and psychoanalytic transference in its positive and negative forms. Such repetition of the mastery and regressive type is important for understanding interpersonal relations, individual productivity, occupational choices, and the capacity to engage in degrees of love or social interaction (Swanson, 1961b).

When these processes can be studied as persons become *socialized, genderized,* and *ideologized*—that is, as they adapt to the cultural and societal apparatus and as they choose occupational roles and become creators of new knowledge, producing artistic and scientific achievements—we will be able to develop our field in depth with greater precision and understanding. Now we only dimly perceive some of these complexities.

This brief introduction to psychoanalysis, sociology, and its integration sets the stage for the chapters and articles that follow. The text you will be reading contains six more chapters with two or three articles in each chapter. Each of the chapters may be read independently, for we have organized the chapters around major fields of sociology. These include the fields of gender, deviance, collective behavior, and scientific activity, fields where psychoanalytic sociological integrations are being made.

The articles in each of these fields touch upon familiar issues in sociology: culture, socialization, revolution, social change, values, labeling, and analysis of society. All of the writers in this text are struggling with the development of a more adequate and comprehensive theory that integrates a social and psychoanalytic level of analysis. The writers all recognize how our traditional theories in sociology—theories of functionalism, Marxism, conflict theory, exchange theory, and structuralism—have all fallen short and need to be supplemented or replaced by a more comprehensive theory. This integration requires a great deal of each writer. It requires mastery of knowledge in two different fields or disciplines. It requires the ability and desire to maintain the integrity of each discipline (to not reduce one to another). It requires skills of observation, listening, and reading that are rather extraordinary. It also requires us to move away from the commitment to the discipline of sociology toward the study of human activity in its fullness (Stinchcombe, 1984). Yet this subfield promises much. It holds out the promise that many envisioned when the social sciences came to the fore.

This vision is what will help maintain an interest in psychoanalytic sociology. The interest is also driven by the crisis in sociology. What is the vision and what is the crisis about? Let me quote one of our own authors:

The social sciences are undergoing a general crisis. Quantitative and structural sociologies, those found in the various versions of positivism, Marxism, functionalism, cannot provide the understanding of social behavior equal to their original promises. This volume on forms of psychoanalytic sociology is a reflection of this crisis. A group of sociologists is looking to another discipline to find the intellectual stimulation and new lines of thought to revitalize sociology: that is, to develop better social theory.

Underlying all of this is the realization that social life is more complex, more multilayered than we ever thought—if that point needs to be underlined one more time after all that has been said. This group of psychoanalytically oriented sociologists has come to realize that traditional social theories just will not do. Sociology must develop theory adequate to the task of explaining the complexity and the multidimensionality of social life. Such theorizing needs to provide for cultural and institutional influences, for personal development and for conscious, unconscious, rational, nonrational and irrational subjective thought (Goldman, this book).

The development of psychoanalytic sociology is a symptom of the underlying problem in sociology and a clue to its possible and needed improvement. Like other indicators, they may lead us to understand the causes of the problem and to suggest a way to improve our current state of affairs. The cure, in this case, will be a more comprehensive theory that addresses the fullness, richness, and complexity of human activity.

NOTES

1. See Breger (1981) for a deeper analysis of development of this psychological model and its comparison to a positivistic model. See Sulloway (1979) for the most recent effort to argue that Freud's psychological theories had a hidden biological agenda. These differences are not as unresolved as I imply. They still persist.

2. Robert Byck has edited Freud's papers on cocaine indicating

Freud's extensive involvement with this drug. In 1884 he used cocaine for the first time, wrote his first research paper on the drug, and started to treat a friend, Ernst von Pleischl-Marxow, who was a morphine addict, with cocaine. In 1885 Freud backed off from his early position about the harmlessness of cocaine. He moved more rapidly than the Coca-Cola Company, which did not remove cocaine from Coca-Cola until 1903 (see Freud, 1974).

3. This is one of Freud's famous five cases (see "Studies on Hysteria" v.2, S.E., 1893). Anna was to become the famous Bertha Pappenheim, a leading social worker and feminist.

4. Whether, in fact, Freud did lie is a topic of considerable current debate. Janet Malcolm's (1984) penetrating essay on Jeffrey Massons's efforts to indicate that Freud lied and Massons's own work (1984) have raised a number of seemingly unanswerable questions. My own view is that even if Freud had "lied," the evidence for the "reality" of seductions would not refute the evidence for unconscious wishes and desires on behalf of children. This in no way supports the idea that fantasy and reality are equal in kind or consequence.

BIOGRAPHICAL NOTE

Jerome Rabow was born in Brooklyn, N.Y. and grew up in the same borough. He went to Brooklyn College and majored in Sociology and Psychology. After college, he worked with delinquent boys at the High-fields Residential Treatment Center in Hopewell, New Jersey and was the Group Therapist at the Provo Experiment in Deliquency Rehabilitation in Utah. Professor Rabow did graduate work at Columbia University and at the University of Michigan. Professor Rabow teaches at the University of California, Los Angeles, where he offers courses in psychoanalytic sociology, social psychology, and the sociology of education, and war and peace in a nuclear age. Professor Rabow is also a practicing therapist. His research interests in the past few years have been in psychoanalytical sociology, alcohol availability and college students drinking and driving. His published works include three texts, *Vital Problems For American Society, Sociology, Students and Society*, and *Cracks in the Classroom Wall*.

REFERENCES

BREGER, L.
  1981 Freud's Unfinished Journal: Conventional and Critical and Lower Perspectives in Psychoanalytic Theory. London: Routledge and Kegan Paul.
BRENNER, C.
  1974 An Elementary Textbook of Psychoanalysis, Rev. ed. Garden City: Anchor Press.

BRONFENBRENNER, U.
1960 Child Development. New York: Cornell University.
ERIKSON, E. H.
1950 Childhood and Society. New York: W. W. Horton.
FRANK, J. D.
1974 "Therapeutic Components of Psychotherapy." Journal of Nervous and Mental Disorder 159: 325–43.
FREUD, S.
1900 "The Interpretation of Dreams." Vol. 4, S.E. London: Hogarth Press.
1901 "The Psychopathology of Everyday Life." Vol. 6, S.E. London: Hogarth Press.
1905 Three Essays on Theory of Sexuality. Vol. 7, S.E. London: Hogarth Press.
1905 "Jokes and Their Relationship to the Unconscious." Vol. 8, S.E. London: Hogarth Press.
1909 "Analysis of a Phobia in a Five-Year-Old Boy." Vol. 10, S.E. London: Hogarth Press.
1909 "Notes on a Case of Obsessional Neurosis." Vol. 10, S.E. London: Hogarth Press.
1914 "On Narcissism." Vol. 14, S.E. London: Hogarth Press.
1920 "Beyond the Pleasure Principle." Vol. 18, S.E. London: Hogarth Press.
1921 "Group Psychology and the Analysis of the Ego." Vol. 18, S.E. London: Hogarth Press.
1923 Two Encyclopedia Articles. Vol. 13, S.E. London: Hogarth Press.
1924 "The Dissolution of the Oedipus Complex." Vol. 19, S.E. London: Hogarth Press.
1925 "Some Psychological Consequences of the Anatomical Distinction Between the Sexes." Vol. 19, S.E. London: Hogarth Press.
1974 The Cocaine Papers. R. Byck (ed.). New York: New American Library.
FREUD, S., AND BREUER, J.
1893–5 Fraulein Anna O. Vol. 2, S.E. London: Hogarth Press.
GILLIGAN, C.
1982 In a Different Voice. Cambridge: Harvard Press.
HOLT, R. R.
1965 "A Review of Some of Freud's Biological Assumptions and Their Influence on His Theories," pp. 93–124 in N. S. Greenfield and W. C. Lewis (eds.), Psychoanalysis and Current Biological Thought. Madison: University of Wisconsin Press.
KOVEL, J.
1980 "Marx and Freud," pp. 21–26 in M. Albin (ed.), New Directions in Psychohistory. Toronto: Lexington Books.
LEWIS, H. B.
1980 Freud and Modern Psychology. Vol. 1. New York: Plenum.
LOEVINGER, J.
1966 "Three Principles for a Pschoanalytic Psychology." Journal of Abnormal Psychology 71 (6): 432–443
LUBORSKY, L.
1976 "Helping Alliances in Psychotherapy," pp. 92–111 in J. Claghorn (ed.), Successful Psychotherapy. New York: Bruner/Mazel.
1977 "Measuring a Pervasive Psychic Structure in Psychotherapy: The Core Conflictual Relationship Theme," in N. Feedman and S. Grand (eds.), Communication Structures and Psychic Structures. New York: Plenum.
MALCOLM, J.
1984 In the Freud Archives. New York: Knopf.

MASLING, J. (ED.).
1983 Empirical Studies of Psychoanalytic Theories. Vol. 1. Hillside, N. J.: The Analytic Press.
MASSON, J. M.
1984 The Assault on Truth: Freud's Suppression of the Seduction Theory. New York: Farrar, Straus & Giroux.
MILLER, D. R., AND SWANSON, G. E.
1968 Inner Conflict and Defense. New York: Holt.
RABOW, J.
1979 "Psychoanalytic Sociology and Thomas Szasz: Transmogrifier, Traditionalist and Translator." Small Group Behavior 10 (3): 316–322.
1981 "Psychoanalysis and Sociology: A Selective Review." Sociology and Social Research 65 (2): 117–28.
RABOW, J., AND PINCUS, F.
1971 "Social Organization and Risk Taking," p.11 in Risk Taking Behavior. R. E. Carney. Springfield, Ill.: Charles C. Thomas
RABOW, J., AND MANOS, J. J.
1980 "Values in Psychotherapy." Humboldt Journal of Social Relations. 7 (2) Summer/Spring.
RABOW, J., AND LOMAN, S.
1985 "You've Come a Long Way, Daddy: Rethinking the Father-Son Relationship." Unpublished ms.
ROSSNER, J.
1983 August. New York: Warner Books.
SCHAEFER, R.
1976 A New Language for Psychoanalysis. New Haven: Yale University Press
SEARS, R. R.
1957 Patterns of Child Rearing. Evanston: Row, Peterson.
STINCHCOMBE, A.
1984 "The Origins of Sociology as a Discipline." Acta Sociologica (1): 51–61.
SULLOWAY, F. J.
1979 Freud: Biologist of the Mind. New York: Basic Books.
SWANSON, G. E.
1961a "Mead and Freud: Their Relevance for Social Psychology." Sociometry 24: 319–339.
1961b "Determinants of the Individual's Defenses Against Inner Conflict: Review and Reformulation," in J. C. Glidewell (ed.), Parental Attitudes and Child Behavior. Springfield, Ill.: Charles C. Thomas.
TERMAN, L. M., AND MILES, C. C.
1936 Sex and Personality. New York: McGraw-Hill.
TURKLE, S.
1978 Psychoanalytic Politics: Freud's French Revolution. New York: Basic Books.

II
INTEGRATING THE DISCIPLINES

Introduction

Having addressed the virtues of integration, we need now to address some of the problems and issues involved in integrating psychoanalysis and sociology.

The first reading in Chapter 2 highlights and underscores for the reader some of the issues raised in Chapter 1. The article by Waud Kracke, an anthropologist, makes use of Erikson's field work to illustrate the issues and complexities of explaining and understanding the individual and social levels of reality. These different realities must be approached as separate, though connected, and cannot be reduced to each other. Most of us who have traveled and lived in a foreign culture or have had extensive contacts with members of different social classes and cultures have encountered difficulty in comprehending another culture. There are the obvious ethnocentric judgments, such as laziness, after discovering that Italians take a two hour siesta. Within the United States alone, misinterpretations may occur between individuals and groups from various cultural backgrounds. In psychotherapy, a family spent the full hour before beginning to speak about the problem they came into the clinic for. Since it was a Japanese family, their rules of respect for the authority of the therapist precluded them from speaking directly about any problems. Instead, they were showing respect by making small talk about the weather, the room, and other items of seeming insignificance. This practice continued for a few sessions. Given the cultural differences, the therapist would have probably been incorrect to interpret resistance.

Such misjudgments are made even by sophisticated and trained persons. Kracke describes the source of Erikson's error in his work on the Yurok. Professor Kracke also alerts and sensitizes us to errors that sophisticated psychoanalysts, trained in social science, have committed by not recognizing the independent levels of two social realities.

Although Kracke is an anthropologist, his comments are germane for sociologists. First he raises the fundamental question of determining what is true about a society as we try to understand a culture and its individuals. Culture at a social level can not be inferred by individual traits or qualities. Individuals may not be understood by determining the overall values or blueprint for social behavior. All of us who wish to understand others; the analyst, the anthropologist, and the sociologist, need to recognize the simultaneous weaving and interaction of culture and person.

Any participant observation efforts, which are part of our sociological tradition, must be sensitive to sampling problems: (Is what we believe to be true about A, true about others?); interpretation: (can our interpretation of A's behavior be validated by others?); conflicting reports: (whose report is more correct—how do we resolve contradictory evidence?), and going "native." The latter refers to a total acceptance and immersion in a new group to the point of its view and values being absolutely correct.

Kracke's suggestions for achieving a blend of social and individual, of culture and personality, of society and psyche, are not without their problems. As Kracke notes, Erikson's efforts to focus at a midpoint between the individual and the culture has upset psychoanalysts and anthropologists who feel that their own domains are not given enough weight and force in Erikson's work. However, Erikson's description of two American Indian cultures serves, in our opinion, as both an example of the value of integrative work and the problems in doing such work.

The discussion of affects in Chapter 1 highlighted the point that Freud's attention to the analysis of feelings was minor, in part because of his ambivalence and conflict over the two multiple paradigms. Yet feelings and affects are becoming the focus of more modern research (Gordon, 1981; Hochschild, 1983; Scheff, 1983). In the second article Thomas J. Scheff develops a method and analyzes the impact of some major emotions and how they might be better understood. Scheff makes some suggestive notions regarding grief and loss and their impact in human affairs. His work, like Kracke's, integrates levels of analyses but does so not in the role of observer and participant, as Erikson did, but in the role of thinker and modern empirical researcher. His article raises questions about the organization of grief and mourning in our society and the way in which the repression of these emotions occurs at the cost of creativity for the person. We would like to underscore his suggestion that the failure to grieve effectively is a source of many repetitious compulsions—involved in much neurotic behavior. The failure to mourn may result in an inability to commit to a new relationship as well as the compulsive desire to seek out new relationships.

Scheff shows us how a more traditional sociological analysis of role behavior needs to be supplemented by a psychoanalytic level of understanding, which would further illuminate organizational concepts like commitment, or an interactional concept like gender relations, and a personal construct such as creativity.

REFERENCES

GORDON, S. L.
1981 "The Sociology of Sentiments and Emotions," p.p. 562–592 in M. Rosenberg, R.H. Turner, (eds.), Social Psychology: Sociological Perspectives. New York: Basic.
HOCHSCHILD, A.
1983 The Managed Heart: The Commercialization of Human Feeling. Berkeley: University of California Press.
SCHEFF, T. J.
1983 "Toward Integration in the Social Psychology of Emotion." Annual Review of Sociology 9:333–56, California: Annual Reviews.

A Psychoanalyst in the Field: Erikson's Contributions to Anthropology[1]

WAUD H. KRACKE

GOING into a new culture for a long period, one finds oneself alternating between two kinds of experience. At one moment, one feels—after meeting a completely unexpected response in a situation that one thought was familiar—that the people one has come to live among are completely alien, and one despairs of coming to understand them. Yet before long, one may have an experience of meeting of minds, of sympathetic contact, rendering immediate and humanly understandable what had seemed a perplexing way of reacting. One comes to feel that, after all, all human beings share a fundamental ground of experience, and that in the end all people are alike. At successively deeper levels, these alternating experiences are likely to recur throughout one's contact with the culture.

Anthropologists do not often describe such encounters—particularly in their professional writings.[2] Yet this alternation of experiences is perhaps the essence of anthropology (Read, 1965; Bowen, 1954; Briggs, 1970; Caudill, 1961). Every science defines certain experiences as "real data" for its schemata and makes its theories about them; for anthropology, such crucial experiences are those of the person immersed in a culture different from his own, struggling to understand it.

Much theoretical controversy in anthropology implicitly boils down to an emphasis on one or the other of the alternating experiences I have just described. Many anthropologists insist that there is a core way of perceiving the world—one that is shared by those who "belong" to any particular culture—so irreducibly different from the way people of another culture perceive the world that empathy across cultural boundaries is at best tenuous, perhaps impossible. Others hold that behind all differences in the way that people express their emotions or suppress them,

Abstracted from article previously published in Peter Homans, ed. *Childhood and Selfhood: Essays on Tradition, Religion, and Modernity in the Psychology of Erik H. Erikson* Lewisburg: Bucknell University Press 1978

the feelings and reactions that individuals have in one society are ultimately the same as in any society—ultimately human. As Robert Redfield
and Alfonso Villa-Rojas put it in their noted collaborative ethnography
of a Mexican village:

Beneath any culture are the same people one has always known. There are always
the shy and the bold, the excitable and the phlegmatic, the intelligent and the
stupid, the leaders and led (1934:212).

Neither of these positions, of course, is widely held in pure form—at
least, not today. Clifford Geertz[3] offers a sophisticated statement that
leans toward the position of cultural relativism without espousing it. He
argues that culture, in all its variable forms, is an essential part of human
nature and that one can never be sure that one can empathize with
someone of another culture. Melford Spiro (1978), on the other hand,
in a searching and insightful intellectual autobiography, describes how
successive fieldwork experiences gradually convinced him that much he
had thought culturally relative in human nature was in fact universal.
(See Kracke, 1980a).

These issues are of considerable import in Erik Erikson's work. Having
undergone repeated sojourns (some by necessity, others of his own vo-
lition) for substantial periods in unfamiliar cultures, Erikson can claim
considerable experience with the ebb and flow of communicating with
someone of another culture. The issues just referred to—the question
of how and at what level an individual's experience is shaped or determined by his culture, and the closely related one of the degree of empathic communication possible between people of different cultures—
occupy an important place in his writing. My intent here is to appraise
his contribution to the discussion of these issues, in the context of current
anthropological thinking on them.

As a psychoanalyst, Erikson had certain special tools for approaching
these problems. Where personal experiences and communication between individuals are central to the issue, the psychoanalyst's skill and
training in listening to the emotional communications of others, and to
his own feelings, give him something special to contribute. Indeed, most
of the early anthropologists who interested themselves in such problems—Edward Sapir, Clyde Kluckhohn, and many others—turned
particularly to psychoanalytic theory (with varying degrees of understanding) for the tools to glean further insights in this area. Sapir and
Kluckhohn did put their knowledge to good use; but theorizing—especially by those not trained in the special kind of attention appropriate
to evaluating data in ways relevant to the theory—can go only so far.

What is needed are trained psychoanalysts willing to collaborate with anthropologists in gathering data on personalities in other cultures, sharing the experience of coming in contact with an alien culture and the people in it. Sapir closed one of his articles with the plea:

> Perhaps it is not too much to expect that a number of gifted psychiatrists may take up the serious study of exotic and primitive cultures in order to learn to understand more fully than we can out of the resources of our own cultures, the development of ideas and symbols and their relevance for the problem of personality (1932:521).

Erikson was not the first psychoanalyst to interest himself in cultural differences; Abram Kardiner (1963) was already collaborating with anthropologists in developing his strongly relativistic theory of "basic personality," and Geza Roheim (1932) preceded Erikson in exposing himself to field work with primitive cultures. But Erikson undertook the task with appreciation for both the theoretical complexity of each discipline and for the subtle differences between their perspectives on man. He exposed himself not only to the cultures that he wrote about, but also to anthropological ideas, through his friendships with the anthropologists who studied those cultures. Perhaps Erikson, himself something of a wanderer in his youth, had some temperamental affinity with anthropologists, who are of necessity mobile. In any case, as much as any analyst who has retained the basic psychoanalytic framework of Freud, he has shown an understanding of anthropologists' ideas, and of some of the uneasiness anthropologists feel, as Sapir put it, about "the particular ways in which psychoanalysts appreciate anthropologists' data" (1932:514).

Erikson did more than take anthropology seriously; he wove it into the fabric of his thought. Every one of his clinical contributions includes careful consideration of the social context of the case or personal document under discussion; his eye for the mutual relevance of social patterns and individual lives makes each of his case histories a rich social document as well as a clinical one. He is certainly the closest thinker in the field today to Sapir's vision of

> a field of social psychology which is not a whit more social than it is individual and which is, or should be, the mother science from which stem both the abstracted impersonal problems as phrased by the cultural anthropologist and the almost impertinently realistic explorations into behavior which are the province of the psychiatrist (1932:513).

But while this blend of psychoanalysis with social science offers many insights into the interactions between culture and personality, it also presents a danger: in achieving a blend, one risks losing sight of crucial distinctions between the very different points of view of the two disciplines. Anthropology and psychoanalysis focus on two very different levels of human experience, from totally different perspectives. Their propositions, therefore, apply to quite different kinds of phenomena. Psychoanalysis is directed to the innermost subjective experience of the individual, which in oneself is accessible directly through introspective-self-observation, in others less directly through empathic communication (Erikson, 1964a; Kohut, 1959; George and George, 1964:5–14; LeVine, 1973:182–202). Anthropology by contrast, formulates the public symbols by means of whose *shared* meanings we communicate with the fellow members of our society, and those shared ideas and orientations that make it possible for us to interact with others in our society in an organized way. While these two aspects of experience are obviously related, the kinds of propositions made from one perspective may be quite meaningless or misleading if they are applied in the domain of the other.

Many psychoanalysts question whether Erikson has not, by focusing his gaze midway between the experiencing individual and his culture, compromised an essential element of the psychoanalytic view—its profound sensitivity to, and sympathy with, the individual's innermost experiences of himself and the world, which may be very much at odds with what his culture defines as "rational" or "correct" or "moral," and which may always retain some patterns and assumptions characteristic of a child's thought. Anthropologists, on the other hand, accuse Erikson of "psychologizing" culture—treating a culture and its institutionalized ways of thinking as if they were the fantasies of an individual.

The difficulty is compounded by the very fluidity of Erikson's style, rich in metaphor and innuendo, which enhances the readability and literary value of his work—making him one of the more readable contributors to psychoanalytic literature—but not always to the benefit of clarity of communication or precision in his explicit formulations.

Erikson has been aware of these conceptual hazards. He has made a resolute effort to avoid the mistakes of psychoanalysts who preceded him in the endeavor to understand individual psychology in other cultures— Abram Kardiner, Geza Roheim, Theodor Reik (1946), and Freud himself (1913, 1914:75).[4] The extent to which he has managed to steer between the twin dangers of psychologizing culture and of what Dennis Wrong (1961) has called "the oversocialized conception of man" is a measure of his contribution to the field. But inevitably, such an attempt to fuse the insights of psychoanalysis and anthropology must end by diluting both.

In this paper, I shall examine the fresh perspectives and experiences that Erikson brings as a psychoanalyst to the questions of cross-cultural communication and understanding, and of the ways in which an individual participates in his culture. I am not concerned here with Erikson's more popularized ideas—the eight stages of life, for example, and the concept of identity—with which other writers have dealt more than adequately. What interests me are his subtler insights into how an individual's unique, subjective experience articulates with the world of beliefs, values, and modes of expression that he shares with other participants in his culture and that forms the ambience of the individual's experience. Many of these insights adumbrate or anticipate ideas now achieving influence in anthropology about the personal use of cultural forms; yet they have been neglected by other writers, and Erikson himself has not developed many of them, at least explicitly, although some of them continue implicitly to guide his thought. In this paper, I shall set Erikson's thought in the context of current anthropological thinking on these problems (with occasional historical excursions into the field of culture and personality for background), showing how Erikson's ideas relate to current trends of thought—how he contributes to such trends, how he has influenced or presaged them, or where he goes against the grain.

Everything that Erikson has written probably bears to a greater or lesser degree on the problem of this paper. From his impressive output, I will limit myself to commenting on those of his writings that deal directly with his experience in cultures quite different from our European-American milieu: his brief but significant contacts with two American Indian cultures, written up in several reports and articles before being encapsulated in *Childhood and Society* (Erikson, 1939, 1943, 1945, 1946, 1964b); and his visit to India, "in search of Gandhi" (1966, 1969, 1975).[5]

Erikson himself, as I have remarked, has repeatedly undergone the experience of contact with cultures different from his own. Like many European analysts, he suffered politically enforced transplantation from Vienna to the United States in the 1930s. But Erikson went further, and sought out opportunities to expose himself to more radically different cultural contexts, in situations approximating anthropological fieldwork.

To anthropologists today, Erikson's first field experiences seem disappointingly brief—a "part of a summer" with the Sioux, just a few weeks with the Yurok. This brevity must be kept in perspective, however, with the practices of the time: anthropologists may be shocked to learn that Ruth Benedict's and Esther Goldfrank's forceful portraits of Pueblo culture are both based on only a few months of field contact (Sack, 1975). In each of Erikson's visits, he had the advantage of extensive familiarity with the literature on the particular culture, as well as the company of an anthropologist deeply familiar with the culture.

The visit to the Sioux, whom he visited in an official capacity, seems to have gone smoothly. The Yurok, however, presented him with problems of a sort familiar to anthropologists: then at odds with the government over a policy of land ownership, they suspected him of being a government agent, and apparently did not permit him to work in their traditional villages, forcing him to depend almost entirely on interviews with a very few informants for his data on their culture. This had some rather interesting effects, which I will discuss, on his data.

Later in his life, Erikson returned to anthropological interests, and to "fieldwork" of a somewhat different sort, with his visit to India to pursue the life of Gandhi. Now, of course, his focus was not on anthropology as such—that is, it was not on Indian culture, but on one Gujarati—but the work on Gandhi can certainly be seen as the fruit of his lifelong interest in other cultures. A central theme of the book is the relationship of Gandhi the man and the Indian culture in which he was raised, contributing insights that are very much in line with some current thinking in anthropology about the way an individual grows into and uses his culture. Furthermore, one has the impression that Erikson spent considerably more time in India than he did in either American Indian society, and that, while there, he became much more fully absorbed in Indian life and friends.

In his sojourns with the American Indians, brief though they were, Erikson did have an immediate and personal taste of the cultures of which he wrote. At a point of major transition in his life, these experiences certainly had an impact on his intellectual development. Some of the personalities he met among the Sioux, and the situations of culture conflict that he observed there, are vividly described in *Childhood and Society*, while one woman "colleague" whom he met among the Yurok made an impression on him that lasted through his life.

THE SIOUX AND THE YUROK: CHILDHOOD EMOTIONAL PATTERNS AND THE INTEGRATION OF VALUES

When Erikson met Sioux and Yurok—and later Gujarati—Indians, he was less impressed with their total difference from people of Euro-American culture than he was with their common humanity. The differences that struck him were in the realm of values, of conceptualization of the world, and of ways in which people of different cultures express themselves—all, to be sure, aspects of personality, but of a somewhat less fundamental nature than the characteristics Abram Kardiner (1963) attributed to the Comanche (absence of repressions) or to the Alorese (fragmented ego, no superego). With Roheim, Erikson could see the same conflicts in Sioux and Yurok children that psychoanalysis had discovered in Europeans; through the eyes of his anthropological colleagues, he could also see the importance of the world views and values of the cultures, and how these were adapted to their economy and environment. His observations confirmed Roheim's that "there is a correlation between the habitual infancy situation and . . . the dominant ideas of the group," but he distinguished his position sharply from Roheim's, in not being able to "conceive of the second as being 'derived' from the first, nor of primitive societies as being solutions of specific infantile conflicts" (1945:330). Later, he distinguished his position from Kardiner's as well:

In describing conceptual and behavioral configurations in the Yurok and in the Sioux world, we have not attempted to establish their respective "basic personality structures." Rather, we have concentrated on the configurations with which these two tribes try to synthesize their concepts and their ideals in a coherent design for living (1964b:185).

A child analyst like Roheim, Erikson was also interested in childhood and in how the child was introduced to his culture. But, with greater respect for the active, self-determination of the individual, and for the economic and historical forces that shape culture, he posed his questions about the process somewhat differently from Roheim and Kardiner. He asked how the culture's values are successively presented to the child, and how a culture permits and encourages certain forms of childhood expression to continue through to adulthood, while discouraging others that are less compatible with its ideal style.

The Sioux: passing on the values. What interested Erikson as a child analyst about the Sioux and later the Yurok was how their "design for living" was itself inculcated into their children, becoming an integral part of each child's personality, but not necessarily molding the child into a "typical Sioux" or a "basic Yurok." Erikson sees the cultural systems of upbringing much more positively than did either Kardiner or Roheim—not as parents unwittingly (and often sadistically) inflicting on their children the same traumata to which they were subjected, but rather as a set of rules that embody a great deal of developmental wisdom. The child-rearing system builds on the conflicts and concerns that all children go through, using them as a medium for presenting the culture's values to the child. In a very important passage for understanding his approach, Erikson asserts (1964:137–38):

We are not saying here that their treatment in babyhood *causes* a group of adults to have certain traits—as if you turned a few knobs in your child-training system and you fabricated this or that kind of tribal or national character. In fact, we are not discussing traits in the sense of irreversible aspects of character. We are speaking of goals and values and of the energy put at their disposal by child-training systems (1964:137–38).

What a culture "builds into" the personalities of its children are values, attitudes, and cognitive orientations more or less shared by most people in the culture; but these do not constitute all of personality.

This point of view has something in common with Melford Spiro's early "functionalist" formulation (1961), and, insofar as Erikson stresses the importance of economic adaptation as a determinant of world view ("values do not persist unless they work, economically, psychologically, and spiritually") (1964b:138), his formulation is very close to Clyde Kluckhohn's that a custom or belief persists only if it is "adaptive for the society and adjustive for the individual,"[6] satisfying individual emotional and physiological needs as it furthers the survival of the society.

Erikson, as a child therapist, is acutely aware of the interplay between a child's needs and capacities at a particular age and the way in which the culture's values are presented to the child at that age. The parents have a timetable for presenting the child with tasks he is ready for, often (in primitive tribes) the more closely geared to the child's *maturational* readiness because they do not insist on measuring a child's performance against his "years." A particular value is presented to the child in a form appropriate to his level of maturation and is presented through the medium of the particular emotional task facing the child at that point, expressed in parental responses appropriate to that task. Thus, the foundation for the later development of generosity, in a society such as the Sioux that stresses this value, is presented first by indulging an infant's needs at the stage when he is learning to cooperate with his mother to fulfill them, which encourages a later conviction that he will be taken care of when in need, so that he can afford to be generous with what he has. A relaxed attitude toward toilet training further encourages a sense of comfort in parting with valuable things, since young children often think of feces as things of great value—babies or parts of their body.

Erikson does not see these "communications" to the child as causing him to become generous, but simply as laying the groundwork; the value itself must be presented later in a more explicit form, by example and exhortation to share with his siblings. Ideally, these should be presented at a time when the child is capable of perceiving others as separate people who, like himself, like to have things given to them— and when he is inclined to imitate and identify with adult models.[7]

An important difference between Erikson's formulation and earlier ones is the active role he allows the individual, portraying him as choosing and molding his own destiny rather than simply submitting to his culture's design for it. The child actively integrates into his personality the values presented to him in age-appropriate forms, or if he feels unable to do so, he chooses one of the alternatives that his society offers. The child himself, with his needs and potentialities and capabilities, builds his own particular personality out of the materials that his culture provides.[8]

Childhood emotional expression and its cultural regulation: the illusion of archaism. In his work with the Yurok, Erikson turned to a slightly different aspect of the relationship between personality and culture—the culture's expressive style. He undertook to find in the beliefs, values and conventional behavior patterns of the Yurok an indication of their ideal personality type, or their preferred style of emotional expression—something very close to what Gregory Bateson, in an earlier study of the Iatmul of New Guinea, had termed a people's "ethos." (1936).

The task that Erikson chose for his work among the Yurok was subtler than what he was trying to do with the Sioux—and, as we shall see later, more perilous. Instead of merely showing how cultural values are presented to the child, he portrayed the particular kinds of emotional expression permitted by Yurok culture—even prescribed by the culture in certain situations—and the cultural prescriptions for how emotions should be handled. All these he traced back to the culturally shaped situations a Yurok child faces as he grows up; yet he still eschews the notion that culture *molds* the personalities of those who grow up in it, carefully distinguishing his position from Roheim's and Kardiner's. The above quoted disavowal of Kardiner's "basic personality type" is, in fact, taken from Erikson's Yurok discussion in *Childhood and Society*, and his criticism of Roheim's deriving social structure from culturally typical childhood traumata is from an earlier version of the same discussion. He carefully avoids labeling the culture either consisting of a particular personality type or as producing one. Choosing his words carefully, he speaks of cultures trying "to synthesize their concepts and their ideals in a coherent design for living," and asserts:

To accomplish this a primitive culture seems to use childhood in a number of ways: it gives specific meanings to early bodily and interpersonal experience in order to create the right combination of organ modes and the proper emphasis on social modalities; it carefully and systematically channelizes throughout the intricate pattern of its daily life the energies thus provoked and deflected; and it gives consistent supernatural meaning to the infantile anxieties which it has exploited by such provocation. (1964b:85).

Here again, Erikson stresses the active role of the individual, *using* the modes of emotional expression his culture provides him, and using them for his own ends, rather than being passively "subject" to them (in the involuntary sense that a neurotic may be "subject" to attacks of anxiety).

Describing, for example, the "institutionalized helplessness" expected of a Yurok in certain situations, he insists that the ability to dramatize an attitude of helplessness in such situations is not at all the same thing as actual, childish helplessness:

Such an institutionalized attitude neither spreads beyond its defined area nor makes impossible the development to full potency of its opposite: it is probable that the really successful Yurok was the one who could cry most heartbreakingly or bicker most convincingly in some situations and be full of fortitude in others, that is, the Yurok whose ego was strong enough to *synthesize orality* and *"sense"*. (1943:295, repeated with slight variations in 1964b:183).

A culture may encourage the expression of a certain childhood attitude and elaborate it into an expected form of behavior; but this kind of dramatization, even though it may involve a kind of intentional "giving way" to the feeling in question—such as our giving way to anger when we are struck with righteous indignation—can be regulated, more or less limited in expression to the appropriate situation. In an effective, mature member of the society, it will be so.

Such culturally patterned differences in the manner of expressing emotions, and of handling and regulating them, may be one of the greatest sources of initial discomfort for someone visiting another culture. A particularly interesting feature of such differences—and one that is rather neatly illustrated in Erikson's description of certain Yurok emotional expressions on particular occasions—is the frequency with which another culture's emotional expressions strike us, strongly, as *childish*—in the very specific sense of reminding us of a child's behavior. Erikson noted that certain instances of institutionalized Yurok behavior—such as the accepted manner of claiming recompense in an economic transaction—could so impress even as sophisticated an outside observer as Kroeber, who described the comportment of the Yurok in this transaction in such terms as "whining around," "bickering," and offering "excuses as a child might give." Erikson himself, comparing the Yurok's pleading with the supernatural with their "bickering" transactions with each other, was

immediately reminded of the way in which a whining child, now so touchingly helpless in the presence of the mother, uses an instant of her absence to turn on his sibling and to protest that this or that object—anything will do—is his (1943:295, 1945:340).

An earlier generation of psychoanalysts would have seized upon this observation as evidence that, as many of Freud's statements on "primitives" imply (e.g. 1914:75), the "primitive mind" is closer to that of the child (or to neurotic ideation) than to the rational thought of our own society. Erikson, however, knowing from personal experience that adults in a primitive society are quite as rational in terms of their world view as we are in ours, is more circumspect: "Such an institutionalized attitude does not interfere with the individual's efficiency in meeting technological demands." (1964b:183).

Nor is he satisfied, though, with the simplest explanation that what is different strikes one as childish simply because it is different. The way in which Yurok behavior reminds him and Kroeber of "childish" behavior is far too specific: his practiced eye, as a child analyst, picks up a *real* similarity.[9]

What happens, Erikson suggests, is that a particular culture permits certain ways that children everywhere have of expressing their emotions, and certain universal patterns of childhood thought, to be expressed in specified situations, and even elaborates on them. Such culturally elaborated behavior is "neither a [personality] trait nor a neurotic symptom," but

a learned and conditioned ability to dramatize an infantile attitude which the culture chooses to preserve and to put at the disposal of the individual . . . to be used by him and his fellow men in a limited area of existence (1943:295, 1964b:183).

The reason that these kinds of behavior strike us as "childish," then, is because (since they are not permitted or elaborated in our adult life) we see such behavior only in our children, or in neurotics, "bewildered people who find themselves victims of an overgrown and insatiable potentiality without the corresponding homogeneous cultural reality" (1943:296, 1964b:296).

Erikson has a very important point, but where he stops too short, in my opinion, is in limiting it to "primitive" societies. What I think he did not quite fully appreciate, at least at the time that he wrote *Childhood and Society*, is that exactly the same can be said of the way *we* strike people of *other* cultures—including primitive ones. Any ethnographer will tell you that some of our behavior inevitably appears childish to people of the culture he studies. What North Americans regard as being "direct" and "forthright" is often experienced by Brazilians, for example, as childishly and naively blunt, and expressions of anger that we regard as justifiable "righteous indignation" are regarded by Eskimo as embarrassing infantile temper tantrums—as Jean Briggs (1970) so beautifully shows in her personal account of fieldwork with the Eskimo. Every society, including our own, dramatizes some emotions and thought patterns that first appear spontaneously in a child's outbursts or fantasies, and suppresses others that are therefore "childish" when seen in adult emotional displays. But since each society chooses different emotions to dramatize, behavior that is acceptable in one society appears childish to people from another.

Claude Levi-Strauss, in his early opus, *The Elementary Structures of Kinship*, points out an analogous problem—the intercultural distortions of perception by which another culture's thought patterns seem "infantile." He calls this "the illusion of archaism," explaining it as follows: the cognitive "schemata" of adults, he suggests, though varying from culture to culture,

are all derived from a universal resource which is infinitely more rich than that of a particular culture. Every newborn child provides in its embryonic form the sum total of possibilities, but each culture and period of history will retain and develop only a few of them . . .

. . . When we compare primitive and child thought, and see so many resemblances between them, we are victims of a subjective illusion, which doubtless recurs whenever adults of one culture compare their children with adults of another culture. . . The analogies between primitive and child thought are not based on any so-called archaism of primitive thought, but merely on a difference of extension which makes child thought a sort of meeting-place, or point of dispersion, for all possible cultural syntheses. (1969:93–95).

Erikson similarly sees childhood as a "meeting place" for cross-cultural communication. He sees all human experience as fundamentally similar enough to allow considerable empathy from one culture to another—for someone who is able to relax his defenses, and willing to make the effort. One message of *Childhood and Society* is that since any culture's values are built into the personality through childhood experiences that are in a general way common to all humans, empathy and communication with people of other cultures is possible through childhood. Access to one's childhood experiences, and an acceptance and some understanding of children's ways of thought and expression in one's own culture, may give one an added access to empathy with people in other cultures. At the very least, the experiences and problems of children in growing up are universal, and provide a universally interesting topic of conversation:

The interesting thing was that all the childhood problems we had begun to take seriously on the basis of pathological developments in our own culture, the Indians talked about spontaneously and most seriously without any prodding. They referred to our stages as the decisive steps in the making of a good Sioux Indian or a good Yurok Indian (Evans, 1969:62).

Fanny: Distinguishing the Individual from Her Culture

For all these theoretical insights, Erikson's picture of the Yurok in *Childhood and Society* does not come off as well as his study of the Sioux. While his ideas about the Yurok are intriguing, they seem less convincing than his portrayal of Sioux values. His portrait of the "ideal Yurok personality," built up largely of scraps of myths, ritual attitudes, and social institutions described by old informants, along with a rather formal outline of the process of child rearing, seems stereotyped. One has few of those intimate glimpses of individuals, or of apparently trivial but revealing bits of shared behavior, that bring his picture of the Sioux to life.

It is instructive to probe some of the shortcomings of Erikson's treatment of the Yurok, weighing them against the insights I have just discussed; such a balancing reveals some of the dangers inherent in Erikson's otherwise fruitful program of blending an anthropological perspective with a psychoanalytic one.[10]

Erikson was certainly aware of the difference between formally expected behavior and the expressions of personal proclivities in spontaneous acts. In much of his discussion of the Yurok, he carefully draws the distinction. Thus, he comments in the Yurok monograph:

There is rarely available the material which would indicate whether or not traditional traits (such as nostalgia or avarice or retentiveness) are also dominant personal traits in typical individuals. (1943:295).

When he compares Yurok "official behavior" with the obsessive or "anal character" described by Freud and Abraham (Erikson, 1964b:178), he goes on to ask himself: "Am I trying to say the Yurok *is* all of this or that he behaves 'as if'?" (Erikson, 1964b:182–183). He answers himself clearly in favor of the latter alternative.

Yet in his actual analysis of the Yurok style, Erikson at points slips into treating the beliefs, institutions, and ethos of Yurok society as if these *were* personal inclinations or the fantasies of an individual. His thesis that Yurok "retentiveness" is "alimentary" rather than "anal" rests not so much on his observations of personal trends or fantasies of Yurok individuals, or even on observations of Yurok upbringing, as on the myths, rituals, and concepts of the tribe that emphasize bodily fluids, digestive tubes, and the dangers of greediness, and such "oral" attitudes as ritual helplessness before deities. Erikson appears to treat the society as if it were itself a psychological product, derived from a specific infantile conflict—a reduction for which Erikson had earlier taken Roheim to task. Though Erikson takes pains, as I pointed out earlier, to distinguish his position from Kardiner's, it is not easy to see where the analysis itself differs from one Kardiner might have made, or even Roheim. One does not see the nice interplay between the personal and the social that comes across in the Sioux analysis. What led Erikson to court the fallacy of which he was so well aware, characterizing social institutions themelves in terms of ontogenetic development?

One factor, certainly, was the difficulty he encountered in studying the Yurok. As I have mentioned, Erikson was prevented by circumstances from becoming as familiar with the Yurok as with the Sioux. Now, it is a common experience that the less familiar one is with a culture, the more one is apt to personify it—to mistake the culture's style (Sapir, 1927) for the spontaneous self-expression of those who adopt the style.[11] At first, all the individuals seem to blend into one another, and one perceives them as all sharing a particular kind of "personality." Gradually, one learns enough of the culture's expressive symbolism to recognize the meanings conveyed by particular acts and gestures, and to distinguish the personal self-expression of individuals from their formalized role behavior. Only then can one detect the individual personalities expressed through their actions.

Accentuating the effect of the brevity of Erikson's contact with the Yurok was the small number of its exemplars to whom he had access. Erikson's psychological study rested on the few representatives of Yurok culture who presented themselves to him as informants. Their individual personalities would undoubtedly tend strongly to color his picture of the Yurok and to magnify his tendency to personify the society.

One informant, in particular—an obviously imposing woman—does stand out as having struck up a warm and communicative relationship with Erikson: the Yurok lady shaman he calls "F." in the original report, "Fanny" in *Childhood and Society*, with whom he reports having such a delightful time comparing professional notes (Erikson, 1964b:171–175). In Erikson's more comprehensive original report this dramatic and evidently personable old lady is presented in much fuller detail. Her life story and the story of how she became a shaman occupies nearly a fifth of the short monograph (Erikson, 1943).[12]

Fanny made a deep impression on Erikson. In a difficult field situation, she was the one Yurok who opened herself up to him. Other informants seemed to remain opaque to him: "I know little about him," he remarked of the old man who gave him much of his material on myth and the old ways. Fanny presented herself vividly to him and seems to have been an unusual and impressive person. In a paper he wrote fifteen years later on clinical methods (Erikson, 1964a (1964a:55), he describes her approach to her patients, and recalls of their conversation: "We felt like colleagues." One senses that meeting with her was of some personal significance to Erikson.

Fanny's story corresponds strikingly to Erikson's portrait of Yurok personality. It is dominated by an alimentary theme: the dream that ushered in her adolescent symptom, which led her to become a shaman, was of eating secretions that dropped from a woman's basket, and the symptom itself was hysterical vomiting—a common enough symptom, Erikson commented, in adolescent girls. The process of her becoming a shaman, again, involved swallowing and vomiting, and prohibitions on eating and drinking, and the profession itself includes sucking out and swallowing the illness. Erikson comments how well her particular choice of profession suits her emotional conflicts, "lifting her oral desires and aversions to a plane of magical usefulness" (Erikson, 1943:266).

Given the situation, it would be highly understandable that much of what Erikson said about the Yurok might have reflected the one Yurok he knew well and with whom he felt a deep kinship. One may hazard a guess, then, that his sketch of the Yurok may be less a rounded analysis of Yurok culture than it is a kind of psychobiography—or "ethnobiography"—of Fanny.

CULTURE AND INDIVIDUALITY

A culture cannot be portrayed on the basis of a single informant; nor can any single individual be taken as a typical representative of the personaliy of members of a culture. To do so would be to neglect the widely diverse individualities of the different, actively responding people who make up a society. From birth, different individuals respond quite differently even to very similar situations, increasingly so as they respond to later situations in terms of a past each has carved out for himself by his earlier responses. Even if all family environments in a culture were identical, which is never even approximately the case, people growing up in the same culture would come out different from one another simply because of the active, choosing nature of the human being, each person to some degree molding his own experience. Since parents, siblings, and other significant persons with whom a child interacts in growing up have their own individualities, the scope of variation increases. Some people in a culture, to be sure, may show similar patterns of response on the basis of having experienced in the same way a particular situation typical of their culture early in life; yet others may have experienced even that initial situation quite differently, and gone on to develop quite a different adult personality. Certain situations may call forth identical *outward* responses from all members of the culture, as in following certain customary rules of avoidance; but even in such cases, the feelings and personal ideas associated with the outward behavior may differ considerably from person to person, or people may integrate the pattern quite differently into their lives and overall personalities.[13]

Ethnographers, dealing directly with individuals of other cultures, have long been aware of this. Ralph Linton commented more than thirty years ago:

All anthropologists who have come to know the members of non-European societies intimately are in substantial agreement on certain points. These are: (1) Personality norms differ in different societies. (2) The members of any society will always show considerable individual variation in personality. (3) Much of the same range of variation and much the same personality types are to be found in all societies (1945:127–38).

Edward Sapir, the philosopher of early American anthropology, pointed out quite early some of the conceptual dilemmas arising from such variations among individuals in a society. Culture, he points out, consists of beliefs, symbols and their meanings, values, and such, which are shared by a number of individuals. If these "exist" anywhere, they exist only as a part of the experience of the individuals who hold them or believe in them. But if different individuals have quite different experiences, if some are ignorant of the meanings of symbols that are central for the lives of others, or disagree about the meaning or interpretation or implications of a symbol, or about their central values, how can they be said to share the same culture? Quoting a phrase in Dorsey's *Omaha Sociology* that had shocked him as a student—"Two Crows denies this"—Sapir asserted (1938) that every informant's opinion, every disagreement with other informants, was as important a cultural datum as the consensus of all the rest.

Kluckhohn almost alone followed his prescription in full in his book on *Navajo Witchcraft*, documenting every disagreement among his informants; but for the most part anthropologists, including those interested in personality, preferred to ignore variation, or sweep it under the rug. Margaret Mead (1928) described numerous variations in personality among the Samoan adolescent girls she studied, but dissolved their differences into generalizations in her conclusions. In interpreting Rorschach responses taken by the anthropologist Cora DuBois from her informants on the Pacific island of Alor, Emil Oberholzer observed that "the variability [among] Alorese. . . is considerably larger than [among] Europeans" (1961:630), but his conclusion is dismissed by Kardiner as reflecting accidental variations in childhood conditions, and as being, in any case, minor compared to the differences he postulated between the Alorese and any other culture.

Ruth Benedict, a close friend of Sapir's, was another anthropological theorist who took variation of personalities in a culture more seriously. She proposed a rather interesting relationship between the range of variability of personalities in a culture and the culture's ethos, or most valued personality type. In any society, she suggested, personalities range from those who are temperamentally in perfect accord with the ethos (who become the society's leaders and successful people) to those who are temperamentally incompatible with it (who are the "deviants"), with a range of people in between who are flexible and can be molded to the ethos, or at least persuaded to conform to it (Benedict, 1934). But she does not consider the deviants to have any significant place in the society. In the end, then, her formulation simply becomes one more rationale for ignoring personality differences within a culture.

How societies organize differences. Benedict leaves her "deviant" personalities in limbo. Erikson attributes a little more compassion (or at least flexibility) to the social order —at any rate, to the order of the American Indian societies he visited. Each society, he noted, while encouraging its members to conform to certain values, makes allowances for deviation from them—either through flexibility in their application or through providing alternative roles for those "who feel that they are 'different,' and that the prestige possibilities offered do not answer their personal needs" (Erikson, 1964b:150). In discussing Sioux society, for example, he pointed out several alternative roles offered for "those men who do not care to be heroes and those women who do not easily agree to be heroes' mates and helpers" (Erikson, 1964b:150)—roles that, though not free from the "ridicule and horror which the vast majority must maintain in order to suppress in themselves what the deviant represents," at least offer some definite status in society for deviant individuals. The culture's central religious rituals, on the other hand, "permit a few exceptional individuals who feel their culture's particular brand of inner damnation especially deeply . . . to dramatize for all to see the fact that there is a salvation" (Erikson 1964b:149). "Each system, in its own way," he states more generally, "tends to make similar people out of all its members, but each in a specific way also permits exemptions and deductions from the demands with which it thus taxes the individuality of the individual ego" (Erikson 1964b:185), and he concludes with admiration of "the way in which these 'primitive' systems undertook to maintain elastic mastery in a matter where more sophisticated systems often fail" (Erikson, 1964b:153).

Erikson was one of the first, then, to take seriously the question now made more explicit by Anthony Wallace (1970): How does a society organize differences within it—the different personalities of the people that make it up, and the variant beliefs that coexist among them? But the framework that Erikson presented in *Childhood and Society* still bowed to the dominant anthropological assumption of the 1950s: that *differences* are equivalent to *deviance.*

Playing with culture. A second way in which Erikson's approach differs from Benedict's and constitutes an important advance lies in his characterization of the type of individual who will become successful in a given culture. Benedict regards culture as fate: the "configuration" of the culture determines which individuals will be successful, in proportion to the closeness of their temperamental predilections with those favored by the culture. Erikson leaves more room for the initiative of the individual, or for the individual's ability to integrate and direct his native propensities with the culture's expressive patterns. In *Childhood and Society* he comments:

In order to create people who will function effectively as the bulk of the people, as energetic leaders, or as useful deviants, even the most "savage" culture must strive for what we vaguely call a "strong ego" in its majority or at least in its dominant minority—i.e. an individual core firm and flexible enough to reconcile the necessary contradictions in any human organization, [and] to integrate individual differences (Erikson, 1964b:186).

This perspective, emphasizing the way an individual member of the society integrates a value into his ego, brings up the possibility that there may be considerable variation among individuals in the way that they integrate a value into their personalities.

From this, it is not a very long step to the idea that people do not simply conform to norms, or hold certain beliefs, but actively manipulate norms and use their beliefs to gain ends—an idea that has been gaining considerable currency in anthropological studies of local and regional political systems (Turner 1957; Nicholas, 1968; Leach, 1964). As Suzanne and Lloyd Rudolph have put it (in somewhat less Hobbesian language):

Cultural norms are as much an opportunity as a constraint and "compliance" can take so many forms that the word may lose its meaning in certain contexts. . . .
. . . "Playing" the culture, as a harp with diverse strings, is, we assume, as frequent a relation to culture as being molded and programmed by it; the spectrum from compliance to noncompliance to counter-cultural innovation suggest the myriad possible relations of the individual to the culture (Rudolph and Rudolph, 1973).

This perspective is not entirely new. Kroeber, according to Murphy (1971:158), "liked to annoy his colleagues by saying that people 'played' with the systems," and much of Dorothy Eggan's work (1949, 1955), expresses this theme. But it is now becoming a focus of anthropological theory, not a provocative comment.

The perspective is developed more fully, as one might expect, in the psychobiographical studies, such as that of Gandhi (to which, in part, the Rudolphs' remarks refer), where the focus is not on how culture deals with differences among individuals, but rather on how individuals use—and change—their own cultural symbols, beliefs, and norms. In discussing Gandhi's life and the lives of those who influenced his personality development, the emphasis is not on how Indian concepts and norms molded Gandhi's personality, and those of his parents, or guided their acts; it is rather on how Gandhi and those around him embodied Indian norms and ideals in their own particular ways, and how they expressed their own personalities through the medium of Indian ideas, Indian norms, and their particular situation in Indian society of that time.

It is not surprising to see the individual's relationship to his culture in such a perspective in a study focusing on the biography of an individual; so it is difficult to say whether this difference in emphasis represents a change in Erikson's view of society, or simply a shift in his focus from the social to the individual level. Nevertheless, this greater emphasis on the individual's actively expressing his individuality by means of cultural forms, which he can manipulate and not simply conform to, corresponds to a new concept of the relationship between cultural concepts and individual thought and action that is gaining some wide currency in anthropology today. Most strikingly formulated by Edmund Leach (1964) in his ethnography of highland Burma in which he presents Kachin myth and ritual as a kind of language with which to express personal differences (rather than, as anthropologists have traditionally seen it, as a set of symbols expressing social unity), this point of view has been most explicitly developed, and its philosophical foundations and implications (always wittily) pursued, in Robert Murphy's, *The Dialectics of Social Life* (1971)—a landmark book which has still not received its deserved recognition. In this point of view, the contradictions within a cultural system—between thought and act, between social structure and people's concept of it—are all taken as part of the nature of social reality, not to be explained away by a higher unity.

Some comments on identity. The chief concept in which Erikson formulates the active role of the individual in selecting, modifying, and organizing cultural elements as he assimilates them into his personality—

and a concept that one cannot avoid in discussing Erikson's work—is *identity*. It is Erikson's best-known concept, and highlights very important issues, but I do not feel that it is one of Erikson's more felicitous additions to the psychosocial vocabulary.

Certainly the concept of identity has focused attention on the key psychosocial problem that I have highlighted: How does the individual initiative that psychoanalysis stresses—the individual's ability to choose between alternatives and put things together for himself, which is both a postulate of psychoanalytic theory and a goal of its therapy[14]—fit with the anthropological tenet that one's minutest perceptions and the course of one's life are manifestations of inescapable cultural orientations? These apparently contradictory orientations, products of the two major discoveries of this century in the study of man, were bound to come into collision—as they did quite promptly, in the controversy between Malinowski and Ernest Jones[15]. The concept of identity is one attempt to bridge these two orientations.

Perhaps the most important contribution of the concept of identity has been to underline an idea that has been around in the background and that may go some way toward providing a way of reconciling the two viewpoints. One does, as W. E. Hocking puts it, "build" a self (1957:146), though the materials of which one builds it can be only those at hand—the ideas and values of one's culture (in the particular form in which they are presented to one through one's parents), modified by and integrated with one's own particular needs, abilities, and ways of seeing things. As Sapir puts it:

A personality is carved out by the subtle interaction of those systems of ideas which are characteristic of the culture as a whole, as well as of those systems of ideas which get established for the individual through more special types of participation, with the physical and psychological needs of the individual organism, which cannot take over any of the cultural material that is offered in its original form but works it over more or less completely, so that it integrates with those needs (Sapir, 1932:518–19).

But, though this idea was around, it did not receive much attention until it received embodiment in a word.

The concept of identity, then, points to a problem area. It is a whole set of questions, not an answer: *How do* people integrate values and shared symbols into their personalities? How differently can two people integrate a particular value? And so on. The problem is that when such questions are embodied in a word—and particularly a catchy one like "identity"—the word very quickly becomes an answer in itself. Intended to raise questions, it is often used, even by Erikson himself, as an explanation: Gandhi stood up to his caste elders, for the "survival" of his identity (1969:141). Even when it is used to define an area of investigation, a set of questions, "identity" has very wide boundaries: when introduced as an explanatory concept, it leaves at least one reader with more of a sense of blur than of clarification. (Much the same has happened with the word "culture", as Meyer Fortes has observed.[16])

Perhaps Erikson intentionally keeps the concept vague, to prevent it from becoming rigidified, as Coles (1970:82, 166) suggests, and to allow himself a certain impressionistic freedom in his style. Others of his images convey a similar sense of things blurring into one another. It is a theme, particularly in *Gandhi*: "It is always difficult to say where, exactly, obsessive symptomatology ends and creative ritualization begins" (Erikson, 1969:157); and a bit earlier in the book he mentions learning

how difficult it is to differentiate between stubborn and superstitious remnants of an orthodox world image, personal and conscious emphases and omissions, and repressions and denials coming from irrational recesses. The fact is that none of these can be separated, for in any given life they have become intertwined (1969:76).

Nature knows no boundaries, as the impressionists have taught us, and Erikson, an artist as much as he is a scientist, may wish to point this out as a corrective to our perhaps overly analytic, scientific view of man. But if this is the case—and if this is one reason that he keeps concepts like identity purposefully vague—it only adds a twist of irony to turn and use the very same concept as an analytic and explanatory tool!

Certainly, much of what Erikson discusses under the rubric of identity are fascinating points and humanly moving clinical observations. One cannot but be intrigued, for example by his insights in the discussion of "grandfathers" (1946) and recognize in one's own experience the difficulties caused by radical change in the historical situation for an adolescent's identification with his forebears. Yet the concept simply seems to include too much. One fears that Robert Coles (1970:166) is all too correct when he suggests that "identity has to do with everything that Erikson wrote about in *Childhood and Society*"—an awesome range of phenomena!

An additional problem is that the term had a prehistory, or several prehistories. "Identity" had at least one meaning in sociology before Erikson picked it up, and a complex of meanings in psychiatry, and, rather than exclude them from his concept, Erikson seems to have incorporated all of these into it. In social psychology, the term has long referred to those features by which one is identified as a social person—beginning with one's name, address, and social security number, and going on through the cost and style of one's house and the sort of people with whom one associates, and all the other ways by which one is "assigned a specific place in the world."[17] In psychiatry, on the other hand, "identity" has referred (among other things) to that basic sense of being a self—separate from others, the same as one was a moment ago, and in voluntary control over the parts of one's body—whose crucial period of development is in the first year and a half of life, and which an adult can lose, really, only in psychosis or in transient and unusual states of mind.[18] In this sense, it is very close to what is currently much discussed under the term "self-cohesion" (Kohut, 1971). Erikson's definitions seem to encompass all of these meanings; and, in addition, he brings in an idea of "group identity," which ranges from a consensus among a number of individuals that they have enough in common to constitute a group, to what Redfield refers to as a culture's "world view" (1953; Caudill, 1962:177–78). One is still left with the impression expressed by H. C. Rümke after a 1951 conference in which the concept was discussed:

We all felt that this 'concept of identity' was extremely important, but it was not clear what the exact meaning was, so loaded with significance was the new term (1965).

CONCLUSION

Psychoanalysis is, and must be, the most sedentary of all professions. It requires a constancy of perception of self, other, and reality: skeptical though he must be of his own motivations and of the possibility of distorted perceptions on his own part, the psychoanalyst, ever contending with human emotional upheaval, must at bottom retain a profound conviction of the rightness of his own perceptions of reality and of himself. The greatest challenge he faces every day is to remain open and sensitive to another person through all that person's determined efforts to close off communication, and through onslaughts of vituperative attack. The anthropologist, by contrast, is probably the most mobile of academics. He must steel himself emotionally for long periods of being out of contact with his consociates, often undergoing physical hardship and sometimes danger to his life, but, most difficult, of being deprived of his essential bearings—the coordinates provided by his familiar social and cultural postulates about reality and human relationships. One can see many similarities between the demands of psychoanalysis and of ethnography—similarities that perhaps partly account for the constant intercommunication and sense of mutual relevance that has characterized the parallel developments of the two disciplines.[19] Both anthropologists and psychoanalysts must ultimately retain their own cultural commitments, their own sense of who they are, through assaults on their identity by intimate association with quite different ways of experiencing the world. Both must at the same time remain open to the other worlds with which they are confronted, maintaining the attitude of "suspension of disbelief," like that more temporarily required (says Coleridge) of the reader of poetry. Yet the essential difference between the demands on the practitioners of the two professions make it difficult indeed to combine them: the one being required to remain constant and emotionally available to a patient torn by his emotions, the other required to adapt himself to very different ways of living and to accept them, at least for the duration of his fieldwork, as the right way to do things.

It takes an unusual person to combine the sedentary occupation of a psychoanalyst with the mobility—one might say wanderlust—necessary for anthropological fieldwork, and to combine the introspective self-awareness and ability to be tuned into others' emotions one needs in psychotherapeutic work, with the social scientist's awareness of social context. Erikson, from his work, seems to combine these qualities well; perhaps the coexistence of such opposites in his character and intellectual framework contributes to his fondness for paradoxical formulations. He is unquestionably an astute and sensitive clinical observer, and at the same time his awareness of the social context makes his case histories most illuminating studies of the social forces impinging on the subjective lives of individuals. To this he adds a literary gift—not an unimportant asset for someone who has chosen to communicate with such a wide audience as has Erikson, particularly in communicating the flavor of a case history to an audience who has had no direct exposure to the clinical situation, and in presenting individuals of other cultures to people with no experience in those cultures.

In dealing with individual life histories, Erikson is on his home ground as a clinician. It is here—from his sketch of "Fanny," the Yurok shaman, to Gandhi's life—that one finds his richest contributions to anthropological thought on how the individual interlocks with his social context. Here, though, more than in the rest of his anthropological work, one must look not primarily for the theoretical formulations that he makes explicit; those on Gandhi are relatively simple and not very different from those in his earlier analyses of great (or infamous) men and their messages. The richest vein of insights in these works lies in his passing comments, or in descriptions that simply bring out (in painterly fashion) particular facets of the interplay between personal emotions and cultural symbols, or psychological themes in social interactions. This kaleidoscopic variety of psychological comments on social process is refreshing, bringing out the various parts that personal psychology can play in the culturally defined social environment—the interplay between the emotional and ideological meanings of symbols (cf. Turner, 1964: esp. Chap.1; Geertz, 1972), the intricacies of the psychological relationship between a leader and his followers (cf. Kohut, 1976; Kracke, 1978; Redl, 1942; Smelser, 1968), and many other kinds of relationship between personal emotions and culture.

Some of these strengths also have their dangers, as does the task of relating social with intrapsychic reality. At times, I have suggested, Erikson is guilty of applying psychoanalytic formulations where analysis at the cultural level might be more appropriate, and at other times, as many psychoanalysts accuse, of making the social *context* of an individual's action seem as if it were the *determinant* of his behavior. Such weaknesses, I think, are inherent in the effort to interweave or (as many of Erikson's metaphors suggest) blend psychological and social models into a single "psychosocial" framework (as Sapir advocated). I would prefer, with Caudill (1962:176–178, 1973b), to maintain the complementary separateness of social and psychological perspectives (see Kracke, 1979, 1980b).

Each of Erikson's best-known anthropological works begins with observations on problems of communication engendered by cultural differences, drawn directly from his experiences in that culture. His various writings on the Sioux (1939, 1945, 1964b: chap. 3) begin with accounts of a seminar with both white and Sioux participants, in which Erikson offers observations on the ways in which the two groups' beliefs and values distort their perceptions of one another and block communication. Beginning the book on Gandhi, he shows how such culturally induced distortions of perception impeded communication in his interviews with friends of Gandhi. Their perception of him, he pointed out, was influenced not only by transferences from their childhood, but more immediately by a "transference" to him of attitudes that they had toward individuals in analogous roles in their own culture. In at least one situation—with Ambalal Sarabhai—Erikson was able to see that a certain impediment to their communication arose from their different cultural perceptions of the situation: "Once fully understood that Ambalal could take our encounter to be only that of two individuals with allegiances to their respective occupational *dharmas*," Erikson says, "things became easier, and he eventually expressed his full confidence in my work" (1969:76).

Erikson certainly seems to feel that, though culturally different modes of expression and ways of thinking may at first hinder communication,[20] once these differences are perceived, empathic communication is possible, and, indeed, enriching. Being able to understand Sioux patterns of emotional expression (better than a cynical teacher who had concluded from their external reserve that Sioux parents did not love their children), Erikson was able to establish enough rapport with a Sioux father to discuss the man's problems in relation to his children—and was able to recognize the "wordy praise" in the man's laconic comment: "I guess you have told me something" (1964b:120–24).

The very differences of another culture can, once one sees the perspective implicit in them, offer personal rewards for such communication. Mary Catherine Bateson, in a beautiful article on her fieldwork in the Philippines, learned that the Philippine way of dealing with mourning can be more satisfying than the personal isolation to which we in our culture subject the mourner.[21] The readiness with which some people can come not only to understand another culture, but also to adapt to its style of expression and to learn to communicate with its members, suggests that—for them at least—there is no insuperable barrier between different cultures' patterns of thinking and feeling. Thus, Napoleon Chagnon, whose descriptions of Yanomamö bring them to life as live and distinct individuals, knew he had been long enough among the Yanomamö when he found himself having all *too* appropriate Yanomamö responses in situations where these responses could have cost him his life (Chagnon, 1968:14–17, 1974:1–45, 162–197, esp. 194–7).

Chagnon spent an unusually long time, even for an anthropologist, among the people he studied. Yet other anthropologists of equal experience and perceptiveness assert just as firmly that there is an unbridgeable difference between, say, a Balinese individual's way of experiencing the world and our own (Geertz, 1966a). The testimony of these ethnographers certainly is not to be dismissed.[22]

The issue we are talking about is essentially one of human experience and human communication. The observer is an essential part of the phenomenon itself (Devereux, 1967). It may well be that the reality of intercultural communication and sympathy (in the literal sense of sharing feelings) across cultural boundaries, may differ from one person to another. One person may experience a deep communication with individuals of another culture, where another experiences a subtle barrier; one person may be more keenly aware of the common experiences with members of the other culture, another more attuned to aspects of the experiences of members of the other culture intrinsically alien to his own. Or two individuals may have different degrees of personal affinity for the way members of a particular culture experience the world.

The psychoanalyst is not only a person trained in certain empathic skills; he is also apt, if he is good at his trade, to be a certain kind of person—one who values the timid, tender core of another's experience, and is able to communicate an appreciation for those personal experiences of the other. He may be especially apt, therefore, to elicit some of the more hidden human feelings of an individual—perhaps more universal ones. These, if they are universal, would not necessarily be those of greatest interest to the anthropologist looking for the experiences his informant has that are distinctive to members of his culture. The anthropologist is more likely to be a tough romantic, willing to undergo hardships to pursue in distant and difficult terrains some personal quest—perhaps, as Susan Sontag (1966) said of Lévi-Strauss, pursuing his vision of the ideal society he does not find at home. He is not likely to take kindly to the suggestion that what he has gone so far to uncover is a mere replica of his own society, in which people pursue the same, humdrum human problems.

A point that Erikson might add to this discussion—though it is only to be teased out of his writings, never made explicit—is that the experience, or experiences, we share most intimately as human beings, are those of having been a child. Perhaps the people who can most easily find common emotional ground with someone of a very different culture from their own, are those who have access to the whole range of their own childhood experiences.

NOTES

1. This article was largely written while I was a fellow of the Center for Psychosocial Studies in Chicago, Autumn Quarter, 1973. I am indebted to the Center staff for their help and support, and I would like to express appreciation for the opportunity to exchange ideas with the Center staff and fellows: Robert LeVine, George Pollock, Bernard Weissbourd, John and Virginia Demos, Mark Gehrie, and Marvin Zonis. Conversations with all of these persons contributed considerably to my appreciation and understanding of Erikson's work, and of the issues discussed in this article. I also owe special thanks to my wife, Laura Huyssen Kracke, for her patient editorial work.

2. What I am here formulating is poignantly described by Kenneth Read in *The High Valley* (New York: Scribner's, 1965), esp. pp. 73–87. He describes a moment of communication with a Gahuku (New Guinea) headman, Makias, in which he suddenly understood the man's feelings for his pregnant wife, who was in danger of dying—feelings hitherto masked by a callous exterior of Gahuku manliness. Another excellent account of such experiences is Laura Bohannon's fictional account of fieldwork with the Tiv, written under the pseudonym of Elenore Smith Bowen, *Return to Laughter* (New York: Harper & Row, 1954). See also

Jean Briggs, *Never in Anger* (Cambridge, Mass: Harvard University Press, 1970), pp. 225–310; William Caudill, "Some Problems in Transnational Communication (Japan-United States)," in *Applications of Psychiatric Insights to Cross-Cultural Communication,* Symposium no. 7, Group for the Advancement of Psychiatry (1961), pp. 409–21. (See also notes 19 & 20 below.)

 3. Clifford Geertz, "The Impact of the Concept of Culture on the Concept of Man," in *New Views of the Nature of Man,* ed. J. Platt (Chicago: University of Chicago Press, 1966), pp. 93–118. See also idem, *Person, Time, and Conduct in Bali,* Yale University Southeast Asia Studies Cultural Report Series, no. 14 (New Haven, Conn., 1966). Both are reprinted in idem, *The Interpretation of Cultures* (New York: Basic Books, 1973). For another view with a relativistic emphasis, see Robert Levy, *The Tahitians: Mind and Experience in the Society Islands* (Chicago: University of Chicago Press, 1973). A psychiatrist, Levy stresses that "one must understand something about shared or prevalent psychological qualities before one can study and understand variations," but he acknowledges that his "interest in *Tahitian* qualities [produces] a partial portrait," and that his subjects' "common humanity" is the "first basis of our relationships and of my understanding of them" (p. xxiv).

 4. LeVine (1982:48–52, 204–5) gives a sound critique of early psychoanalytic writing on primitive cultures.

 5. For a thoughtful review of *Gandhi's Truth,* see Geertz, 1969.

 6. Clyde Kluckhohn, *Navaho Witchcraft* (Boston: Beacon Press, 1944). Kluckhohn later abandoned this formulation as *too* functionalist, implying a greater degree of harmony among the parts of a society than is usually the case, and a degree of satisfaction provided by a social system for its members that is rarely observed. Idem, "The Limitations of Adaptation and Adjustment as Concepts for Understanding Cultural Behavior," in *Culture and Behavior: The Collected Essays of Clyde Kluckhohn,* ed. Richard Kluckhohn (New York: Free Press of Glencoe, 1964), pp. 254–64.

 7. Erikson conceded, though he did not stress or take fully into account, that the same custom of child rearing may have different effects on different children, depending on the child, the parent, and the circumstances. This point is discussed later.

 8. Meyer Fortes, writing around the same time (1938) about the bringing up of Tallensi children in Africa, put a similar emphasis on the child's native mastery of his culture. "Social and Psychological Aspects of Education in Taleland," reprinted in idem, *Time and Social Structure and Other Essays* (London: Athlone Press, 1970), pp. 201-59.

 9. For those who do not have access to a strikingly different culture

to test this kind of observation, ethnographic films—a medium gaining considerable place in anthropology (cf. Paul Hockings, ed., *Principles of Visual Anthropology,* The Hague: Mouton, 1975)—provide an opportunity for vicarious cross-cultural experience in cultures quite different from our own. In *The Feast,* for example, a film by Timothy Ash and Napoleon Chagnon portraying a festive visit by one village of a South American Indian tribe to another, one scene depicts a trading session during the visit, showing one individual almost jumping up and down, complaining in a whiny, sulky voice, "Doesn't anybody see I need a hammock?" and another, "I'm tired of nobody paying any attention to me!" The emotional tone of these outbursts strikes most viewers of our culture as decidedly childish; yet in the society portrayed (Yanomamö), and in that situation, I suspect that the behavior was perfectly appropriate. Close observation suggests that the men were performing for a calculated effect rather than being "carried away" in a childish tantrum. In our society, we do not see such behavior except in a child (or in a very "childish" person), so that, though the man's fellow Yanomamö seemed to regard it as perfectly normal, it strikes us as "childish." But this does not mean that the Yanomamö are at a lower level of maturity than us, for some of our behavior—flinching at pain, for example—would strike *them* as childish.

10. Robert LeVine offers a comprehensive discussion of methodological problems in the psychoanalytic understanding of social phenomena in his book, *Culture, Behavior, and Personality.* See esp. pp. 203–48 for discussion of problems of field methodology. See also Herbert Phillips, "The Use and Misuse of Psychoanalysis in Anthropology" (paper delivered at the Seventy-third Annual Meeting of the American Anthropological Association, Mexico City, November 22, 1974).

11. Thus an Italian might at first strike an Anglo-Saxon as "expressive," though he may in fact, for all his expansive gestures, be "as reserved as an Englishman." Edward Sapir remarks:

It is the failure to understand the relativity of gesture and posture, the degree to which these classes of behavior are referable to social patterns while transcending merely individual psychological significances, which makes it so easy for us to find individual indices of personality where it is only the alien culture that speaks. (1927:557)

12. I was fascinated to discover this original report of Erikson's visit, the impressions of a psychoanalyst soon after his first encounter with the Yurok, which I read for the first time in preparing this article. Erikson's presentation in this report of his cultural analysis of myths, rituals, and cosmological beliefs of the Yurok renders far clearer and more

convincing some of the cryptic statements he makes in the much-abbreviated analysis in *Childhood and Society*. The metaphor in which he summarizes the Yurok world view—"peripheral wombs" whence come fish and game, "joined by the human womb" ("observations on the Yurok," p. 275)—shows an intriguing resemblance to the imagery of the universe that Gerardo Reichel-Dolmatoff worked out with his gifted Desana informant, Antonio Guzmán, in Colombia, South America: *Amazonian Cosmos* (Chicago: University of Chicago Press, 1971).

For all its rough edges (and a few unguarded bows to psychoanalytic mythology, such as the "primal horde" story). it is unfortunate that this fresh document, so much more immediate than Erikson's later, more polished discussions of the Yurok, should have been left living in the compative obscurity of the technical monograph series where it first appeared. Of particular value is the vivid and forceful portrait of Fanny.

13. Herbert Phillips made similar points in his paper, "The Use and Misuse of Psychanalysis in Anthropology." See also idem, *Thai Peasant Personality* (Berkeley: University of California Press, 1965). An overview of the rising emphasis on divirsity of personalities within a culture is to be found in Pertti J. Pelto's review article, "Psychological Anthropology," in *Biennial Review of Anthropology: 1967*, ed. Bernard J. Siegal and Alan R. Beals (Stanford, Calif.: Stanford University Press, 1967), pp.140–208. For an earlier statement of this point of view, see George Devereux, "Two Types of Modal Personality Models," in *Studying Personality Cross-Culturally*, pp. 227–42. William Caudill presents a somewhat different perspective on the question of individual variation within a culture in his "Psychiatry and Anthropology: The Individual and His Nexus," in *Cultural Illness and Health*, ed. Laura Nader and Thomas Maretzki (Washington, D.C.: American Anthropological Association, 1973), pp. 67–77.

14. See, for example, Freud's succinct statement of the goals of a psychoanalysis in a highly important footnote to *The Ego and the Id*, *Standard Edition*, vol. 19 (London: Hogarth, 1957), p. 50.

15. Bronislaw Malinowski, *Sex and Repression in Savage Society* (1927; reprint ed., New York: Meridian, 1959). This work contains both his attack on the psychoanalytic position and his counterattack to Ernest Jone's reply. "Mother Right and the Sexual Ignorance of Savages," *International Journal of Psychoanalysis* 6 (1925): 109–30. The entire controversy is a study in misunderstanding. Malinowski could not understand that psychoanalytic propositions refer to inner subjectivity rather than directly to observable interpersonal behavior as such. As many anthropologists still do, for example, he took "repression" to be synonymous with moral condemnation or prohibition of a behavior—that is, in the interpersonal sense, as in "political repression"—whereas in psychoa-

nalysis it refers to the subjective act of (involuntarily) banishing an idea from one's *own* thoughts. Jones, on the other hand, could not understand that anthropologists objected to attributing the existence of an institution to its presumed psychological defensive function. The gap between the two points of view is scarcely narrowed. Cf. LeVine, *Culture, Behavior, and Personality,* pp. 48–50.

16. Personal communication.

17. Peter L. Berger and Thomas Luckman, *The Social Construction of Reality* (Garden City, N.Y.: Doubleday, 1966), p. 132. In this sense, the concept has been particularly developed by social psychologists of the "social interactionist" orientation.

18. For a review of the meaning of the term in psychiatry and psychoanalysis—including a critique of Erikson's usage—see Edith Jacobson, *The Self and the Object World* (New York: International Universities Press, 1964, chapter 2.

19. This can be seen in the number of scholars who combine the two disciplines as well as in the degree of interest psychoanalysts have shown in anthropology and vice versa. W. H. R. Rivers, one of the pioneers of British anthropology, was a dynamically oriented psychiatrist, and Meyer Fortes was first trained in clinical psychology—to say nothing of the many anthropologists who had psychoanalytic training after becoming anthropologists, including Alfred Kroeber, George Devereux, and Weston LaBarre, as well as, more recently, Robert LeVine and Melford Spiro. The Institute for Psychoanalysis in Chicago has been especially active in giving research training to anthropologists and other social scientists, particularly through the efforts and interest of its director, George Pollock. More recent graduates and candidates include Mark Gehrie, Katherine Ewing and Marvin Zonis.

20. The observation that cultural differences can magnify problems of communication and empathy is by no means a new one in psychoanalysis. Commenting on a Russian patient—the now famous Wolf Man—Freud observed that "a national character that was foreign to ours made the task of feeling one's way into his mind a laborious one"—but not an impossible one! "From the History of an Infantile Neurosis," *Standard Edition,* vol. 17 (London: Hogarth Press, 1955), p. 104.

Gertrude Ticho (1971) provides a more recent analytic viewpoint on the problem of cross-cultural analysis, with discussions by a Cuban and a Japanese analyst (Charles Chediak and Tetsuya Iwasaki). Vincent Crapanzano (1980) offers an insightful anthropological perspective (see also note 2, above).

21. Mary Catherine Bateson, "Insight in a Bicultural Context," *Philippine Studies* 16 (1968): 605–21, quoted at length in LeVine, *Culture,*

Behavior, and Personality, pp. 16–18. "This is a case," Bateson says in a passage not included in LeVine's excerpt, "where a lack of knowledge would clearly have been painful and led to further misunderstanding, whereas, given sufficient insight, I was even grateful that my loss had occurred here, since I found the Filipino tolerance for the rhythms of life deeply healing" (p. 613). "A sense of discomfort" at the response of people of an alien culture, she concludes, "can be transcended . . . by anthropologists or by any layman who is prepared to look critically at his own responses" (pp. 612–13).

22. One could suppose that different cultures differ in penetrability to members of our culture, but one sometimes finds different individuals making opposite assertions in this regard, even about the same culture.

BIOGRAPHICAL NOTE

Waud Hocking Kracke was born in Peking, China and grew up in Washington, D.C. and Chicago. He went to Harvard College and majored in History and Science. After college, he did graduate work in Anthropology at the University of Chicago and had research training in psychoanalysis at the Chicago Institute for Psychoanalysis. Professor Kracke teaches at University of Illinois at Chicago where he offers courses in psychoanalytic anthropology and South American Indians. His research interests in the past few years have been in cross-cultural psychoanalytic study of dreams and dream beliefs, and psychological aspects of the encounter with cultures different from one's own ("culture shock"). His major published works are: (1) Force and Persuasion: Leadership in an Amazonian Society; (2) "Dreaming in Kagwahiv", in Psychoanalytic Study of Society Vol. 8; (3) "The Complementarity of Social and Psychological Regularities." Ethos, Vol. 8. and (4) "Myth, Dream, Text and Image: an Amazonian Contribution to the Psychoanalytic Theory of the Primary Process," to appear in *Dreaming: the Anthropology and Psychology of the Imaginal*.

REFERENCES

BATESON, G.
   1936 Naven. Cambridge: Harvard University Press.
BATESON, M. C.
   1965 "Insight in a Bicultural Context. Philippine Studies 16:605.
BENEDICT, R.
   1934 "The Individual and the Pattern of Culture." Patterns of Culture. Boston: Houghton Mifflin.
BERGER, P. L., AND LUCKMAN, T.
   1966 The Social Construction of Reality. Garden City: Doubleday.

BOWEN, E. S. [Laura Bohannon]
   1954 Return to Laughter. New York: Harper & Row.
BRIGGS, J.
   1970 Never in Anger. Cambridge: Harvard University Press.
CAUDILL, W.
   1961 "Some Problems in Transnational Communication (Japan-United States)," pp. 409–421 in Application of Psychiatric Insights to Cross-Cultural Communication. Symposium No. 7, Group for the Advancement of Psychiatry.
   1962 "Anthropology and Psychoanalysis: Some Theoretical Issues," pp. 174–214 in T. Gladwin & W. Sturterant, eds.) Anthropology and Human Behavior. Washington, D.C.: Anthropological Society of Washington.
   1973a "Psychiatry and Anthropology: The Individual and His Nexus," pp. 67–77 in L. Nader and T. Maretzki, Cultural Illness and Health. Washington: American Anthropological Association.
   1973b "The influence of Social Structure and Culture on Human Behavior in Modern Japan." *Ethos* 1:343–382.
CHAGNON, N.
   1968 Yanomamo: The Fierce People. New York: Holt.
   1974 Studying the Yanomamo. New York: Holt.
COLES, R.
   1970 Erik H. Erikson: The Growth of His Work. Boston: Little, Brown.
CRAPANZANO, V.
   1980 Tuhami: Portrait of a Moraccan. Chicago: University of Chicago Press.
DEVEREUX, G.
   1961 "Two Types of Modal Personality Models," pp. 227–242 in Abraham Kaplan, ed. Studying Personality Cross-Culturally.
   1967 From Anxiety to Method in the Behavioral Sciences. The Hague: Mouton.
EGGAN, D.
   1949 "The Significance of Dreams for Anthropological Research." American Anthropologist 51:177–198.
   1955 "The Personal Use of Myth in Dreams." Journal of American Folklore 68:67–75.
ERIKSON, E. H.
   1939 "Observations on Sioux Education." Journal of Psychology 7:101–56.
   1943 "Observations on the Yurok: Childhood and World Image," pp.257–301 in University of California Publications in American Archeology and Ethnology. Monograph 35. Berkeley: University of California.
   1945 "Childhood and Tradition in Two American Indian Tribes." Psychoanalytic Study of the Child 1:319–50.
   1946 "Ego Development and Historical Change." Psychoanalytic Study of the Child 2:359–96.
   1964a "The Nature of Clinical Evidence." pp. 47–80 in Insight and Responsibility. New York: W. W. Norton.
   1964b Childhood and Society. New York: W. W. Norton.
   1966 "Gandhi's Autobiography: The Leader as a Child." American Scholar 35:632–46.
   1969 Gandhi's Truth: On the Origins of Militant Non-Violence. New York: W. W. Norton.
   1975 "On the Nature of Psychohistorical Evidence: In Search of Gandhi." Life History and the Historical Moment. New York: W. W. Norton.
EVANS, R.
   1969 Dialogue with Erik Erikson. New York: E. P. Dutton.
FORTES, M.

1970 "Social and Psychological Aspects of Education in Taleland," pp. 201–59 in Time and Social Structure and Other Essays. London: Athlone Press.

FREUD, S.
1913 Totem and Taboo, Complete Psychological Works of Sigmund Freud. Strachey (ed.). S.E. Vol. 13 London: Hogarth Press, 1955
1918 From the History of an Infantile Neurosis. S. E. Vol. 17:1–122 London: Hogarth Press, 1955.
1914 On Narcissim. S.E. Vol. 14:73–102, London: Hogarth Press, 1957.
1923 The Ego and the Id. S.E. Vol. 19:3–66, London: Hogarth Press, 1961.

GEERTZ, C.
1966a "The Impact of the Concept of Culture on the Concept of Man," 93–118 in J. Platt (ed.), New Views of the Nature of Man. Chicago: University of Chicago Press. Also in Geertz, 1973.
1966b "Person, Time and Conduct in Bali." Series No, 14 in Yale University Southeast Asia Studies Culture Report Series. New Haven: Yale University Press. Also in Geertz, 1973.
1969 "Gandhi: Nonviolence as Therapy" *New York Review of Books* 20, Nov. 1969, pp. 3–4.
1972 "Deep Play: Notes on the Balinese Cockfight. Daedalus 101:1–37. Also in Geertz, 1973.
1973 Interpretation of Cultures. New York: Basic Books

GEORGE, A. L., AND GEORGE, J.
1964 Woodrow Wilson and Colonel House. New York: Dover.

HOCKING, W. E.
1957 The Meaning of Immortality in Human Experience. New York: HARPER & ROW.

HOCKINGS, P.
1975 Principles of Visual Anthropology. The Hague: Mouton.

JACOBSON, E.
1964 The Self and the Object World. New York: International Universities Press.

JONES, E.
1925 "Mother Right and the Sexual Ignorance of Savages." International Journal of Psychoanalysis 6: 109–130.

KARDINER, E.
1963 The Psychological Frontiers of Society. New York: Columbia University Press.

KLUCKHOHN, C.
1944 Navaho Witchcraft. Boston: Beacon Press.
1964 "The Limitations of Adaptation and Adjustment as Concepts for Understanding Cultural Behavior," pp. 254–264 in Culture and Behavior: The Collected Essays of C. Kluckhohn. New York: Free Press of Glencoe.

KRACKE, W.
1978 Force and Persuasion: Leadership in an Amazonian Society. Chicago: University of Chicago Press
1979 "Dreaming in Kagwahir: Dream Beliefs and their Psychic Use in an Amazonian Culture." Psychoanalytic Study of Society 8:119–172. New Haven: Yale University Press.
1980a "Amazonian Interviews." The Annual of Psychoanalysis 8:249–267
1980b "The Complementarity of Social and Psychological Regularities." Ethos 8:273–285
n.d. "Encounter with other cultures: Psychological and Epistomological Aspects," in G. Herdt & W. Kracke, eds New Approaches to Interpretation in Psychoanalytic Anthropology, forthcoming.

KOHUT, H.

1959 "Introspection, Empathy, and Psychoanalysis," in Journal of the American Psychoanalytic Association, 7:459–483.
1971 The Analysis of the Self. New York: International Universities Press.
1976 "Creativeness, Charisma, and Group Psychology," pp. 379–425 in J. Gedo and G. Polluck (eds.), Freud: The Fusion of Science and Humanism. New York: International Universities Press.

LEACH, E.
1964 Political Systems of Highland Burma. Boston: Beacon Press.

LeVINE, R.
1982 Culture, Behavior, and Personality. 2nd ed. New York: Aldine.

LEVI-STRAUSS, C.
1969 The Elementary Structures of Kinship. F. J. Bell, J. von Sturmer, and R. Needham (eds.). Boston: Beacon Press.

LEVY, R.
1973 The Tahitians: Mind and Experience in the Society Islands. Chicago: University of Chicago Press.

LINTON, R.
1945 The Cultural Background of Personality. New York: Appleton-Century Crofts.

MALINOWSKI, B.
1927 Sex and Repression in Savage Society. New York: Meridian, 1959.

MEAD, M.
1928 Coming of Age in Samoa. New York: Morrow.

MURPHY, R.
1971 The Dialectics of Social Life. New York: Basic Books.

NICHOLAS, R.
1968 "Rules, Resources, and Political Activity," pp. 295–321 in M. Swartz (ed.), Local Level Politics. Chicago: Aldine

OBERHOLZER, E.
1961 "Rorschach's Experiment and the Alorese," pp. 588–640 in Cora DuBois, The People of Alor. New York: Harper & Row.

PELTO, P. J.
"Psychological Anthropology," pp. 140–208 in B. J. Siegal and A. R. Beals (eds.), Biennial Review of Anthropology. Stanford: Stanford University Press.

PHILLIPS, H.
1974 "The Use and Misuse of Psychoanalysis in Anthropology."

READ, K.
1965 The High Valley. New York: Scribner's.

REDfIELD, R.
1953 The Primitive World and Its Transformations. Ithaca: Cornell University Press.

REDfIELD, R. AND VILLA-ROJAS, A.
1934 Chan Kom: A Maya Village. Chicago: University of Chicago Press, 1962

REDL, F.
1942 "Group Emotions and Leadership." Psychiatry 5: 573–596.

REICHEL-DOLMATOFF, G.
1971 Amazonian Cosmos Chicago: University of Chicago Press.

REIK, T.
1946 Four Psychoanalytic Studies. Trans. D. Bryan. New York: Grove Press.

ROHEIM, G.
1932 "The Psychoanalysis of Primitive Culture Types," International Journal of Psychoanalysis 13: 1–224.
1974 Children of the Desert. New York: Basic Books.

RUDOLPH, S., AND RUDOLPH, L.
1973 "Comments on 'The Study of Life History: Gandhi'. by D. Mandelbaum." Current Anthropology 14: 201–203.
RÜMKE, H. M.
1965 Preface to The Concept of Identity, by D. de Levita. Paris and The Hague: Mouton.
SACK, E.
1975 "The Anthropologist as Individual: Ruth Benedict and Esther Goldfrank." Master's Thesis. University of Illinois at Chicago Circle.
SAPIR, E.
1932 "Cultural Anthropology and Psychiatry," pp. 509–521 in D. Mandelbaum (ed.), Selected Writings of Edward Sapir. Berkeley: University of California Press, 1949.
1927 "The Unconscious Patterning of Behavior in Society," pp. 544–559 in D. Mandelbaum (ed.), Selected Writings of Edward Sapir Berkeley: University of California Press, 1949.
1938 "Why Cultural Anthropology Needs the Psychiatrist," pp. 569–577 in D. Mandelbaum (ed.), Selected Writings of Edward Sapir. Berkeley: University of California Press, 1949.
SMELSER, N.
1965 "Social and Psychological Dimensions of Collective Behavior," pp. 92–121 in Essays in Sociological Explanation. Englewood Cliffs, N.J.: Prentice-Hall.
SONTAG, S.
1966 "The Anthropologist as Hero," pp. 69–81 in Against Interpretation. New York: Dell.
SPIRO, M.
1961 "Social Systems, Personality Theory, and Functional Analysis," 93–127. In, Studying Personality Cross-Culturally, B. Kaplan (ed.), New York: Harper & Row.
1978 "Culture and Human Nature." pp. 330–360 in G. Spindler, ed., The Making of Psychological Anthropology. Berkeley: the University of California Press.
TICHO, G.
1971 "Cultural aspects of Transference and Countertransference." Bulletin of the Mennniger Clinic 35:313–334
TURNER, V.
1957 Schism and Continuity in an African Society. Manchester: Manchester University Press.
1964 The Forest of Symbols. Ithaca: Cornell University Press.
WALLACE, A.
1970 Culture and Personality. 2nd edition. New York: Random House.
WRONG, D.
1961 "On the Oversocialized Conception of Man In Modern Sociology." American Sociological Review 26: 183–193.

Creativity and Repetition: A Theory of the Coarse Emotions[1]

THOMAS J. SCHEFF

T HIS article seeks to account for the extremes of human accomplishment and failure in terms of a single theory. It is proposed that both creative and rigid behavior depend on the outcomes of basic emotional sequences, particularly grief, fear, rage and shame, with shame occupying a prominent role. These emotions are described in terms of three interacting systems: a biological system, referred to as the emotion response cycle, a psychological system, referred to as self-process, and a social system, the social institution of emotional expression. Consideration of these three systems gives rise to a theory of the conditions under which emotion response cycles are initiated and completed or arrested, and the effects of these alternative outcomes on behavior.

Although Einstein and Freud's patient "the Rat-man" (Freud, 1909) were born in the same country and era, they would seem to be so different from one another as to belong to different species. Einstein, virtually single-handedly, rebuilt a broken universe. The Rat-man's own personal universe was seemingly broken beyond repair. Is it possible that the behavior of both these men can be explained by a single theory? In this article I will argue that they can, that creative genius and rigid neurosis can both be understood in terms of emotions. Needless to say, at this early stage of its development, the theory will be crude and incomplete, a sketch of possibilities rather than a completed statement. Because of space limitations in this volume, the presentation of the theory will also be extremely abbreviated. For a fuller treatment, the interested reader is referred to a book-length statement (Scheff and Retzinger, 1985).

CREATIVE INTELLIGENCE

The first step in the proposed theory is to define the range of human behavior. At one extreme is what will be called creative intelligence, the construction of a new solution to a new problem. Einstein's theory of relativity is one example of creative intelligence. Faced by a new problem,

---

1. I am indebted to discussions with my colleagues Michael Ingham and Ursula Mahlendorf for the distinction between "easy" and "hard" creators, and for their knowledge of the details in the lives of writers and composers.

the failure of Newtonion physics to account for a rapidly growing number of facts, he discarded the old system for a completely new one. At the other extreme is rigid behavior, the repetitive application of old responses to a new problem, even though they clearly are not the needed solution. "The Rat-man" sought to allay his overwhelming feelings of dread and guilt by rituals which were clearly ineffective. Nevertheless, he persisted with them.

Rigid behavior is found not only in neurosis but in many realms of human affairs. As is frequently noted, the actions of bureaucracies are often totally unresponsive to the problems at hand. The nineteenth century physicist Boltzmann foresaw that even science could be riddled with rigid responses. When a new theory or method initially gives promising results, many who are converted to its use become wedded to it; they come "to believe that the development of science to the end of all time would consist in the systematic and unremitting application of it," even in the face of virtually overwhelming contrary indications (Boltzmann, 1899).

The method of "unremitting" repetition of a method that originally was useful is the pattern of all life outside of the human world. Among all living things other than humans, patterns of behavior are rigidly fixed during the lifetimes of individuals by genetic inheritance. New solutions to new problems occur, but only over immense spans of time, through natural selection of chance variations among members of a species.

Unlike all other living creatures, humans seem to have the ability to create new solutions to new problems as they arise. Geniuses like Einstein and Boltzmann realized this potential in their work by creating dramatic solutions to new problems in the world of science. In the world of everyday life, ordinary human beings who are not called geniuses also create new solutions to new problems. In most realms of activity, creative acts are somewhat unusual. There is one realm of behavior, however—language use—in which most humans are extraordinarily creative. Recent attempts to program computers to translate natural languages show that competent language use involves complex creative thought, far beyond the ability of any existing program, and probably any conceivable program (Winograd, 1984). The use of metaphors and puns is a creative act, yet it is so easy for humans that they often do it for sport, as in witticisms or games like charades.

CREATIVITY AND PAINFUL EMOTION

The problem posed here concerns the prevalence of rigid behavior among humans. If all humans have the ability for almost continuous creative activity, why is most of their behavior rigid, or at best routine?

The answer I will suggest is that creativity is severely hampered by pain, not only physical pain, but also emotional pain. Creative acts require all of one's attention. If attention is absorbed by pain, either one's behavior will be disrupted, or at best, one will go into a holding pattern, selecting an already existing sequence from one's repertoire, rather than constructing a new one which is exactly appropriate to a new situation.

In the following discussion of distancing, the rigid response that is signaled by disrupted behavior corresponds to what I will call underdistanced emotion, an arrested emotion response cycle involving overt painful feelings. The holding pattern response, which is the other variant of rigid behavior, corresponds to overdistanced emotion, an arrested cycle expressed as compulsive speech or thought, rather than as overt emotion.

The human brain is capable of functioning as a high speed computer with vast storage capacity and extraordinary sophistication. Von Neumann estimated that it is capable of processing 120 million bits of information per second. This capacity would seem to be necessary for creative intelligence. In order to construct a new solution that is exactly appropriate to a new situation, a person needs to compare the new situation to every other situation in his experience, first for similarities, then for differences—a computation of staggering size and complexity. Pain appears to disrupt this process, whether the pain is in its overt or covert form.

Both types of rigid behavior, the disruption marked by painful fluster and confusion, and the holding pattern in which a person is seemingly cogent but actually deadlocked, are marked by repetition. In underdistanced emotional states, a person appears to be reliving an experience of arrested emotion which is so overwhelming that thought and behavior are disrupted. In overdistanced states, repression of emotion is almost complete, there seems to be little awareness of pain. But thought and behavior in this state have an obsessive or compulsive character; they are slightly off the mark, and not completely under control. What appears to be involved is the repetition of old sequences which are not constructed especially for the new situation, and are therefore somewhat inappropriate.

The part of the present theory dealing with repetition is derived from Freud's theory of neurosis and repression (1916). Overdistancing corresponds to the success of repression and the use of mechanisms of defense, underdistancing to what Freud called "the return of the repressed," the reliving of emotionally unresolved scenes from the past. Freud's theory of neurosis as repetition, in the present context, can be considered to be a theory of noncreative behavior. The proposed theory seeks to extend Freud's work in two ways: first, by including in the theory not only rigidity, as Freud did, but creativity as well; second, and most elaborately, by basing the theory on emotions rather than instincts and drives. To this end, I will also call upon the work of G. H. Mead (1934), particularly his models of consciousness and of self-process, and Helen B. Lewis's (1971) study of the dynamics of shame. The basic emotions will be defined in terms of three component systems: one biological; one psychological; and one social.

THE BIOLOGICAL COMPONENT: THE EMOTION RESPONSE CYCLE

For purposes of argument, let us suppose that there is a purely biological component to emotions and that this component is a stereotyped, genetically inherited sequence. We know that infants don't have to learn how to weep. The weeping reflex is available at birth. Although the picture is not as clear for the other emotions such as fear and anger, it seems plausible that they also have a similar component. If we make this assumption, we can formulate a definition of emotion which encompasses both physical actions and subjective experience. We will begin with the emotion of grief.

A complete definition of grief should involve the concept of an emotion response cycle analogous to the sexual response cycle defined by Masters and Johnson (1966). Following the descriptions of grief by Engel (1961) and others, we can say that the grief response cycle is triggered by the loss of "objects" (persons or things) to which one is emotionally attached. The second phase, arousal, is signaled by certain universal, invariant subjective feelings of sadness, and objective signs, particularly by facial actions which are usually labeled as expressions of sadness. The universality across cultures of the recognition of facial expressions of sadness and other of the coarse emotions in photographs has been established by Ekman and Friesen (1972) and independently by Izard (1971). The third phase, climax, is signaled by weeping—sobbing with tears. As will be indicated below, in the discussion of distancing, weeping is only a necessary condition for climax, not a sufficient one. Not all weeping is climactic. The fourth phase, resolution, in analogy with the last stage of the sexual cycle, is marked by the extremely rapid and virtually complete relaxation of the tension of sadness in the face and body, and rapid diminution of subjective feelings of sadness. A particularly vivid manifestation of the stage of resolution is the marked decrease of tension in the face, either in the form of a more relaxed repose than occurred before the cry, or of authentic or what Ekman and Friesen (1982) call "felt" smiles, in contrast with forced smiles.

The analogy between emotion response cycles and drives like sex has an important implication, the hypothesis of the asymptote. Suppose a person suffers a significant loss, the grief response cycle is triggered, but no climax occurs. What is the fate of the sadness that is aroused? We can answer a similar question about the fate of sexual arousal in the absence of orgasm. Without orgasm, the arousal is dissipated, but over a much longer time period. One minute after orgasm almost all of the sexual tension, as evidenced by myotonia (muscle contraction) and engorgement of blood in the erectile tissue, has disappeared (Masters and Johnson, 1966).

Masters and Johnson also report a study they made of prostitutes who experienced hours of sexual stimulation without orgasm. In these cases, the lips of the vagina were so engorged as to be painful to the touch, as much as six hours after the last sexual stimulation. Apparently the duration of sexual tension is greater by some four-hundred fold without orgasm than with it.

Does the analogy hold for grief and other emotions? If so, it would be a way of modeling the physical component of a chronic emotion: pathological grief, for instance, or chronic anger. A recent study of resentment suggests that facial expressions of anger are of much longer duration before climactic laughter than after (Retzinger, 1985). The same study indicates that the dissipation of the anger expressions before the climax seems to be asymptotic. That is, without climax, the tensions in the facial muscles that are indicative of anger return to normal so slowly that, in principle at least, they never quite make it. Without climax, emotional tension could go on forever, albeit at a vanishingly small intensity.

To this point we have been outlining a model of the biological component of the coarse emotions in general, and grief in particular. If we assume that grief is a stereotyped biological action sequence, a definition of this emotion results which fits Mead's model of consciousness and satisfies many of the clinical findings concerning bereavement, pathological grief, and grief therapy. In this model, a feeling of sadness is a result of a two-step sequence: the grief cycle is triggered by loss, but the climax, crying, is delayed (Nichols and Efran, 1983).

The connection between delay and conscious feeling is the chief feature of Mead's theory of consciousness. According to that theory, when a behavioral sequence (what Mead called an "attitude") is triggered but blocked from completion, the result is consciousness. For example, it is the delay in consuming food, once the eating sequence has been triggered, that results in the consciousness of hunger. By analogy, felt emotion occurs when an emotion response cycle is triggered, but is blocked from completion.

I will apply this theory only to four basic emotions, which James (1890) referred to as "the coarse emotions." I find it convenient to use James's term, although my list of coarse emotions is somewhat longer than his. He named only four: grief, fear, rage, and love. I would add two more: joy and shame. In this paper, I deal only with grief, fear, anger, and shame because I think that love and joy are not directly subject to repression.

Neither Mead nor Dewey (1894) took the theory of consciousness very far into the realm of emotions. In their era, and still today, there is little agreement or knowledge of the response cycles of the coarse emotions. There is considerable clinical literature, however, suggesting that loss is the stimulus, and crying the climax of what I am referring to here as the grief response cycle (e.g., Bowlby 1960, 1961, 1963). In an earlier paper, I delineated the elements of the other three coarse emotion response cycles (Scheff and Bushnell, 1984). For the purpose of the present discussion, only the climax signals will be mentioned: shivering and cold sweat for fear, body heat and flushing for rage, and spontaneous laughter for shame.

If this definition of grief is accurate, then a new question arises. We are saying that crying is a natural, unlearned reaction to loss. Since loss pervades human life, then why is it we so seldom see an adult cry? To answer this question, we need to leave the biological realm and enter the realm of culture. Crying is a biological response to loss, delaying the cry, a cultural one.

In his seminal book, *Affect/Imagery/Consciousness* (1963), Tomkins raises what is very nearly the same question:

The reader must be puzzled at our earlier affirmation that distress is suffered daily by all human beings. Nothing seems less common than to see an adult cry (p. 56).

His explanation of this paradox is in two parts. In the first part, he proposes that adults learn to do something else instead of crying:

The adult has learned to cry as an adult. It is a brief cry, or a muted cry, or a part of a cry or a miniature cry, or a substitute cry, or an active defense against the cry that we see in place of the infant's cry for help.

Among the many types of substitute actions, Tomkins offers the following example:

the adult who sits in the dentist's chair and attempts not to cry out in pain commonly braces himself against this innate affective display by a substitute cry which is emitted in advance of the pain. He may tightly squeeze the sides of the

dental chair with both hands, or tighten the muscles of his stomach and diaphragm or tightly curl toes and feet. He senses that if these muscles are in a
stage of massive contraction before and during the experience of pain, this will
help to drain off the massive motor discharges of the cry and interfere with the
innate contractions of the diaphragm and vocal chords which would normally
constitute the cry of distress. Whether by interference or substitution, this enables
the individual to cry as it were in his hands, or feet, or diaphragm, and not cry
in his face and throat.

The massive tensing of the muscles as a defense against crying, especially
those of the stomach and diaphragm, which is described in this example
of reaction to physical pain, can also be used to defend against the cry
which would be a response to emotional pain. This reaction may be
learned in infancy and become so automatic as to be out of awareness,
which is the basis for Reich's (1948) idea of "body armor."

In the second part of his answer, Tomkins proposes that the reason
that adults learn to substitute other actions for crying is that they are
socialized to do so. In modern societies, we are punished for crying rather
than rewarded for it. In the close quarters of a city, crying is seen as
obnoxious, and the first act of socialization of the newborn is directed
toward the cry. Later, but still early in life, the other coarse emotions
such as fear, grief, and anger are socialized.

The socialization of emotions takes place through punishment, reward, and a third means that Tomkins notes, sedation. (A crying child
may be put to sleep, or offered a distraction, such as candy.) For our
purposes here, it will be convenient to think of social control as taking
one of two forms: either permission to express an emotion is granted
or denied. In this formulation, sedation tactics are subsumed under the
denial of permission. As an example of the social control of emotion,
we may contrast the sanctions that can be expected to obtain at funerals
with those at cocktail parties. There will probably be a blanket permission
to weep at funerals, and to laugh at cocktail parties. Obversely, there
will be a blanket denial of permission to laugh at funerals and to weep
at cocktail parties. The sanctions which violations of these expectations
incur may be quite obvious: verbal recriminations accompanied by intense anger, for example. Usually, however, the control is more subtle.

At the interpersonal level, the most pervasive controls are probably
slight changes of facial expression—the parents' frown or gestures of
impatience or ridicule—are usually powerful controls over the children's
expressions. Finally, and most subtle and powerful, are the sanctions
within the individual. One has learned, for example, to deny oneself
permission to be angry, because one may injure another or loose his
esteem. One learns to substitute some other form of expression for overt
anger: silence or a very elaborate courtesy, for example. We will return

to the issue of inner and outer controls in the discussion of the institutions which control expression.

THE SOCIAL INSTITUTION OF EMOTION EXPRESSION

It would appear that all cultures socialize expressions of grief and other coarse emotions. This process begins very near the moment of birth with crying and not much later with the other coarse emotions. In order to define the cultural components of emotion, it is necessary to understand how the pattern of punitive socialization, which characterizes whole societies, affects individuals. It would appear that early in childhood the individual learns to block or delay the climax phase of the coarse emotion cycle by substituting some more socially acceptable response; one, at least, less visible than crying, laughing, or trembling and sweating as implied by Tomkins's discussion of the substitute cry. Interference with crying or other climactic expression, which in early infancy comes from parents and other socializing agents, is internalized. In order to avoid social sanctions such as ridicule, which can be extraordinarily painful, the individual learns how to delay the climax or avoid triggering the emotion response cycle. Social control is transmuted into self-control.

At first these tactics are temporary, aimed at hiding emotional responses from others. After thousands of repetitions, however, inhibition appears to become automatic so that emotional responses are hidden not only from others but from oneself. Under these circumstances, emotional responses may disappear from conscious awareness. In psychoanalytic terminology, they are repressed.

The combination of inner and outer controls over emotional expression, some conscious, others subconscious or unconscious, may be referred to as a social institution. Boys learn to suppress their tears to avoid external sanctions, ridicule from their peers and/or parents. With repetition, the suppression becomes almost, but not completely, automatic. Under unusual conditions, tears may still appear: under extreme conditions of loss, or when permission is fully and flagrantly granted; athletes getting their Olympic medals, for example. The athlete's manhood has been established by victory. No one is likely to think ill of him for a few tears. But the more normal conditions contain the threat of sanction or, at least, the possibility of sanction. The crying male may be derided as weak, out of control, or effeminate.

Social institutions involve the mutually reinforcing interplay of inner and outer controls. As Durkheim (1965) suggested in his discussion of the church as a social institution, religious beliefs reaffirm religious practices, just as religious practices reaffirm religious beliefs, the inner and the outer mutually sustaining each other.

In modern societies, the social institution which controls emotional expression is composed of interlinked and rigid practices of socialization, and the more or less continuous sanctioning of facial and other expressions of emotion in social interaction. The social institution of controlling emotional expression directly impinges on actual behavior through the granting or denying of permission to express a particular emotion in a particular situation.

The suppression of inner and outer sanctions from awareness, which sometimes occurs, has an indirect but nevertheless important effect on emotional expression. Since self-control depends upon self-awareness, unconscious emotional processes become difficult to control. To understand this apparent paradox, that excessive control of emotions in childhood may lead to deficiencies of control in adults, it is necessary to return to another aspect of Mead's theory.

The Dialogue between the I and the Me

For Mead (1934), the crucial step in the development of human beings occurs when the child learns to "take the role of the other." In Mead's scheme, it is this step that establishes the uniquely human potentialities for creative intelligence, self-awareness, and self-control. One becomes fully human only when one can step outside of oneself, imaginatively, and see oneself as from the outside. At first, in the process of maturation, the child is unable to do this. The child plays at the external role of the other, the parent or the postman, as the role appears from the outside. The child goes through the motions of the person in these roles, without understanding what they mean from within.

The first step into the other's viewpoint occurs in what Mead calls the game stage. In organized games like baseball, or in other activities requiring close coordination, to become proficient at one's own role, one needs to learn the role of the others involved, not only from the outside, but from the inside. To execute a double play in baseball, the second baseman must be able to imagine the development of the play, not only from his point of view, but from the point of view of the first baseman, and even from the point of view of the antagonist, the base runner, allowing the coordination of the moves of the players in the three roles to occur with extraordinary rapidity. Since no double play situation is identical to another, each play requires *improvising* one's own action sequence so that it fits *exactly* into the action sequences of the other two players. There is no way out—to be proficient, one must learn to take the role of others.

In the game stage, the child's vocabulary of the other's roles is limited to actual roles that it has dealt with, and therefore to conformity to the concrete games and other institutional arrangements in the particular host society. The child in the game stage is parochial. The coming of human maturation is marked by the ability to take the role of what Mead called "the generalized other." With maturation, the child learns to extrapolate from the succession of concrete roles he has dealt with to imaginary roles or points of view that have never been dealt with, and probably never will: posterity, or the legal fiction of "the reasonable man." One can then imagine a point of view from which one can view oneself.

To understand the origins of self-awareness and self-control in Mead's scheme, it is necessary to utilize both the model of consciousness discussed earlier, with the concept of role-taking, just described. According to Mead, the first glimpses of consciousness arise in infancy when outside impediments delay the completion of an action sequence which has been triggered. The longer the delay in feeding a hungry baby, the greater the subjective pain of hunger. Through participating in coordinated social activity, the child learns the knack of first initiating, then blocking, its own action sequences, giving rise to the ability to induce consciousness at will. In a typical sequence, the individual might notice that he is aroused in some way, take the role of some other (What would mother say?), continue to inhibit overt action to allow further deliberation, or complete the action sequence that has been initiated, according to the particular situation.

The process of initiation and delay of overt action requires an alternation between two kinds of activities: bodily action sequences, and taking the role of the other towards oneself. Mead named this process of alternation "the dialogue between the I and the me." The "I" is the biologic individual—the bodily action sequences such as the hunger or grief cycle. The "me" is the point of view of the other. It requires one to take a stance outside of oneself, to observe oneself as another might. It is this fundamental process that transforms the animal into a person with a self, capable of self-control, selectivity in the face of thousands of different stimuli and self-awareness. According to Mead, the self is a process, the dialogue between the I and the me, between the participant in one's bodily reality, and the observer of it.

Mead's model of the self solves not only the puzzle of consciousness, but a host of others: the mechanisms of self-control, self-awareness, and particularly, the puzzling issue of creativity, intelligence, and flexibility which humans sometimes exhibit. Mead's scheme speaks not only to the issue of ordinary intelligence, but to extraordinary feats of creative genius.

Mead's model of the self is not complete, however, in that it is not very helpful when applied to the dark side of human behavior: rigidity, stupidity, fixation. Mead's basic concern was human evolutionary adaptiveness: he gives very little attention to incapability. Since any theory of emotion must encompass both sides of human nature, both artistic creativity and hysterical panic, it will be necessary to introduce some new features to Mead's model of the self which he himself did not foresee.

In Mead's discussion, he usually seems to assume complete fluidity in the movement between the I and the me. This is a limitation in his treatment of the self process. To be sure, there are moments when humans are at their highest level of functioning, that his assumption holds. The key concept of aesthetic distance, which will be introduced shortly, is the name for just such a state, involving complete fluidity in the alternation between I and me.

Typically, however, there is usually a lack of complete fluidity in the self process, either in going from the I to the me, or from the me to the I. The impediment may be very slight, and have so little effect on behavior as to be virtually undetectable, or it may be very severe, profoundly affecting aspects of behavior. To take an extreme case, consider two short spans of time in the sexual response cycle that have been described by Masters and Johnson. Just before ejaculation in the male, or contractions of the vagina in the female, there is a point at which the orgasm proper has not begun, but is inevitable. Masters and Johnson refer to this point as the "point of inevitability." After orgasm has run its course, there is a short period of time in which sexual arousal cannot occur, which Masters and Johnson call the "refractory period." Needless to say, during these two short time spans, Mead's assumption of the fluidity of movement between I and me does not obtain. During the period between the point of inevitability and the end of orgasm, the aroused individual can no longer enter the "me" phase, but has become totally an "I." Similarly, in the refractory period, there is no entry into the "I" phase. With respect to the sexual response cycle, at least, the individual has become totally a "me."

Obviously, these two limitations on Mead's assumptions are fairly trivial, since they are so brief and circumscribed. They are undoubtedly genetically determined, and do not seem important exceptions to the general applicability of Mead's treatment of the self process.

In Freud's (1916) concept of repression, however, a parallel, and much more general process of impediment in movement between I and me is intimated. Two forms of repression, which parallel the two types of impediment in the sexual response cycle, are suggested. Freud referred to certain types of hysterical emotional episodes as the "return of the repressed." In these episodes, Freud thought that the individual relived episodes which had not been resolved emotionally. These episodes were thought to be exact repetitions of the emotional content of the earlier experiences. If Freud's idea is accurate, such an episode would be an exact emotional analog of the physically caused period of inevitability in the sexual cycle. Once the episode is triggered by some stimulus which is reminiscent of the original situation, the person is all "I," and has little if any control over the unfolding incident. Similarly, the other form of repression involves the absence of feeling, as in obsessive-compulsive or schizoid episodes; it parallels the "me" phase of being only an observer, that occurs during the refractory period of the sexual response cycle.

The Distancing Process

The concept of distance provides a model of self-process which subsumes both Mead's assumption of fluidity and Freud's conception of impeded movement in the self-process. This idea originated in dramatic criticism. Drama critics understand audience response to occur at one of three distances: too little distance means that the members of the audience react with raw emotion, even forgetting, perhaps only briefly, that they are in the theater. These kinds of drama, whether they produce fear, embarrassment, anger, or grief in the audience, are referred to as "underdistanced." At the opposite extreme is the drama which produces very little, or no observable emotional reaction in the audience, which is referred to as "overdistanced." Such dramas do not "work" in the sense that they do not seem to arouse the overt feelings of the audience, and are usually critical and economic failures. Finally, there are the dramas which arouse the feelings of the audience, but not to the point that the members of the audience forget, even for a moment, that they are in a theater. These dramas, which are said to create "aesthetic distance" in the audience, lead to both an emotional and an intellectual reaction in the audience.

The concept of aesthetic distance corresponds, in part, to a process described by psychoanalysts as "the splitting of the ego": In order for psychoanalysis to be successful, there must be a split in the patient's ego between a "reasonable, observing, analyzing ego, and an experiencing, subjective, irrational ego" (Greenson, 1967). This is exactly the split between observer and participant that characterizes aesthetic distance.

But the two conceptions are distinct, because two different temporal processes are envisioned. Psychoanalysts visualize the two sides of the ego as mutually exclusive; either one or other is dominant, but not both:

When the patient permits himself to be carried away by a painful memory or fantasy, the experiencing ego is in the foreground, and there is no awareness of the meaning or appropriateness of the emotion at the time.

If the analyst were to intervene at this point, the patient's reasonable ego would come back into the fore and, the patient would now be able to recognize that the affects in question came from the past . . . (47–48).

   At aesthetic distance, however, the two states are experienced seemingly simultaneously: there is a double vision; one is both participant and observer. Applied to the process of recollection, the same dynamics of distancing may occur: *reliving* the past is underdistanced, one is entirely a participant. *Remembering* the past is overdistanced, one is entirely an observer. Aesthetic distance corresponds to *returning* to the past; one is simultaneously participant and observer.

   Psychoanalysts believe that the successful patient is able both to participate in and observe his distressful emotions, and to move freely back and forth between the two states. The concept of aesthetic distance takes this idea a step further, by positing a third state, a process in which the patient moves so rapidly between participation and observation that the two states are experienced as simultaneous. When this occurs, the paradox of repression is resolved: how can unbearable pain be borne? When it is both felt and observed, simultaneously.

   An anticipation of the concept of aesthetic distance can be found in Arthur Koestler's (1964) concept of *bisociation*: the simultaneous experience of a situation "in two (internally) self-consistent but habitually incompatible frames of reference" (p. 35). Koestler illustrates this idea with tickling: "It is probably the first situation encountered in life which makes the infant live on two planes at once, the first delectable experience in bisociation—a foretaste of the pleasures to come at the pantomime show, of becoming a willing victim to the illusions of the stage, of being ticked by the horror-thriller- . . . the tickled child's laughter is the discharge of apprehensions recognized as unfounded by the intellect" (p. 81). Implicit in Koestler's comments is the generalization that any situation which gives rise to a precisely balanced experience of distress on the one hand, and safety on the other, will result in laughter.

   An analysis of the childhood games of tickling, peek-a-boo, and mistake games fits very well into the distancing paradigm. These games can be spoiled through underdistancing, as when the stranger, rather than the mother, tickles the child, restimulating too much distress at too little distance; or when the mother hides her face too long; or the leader in a mistake game makes the commands and ridicule of mistakes too much like real life. On the other hand, these games can also be spoiled by overdistancing: one cannot tickle oneself; the mother doesn't hide her face long enough to arouse the baby; or the commands of the leader in a mistake game are slow and lifeless. The distance is too great, and the amount of distress restimulated too small. The theory of distancing outlined here subsumes and broadens Koestler's analysis of the mixture of the elements of safety and distress that produce bisociation and laughter, since it concerns a process: Koestler's idea seems to concern a static state.

The conception of aesthetic distance as a balance between participation and detachment bring us very close to a useable phenomonological definition of the distancing process. As already suggested above, if we understand the "I" in the self-process to represent the participant in bodily processes, and the "me" to be the observer, then we can define the distance as the relative balance between the dominance of the I or the me. In underdistanced states, the participant part of the self is dominant, in overdistanced states the observer part, and at aesthetic distance, the two parts are at parity.

The work of Helen Lewis (1971) on shame and guilt suggests a further modification of Mead's treatment of the me, the phase of the self in which one is observing one's self as if one were an outside observer. In his discussion of this movement of the self, Mead seems to assume that it can occur without emotion. Lewis, however, notes that in the clinical context, at least, when the patient takes the point of view of the therapist, intimates in the patient's life, or just people in general, shame is almost always evoked, since the patient seems to assume that the other is critical or scornful. It seems clear, however, at least outside of the clinical context, that pride also may be evoked by taking the role of the other toward one's self. Such a situation occurs when one basks in the enjoyment of one's appearance or accomplishments, as seen in the imagination through the eyes of the other, another who is laudatory or at least accepting toward one's self. Because of the ubiquitous presence of emotion connected with the observer position of the self, it would seem important to specify that for aesthetic distance to occur, the imagined role of the observer, the me, must be that of an accepting other.

Helen Lewis (1971) also makes another important contribution to this discussion in her distinction between two kinds of affect. In her analysis of shame and guilt, she shows that both of these emotions have two different manifestations. In the first kind, which she refers to as overt, unidentified affect, there is considerable feeling but little or no ideation. One describes this feeling with non-differentiating words, such as "I felt 'funny,' " (or 'silly,' 'curious,' 'upset,' and so on). There may be considerable bodily changes (blushing, rapid heartbeat) but little or no thought. This type of emotion seems virtually identical to what I have called underdistanced emotion. The second type of emotion she identifies as bypassed affect, where there is considerable ideation but little or no feeling. Lewis describes this type of affect as being experienced with a wince, jolt, or groan, but so quickly that there are virtually no bodily changes, only thoughts, perhaps obsessively. This type seems identical to what I have called overdistanced emotion. Since, as indicated earlier, Lewis also states that laughter dispels shame, she seems to have independently identified the three main states of distance, although she does not use that terminology.

Because of the extremely detailed and concrete description of large numbers of actual episodes, Lewis's work supplements my theoretical analysis of distancing, filling in the gap in this paper caused by the paucity of concrete indicators of each of the three distances. To get an understanding of the phenomena of distancing, it is necessary to give Lewis's work a very careful reading.

Lewis's examples and her interpretations give rise to many implications, but I will take up only two here: (1) the issue of naming emotions by the person involved in the case of the overt, unidentified emotions. (2) the question of the fate of the feeling component in the case of the bypassed emotions. It is clear from Lewis's excerpts that we have many, many terms for emotions that do not differentiate one emotion from another and do not give the particular emotion one is feeling its right name. This seems especially true in the case of shame, which appears to be a very low-prestige feeling. One says instead that one feels "funny," "awkward," "upset," "silly," or "uncomfortable." In the youth culture, there are a few all-purpose words and phrases: "bummed," "freaked out," and "weird." Many similar expressions serve in the case of anger, also. "I am upset with you" rather than "I am angry with you" is one of numberless examples. Lewis's descriptions of overt, undifferentiated affect seems to point back the institution which controls emotional expression, showing how one does not speak (or even think) clearly about one's emotions.

The other issues suggested by Lewis's discussion that will be mentioned here, concerns the fate of the emotions that are "bypassed." Most of Lewis's work was completed before the discovery of "micro-expressions" (Haggard & Isaacs, 1966). These expressions, which last less than a quarter of a second, and are, therefore, unnoticed by the person showing them and by the other interactant(s), occur frequently in clinical interviews, particularly when an emotionally laden topic is being discussed. It seems quite likely that these expressions are the outward manifestation of the bypassing of emotion. Perhaps future research, which involves both the clinical rating of transcripts, as in Lewis's work, and the objective assessment of videotapes for micro-expressions, will be able to show the coincidence of these two effects.

To give examples of these very abstract ideas, let us consider three states connected with the effects of separation. Immediately after separation, the child or other bereaved person may exhibit episodes of hysterical crying and panic. Such states have been described by child psychologists as "separation protest," in the case of young children separated from a parent. In the scheme proposed, such states would be described as underdistanced grief. The departure of the parent triggers a crying episode which, early in the child's life, may be at least partly under conscious control, as a message of protest. According to our theory, however, to the extent that the child is continually unable to complete the grief cycle for any reason, whether the cry is punished severely by others, or whether the prospect of crying alone seems unbearably painful to the child so that the cry is self-inhibited, to that extent, the cry, once triggered, will be less and less controllable. As the layers of asymptotic residues from earlier uncompleted cries mount, the child becomes chronically grief stricken.

Under these conditions, each separation triggers the impulse to an uncontrollable cry. As a defense against such painful crying episodes, the child may adopt a strategy of overdistanced grief, warding off the cry automatically. The strategy is created through selective inattention, both to the outer stimuli, as when the child refuses to acknowledge the separation, and/or to the inner response, as when the tension of grief is denied. In the overdistanced state, the child is either unable to initiate the grief cycle, since she has learned automatically to ignore stimuli of loss, or is trapped in the stage of grief arousal, but is unaware of her bodily reaction through selective inattention to the inner signals of sadness.

Grief at aesthetic distance involves what seems to the individual to be an experience of being both sad and not sad at the same time. At this distance there is the feeling of being in and out of grief simultaneously. Crying when happy provides a common example. This model of self-process suggests an explanation of the otherwise puzzling phenomenon of crying at joyful reunions. When a family greets a returning loved one who has been away for years, often all involved will weep. From what has been said so far concerning the distancing of grief, it is possible that the grief would seem too overwhelming to countenance during the separation. Repression would occur, perhaps in the form of overdistancing, with occasional bouts of hysterical crying. Only when the period of separation was ended would the grief be perceived as bearable. At the reunion, the delayed grief is triggered at aesthetic distance. A similar instance involves the Olympic athletes crying tears of joy when receiving their medals. The pain involved in the long struggle to get to that point is allowed to surface because the pain is no longer unbearable in the context of victory, which gives the detachment necessary to feel and discharge the delayed grief.

I will term crying that takes place at aesthetic distance "effective crying." I use this term to conform to the usage of the psychoanalyst Wetmore (1963) in his discussion of "effective griefwork." In this paper, Wetmore modifies the concept of the "work of mourning" in a fundamental way. According to Freud, the process of emotionally working through a profound loss is complete when the bereaved person is able to become attached to a new person. Wetmore argues, however, that such a move may not signal completion at all, but the repetition of a neurotic relationship. Not all grieving or mourning is effective. To be effective, the nature of the new relationship must be a change, so that it is not a mere repetition of the lost relationship. According to the argument presented here, effective crying should be the exact emblem of the kind of griefwork that Wetmore described.

The parity between the I and the me that occurs at aesthetic distance usually gives rise to heightened feelings of integration, completeness or wholeness and, at times, ecstasy. Proust (1936) described the feelings of his narrator, Marcel, at the moment in *Remembrance of Things Past* after he has dipped the madeleine in the tea, and soon will remember his entire childhood:

No sooner had the warm liquid, and the crumbs with it, touched my palate than a shudder ran through my whole body, and I stopped, intent upon the extraordinary changes that were taking place. An exquisite pleasure had invaded my senses. And at once the vicissitudes of life had become indifferent to me, its disasters innocuous, its brevity illusory. I had ceased now to feel mediocre, accidental, mortal. Whence could it have come to me, this all-powerful joy?

(It should be noted here that Proust may have been prepared to write this description by real incidents in his own life. There is ample evidence from his letters and biographies that he wept frequently and at aesthetic distance.)

Mead refers to such moments of ecstasy as involving the "fusion of the I and me," as if they could be static states. Since attention is probably indivisible, like a single searchlight, the seeming simultaneity of contradictory feelings is probably only apparent. What may happen is that the alternation between the two states is so quick that they appear to fuse. A slower form of alternation can be seen in small children when they cry in the presence of a parent figure. The boy who is hurt on the playground delays the tears until he finds his mother. If a quick look at her expression suggests that she will tolerate them, the tears and sobs are released, with the child looking down to concentrate on the pain sensation, but occasionally looking up at the parent's face to make sure that the crying is still being tolerated. Adults may learn to speed up this process until it occurs so rapidly that the movement is not perceptible, perhaps as fast as every one or two seconds. If this were the case, it would explain Ekman's finding that genuine facial expressions of emotion (in contrast to forced smiles, for example) are very brief, only a second or two, and that some are extremely brief, about a quarter of a second. These latter expressions are referred to as "micro-expressions."

The occurrence of a cycle involving sad expressions which last for a second or two followed by repose or any other socially acceptable expression, lasting 2 or 3 seconds would suggest a slightly overdistanced state. The me would be dominant but only a little higher than parity with the I. On the other hand, micro-expressions of sadness lasting less than a quarter of a second, followed by a repose or smile which lasts two or three seconds, and back to the micro-expression of sadness lasting less than a quarter of a second, followed by a repose or smile which last two or three seconds, and so on, would be suggestive of a highly overdistanced state, with the me dominant by a factor or eight or nine. Most of the studies of micro-expressions have been in a clinical context. Since it has been reported that these expressions cluster during discussions of highly charged topics, the interpretation suggested here is not implausible (Haggard and Isaacs, 1966).

The concept of aesthetic distance is also relevant to the question of whether mental processes occur serially or in parallel, which is currently being argued in cognitive psychology. Some of Hilgard's (1977) findings concerning mental processes which take place under hypnosis seem to suggest parallel processing. In addition to conscious processing, he argues that there is a "hidden observer" such that information is being processed even when the subject is in a deep trance. The present discussion suggests, however, that at least at aesthetic distance, processing is both serial and parallel. There is a kind of time-sharing occurring, so that conscious attention alternates between bodily processes and the point of view of the outside observer.

The concept of distancing subsumes both phenomenological and psychodynamic ideas. The balance between self as participant and self as observer connects distancing to the phenomenal world of subjective experience. In psychodynamic terms, underdistancing corresponds to "the return of the repressed," the repetitive reliving of at least the emotional content, if not the substantive content, of unresolved traumas. Overdistancing signals the success of repression, and aesthetic distance, the balanced experience of feeling and thought that is considered necessary for therapeutic change. The distancing concept may help to integrate two fields that are of great importance for understanding emotion.

STATEMENT OF THEORY

Based on the preceding discussion, we can now state an explicit theory. The first step is to define the fundamental concept in the theory, that of emotion. According to the point of view presented here, an emotion is a social psychophysical sequence which has three interdependent components. First, a physical component, a stereotyped biological sequence. Second, a mental or cognitive component involving the extent to which the individual is a participant or observer. Finally, a third component, whether permission to express the emotion, without shame, is granted.

The theory of emotion implied by the discussion to this point may be stated in a way that involves social, psychological, and biological parameters.

1. Complete cycles of emotion: in a context which initiates a coarse emotion cycle, if permission is perceived as granted, the emotion may be experienced at aesthetic distance, and the cycle will be completed. For example, in a context of loss, if the bereaved perceive that permission to cry has been granted, they may experience grief at aesthetic distance and cry "effectively" until the tension of grief has been relieved.

2. Incomplete cycles of emotion: in a context which initiates a coarse emotion cycle, if permission is perceived as denied, the cycle will be begun but not completed either by denying the stimulus or by repetitive expressions of the emotion. That is, either by overdistanced or underdistanced experiences of the emotion. For example, in a context of loss, an overdistanced experience might take the form of depression, an underdistanced one of hysterical crying.

Given the theory as stated, we are now in a position to generalize Tomkin's question about the rarity of adult crying. The question becomes one concerning all of the coarse emotions: Why do we seldom see adults finish an emotion response cycle? The answer suggested here is that social and psychological controls, the outer and inner constraints, are so powerful that most adults seldom experience the climax of their own emotion cycles. The inner and outer sanctions reaffirm and support each other, as is true in any social institution. It is true that these institutional controls over emotional expression vary somewhat from emotion to emotion and from group to group. Even the less stigmatized climaxes, however, like laughter and yawning are severely sanctioned in most groups. Yawning is usually seen as at least impolite, if not extremely rude, an indication of boredom or fatigue. If this theory is correct, the only relationship between yawning and boredom is a cultural one. Because public yawning is negatively sanctioned, yawns are suppressed until one is alone, perhaps at bedtime, or at some other time of inactivity. The fatigue at the end of the day or the boredom associated with inactivity is erroneously confounded with yawning, which has had other roots in tension during the day.

Laughter is also usually negatively sanctioned, at times with great force. Its hearers often seem to equate it with a lack of seriousness or respect. In the case of laughing fits, they seem to respond to the hint of loss of control, especially in women. The more intensely sanctioned emotional expressions, such as crying (grief), shivering, sweating (fear), and the hot flush of rage may produce profound feelings of apprehension or indignation in the onlooker, leading to a rapid rebuke or attempt at intervention.

Tomkins's question about the rarity of adult crying, and his answer on the self and social control of crying suggests yet another question. What are the personal and social consequences of the inhibition of crying and the other climaxes? Tomkins gives this question very little attention. He assumes, without any evidence, that the various substitute cries are equivalent to the real cry. The theory proposed here suggests another conclusion: the arrest of the coarse emotion cycles in children and adults may have profound consequences for the level of creativity in persons and societies. It also suggests that the catharsis of emotion should lead to creative behavior.

CREATIVITY AND EMOTION

The theory outlined above suggests that there should be an association between creativity and catharsis. If the theory is true, we would expect to find evidence of frequent emotional discharge, such as effective crying, in the lives of highly creative persons. A similar proposal can be found in the work of Koestler. Although he gives no evidence, or even any examples, the central thesis of *The Act of Creation* (1964) is that laughing and crying are the sources of creativity.

An adequate test of the hypothesis connecting creativity and catharsis is not possible at this time. It would require comparing the amount and quality of the emotional discharge in the daily lives of creative and noncreative people. There are many impediments to such a study. One central difficulty is the lack of detailed information about laughing and crying in everyday life. Except in unusual instances, these processes seem to go unrecorded, even in detailed accounts. In the case of non-creative people, there is little evidence of any kind concerning their daily lives, much less the specialized knowledge of their emotional expressiveness that testing the theory would require.

Unlike non-creative persons, the lives of some of the great creators are so celebrated in biographical material that enough evidence concerning their daily lives exists to allow some testing of the theory. In order to make a test, however, it is necessary to further specify the nature of the link between creativity and catharsis. I will argue that among creative persons, the ease and rapidity of creative activity is associated with catharsis. I will divide creative persons into two types: "easy" creators and "hard" creators. I will show how the theory suggests that catharsis should be associated with ease of creative activity and that a preliminary survey of these creators whose daily lives are documented supports the hypothesis.

It would appear that in most cases, the act of creation involves excruciatingly hard work. Edison's dictum, that innovation is only one percent inspiration, and ninety-nine percent perspiration, seems to be literally true for most creators. There are so many illustrations of this type of creator that I will give only a few examples. The poet Yeats apparently labored over each line of his poems. His wife reports that he walked around the house all day long, repeating variations of the same line over and over. The writer Thomas Mann worked at his desk eight hours a day, as if he were an employed laborer. Finally the composer Mahler appeared to have suffered agonies with each of his compositions. In the case of the "hard" creators, their work is produced slowly and with difficulty and is marked by extensive and often almost endlessly repeated revision.

On the other hand, there are the much rarer creators whose work is extremely rapid, seemingly requires little effort, and appears to need almost no revision. Since Shakespeare produced his plays at the rate of two or three a year, most authorities believe that his work was of this type. For example, Samuel Johnson commented that in his comedies, Shakespeare "seems to produce without labour what no labour can improve." There is considerable evidence that among musicians, Schubert and Mozart were easy creators. Schubert's example is particularly striking. Musical ideas seemed to come to him so fast that the only limitation on his productivity was his speed in writing them down. Like Mozart's, many of his compositions required virtually no revision.

Our hypothesis requires that ease of creativity be associated with catharsis. This association seems plausible from the point of view of common sense. The less emotionally repressed the creator, the more quickly the creative work would be done. There is also a more specific prediction generated by the proposed theory, associated with the emotion of shame. Creative activity requires originality, which means that often the creator is violating accepted convention, which generates shame. If the proposed theory is correct, we would expect easily creative persons to be better able to manage shame than hard creators and to be more expressive of the other basic emotions as well.

From my preliminary survey of the biographical materials about the hard creators, such as Yeats, Mann, and Mahler, I find no indication of frequent cathartic episodes. If anything, some of the hard creators seem unusually unemotional, as in the cases of Yeats and Mann. Their excessive detachment and coolness suggests an overdistanced emotional style. The lives of other hard creators, like Mahler, with their emotional agonies, also are not suggestive of cathartic episodes, but of an underdistanced style.

With respect to the easy creators, the available evidence seems to support the hypothesis. There is virtually no evidence concerning the daily lives of most easily creative artists, like Shakespeare, Schubert, and Mozart. But the lives of Goethe, Wagner, and Proust, who were easy creators of the first rank, contain many instances which seem to support and further illuminate the proposed theory.

All three of these creators were of the easy type. During most of their long creative careers, both Goethe and Wagner were spectacularly prolific. Their creativity was marked by rapidity and the absence of revision, and also by its many-sidedness. Wagner once boasted that he had developed all of his musical ideas by the time he was 18, and his career was mostly a matter of executing the ideas. Goethe wrote *Werther*, the most successful novel of its time, in twenty-four days, and many of his greatest poems in a single sitting.

Proust is not in the same class as Goethe and Wagner in terms of the ease of creation and prolificness. He produced only a single masterwork, his novel *The Remembrance of Things Past*. But this novel is vast, the equivalent in length of eight or nine normal novels, and was produced in a relatively short time, twelve years. For this reason, he, also, seems to belong to the easy type of creator.

The link between effective crying and creativity appears to be documented in the life of Proust. His letters make vividly clear that he was neurotically attached to his mother: he complains of the agony of being separated from her even for a few days. His ambivalence is also clear in his letters: he loved and hated her. Both feelings are spelled out in vivid detail. Her death, when he was thirty-five, provides a severe test for the theory. How did he respond? His biographer, Painter (1959), provides a description:

For a month Proust disappeared from the world of the living, almost as if he shared his mother's death. In this twilight half-life, he lay in bed weeping incessantly and entirely deprived of sleep (Painter V 2: 49).

This information seems to support the hypothesis. If one learned that he did no weeping at his mother's death, it would be difficult to use his case to support Koestler's thesis. He apparently did not go through an initial period of shock, as most people do in the event of deeply serious loss (Parkes, 1972). He began weeping immediately and wept for a month.

To support fully the hypothesis, however, it is necessary to find information on the quality of the emotional experience of weeping. Although it is clear that Proust did an extreme amount of weeping in reaction to his mother's death, it is possible that it was not effective weeping, that is, that it was solely painful, and therefore, according to the hypothesis, did not advance the work of mourning.

One of Proust's friends, Reynaldo Hahn, offers a helpful observation. After participating in the funeral, he described the sight of "Marcel by Mme. Proust's deathbed, weeping, and smiling through his tears at her body." This "happy crying" apparently was puzzling and even disturbing to some of Proust's friends who were present at the funeral, but it provides support for the hypothesis. According to theory, this type of cry, balanced between safety and distress, shows that Proust was, in a preliminary way, effectively working through his loss.

It is of great interest for the present thesis also that Proust did not begin his one great creative work, *Remembrance of Things Past* until six years after the death of his mother. It is possible that the work of mourning required by his mother's death unlocked his creative abilities. Many critics have remarked on the transformation that took place in the quality of his work between his earlier writing and his great novel. Many of its themes appear in the early work, but in a distinctly weak and unorganized form.

It can also be shown that Proust's weeping was occurring during the exact period that he began his novel, the first weeks of July, 1909. On the 29th of June, he was reading an article about Charles Haas, the model for Swann (one of the principal characters in the novel). Haas had been dead for seven years at this point. As he was reading the article, apparently in the presence of its author, his friend Robert Dreyfus, he began to weep, to Dreyfus's bewilderment. He also wept, this time publicly, on August 20 or 21 when an orchestra played music written by Hahn.

It would be possible to advance many more instances of Proust's weeping. It is clear that he wept frequently, that the weeping appears to be the type we have called "effective," and that it often occurred at critical junctures in his life. His case seems to support the hypothesis.

It is relevant to the thesis advanced here that Proust shows evidence, in the next to the last component of his great novel, (*The Fugitive*), of psychological understanding of the work of mourning. His understanding is first stated, succinctly, in a single sentence:

"We are healed of a suffering only by experiencing it to the full" (p. 86).

In this sentence, Proust exactly anticipates a modern discovery in psychiatry, "re-grief therapy" (Volkan, 1979). The hundred pages of the first chapter of *The Fugitive*, "Grief and Oblivion," is almost a textbook on this theme, of Marcel reviewing, reliving, and finally, letting go of Albertine's memory.

In the case of Wagner, there is an extensive record of his weeping behavior. His biographer, Glasenapp (1977) states:

Amid his untold cares and humiliations, the young master had one source of unfailing relief, a secret closely guarded from the world. His keenly sensitive and easily inflammable nature made him feel every sting with a double smart; but it also offered him a means of palliation. The secret was—the man of steel could weep.
The hot floods of tears of his infancy never failed him in the sorest trials of his manhood, though his friends were not permitted to be witnesses, still less his foes. "Let me be cursed if an enemy ever hears me moan: in his regard we must be bold as brass and hard as stone."

The source of this information is not revealed. However, since Glasenapp was Wagner's official biographer, it is quite possible that it came directly from Wagner himself. Whatever its source, it clearly concerns Wagner as a young man ("the young master"). What about the mature Wagner? To answer this question, it was necessary to consult the voluminous diaries (2399 pages) of Wagner's wife, Cosima (1976).

Since Wagner married Cosima late in life, the diaries cover only his last 15 years, 1869–1833. During this period, there are ninety dated episodes of weeping recorded in the diary. That is, there are ninety entries in which the date is specified. There are eight additional episodes of Wagner's weeping mentioned but which occurred at an earlier, unspecified date. (In one case, in his childhood.) There are also three dreams involving weeping, which were not counted. The average rate of crying during this period, therefore, was six times per year. The episodes are not distributed equally throughout the whole period. There are sixty-four episodes recorded in the first volume, which covers the period 1869–1877, and twenty-six episodes in the second volume, 1878–1883. The rate decreases from about seven episodes a year to about four. Are these changes correlated with a change in Wagner's creative efforts?

Throughout much of his life, Wagner was a remarkably active artist, writing operas, compositions for the piano and for orchestra, plays, narratives, musical criticism, and other prose. Although he had already passed the peak of his creative years by the time the diary was begun, his pattern of producing operas, as well as other compositions and creative writing, continued through the period of the first volume of the diaries but virtually stopped during the period of the second. In Wagner's case, therefore, the association between weeping and creativity, as required by the hypothesis, is clear.

The life of Goethe also seems to support the hypothesis. Goethe had the unusual distinction of being both an artist and scientific genius. In fact, he was spectacularly creative: he came very near to being a universal genius. He was a virtuoso in the creation of poems, drama, and novels, many of which still have current appeal. He was an actor, composer, painter, and musician. He was also a philologist and a scientist. His work on the subjective side of color vision still stands, as do many of his other findings.

To this point, I have found Goethe's autobiography to be of little help, since it is rather formal. Most of it is given over to matters intellectual, political, and artistic. His biographies are very helpful, however; they provide very strong evidence that he was extraordinarily expressive of all of his emotions, and particularly, that he was given to profound episodes of weeping.

The issue of Goethe's emotionality surfaces in an odd but forceful way in Eissler's (1963) monumental (p. 1538) psychoanalytic study. This study mentions Goethe's emotions only in a very late chapter given over to an analysis of a sexual problem. Eissler discreetly speaks of "Goethe's sexual impediment and his attitude toward emotions," and calls attention to reports that Goethe was bothered by premature ejaculation.

Goethe apparently suffered from premature ejaculation precipitated by sexual foreplay, particularly by kissing, or perhaps even exclusively by kissing. It would fit into the general picture of his hyperemotionality, against which he later often protected himself by ceremoniousness and which, despite all precautions, was even then frequently interrupted by periods of intensely flowing emotions. Instances of his being overwhelmed by emotion can be seen in his reports of weeping when he thought of the vicissitudes of his characters (p. 1058).

Noting the extreme rapidity with which Goethe sometimes created a poem or story, Eissler goes on to trace both Goethe's sexual problem and his vast creativity to the same source, his tendency toward "immediate discharge." Actually, Eissler's speculations in this matter tell us nothing new. He is merely saying, in a ponderous way, that in three different areas, sex, emotional expression, and artistic creativity, Goethe was quick. In the fundamentally important questions of why or how Goethe was quick at artistic creation and how this quickness was linked to emotional expressiveness, Eissler is silent.

Eissler's chapter does establish the fact of Goethe's prodigies of emotional expressiveness. He reports an observation by one of his contemporaries about Goethe's griefwork:

I had been told how he had lost (several children) through death during those years, and how his paternal grief over this overpowered him to such an extent that he threw himself to the ground in unrestrained expressions of grief . . . (p. 1059).

Eissler's coverage of Goethe's emotional expressiveness is not limited to grief and crying, but covers a wide range. For example, Goethe was also capable of sudden happiness, of being surprised by joy:

. . . Once, on a fine summer's day, the great poet was sitting outdoors there in Carlsbad, at a table with wooden benches, together with some Weimarian acquaintances . . . Thereupon, absorbed in conversation, one saw Goethe's son coming down a hill. The young man was at that time studing in Heidelberg and, engaged on a hiking trip, he had directed it towards Carlsbad in order to surprise his father there by a visit. Thus, approaching the party at the table in such a manner that his father had his back turned to him and could not see his approach, he motioned eagerly to those sitting opposite to keep quiet and not to draw his father's attention to his arrival. Thus, finally, he sneaked up behind his father's back and, following a customary Weimarian jest, he suddenly put his hands over his father's eyes. As Goethe now disentangles himself and turns around and thus most unexpectedly sees his son, the joyful paternal feeling gets hold of him in a way that deeply moved those who were present. The boundless expressions of being overwhelmed by emotions which the august man exhibited were of such force that the witnesses of this scene were really frightened, and, out of concern for his mental state, wished his calming down (p. 1059).

Goethe's contemporaries, and even Eissler, saw Goethe's emotional expressiveness in a dubious light:

In view of all these factors, it is not improbable that the psychological basis of his personality tended towards a full emotional discharge on minimal provocation. This must not be thought of as a weakness of the sexual impulse or desire, but rather as a tendency·of the instinct itself—formed in accordance with the way his emotions unfolded—to present itself immediately with its full force. From his letters as a young man, one can see how the emotion, once stimulated, rushed with surprising rapidity to an almost unbearable peak. This, of course, often resulted in contradictory behavior. Also, it gave him at times ..... appearance of unpredictability, since his emotions were prone to develop to a maximum over incidents that looked *inconsequential* to the beholder (p. 1060); (my italics).

Eissler goes on to diagnose Goethe as having a hysterical personality. From the point of view presented in this paper, however, such a negative view of Goethe's expressiveness may be in error. It is conceivable that Goethe's ability to express immediately and fully his emotions, even, or perhaps especially, those engendered by "inconsequential" incidents, was the source of his creative power.

A comparison of the emotional lives of these three creators shows that although they were all three emotionally expressive, there is an important difference between Goethe and Proust, on one hand, and Wagner on the other. There are many indications in the lives of the first two that they wept not only easily and frequently but also unashamedly. Their lack of shame about weeping is particularly striking view of the intensity of many of their public weeping episodes. Although the onlookers of these episodes seem to have been surprised, puzzled and embarrassed, both Proust and Goethe apparently wept without being restrained by the reactions of others.

Wagner's feelings about his own weeping, however, stand in stark contrast to those of Proust and Goethe. As the quote from Glasenapp suggests and as the diaries make clear, Wagner was ashamed of his weeping and kept it secret. During the period of the diaries, it would appear that only his wife knew about this side of his personality. Wagner's attitude is not surprising for a 19th-century German male. As would also be true today, frequent and intense weeping by a grown a man would incur intense disapproval from onlookers. It is not Wagner's attitude toward his weeping that is unusual, but Goethe's and Proust's toward theirs. Even by the somewhat more relaxed standards of Proust's French context and the much more tolerant standards of Goethe's earlier era, their extreme weeping behavior and their own acceptance of it was unusual. I will examine this issue in terms of the affect of shame in order to make inferences about the role of this emotion in the lives of these three creators.

Recent work by Lewis (1971, 1981, 1984, 1985) suggests that shame dynamics are central to the repression of emotion. Her model of repression involves what she calls "feeling traps," emotional arousal which is indefinitely prolonged because of emotional reactions to one's own emotional reactions. Such spirals have no natural limits to their intensity and duration. Unlike simple emotional responses, which are brief and usually very low in intensity, feeling traps may result in almost continuous arousal of unlimited magnitude.

Most feeling traps, according to Lewis, involve shame. For example, the shame-rage spiral occurs when a person is ashamed of being angry. The result is humiliated fury. The anger cannot be discharged or even fully expressed, because it is bound by shame. This feeling trap seems to be identical to the emotional state that plays an important role in Kohut's psychology of the self, narcisstic rage. In his discussion of this state, he explicitly says that it is a compound of shame and rage (Kohut, 1978).

Lewis's concept of the feeling trap supplies the link that is missing from Kohut's idea, the relationship between shame and rage. In a feeling trap of shame and rage, one is enraged because one is ashamed and ashamed because one is enraged, a feedback loop which may never end. The feeling trap appears to offer a very general way of understanding the continuing process of repression.

The idea of the feeling trap may be useful in explaining the difference between the way Goethe and Proust seemed to manage grief, in contrast to Wagner's way. In the case of the former, their unashamed crying suggests the possibility that their grief was less repressed than in other men of their time; their grief was less bound by shame. It is not just the frequency of any type of crying that frees creative potential, but unashamed crying, as in the cases of Goethe and Proust. The many episodes of intense and unashamed crying in their lives suggests the possibility of not only less repressed grief, but of less repressed shame also. As the theory suggests, there seems to be a connection between catharsis and easy creative activity in these two cases.

Wagner's case is quite different, however. Like Goethe and Proust, he was an easy creator who cried quickly, frequently, and intensely. Unlike them, however, he was ashamed of his crying, to the point of keeping it a secret from everyone but his wife. If the theory is true, why wasn't his grief bound by shame? That is, how could he have escaped from the grief-shame feeling trap? A clue to this puzzle is suggested by Cosima's diaries. The entries show that in addition to crying frequently, Wagner was also a prodigious laugher. There were slightly over 300 entries over the fifteen year period. Although a few of the entries concerned minor laughter episodes, most were substantial. Our theory proposes that spontaneous, good natured laughter signals the catharsis of shame (see above). Perhaps the laughter episodes explain what would otherwise be an anomaly in Wagner's emotional life compared with the lives of Goethe and Proust. Wagner may have escaped from the grief-shame trap (and possibly other feeling traps, as well) through frequent episodes of intense laughter.

The scattered incidents from these biographies were presented, not in an attempt to prove the theory under consideration, but only to suggest its plausibility and to flesh out some of the vary abstract formulations. The section on creativity suggests, in a preliminary way, that the cost of the repression of the coarse emotions may be very high, or, more positively, that even the partial lifting of repression may produce creativity to the point of genius. With two colleagues, I am now involved in a study interviewing living geniuses among writers, composers, and physicists. We are attempting to further test the theory.

BIOGRAPHICAL NOTE

Thomas J. Scheff was born in Wewoka, Oklahoma and grew up in Kilgore, Texas. He went to the University of Arizona and majored in Physics. After college, he did graduate work first in Physics, then in Sociology. Professor Scheff teaches at the University of California, Santa Barbara, where he offers courses in Social Psychology. His research interest in the past few years has been in Emotions. His major published works are: (1) Being Mentally Ill; (2) Catharsis in Healing, Ritual, and Drama; and (3) Laughter and Resentment: Theory and Research on Catharsis, with Suzanne Retzinger.

REFERENCES

BOLTZMANN, L.
1899 "The Recent Development of Method in Theoretical Physics." *The Monist* 11: 229–230.
BOWLBY, J.
1960 "Grief and Mourning in Infancy and Early Childhood." *Psychoanalytic Study of the Child.* Reprinted in G. E. Daniels, ed., *New perspectives in Psychoanalysis* 15: 9–52. New York: Grune & Stratton. 1965.
BOWLBY, J.
1961 "Process of Mourning." *International Journal of Psychoanalysis*, 42: 317–340, reprinted in G. E. Daniels (ed.), *New perspectives in psychoanalysis*, 1965. New York: Grune & Stratton.
BOWLBY, J.
1963 "Pathological Mourning and Childhood Mourning." *Journal of the American Psychoanalytic Association*, 11: 500–541.
DURKHEIM, E.
1915 *The Elementary Form of Religious Life.* New York: Macmillan
EISSLER, K. R.
1963 *Goethe: A Psychoanalytic Study.* Detroit: Wayne State University Press.
EKMAN, P., FRIESEN, W., AND ELLSWORTH, P.
1972 *Emotion in the Human Face.* New York: Pergamon.
EKMAN, P., AND FRIESEN, W.
1982 "Felt, False, and Miserable Smiles." *Journal of Nonverbal Behavior.* 6: 1–25.

ENGEL, G.
1961 "Is Grief a Disease?" *Psychosomatic Medicine.* 23: 18–22
FREUD, S.
1909 Notes Upon a Case of Obsessional Neurosis. Vol. 10, S.E. London: Hogarth Press.
1916 Introductory Lectures on Psychoanalysis. Vol. 16, S.E. London: Hogarth Press.
FREUD, S.
1927 *Standard Edition.* 21: 61–166 London: Hogarth Press, 1961.
FREUD, S. & BREUER, J.
1895 *Studies on Hysteria.* New York: Avon Books, 1966
GLASENAPP, C. F.
1977 *Life of Richard Wagner.* New York: De Capo Press.
GREENSON, R.
1967 *The Technique and Practice of Psychoanalysis.* New York: International Universities Press.
HAGGARD, E. A., AND ISAACS, K. S.
1966 "Micromomentary Facial Expressions as Indicators of Ego Mechanisms in Psychotherapy" in L. A. Gottschalk and A. H. Auerbach (eds.), *Methods of Research in Psychotherapy.* New York: Appleton-Century Crofts.
HILGARD, E.
1977 *Divided Consciousness.* New York: Wiley.
IZARD, C.
1971 *The Face of Emotion.* New York: Appleton-Century Crofts.
JAMES, W.
1890 *The Principles of Psychology.* New York: Holtz.
KOESTLER, A.
1964 *The Act of Creation.* New York: Dell.
KOHUT, H.
1972 "Thoughts on Narcissism and Narcissistic Rage." *The Search for the Self.* New York: International Universities Press.
LEWIS, H. B.
1971 *Shame and Guilt in Neurosis.* New York: International Universities Press.
1981 *Freud and Modern Psychology.* New York: Plenum Press.
1984 *Freud and Modern Psychology.* Vol. 2. Emotions and Human Behavior. New York: Plenum Press.
1986 *The Role of Shame in Sympton Formation.* Patterson, N. J.: Lawrence Earlbaum Associates.
MASTERS, W., AND JOHNSON, V.
1966 *Human Sexual Response.* Boston: Little, Brown.
MEAD, G. H.
1934 *Mind, Self, and Society.* Chicago: University of Chicago Press.
NICHOLS, M. P., AND ZAX, M.
1977 *Catharsis in Psychotherapy.* New York: Gardiner Press.
NICHOLS, M., AND EFRAN, J. S.
1983 "Catharsis in Psychotherapy: A New Perspective." Unpublished manuscript.
PAINTER, G.
1959 *Marcel Proust: A Biography.* New York: Random House.
PARKS, C. M.
1972 *Bereavement: Studies of Grief in Adult Life.* New York: International Universities Press.
PROUST, M.
1978 *Remembrance of Things Past.* New York: New American Library. 1934.

REICH, W.
  1948 *Character Analysis*. London: Vision Press.
SCHEFF, T. J., AND BUSHNELL, D. D.
  1984 "A Theory of Catharsis." *Journal of Research in Personality 18: 238–264.*
SCHEFF, T. J., AND RETZINGER, S.
  1986 *Laughter and Resentment*: Theory and Research on Catharsis. Stanford: Stanford
  University Press.
TOMKINS, S. S.
  1963 *Affect/Imagery/Consciousness*. Vol.2. New York: Springer.
VOLKAN, V. D.
  1979 "Brief Psychotherapy and Pathological Grief: Re-Grief Therapy." T. B. Karasu
  and L. Bellak. (eds.) Specialized Techniques in Individual Psychotherapy. N.Y. Brunner,
  Mazel
WAGNER, C.
  1976 *Diaries, VI and V2*. New York: Harcourt Brace Jovanovich.
WETMORE, J.
  1963 "The Role of Grief in Psychoanalysis." *International Journal of Psychoanalysis* 44:
  97–103.
WINOGRAD, T.
  1984 "Computer Software for Working with Language." Scientific American 251: 130–
  145.

III

THE PSYCHOANALYTIC SOCIOLOGY OF GENDER

Introduction

THIS section investigates gender and psychoanalysis. Our three authors, Nancy Chodorow, Miriam Johnson, and Susan Contratto all attempt to understand and locate the sources of gender inequality, and all three find Freudian theory valuable in helping us understand gender inequality and male dominance. Each approaches the issue, however, from a slightly different perspective.

In the first article, "Feminism, Femininity, and Freud," Professor Nancy Chodorow investigates the seemingly opposing stances of feminism and Freudian theory. She concludes that this political movement and psychological theory *complement* rather than *contradict* one another. Chodorow begins by adopting a set of feminist questions and shows how satisfying answers may be derived from Freudian theory. She notes that feminists often ask: (1) What does Freud have to do with feminism? (2) Why is a complex psychological theory needed to explain a political movement? (3) How can the views of a sexist theorist be useful to an anti-sexist movement? Conversely, the author adopts a set of Freudian questions. What does feminism have to do with Freud? (2) Why can psychological theory be useful to a political movement? (3) How can a value-free science (psychoanalysis) learn from a value-laden social movement (feminism)? Chodorow's answers to each set of questions lead us to comprehend the deep connection between politics, social movements, sex, and gender.

Professor Miriam Johnson contends that internalized conceptions of masculinity and femininity derive from such social structural features as: the centrality of female figures in infant care, the mother-son incest taboo, and male-controlled marriage institutions. Johnson especially stresses the significance of fathering as a means of reproducing male dominance in a marriage system in which husbands are expected to be dominant over mothers/wives. This is the system that Freud assumes in his description of the Oedipus complex. In sociological terms, it is the "husband superiority" expected in the husband-wife relationship and magnified in the father-daughter relationship (because of the generational difference) that reproduces the feelings of "psychological dependence on men that can prove incapacitating to women as adults." It is also husband dominance that reproduces in sons a feeling of superiority to women that assuages the son's early fear of being psychologically overwhelmed by the mother. These psychic underpinnings of male dominance are reinforced by structural arrangements outside of marriage, itself, in the economy and polity. In the light of these considerations, Johnson suggests that the "equal parenting" solution to male dominance advocated by some feminists needs to be examined more critically.

While accepting many aspects of Freud's analysis, Johnson takes issue with his assumption that femininity *means* taking a subordinate stance with men and that masculinity *means* superiority to women. She argues that "if (psychoanalytic theory) is not to be oppressive to women, it must come to terms with the fact (which Freud recognized but did not deal with sufficiently) that gender identity is established prior to the Oedipal period and probably does not rest on either heterosexuality or dominance/submission."

Professor Contratto's article shows more concretely the effects, conscious and unconscious, of the patriarchal family culture frequently internalized by women. In "Father Presence in Women's Psychological Development," Contratto demonstrates how the power and control that fathers have in the family have a major impact on their own daughters' development and autonomy. On the basis of her clinical work Contratto argues that twenty-two women, all of whom are upper middle-class, have gone through a very "normal" childhood development but with some disturbing consequences. For almost all of these women, "father" was a very special person. He was the "head of household" dominant, persevering, and privileged. He was also fun, energetic, and charismatic. Mom, on the other hand, who was perceived as more accessible and more familiar, was also often seen as boring, submissive, dominated, and controlled by the husband. Identification with the mother by these daughters often meant that in being feminine, in being like mommy or a wife, they would have to be submissive and, hence, dominated. Identification with the father often meant that if they were independent and assertive, they felt they were being masculine. Identification with either or both parents involved gains and losses. One could gain a sense of femininity, but in doing so, one would be dominated and lose a sense of power, control, and independence. One could move towards independence and power and fear a loss of femininity.

Contratto describes the struggles and goals of her patients as they attempt to become independent and assertive, while trying to develop a commitment to a male partner. Contratto helps us feel the painful struggles that women and men have with control, autonomy, and intimacy, which are engendered by the organizational forms elaborated by Chodorow and Johnson.

Feminism, Femininity, and Freud

NANCY CHODOROW

In the last several years, there has been significant interest in psychoanalytic theory among feminists and many major, varied attempts to draw upon psychoanalysis as one basis of feminist social theory.[1] This interest would have surprised members of the women's movement in the late sixties and early seventies. The dominant feminist stance during this period, beginning with Betty Friedan, and continuing with major statements by Firestone, Millett, Weisstein, and others, was an enormous hostility to and condemnation of Freud. Freudian theory and therapy were taken as major factors in women's oppression (Bart, 1983).

The response to this feminist debate was quite mixed within psychoanalysis itself. The women's movement has spurred extensive rethinking, revision, and critique of Freud, especially in what are considered the "neo-Freudian" or cultural schools—Sullivanians, and the followers of Horney and Thompson (Miller, 1973, 1976). Within orthodox psychoanalysis as well, there has been a resurgence of interest in questions of female sexuality, female development, and the psychology of women more generally (Blum, 1977; Rolphe and Galenson, 1981). But also its seems there has been a strict attempt to keep this new research and interest scientific and sober, to make sure it is not influenced by what are seen as such extraneous considerations as politics or cultural values.

INTRODUCTION

In this paper I address two general questions (or objections) posed by feminists and Freudians which are related to these developments and to each other. Mainly, I address questions asked by feminists, but I also address questions asked by Freudian scholars and clinicians. Both sets of questions concern a claim put forth by feminist psychoanalytic theory: That femininity, feminism, and Freud are in many was related and gain meaning, one from the other.

What are these two general questions? The feminist asks: What does

Freud, or psychoanalysis, have to do with feminism? Does psychoanalysis have anything to do with "femininity," or anything meaningful to say about women? The Freudian's question is the obverse. The clinician or psychoanalyst asks, what does feminism have to do with Freud? Does feminism have anything to do with our psychoanalytic understanding of female psychology?

THE FEMINIST'S QUESTIONS

Let us expand the feminist's questions. The person who asks what Freud has to do with feminism may have in mind a number of objections. The first and most extreme position holds that women's oppression is political, economic, and social and that psychology has nothing to do with it.

A second position claims that women are certainly psychologically oppressed, but that we do not need a theory as mystified or complicated— relying on the unconscious and intrapsychic—to explain and understand female socialization and how women turn out the way they do. It has nothing to do with the unconscious but is obvious in daily life. Children grow up in a male-dominated society, channeled from the day they are born into pink and blue blankets, into playing with trucks or dolls, through books with sexist messages, and gender differentiating schools. Girls learn that they are supposed to be good and to please men, boys to be strong. "Society" imposes values on people, and they have to behave according to societal expectations. "Society" expects that women will not achieve or be active, so they are not. People respond according to the social situation they are in and the rewards they get. This was the argument made early by Betty Friedan (1963), and by Naomi Weisstein (1968), in her widely influential piece. It is made repeatedly by many others.

Third, the feminist argues, Freud's theory was sexist, anti-woman, misogynist. Freud denied women their own orgasms; he thought that women were without as great a sense of justice as men, that they were vain, jealous, full of shame, and have made no contributions to civilization except for weaving. He thought it obvious that any three-year old would think the masculine genitalia better than the feminine.

THE FREUDIAN'S QUESTIONS

We can also expand the Freudian's questions. The person who asks what feminism has to do with Freud may also have several objections in mind. First, according to the Freudian, psychoanalysis is a psychological theory and clinical practice: by contrast, feminism is a political movement, or at most a political theory. Psychoanalysis does not have to do with questions of politics, equality, or inequality.

The Freudian makes a second, related claim; the methodological claim that psychoanalysis is a value free science, simply recording the truth about human development and human psychological life and not taking sides. Feminism, by contrast, is value laden, and has an axe to grind.[2]

These are the sorts of questions and considerations I will discuss. I will address the feminist questions first, because I believe that this provides insight into the clinician's, or Freudian's, question as well. Let me say parenthetically that I consider feminism here as a theory and practice. Feminist theory must understand the social organization and dynamics of women and men in their life situations—of sexual inequality and asymmetry, of sexuality, of gender, parenting, children, of the relations between the sexes. But feminist theory must also contribute to a liberatory practice, to a practice that will free women from sexual inequality and enable things to change.

ANSWERING THE FEMINIST: THE IMPORTANCE OF FREUD FOR FEMINISM

To take on the feminist's questions: what does Freud have to do with feminism? Does psychoanalysis have anything meaningful to say about women and "femininity"? Recall the first objection: women's oppression is social and not psychological. It is concerned with wage inequality, job segregation, rape, wife-abuse, the unequal sexual division of labor in the home, men's power over women. Let us develop an answer.

To start, this social and political organization of gender does not exist apart from the fact that we are all sexed and gendered in the first place— that we all have a particular sexual organization and orientation, that we are all either men or women—which is a part of our fundamental identity and being in the world. We cannot understand the social and political organization and history of gender without simultaneously taking people's sexualization and engendering into account. So we are not talking here about external roles, as, for instance, some sociologists might want us to do: that people are workers, parents, teachers; that we differentiate occupational from family roles, the mother role from the father role; that people are personifications of economic categories. This is not the case with gender. People do not just play out a gender role that combines with other roles, or that they can step out of. We cannot step out of being sexed and gendered; this is *who we are*. We do not exist apart from being gendered, or have a separate self apart from our engendering. So, when we are interested in questions of gender and sexuality—even when our questions are in the first instance social, political, or economic—there is no easy line between psyche and society. The social organization of gender and people as sexed and gendered are an inextricable totality or unity: the social organization of gender is built right into our heads and divides the world into females and males. Our being sexed and gendered (our sexuality and our gender identity) is built right into social organization. They are only given meaning one from the other.

Feminist theory must be able to encompass these linkages, this totality. For our purposes, feminist theory must include the fact that we are psychologically gendered and sexed as part of who we are. The social organization of gender is not an organization of empty places or role categories that anyone can fill, as people have argued about places in the economy or polity. In the social organization of gender, only particular people can fill particular places.

But feminism also wishes to change the social organization and psychology of sex and gender. Its basic argument is that gender and sexuality, whatever the biology that helps to inform these, are *created* culturally and socially; they are not immutable givens. Therefore, feminism demands a theory of how we *become* sexed and gendered.

Freud has given us such a theory. He has given us a rich account of the organization and reproduction of sex and gender, of how were are *produced as gendered and sexed.* Psychoanalytic theory is almost by definition a theory of sexuality and the way sexuality develops in women and men. Freud shows us why we do not exist apart from our particular sexualization and gender identification, even though that sexualization and that gender identification are created. Let me mention a few important elements in Freud's argument.

First, Freud divorced, or liberated, sexuality from gender and procreation. As Freud argues, there is nothing inevitable about the development of sexual object choice, mode, or aim; there is no innate femininity or masculinity. We are all potentially bisexual, active or passive, polymorphous, perverse, and not just genital. How any woman or man understands, fantasizes about, symbolizes, internally represents, and feels about her or his physiology is a developmental product, and these feelings and fantasies may be shaped by considerations completely *apart* from biology. *Woman is made, not born, Freud tells us*, and he describes quite openly the special difficulty girls have in attaining an expected passive, heterosexual, genital adulthood. Freud argued, as well, that *both* homosexuality and heterosexuality, for *both* sexes, are products of development. Neither is innate.

Freud demonstrated that all sex—procreative and non-procreative, genital and non-genital, heterosexual and homosexual, autoerotic and

other oriented, child and adult—is on a continuum and related in man-
ifold ways. There is nothing special about heterosexual coitus for purposes of reproduction, which is just one kind of sex among many. Any
organ, almost any object, can have erotic significance.

Second, Freud tells us how, in spite of the fact that sexual and gender
development as we know them are not inevitable, *the development of gender,
personality, and sexual orientation tend to happen in regularized ways for women
and for men.* We find this in the classic account of the Oedipus complex,
which explains the development of masculine identity, the development
of female heterosexuality and love for the father, and differential forms
of superego formation. We find it in the important, late account of the
special nature of the pre-Oedipal mother-daughter relationship and the
effect this relationship has on a woman's later life. And we find that
Freud is quite candid about the fact that "normal" female development
is very costly to women. In a passage in his lecture on "Femininity," he
says:

I cannot help mentioning an impression that we are constantly receiving during
analytic practice. A man of about thirty strikes us as a youthful, somewhat un-
formed individual, whom we expect to make powerful use of the possibilities
for development opened up to him by analysis. A woman of the same age,
however, often frightens us by her psychical rigidity and unchangeability. Her
libido has taken up final positions and seems incapable of exchanging them for
others. There are no paths open to further development; it is as though the
whole process had already run its course and remains thence forward insuscep-
tible to influence—as though, indeed, the difficult development to femininity
had exhausted the possibilities of the person concerned (Freud, 1933a).

In this discussion of how gender personality and sexual orientation
develop in regularized ways for women and for men, there are two things
of particular note for feminist theory:

First, Freud demonstrates that *women's heterosexual attraction to men is
very tenuously achieved* and even then only partially. In the developmental
account, a girl wants a *penis* from her father, not him for his own sake.
Or she wants him as a refuge from mother, and always remains involved
with mother, taking the character of her relationship with her *mother* to
her relationships with men. Freud also implies that women only achieve
"true" object love in relation to children, not to men (he never looks to
see if women achieve true object love with women, which would be the
logical extension of his theory) (1933b). Women have no "natural" attraction to men; this attraction must be created.

Second, *the theory of the masculine Oedipus complex is a theory of the reproduction of male dominance.* Contempt for women, as penisless creatures,

and identification with his father in their common masculine superiority, are normal outcomes of the masculine Oedipus complex. The masculine Oedipus complex results in what Freud's follower, Ruth M. Brunswick (1940), calls "what we have come to consider the normal masculine contempt of women." This is the manner by which a boy comes to give up his mother as a love object and the reason he is willing to do so. Freud doesn't extend his insight here, but later analysts, like Karen Horney (1942) and Grete Bibring (1953), were able to do so. They demonstrated that the intertwining of contempt for women, fear of women, devaluation of women, feminine activities, and ways of being, are *developmental products*, resulting from a boy's first love object and primary parent being a woman. (Women, also, as a normal outcome of their Oedipus complex, come to devalue their own gender. We become who we are as men and women, with differential valuations of masculinity and femininity.

Finally, *Freud provided perceptive social analyses concerning oppressions of gender and sexuality*. Two examples must suffice here. First, in " 'Civilized' Sexual Morality and Modern Nervousness," Freud analyzed how sexual repression in childhood created conflictual and strained marital relationships which, in turn, affected the children of these marriages in ways that reproduced the whole situation in the next generation (Freud, 1908). A bourgeois woman, Freud argues, brings the sexual repression forced upon her into marriage, along with her dependence on her parents. These together lead her husband to turn elsewhere for sexual satisfaction. As she matures, however, her sexual interests awaken, but by then her husband is no longer around. As a substitute, she sexualizes her relationship to her children, awakening their sexuality, which must then be repressed (helping to create their neuroses). She also feels guilty about the resentment she has toward her husband because of his marital and sexual failures. She turns this resentment inward into neurosis, which hurts her, her children, and her marriage. Second, *Studies on Hysteria* gives us the glimmering of an argument for a relationship between constraint on women and neurosis. Here, Freud argues *against* the view prevalent in his time—that hysterics are degenerate and weak— and *for* the view that the women he treated were especially intelligent, creative, and moral. He suggested it was confinement, in caring for the sick, for instance, that did not allow the expression of a woman's gifts and capacities; her neurosis was a reaction (Freud, 1893–1895).

Thus, in answer to the first feminist question, I would suggest that Freud demonstrates the intertwining of psychological and social forms of gender oppression, and especially, that he provides an account of the genesis of phychological aspects of gender and sexuality in their social context.

To turn to the second feminist objection: why do we need such a complicated theory, one relying on unconscious mental processes, when it is obvious that society treats women and girls differently and pushes them into certain roles. Two issues are relevant here. We need to explain and understand the *tenacity* of people's commitment to our social organization of gender and sex: the *intensity* of the taboo on homosexuality; *why* people often cannot change even when they want to; *why* a "liberated" man still has difficulty with equal parenting or being completely happy about his successful, independent, liberated wife; or *why* a feminist woman might find it hard to be attracted to a non-macho, non-traditionally masculine man just because he's "nice" and egalitarian or to be unambivalent about choosing not to have children. Psychoanalysis helps here because it shows us that we also live our past in the present. We do not just react to our contemporary situation and conscious wishes, nor can we easily change values, feelings, and behavior simply if we have an encouraging social setting. Moreover, psychoanalysis explains our *commitment* to this past, which arose at a time of huge feelings of helplessness and dependency, a commitment now repressed, unconscious, and inaccessible to our conscious self. It is who we are, and changing that is very difficult. Role training theories, social learning theories, situational theories, cannot explain this tenacity as well. They suggest that gender and sexuality are added onto something else, to our "real" selves and can presumably be dropped at will. They also suggest that changing the social setting and nature of reinforcement should automatically change behavior, which we know from experience is not true. (This is not say that change is impossible. Psychoanalysis also argues for the replacement of unconscious determination by conscious choice: "where id was, there shall ego be." It is only to say that change is more, and often much more, than a matter of will, and that—as we know from contemporary politics—people's feelings about changes in the organization of sex and gender run very deep). To understand what we observe about gender psychology and behavior, we need a theory which includes unconscious mental factors.

Second, role learning theories and theories of situational reinforcement in fact make people (women in this case) into *passive reactors* to society. Where can the initiative for change come from in a theory in which people only react? Psychoanalysis, by contrast, is a theory *founded on people's creativity*. People always *make something* of their situation, even if that something is neurotic. (Neurosis, as we know from Freud's case studies, is highly original and individual.) People appropriate, fantasize, transform, react against, repress, resist, and symbolize their experiences. They create their inner object world and self. The goal of psychoanalysis is to make this individually created unconscious conscious, to move beyond being powered or directed by these active, though not always desirable to the individual, fantasies. Psychoanalysis, then, is a theory of human nature with positive, liberatory implications, a theory of people as active and creative.

Let us turn now to the third feminist objection, that Freud was sexist, and that psychoanalytic theory and practice have been oppressive to women. A few words must suffice on this very complex topic (Chodorow, 1978: Ch.9). First, we have to acknowledge that this criticism is not entirely wrong; Freud was indeed sexist. He wrote basically from a male norm and ignored women. He repeated cultural ideology in a context where it can be mistaken for scientific findings. He talks, for instance, about women's lesser sense of justice, jealousy, shame, vanity, and lack of contribution to civilization as if these were clinical findings, but then claims that these are "traits which critics [masculine critics, we may assume] of every epoch have brought up against women" ("Some Consequences"). He finds it perfectly natural that girls would find their own genitals inferior, talks of these girls' "genital deficiency" ("Femininity") and the "fact [note, not the fantasy] of her being castrated" ("Some Consequences"). He recognizes the costs to women of female development, as I mentioned, but he is quite cavalier about it and does not care much. It seems that "Nature" has taken less care of the feminine function than the masculine, but this does not really matter, since the "accomplishment of the aim of biology [i.e., procreation] has been entrusted to man's aggressiveness and left to some extent independent of women's consent" ("Femininity"). The evidence seems very clear that psychoanalytic theory has been used against women, for instance, when they were labelled frigid because they did not have what turned out to be a non-existent vaginal orgasm; when they were called masculine for wanting careers.

But there is a method to Freud's misogyny, and this method can be used against him.[3] Freud goes wrong, it turns out, when he undercuts his own psychoanalytic methodology and findings. I will give a few examples here. I suggest, however, that this is very widespread.

As we have seen, psychoanalysis is founded on Freud's discoveries that there is nothing inevitable about the development of sexual object choice, mode, or aim, and that all sexuality is qualitatively continuous. Freud argues explicitly that nothing inherently distinguishes procreative sex from any other sex (Three Essays; Introductory Lectures). But Freud implicitly has a functionalist, teleological theory that gender differentiation is *for the purposes* procreation. He defines procreative sexuality in a particular way: procreation is a product of *active, genital*, masculine heterosexuality and *passive, genital* feminine heterosexuality (Schafer, 1974). The theory becomes coercive, as Freud talks of Oedipal "tasks," and claims that "anatomy is destiny," in a functionalist sense rather than a maturational sense. These tasks and this destiny are not at all inevitable biologically, but they "must" happen for nature's requirements to be met.

But, this functionalism is not inherent to psychoanalysis; it comes in as Freud's value system. Similarly, women's passivity is not biologically inevitable, or even necessary to procreation. It is only necessary to *male dominant* sex, which Freud also takes for granted (Johnson, 1981).

In psychoanalytic theory, *traumas need explaining*. Psychoanalysis *always* looks for the *history* of something conflictual and powerful in previous individual history, *except* in the case of penis envy. Penis envy is self-evident, and not in need of any explanation: "she sees one and she knows she wants one." If we employ psychoanalytic methodology and look to the *history* of this powerful conflict, we can learn a lot about the origins of penis envy. We can learn about the pre-Oedipal girl's relation to her mother and early development; about her desire for autonomy and for something that can symbolize that autonomy; about symbols of male supremacy in the culture and in her family.

In addition to the male genitals being self-evidently better than female genitals, penis envy *is* "necessary" to the creation of female passivity. This is another reason why Freud does not take it as problematic or in need of explanation. In Freud's theory, girls come to want babies as a substitute for the penis (the penis-baby equation). But Freud also admits that girls *already* may want babies, as part of their identification with their mother. This won't do for Freud, however, who has to get the girl's passive heterosexuality and a man into the baby picture. So, he claims, wanting a baby as identification with mother is "not an expression of femininity"! Only when the baby becomes a baby from the father as a substitute for a penis is it a *feminine* wish. Penis envy here becomes a *developmental task*, not inevitable or biologically determined but necessary for a girl to achieve her "destiny."

A third example of Freud"s undercutting his own methodology is his claim that "woman is made, not born." The little girl is originally a "little man," because she loves her mother with an active sexuality. Both sexes are originally masculine. But there is a peculiar asymmetry in the developmental account here. Either, it would seem, you need to take a biological determinist view, in which case both women and men are born, or a developmental/cultural view, in which case both women and men are made. But if the little girl is a little man, then, seemingly, man is born but woman is made.

I could go on. The point is, that unless you think Freud took an extreme "biology of the sexes" position, and he did not (although many psychoanalysts do), his anti-woman statements are not intrinsic to psychoanalytic theory and modes of theorizing or to clinical interpretation, but *counter to them*. This is why there has been, and has needed to be, such extensive feminist critique and revision of Freud. But because the theory is so useful, the critique and revision have often been rich and provocative.

Answering the Freudian: Why Psychoanalysis and Feminism are Intrinsically Linked

I would now like to turn briefly to address the questions of the Freudian who wonders what feminism has to do with Freud, who thinks and argues that feminism has nothing to do with Freud. We can use our insights from the previous discussion to address these questions. The first question, or objection, argued that psychoanalysis is only a psychological theory. Clinical practice, interested in psychic structure, mental processes, and the development of sexuality has nothing to do with politics, equality, or inequality.

My argument for why feminists must incorporate an understanding of Freud into their theory and practice should make the response here obvious. Freud *made* gender and sexuality central to his theory. Psychoanalysis is first and foremost a theory of femininity and masculinity, a theory of gender inequality, and a theory of the development of heterosexuality. Freud did not develop just any theory or clinical practice, but this specific one. Moreover, psychoanalysis makes a feminist argument, that women "and men" are made and not born, that biology is not enough to explain sexual orientation or gender personality.

Just as we cannot have a theory of the social organization of gender and sexuality apart from a psychological theory, so we cannot have a psychological theory of sex and gender apart from the social and political. *Freud's theory is a social and political theory.* The analysis of development that Freud puts forth is not the analysis of *any* development, but of *development in a particular social situation which is intrinsic to the theory.* That children develop in a family where *women* mother or perform primary parenting functions explains the development that Freud found; biology does not explain this development. *Psychoanalysis shows that women and men and male dominance are reproduced in each generation as a result of a social division of labor in which women mother* (recall the account of men's psychology and ideology of male superiority, of the nature of women's heterosexuality and connections to women and children, of women's self-valuation, of the development of attitudes toward women). *That people*

develop in a society with a heterosexual norm and with parents who are hetero-
sexual, is also intrinsic to Freud's theory and explains development, whereas
biology does not. (Otherwise, why should a girl turn from the mother whom
she loves? Why should the mother experience her son and daughter
differently and treat them differently? Why should father-daughter attraction develop?)

Further, *Freud's theory assumes, and is founded on, "politics" in a wide sense.*
The inequality of child and adult, the child's powerlessness, is *central* to
the explanation of character and neurosis development and of the formation of defenses. The inequality of women and men is central to the
theory. Freud does not give us a theory which explains what is necessary
for species survival or the survival of *any* society. He constructs his theory
around what is necessary for the perpetuation of a male dominant social
organization; for the restriction of women's sexuality to be oriented to
men's; for the perpetuation of heterosexual dominance.

What about the second psychoanalytic objection, that psychoanalysis
is a value-free science with no axe to grind, that psychoanalysis doesn't
take sides about anything, whereas feminism is value-laden and by definition takes sides. I would give two kinds of answers to this objection.
Most generally, I would say, psychoanalysis is not a behavioral or medical
science; it cannot be, and should not be, a value-free positivistic description and explanation of behavior. Rather, it is an interpretive theory of
mental processes, and with an interpretive theory, we can only say that
an interpretation makes better or worse sense, not that it is true or false,
right or wrong. Similarly, psychoanalysis is not founded on the objective
description of someone out there about someone studied, but comes out
of the *transference situation*: a mutually created interpersonal situation
which in its turn reflexively informs the processes of free association,
interpretation, and the further working through of the transference.
"Observer" and "observed" together create psychoanalytic theory and
clinical practice through their interaction and the interpretation of that
interaction.

On a completely different track, but in answer to the same objection,
it must be pointed out that Freud, himself, made the "mistake" of constantly intertwining ideological positions with clinical interpretation and
theory. Freud made an insistence on inequality central. There is nothing,
for instance, inherently valuational in saying that women and men have
differently formed superegos, or different modes of object-choice, or
differently formed body images. But Freud insisted on introducing value
and judgment, in arguing that men's mode of superego development
and function, men's mode of object choice, and men's body image were
better and more desirable.

Finally, we must recognize that Freud did not content himself with simply making *ad hominem* claims about women. *He actively threw down the political gauntlet at feminists* in ways which make unclear whether it was he, himself, or feminists who first chose to make psychoanalysis a center of ideological struggle. In "The Dissolution of the Oedipus Complex," published in 1924, he claims that "the feminist demand for equal rights between the sexes does not take us far." In 1925, in "Some Psychological Consequences of the Anatomical Distinction between the Sexes," he argues that "we must not allow ourselves to be deflected from [conclusions about women's lesser sense of justice, vanity, envy] by the denials of feminists, who are anxious to force us to regard the two sexes as completely equal in position and worth." When such criticism begins to creep into the psychoanalytic ranks themselves, and women psychoanalysts begin to object to his characterizations of women and claim that it may be biased, he responds with a more subtle anti-woman put-down: women psychoanalysts were not afflicted with the negative characteristics of femininity but were special and unlike other women. "This doesn't apply to *you*. You're the exception; on this point you're more masculine than feminine."

CONCLUSIONS

Let me try to bring my original query together, a query about the relation of femininity, feminism, and Freud. We started with the justifiable anger of past feminists. Freud does give us a prime example of an ad hominem, distorted ideology about women and women's inferiority, an ideology which feminists must confront, challenge, and transform.

More importantly, Freudian theory does not just oppress women. Rather, Freud gives us a theory concerning how people—women and men—become gendered and sexed, how femininity and masculinity develop, how sexual inequality is reproduced. With the exception of anthropological kinship theorists like Malinowski, Fortes, Levi-Strauss, Schneider, and others, no major classical social theorist has made sex and gender central to his theory. In telling us how we come to *organize* sexuality, gender, procreation, parenting, according to psychological patterns, Freud tells us how nature becomes culture and how this culture comes to appear as and to be experienced as "second nature"—appears as natural. Psychoanalytic theory helps to demonstrate how sexual inequality and the social organization of gender are reproduced. It demonstrates that this reproduction happens in central ways *via transformations in consciousness*, in the psyche, not only via social and cultural institutions. It demonstrates that this reproduction is an unintended product of the structure of the sex-gender system itself—of a family division of labor in which women mother, of a sexual system founded on heterosexual norm, of a culture that assumes and transmits sexual inequality. Freud, or psychoanalysis, tells us how people become heterosexual in their family development (how the originally matrisexual girl comes to be heterosexual rather than lesbian); how a family structure in which women mother produces in men (and in women, to some extent) a psychology and ideology of male dominance, masculine superiority, and the devaluation of women and things feminine; how women develop maternal capacities through their relationship to their own mothers (which I do not discuss in detail here). Thus, psychoanalysis demonstrates the internal mechanisms of the socio-cultural organization of gender and sexuality and confirms the early feminist argument that the "personal is political." It argues for the rootedness and basicness of psychological forms of inequality and oppression.

Psychoanalysis does not stop at this demonstration. Freud suggests that these processes do not happen so smoothly, that this reproduction of gender and sexuality is rife with contradictions and strains. People develop conflicting desires, discontents, neuroses. Psychoanalysis *begins from psychic conflict*; this is what Freud was first trying to explain. Heterosexuality is not constituted smoothly for all time: Women still want relationships and closeness to women, and male heterosexuality is embedded in Oedipal devaluation, fear and contempt of women as well as a fear of the overwhelmingness of mother and of acknowledging emotional demands and needs. Male dominance on a psychological level is a masculine defense and a major psychic cost to men, built on fears and insecurity; it is not straightfoward power. Psychoanalysis demonstrates, against theories of over-socialization and total domination, a *lack* of total socialization. It demonstrates discontent, resistance, and an undercutting of sexual modes and the institutions of sexual inequality.

Psychoanalysis is also a theory that people *actively* appropriate and respond to their life environment and experiences, make something of these psychologically, and, therefore, presumably can act to change them.

NOTES

1. See Benjamin, 1977, 1978, 1980, 1981; Dinnerstein, 1976; Flax, 1978a, 1978b, 1981, 1983, n.d.; Johnson 1981a & b; Keller,n.d.; Mitchell, 1974: Rubin, 1975.

2. Sociologists are in the middle here. Traditional sociology would agree with the feminist that gender is social and not psychological; or if

it is psychological; a social learning perspective explains it. A feminist sociologist would also be critical of Freud's misogyny. But a traditional sociologist would also take the psychoanalytic methodological position in favor of value-free theory and method, against the feminist sociologist who would argue for a "sociology for women," and that traditional science is male-biased, as psychoanalysis is.

3. I am indebted in this discussion to Roy Schafer.

BIOGRAPHICAL NOTE

Nancy Julia Chodorow was born in New York City and grew up in Menlo Park, California. She went to Radcliffe College and majored in social anthropology. After college, she did graduate work in sociology. Professor Chodorow teaches at the University of California, Santa Cruz, where she offers courses in feminist theory, psychoanalytic sociology, and family sociology. Her interests in the past few years have been in psychoanalytic social theory; early women psychoanalysts. Her major published works are: *The Reproduction of Mothering: Psychoanalysis and the Sociology of Gender*; "Gender, Relation and Difference in Psychoanalytic Perspective:" and "Beyond Drive Theory: Object Relations and the Limits of Radical Individualism."

REFERENCES

BART, P.

1983 A Review of the Reproduction of Mothering, in J. Trebilcot (ed.). Rowman & Allenheld.

BENJAMIN, J.

1977 "The End of Interalization: Adorno's Social Psychology." 32 in *Telos*.

1978 "Authority and the Family Revisted, or A World Without Fathers?" 13 in New German Critique.

1980 "Rational Violence and Erotic Domination," in H. Eisenstein and A. Jardine (eds.), The Future of Difference. Boston: G. K. Hall.

1981 "The Oedipal Riddle: Authority, Autonomy, and the New Narcissism," in J. Diggins and M. Kamm, The Problem of Authority in America. Philadelphia: Temple.

BIBRING, G.

1953 "On the 'Passing of the Oedipus Complex' in a Matriarchal Family Setting," p. 278–284 in R. M. Lowenstein (ed.), Drives, Affects, and Behavior: Essays in Honor of Marie Bonaparte. New York: International Universities Press.

BLUM, H. P.

1977 Female Psychology. R. M. Brunswick New York: International Universities Press.

1940 "The Pre-Oedipal Phase of the Libido Development," p. 231–253 in Robert Fliess (ed.), The Psychoanalytic Reader. New York: International Universities Press.

CHODOROW, N.

1978 The Reproduction of Mothering. Berkeley: University of California Press.

DINNERSTEIN, D.

1976 The Mermaid and the Minotaur. Harper & Row.

FLAX, J.
1978a "The Conflict Between Nurturance and Autonomy in Mother-Daughter Relationships and Within Feminism." Feminest Studies 4 (1): 171–189.
1978b "Critical Theory as a Vocation." 8, 2 Politics and Society.
1981 "Mother-Daughter Relationships: Psychodynamics, Politics and Philosophy," in H. Eisenstein and A. Jardine (eds.), The Future of Difference. Boston: G. K. Hall.
1983 "Political Philosophy and the Patriarchal Unconscious," in S. Harding and M. B. Hintikka (eds.), Discovering Reality: Feminist Perspectives on Epistemology, Metaphysics, Methodology, and the Philosophy of Science. Reidel.
n.d. "On Freud: Narcissim, Gender and the Impediment to Intersubjectivity." Unpublished ms. paper.
FREUD, S.
1893–95 Studies on Hysteria. Vol. 2, S. E. London: Hogarth Press.
1908 Civilized Sexual Morality and Modern Nervous Illness. 9: 179–204, S. E., London: Hogarth Press.
1933a "Femininity." New Introductory Lectures on Psychoanalysis. S. E. Vol. 22, S. E. London: Hogarth Press.
1933b On Narcissism: An Introduction. 14: 69–102, S. E. London: Hogarth Press.
FRIEDAN, B.
1963 The Feminine Mystique. New York: Dell.
HORNEY, K.
1942 "The Dread of Women." International Journal of Psychoanalysis 13: 348–360.
JOHNSON, M. M.
1975 "Fathers, Mothers and Sex Typing." Sociological Inquiry 45:15–26.
1981a "Heterosexuality, Male Dominance and the Father Image," Sociological Inquiry 51:129–139.
1981b "Reproducing Male Dominance." This volume.
KELLER, E. F.
n.d. Reflections on Gender and Science. New Haven: Yale University Press.
MILLER, J. B.
1976 Toward a New Psychology of Women. Beacon.
1973 Psychoanalysis and Women. Baltimore: Penguin Books.
MITCHELL, J.
1974 Psychoanalysis and Feminism. New York: Pantheon Books.
ROLPHE, H., and GALENSON, E.
1981 Infantile Origins of Sexual Identity. New York: International Universities Press.
RUBIN, G.
1975 "The Traffic in Women: Notes on the Political Economy of Sex," in R. Reiter (ed.), Toward an Anthropology of Women. Monthly Review Press.
SCHAFER, R.
1974 "Problems in Freud's Psychology of Women." Journal of American Psychoanalytic Association 22 (3): 459–485.
WEISSTEIN, N.
1968 "Kinder, Küche, Kirche: Psychology Constructs the Female." New England Free Press.

Reproducing Male Dominance: Psychoanalysis and Social Structure

MIRIAM M. JOHNSON

SOCIAL learning theorists imply that male dominance is a relatively superficial phenomenon which can be eradicated by getting rid of outmoded stereotypes concerning female inferiority or by encouraging a more androgynous set of traits in both sexes (Kaplan and Bean, 1976). In contrast, feminists using psychoanalytic theory in conjunction with an analysis of social structure suggest that male dominance is far from being superficial. It is built into our deepest feelings and understandings about what being masculine or being feminine means. These conceptions of gender, in turn, derive from certain basic (but not invariant or inevitable) features of social organization. They include not only economic and political organization but also, and more fundamentally, such things as the social assignment of "mothering" to women, marriage, the taboo on incest, and other aspects of kinship organization. These latter aspects of social organization impinge most directly on the gender development of the young child.

Some feminists, who have utilized psychoanalytic theory along with an analysis of the social organization of biological reproduction, have concentrated their attention on the psychic consequences for male and female children of women's mothering. Others have focused on the psychic consequences of the mother-son incest taboo and men's dominance as fathers. Specifically, Nancy Chodorow (1978) has discussed how women's mothering reproduces a more relational orientation in females and a more distanced orientation in males. Both Chodorow (1974) and Dorothy Dinnerstein (1976), among many others, have argued that women's mothering reproduces the motive to devalue females in both sexes. While these theorists tend to "locate" the reproduction of male dominance in women's mothering, other feminist theorists, most notably Juliet Mitchell (1974 a and b) and Gayle Rubin (1975), structurally "locate" the reproduction of male dominance in other aspects of human kinship arrangements. This is found especially in the mother-son incest taboo enforced by the father and in male controlled marriage institutions.

Juliet Mitchell, principally, sees "feminity" in women as being reproduced through a girl's relationship with her father. "Masculinity" in men is reproduced by the boy's understanding that the father "owns" the mother.

In this paper, I will be concerned with extending and modifying these latter analyses in order to argue that, while the social assignment of mothering to women produces a generalized motive in males to devalue and dominate women, marriage institutions tend to give males control over women's mothering. Male dominated marriage is the context in which women's mothering takes place and is the context in which children in this society grow up. Analyses of the effects of women's mothering, then, need to be accompanied by an examination of the organization of male hegemony over women in marriage. How the role of husband-father, at least as presently constructed, contributes to the internalization of attitudes fostering male dominance in sons' acquiescence in that dominance by daughters must also be considered. It is the "husband superiority" expected in the husband-wife relationship that, I will argue, reproduces in female offspring the feelings of psychological dependence on men that can prove incapacitating to women as adults. It is also the husband's hegemony over the wife that reproduces in sons a feeling of superiority to women that assuages their earlier fear of being psychologically engulfed by the mother.

While Mitchell's and Rubin's reading of Freud correctly highlights his own emphasis on the husband-father and marriage institutions, their conclusions arc problematic. They carry over certain unexamined assumptions from psychoanalytic theory which cause them to believe that in order to do away with male dominance, we must do away with gender identity and all differentiation between the sexes. I contend that this is not necessarily so, and that if it is not to be oppressive, psychoanalytic theory must come to terms with the fact (which Freud recognized but did not deal with explicitly) that gender identity is established prior to the Oedipal period and probably does not rest on heterosexuality or dominance/submission. In Freud's paradigm, femininity is not defined in terms of women's capacity to bear children but on women's capacity to be impregnated by men. In social structural terms this view subsumes motherhood under heterosexual marriage; in role terms, it assumes that women's sense of self is based on the relatively subordinate wife role, not on the considerably more powerful, mother role. The Freudian paradigm does, however, reflect the structure of the contemporary nuclear family. Mitchell and Rubin are correct in seeing male dominance in this structure, but incorrect in seeing male dominance as inherent in gender difference.

Gynocentric Psychoanalytic Perspectives on Male Dominance

As noted, in its various forms, the "gynocentric" argument maintains essentially that male misogyny results from the fact that women are the primary caretakers of infants. One version has it that women's mothering generates fear and envy of females in males and causes them to have a psychological need to constrain women. Dorothy Dinnerstein (1976), has argued that men and women "collude" to allow men to dominate because it appears to be less of a psychological threat than the primitive, intense, all encompassing power infants attribute to mothers and from which they never quite recover as adults. Another version of gynocentric theory maintains that women's mothering causes males to feel less securely masculine and leads them to deny in themselves the femininity acquired from the mother. This is accomplished by devaluing all things female and assigning greater value to whatever tasks and traits are considered especially appropriate to males in a given society. (For a summary of both versions see Stockard and Johnson, 1979).

Nancy Chodorow's elegantly argued book, *The Reproduction of Mothering* (1978) reflects a gynocentric view to some extent. She is concerned with women as mothers. In this book, as opposed to her earlier writings, she is not primarily concerned with gender inequality but with gender *differences* in relational capacities. She contends that women's greater relational capacities and their interests in mothering and men's more rigid and distanced egos are created by mothers' propensity to bind their daughters to them more closely than their sons. She sees these differences as being related to male dominance because they tend to perpetuate women's association with the domestic sphere and men's association with the public sphere, which in turn gives males greater authority. Chodorow maintains that equal parenting by a male and female would help eliminate the male motive to dominate and would eliminate the extreme versions of both women's relational ego and men's non-relational ego.

Phallocentric Perspectives on Male Dominance

Gynocentric arguments, however, focus only on women as mothers and not on women as wives. Within the mother-child dyad, *the mother* has power, but within the context of marriage, it is the husband-father who is perceived as having power and who embodies male dominance. The phallocentric analyses of Juliet Mitchell and Gayle Rubin virtually ignore women's mothering and attempt to link Freud's description of the Oedipus complex to Levi-Strauss's theories about the consequences of incest taboos for the exchange of women by men in human marriage systems.

JULIET MITCHELL AND MEN AS FATHERS

In her book, *Psychoanalysis and Feminism,* Mitchell justified taking Freud's analysis of male and female psychosexual development seriously in terms of the necessity for women to know "the devil you have got" (1974a: 361). Mitchell thought Freud should be understood as providing a description of psychic reality, the often unconscious ideas in people's heads in patriarchal culture. The fact that the content of these ideas is oppressive to women, she says, makes it all the more important that we study them to understand the true enormity of the problem women face. Mitchell essentially follows the French philosopher, Lacan's, interpretation of Freud which, in effect, erects the ordinarily flaccid anatomical penis into a cultural "phallus" symbolizing "everpresent potency" and the right to the possession of women.

The Oedipus complex is precipitated in the girl, according to Mitchell's reading of Freud, when she finds out that she "has no phallic powers and thus will not now or ever possess her mother or her later substitute (a wife) . . . .she recognizes her castration, envies the phallic power, and has to do her best to overcome this envy" (1974b:34). The girl then turns to her father in the hope of obtaining a phallus in the form of a male child and only gradually relinquishes this hope. The little boy resolves his Oedipus complex by accepting the fact that his phallic powers are inferior to his father's but understands that "he will later have the same patriarchal rights and a woman of his own" (1974b:34). The above statements emphasize a crucial point: for Freud, and for psychoanalytic theory in general, masculinity *means* possessing a woman and femininity means being possessed by a man. Thus when females resign themselves to "femininity," if we accept Freud's premise, it means resigning themselves to passivity vis-à-vis males. This is the "normal" outcome of the Oedipal conflict for women.

Mitchell does not challenge this interpretation; she emphasizes it. The only hope for change that Mitchell can give us is her contention that the phenomena she describes are ideological instead of biological.

In order to give these ideas some basis in institutional reality, Mitchell does try to relate Oedipal events to institutional arrangements by using the work of the anthropologist, Claude Levi-Strauss who, like Freud, deals with the incest taboo. Levi-Strauss (1969) argued that the mother-son and brother-sister incest taboo had the effect of forcing men to marry outside their own kin group and in so doing, to form solidarity bonds with non-kin males, thereby creating and sustaining a wider sense of bondedness and community among males. Reciprocity between unrelated men was thus established by means of the exchange of sisters, and thereby, society and human culture came into being. The argument that marriage serves to unite kin groups, and makes society possible can be made without calling it the "exchange of *women*," but it was important to Levi-Strauss that it was women who were exchanged.

As far as I can tell, Mitchell does not really answer the question of why it is men who exchange women and not vice versa. Instead, she repeats Levi-Strauss's argument that this is the very basis of human society. Thus Mitchell assumes the position that the "patriarchal culture" we want to change cannot change because it is the basis of our humanity. In the end, such analysis leads us to the conclusion that there is nothing to be done to end male dominance or that a revolution of such vast proportions must take place that it is unlikely to occur. Essentially, because of its ahistorical nature, Mitchell's scheme is just as deterministic as any biological determinism might be.

Mitchell's service to feminism lies not in her attempts to find structural correlates of psychological phenomena by way of Levi-Strauss, but in the way she highlights the issue of male dominance in her reading of Freud. Her interpretation stresses Freud's own emphasis on the father as the key figure for both sexes in the Oedipal conflict. It is the father who comes to be seen as threatening by the boy and loving by the girl. Both male and female infants love the mother and both abandon her for the father (1974b:34). Mitchell explicitly states that it is the central role played by the father, or "the name-of-the-father," or the father image, that lies behind her own use of the term "patriarchy" rather than "male dominance(1974b:36)."

"Patriarchy" does not mean, for Mitchell, a particular kind of kinship structure in which the father holds the power of life and death over family members but refers to the role the father image plays in the acquisition of masculinity in males and femininity in females during the Oedipal period. She follows Freud in seeing "femininity" as passive submission to males and fails to consider the possibility that "femininity" may rest on active caring and nurturant orientations rather than on being a passive object.

Gayle Rubin and the Exchange of Women

Perhaps because she is an anthropologist, Gayle Rubin does not treat Levi-Strauss's ideas as abstractly as Mitchell. She uses ethnographic materials to spell out the sense in which Levi-Strauss's contention that marriage systems involve "the exchange of women by men" is true. The exchange of women by men, says Rubin, must be interpreted to mean that men everywhere have "certain rights in their female kin, and that women do not have the same rights either to themselves or to their male kin" (1975:177). Rubin stresses that the "exchange of women" idea should not be taken literally but that it can become a beginning point for understanding what she calls sex/gender systems.

While Mitchell's (and Freud's) real interest is in fathers, Rubin is concerned with analyzing the sexual division of labor and marriage. Levi-Strauss argued that in human societies, not only is there a taboo on incest which forces outside marriages, but there is also a taboo on one sex doing the work of the other, which forces people to marry in the first place. In other words, while the exact tasks that are considered appropriate for each sex vary from society to society, all societies have a division of labor based on sex, which causes males and females to need marriage to survive. Rubin takes this further and suggests that cultural norms prescribing heterosexuality are themselves devices to reinforce this cross-sex bonding. Ultimately, then, kinship arrangements which put women at a disadvantage depend on heterosexuality in both men and women. This heterosexuality, like the wider division of labor, requires the repression of half of what one might be. Rubin's analysis leads her to call for a revolution in kinship. The Oedipus complex must be dismantled and along with this, gender differentiation itself. Rubin describes her vision of the future as a "genderless (though not sexless) society, in which one's sexual anatomy is irrelevant to who one is, what one does, and with whom one makes love"(1975:204). I do not expect to see all gender differentiation end. Rather, a more realistic hope is that we can move toward a society in which each individual's basic sense of gendered self can be separable from heterosexuality as a way of life and from expectations of male dominance in heterosexual relationships.

In sum, Mitchell and Rubin provide an important supplement and counter to those who look to women's mothering for an explanation of gender differentiation. In differing ways, both are arguing that it is men's dominant position in marriage, or as fathers—not women's motherhood—that must be examined if male dominance is to be eradicated. The problem with both Mitchell's and to a lesser extent, Rubin's analyses, is that they overgeneralize to all societies. Neither of them questions Freud's assumption that the core of gender differentiation is being desirous of the other sex.

FREUD'S CONCEPTION OF GENDER DIFFERENCE

As both Mitchell and Rubin show, Freud, to his great credit, did not take masculinity in males and femininity in females as being given at birth. While there may be disagreement about how large a weight Freud gave to biological factors, there can be no doubt that gender differentiation for Freud was something which was, at least in part, "accomplished" rather than given. Freud saw each sex as possessing elements of both masculinity and femininity and referred to this as bisexuality. These elements were both physiological and psychological in nature. For Freud the psychic manifestations of bisexuality included a wide range of behaviors from overt homosexuality to cross gender, non-erotic behavior. While bisexuality lay at the basis of all psychopathology, according to Freud, he was also quite clear that normals were never totally masculine or feminine in their behavior (See Stoller, 1974).

The problem with Freud arises not with regard to any insensitivity on his part as to the precariousness of gender, but with the fact that he equated what we now call gender with issues of sexuality and dominance. Even though Freud treated bisexuality as a highly inclusive category, heterosexuality was built into his definition of masculinity and femininity in such a way that masculinity meant an active heterosexual orientation toward females and femininity meant a passive, heterosexual orientation toward males. One could deviate from femininity by being active and/ or by choosing a female object. What one cannot do within the scheme is deny the centrality of heterosexuality and male dominance to gender differentiation.

When Freud says that the orientation of both pre-Oedipal boys and pre-Oedipal girls is predominantly masculine, he clearly defines masculinity as meaning a phallic (which for Freud is by definition active) orientation toward the mother.[2] Freud argued that a female first loved her mother as a little man, as does the little boy. The little boy then has a head start on masculinity because of his early relationship with his mother; and as Stoller recently stated, Freud never doubted that this relationship was "fundamentally heterosexual." (Stoller, 1974:356–57). Even though Freud did make a few statements concerning the possibilities of affectionate identification with the parent of the same sex (Burlingham, 1973:26–27), he generally thought of same sex relationships as threatening gender identity. Opposite sex relationships affirmed it. This conclusion results from his equation of masculinity with an active orientation toward females—an attitude Freud saw as being symbolized by the phallus.

Freud's commitment to the mating, as opposed to the nurturing aspects of reproduction, seems related to his claim that parenting was not a primary wish in either sex. Motherhood was not feminine, being loved by a man was. As late as 1933, Freud explicitly stated that the doll play of a young girl is "not in fact an expression of her femininity." He explained this by saying it could not be feminine because "it served as an identification with her mother with the intention of substituting activity for passivity" (Freud, 1974:87). For Freud, femininity is not active mothering, nor is femininity acquired by identifying with the mother.

In dealing only with Freud, because Mitchell and Rubin dealt only with Freud, I do not wish to imply that others in the psychoanalytic tradition have avoided his merger between gender, heterosexuality, and male dominance. Even gynocentric psychoanalytic thinkers who have stressed womb and breast envy in boys and who see penis envy in girls as a secondary rather than a primary development, maintain the connection between gender identity and heterosexuality. Karen Horney, for example, was one of the first to argue against Freud's ideas concerning females' initial penis envy. She did so only to conclude that penis envy was a secondary development in females which acted as a defense against their *innate heterosexual* desires for the father. (Horney 1974:179-80). Even though Freud's phallocentric conclusions were related to his merger of male dominance, heterosexuality, and masculinity, it does not follow that those who stress women's mothering make a total break with his conceptualization. Sometimes, as with Horney, they draw the connections between sexuality and gender even more firmly by making them biologically given.

Perhaps the person who comes closest to a full-fledged reconceptualization of gender development within the psychoanalytic tradition is Robert Stoller. He concludes that the boy's first interaction with the mother is *not* heterosexual but involves a merging with the mother's femininity, just as the girl merges with her femininity. The nature of this femininity is recognized, at least implicitly by Stoller, as being essentially a maternal impulse as opposed to a heterosexual one. Stoller argues that Freud misinterprets the famous Schreber case when he labels Schreber's fantasies "homosexual." Schreber's fantasies were actually about his body changing to female and procreating a new race. Schreber was thinking in terms of maternal creativity, not sexual relations (Stoller, 1974:351–53). Thus Schreber wanted to *be* a *mother* (not *have* a *man*). Stoller's work can offer a basis for defining core femininity, itself, as being maternal rather than heterosexual. Stoller does not develop this insight in a feminist direction, nor does he offer a full-fledged alternative to Freud's scheme.[3]

It may be that only in the male psyche does heterosexuality become important to gender identity. In the early process of separating self from mother, the male child may well "dis-identify" with her by coming to want to "have" the mother rather than to "be" her. The pre-Oedipal girl can identify with her mother directly in her maternal role, which involves nurturing children regardless of sex. The boy may tend to define himself more in terms of being husband of mother. Being like the father becomes desirable because the father is husband to mother.[4] Another way of putting this is that the girl seems first to attempt to enact a maternal identity while the boy avoids this by enacting a heterosexual identity.

The Oedipus Complex and Male Dominance

For Freud, heterosexuality is problematic only in the sense that a person's becoming entirely "masculine" or entirely "feminine" is problematic. On the other hand, he makes the incest taboo highly problematic and central to his theory of Oedipus complex. Actually, it is the taboo on mother-son incest that interested Freud so much, and I believe that this, in turn, relates to the internalization of male dominance. In Freud's terms, the father threatens the son's masculinity if the son continues his heterosexual attachment to his mother. But why, since this attachment is heterosexual, doesn't that, in terms of Freud's own analysis, ensure masculinity in the boy? The answer is that love of the mother, this heterosexual love which becomes part of masculinity, is not the heterosexuality a male dominant society expects of the adult male. In the mother-son relationship, the mother is clearly the more powerful individual by virtue of the generational difference and by virtue of the relative helplessness and dependence of the child. If the mother-son relationship were not radically rejected by the boy, male dominance in heterosexual relations would be threatened.

This, of course, is not the way Freud looked at the situation. In his initial analysis, he assumed male dominance already installed. Mothers were seen *not* as powerful in their own right but as relatively powerless *wives*. Thus, in the Freudian scenario, the boy is threatened with the loss of his masculinity, not by the dominance of his mother but by the dominance of her husband. The mother, as wife of the boy's father, belongs to the father. He in turn lets the son know that if he gives up his mother, he can have a woman of his own someday.

Thus the son represses his mother love until it can be transferred to a woman who is not his mother in a context where he can be the dominant partner. As a husband, he gets a wife as a mother over whom he has control. A husband, unlike the male child, can receive the benefits of his wife's mothering on his own terms. In Freud's account, the boy resolves his Oedipus complex by massively repressing his love for his mother and identifying with or internalizing the authority of the father. I read this as the point at which the generational difference between parent and child comes to be represented by the father, not the mother, and the point at which male dominance is installed.

While the taboo on incest between mother and son is central in the boy's development, the taboo on incest between father and daughter is only lightly stressed by Freud. The problem for the girl is not to give up her father but to transform what Freud thought of as her "active masculinity" vis-à-vis the mother to "passive femininity" vis-à-vis the father. She cannot become "feminine" until she detaches herself from her mother and attaches herself to the father who is, of course, dominant in the relationship and remains so. In a male dominant society, the father-daughter relationship can remain the paradigm for the girl's adult relationships with men and thus does not need to be radically repressed. The father-daughter relationship reinforces rather than threatens her passive "femininity."

I have argued in some detail elsewhere that while the girl internalizes the maternal aspects of being female from her mother, she acquires the heterosexual (wife) aspects of femininity in interaction with a father figure. The research on fathers consistently shows them to be more differentiating in their behavior toward opposite sexed children than mothers and especially in those areas having to do with male-female relations. (Johnson, 1975 and 1977).[5] Moreover, the body of research comparing homosexuals and heterosexuals of both sexes shows that the groups differ more from each other with respect to their attitudes toward their fathers than they do with regard to their attitudes toward their mothers. This suggests again that it is the father who is the central figure in sexual orientation. (Johnson, 1981).

This research supports Mitchell's stress in her reading of Freud that it is the father who is the key figure in the Oedipal phase for both sexes. Freud is quite correct in the prominence he gives the father in the Oedipal period, although he did not understand that the reason for it lay in male dominance. The father's prominence, which Mitchell calls "patriarchy," means that males are dominant in heterosexual relationships, and this dominance is reflected in the institutionalized rights males acquire in women and their children. In the following section I will extend and specify Mitchell's and Rubin's analyses using Levi-Strauss by showing specifically how marriage institutions relate to and organize women's mothering in this society.

STRUCTURAL CORRELATES OF THE PHALLOCENTRIC VIEW

In general, marriage gives husbands rights in women's sexual and reproductive capacities that are greater than the reciprocal claims wives can make upon husbands. While women may gain power through motherhood and in other kinship roles (mother-in-law, for example) and obtain power in the wife role that is derived from her husband's status, the formal power of wife is generally always less than that of husband.

For present purposes, it is important to stress that it is not women's mothering or the assignment of paternity to men so much as it is a women's status as wife and a man's status as husband that give men key advantages over women.

The particular way that wives are subordinate to husbands varies enormously cross-culturally as does the significance of marriage in the overall lives of women. In societies which emphasize large corporate kin groups, marriage may be less central to the secondary status of women than it is in societies such as ours (and in certain hunting and gathering societies) where the influence of extended kin is minimal. In this society with its emphasis on "the couple" relationship, expectations of male dominance in marriage and in heterosexual relations in general become a major way in which male dominance is expressed and organized.

In contemporary U.S. society, husbands have been defined as providers for the family through their work in the public sphere; "providing" is what husband/fathers are *supposed* to do and what wives are not supposed to do—certainly not better than their husbands. While over half of all married women now work, that work is expected to be secondary to the work of their husbands. The expectations of male dominance in marriage make it very unlikely, in any given marriage in the United States that a wife will make more money than her husband. The likelihood that a couple will divorce is associated with higher earnings or earning potential for the wife relative to the husband. (Cherlin, 1981:53-54; Ross and Sawhill, 1975:57) This is, itself, evidence that marriage stability, at least as marriage is now constituted, rests on the wife's economic dependency and the husband's economic hegemony.

In stressing husbands' income dominance over wives, I do not mean that this is either the root cause of their dominance or that this is the only way male dominance is expressed in marriage. Wives are expected to be younger than their husbands, and age is also associated with superior power. Husbands are expected to take the sexual initiative and resent their wives taking it except under their direction.[6] Husbands have rights of sexual access to their wives, and a husband cannot in many states be accused of raping his wife. The double standard decrees that sexual fidelity is more important for wives than for husbands. When husbands take on roles within the family ordinarily considered women's work, they expect and receive more deference for their performance than when the wife does them. On the other hand, when women take roles outside the family ordinarily considered men's work, their work is perceived as threatening the marriage relationship because it threatens the husband's superiority. Female superiority in marriage runs counter to the implicit rule that heterosexual relationships are to be male dominated.

My own argument is not against male-female bonding per se but is against the unequal structuring of that bonding as it is now constituted. Indeed, from the standpoint of tempering some of the more aggressive aspects of male behavior that occur on the basis of male bonding, marriage may be a very good thing. As I have tried to show, however, marriage now appears to depend on the male being the superior partner. We must face and criticize the fact that the contemporary meaning of being female rests on finding and keeping a male whom one can "look up to."

PSYCHOANALYSIS AS PART OF THE PROBLEM

While the husband-provider role has been the external linchpin to the system of male dominance in this society, the internal linchpin of the system is psychological, one that Freudian analysis did not cause but to which it contributed. Women in contemporary society have been pushed toward marriage not only by economic necessity but also by a general cultural emphasis on male dominated heterosexual relationships as the primary basis for women's psychological fulfillment.

The first time the U.S. Census no longer automatically designated the male as head of household was in 1980. This is a dramatic step toward egalitarian relations within the family, but as Jessie Bernard (1981) points out in her article on the decline of the male provider role, "A host of social-psychological obstacles related to gender identity have to be overcome before a new social-psychological structure can be achieved" (1981:1). I am suggesting that the basic social-psychological obstacle is a conception of gender identity which rests on male leadership in heterosexual relationships.

Freud's formal system, which has never been totally reformulated even by gynocentric theorists, rationalizes and justifies all this by defining the essence of femininity as that of being possessed by a man and having his child. Heterosexuality and male dominance are not mere anachronistic adjuncts to his scheme but lie at the heart of his definition of gender differences. In his scenario, which in fact reflects the general public's position, neither lesbians nor heterosexuals seeking equality in marriage qualify as "feminine."

GENDER IDENTITY AND THE ORGANIZATION OF PARENTING RECONSIDERED

In Freud's formal theory, gender differentiation was a product of the phallic period. Even though gynocentric psychoanalytic theorists considered gender differentiation to be pre-phallic, they related it closely to an unlearned heterosexuality. Since Freud, a great deal of work has been done in psychoanalysis on the mother-child relationship and the pre-Oedipal period. This work has dealt almost exclusively with issues of separation and individuation in relationship to the mother, essentially without regard to the sex of the child. Today, however, traditional psychoanalytic interpretations of gender have been challenged by research on adult transsexuals and on children whose gender identity is for some reason problematic. Money and Ehrhardt (1972) have concluded, on the basis of their work with children with ambiguous genitalia, that gender identity—the gut level conviction that one is a male or female—is formed early, well before eighteen months, and probably prior to anything like the phallic period. Mitchell and Rubin thought gender itself had to be eliminated to end male dominance. But the finding that gender identification occurs so early allows us to speculate that it is the Oedipus complex and perceptions of the father connected with it which are related to male dominance and sexism. A primitive sense of gender difference is not.

Chodorow and other gynocentric theorists tend to argue that sexism and male dominance are a result of women's mothering. Their suggested solution to the negative consequences of women's mothering has been "equal parenting" by fathers and mothers. They feel that the father's parenting would temper girls' interest in mothering and in relationships in general. It may also modify boys' lack of interest in mothering,[7] along with the male tendency to objectify women and emphasize difference. The purpose of this paper is not to invalidate the gynocentric argument but specifically to bring the phallocentric theorists into the picture and show how they relate to it. Those theorists who stress the centrality of the father in the Oedipus complex, the relation of this to the exchange of women by men in marriage, and the dominance of men in marriage need also to be considered in any assessment of "equal parenting" as a solution to male dominance.

PARENTING IN THE OEDIPAL PERIOD

There is a great deal we do not know about gender identity and how it is established, but in view of the fact that the early primitive sense of gender is formed before the Oedipal period, it would certainly make sense for children to be exposed to individuals of both genders very early. It would also seem salutary that both males and females be perceived by children as warm and nurturant, as able to meet basic needs for contact. As Chodorow and others point out, if males were nurturant rather than distant figures, the male child would find it easier to identify with being male and would not have to deny femaleness so compulsively.

While I am in general agreement with the argument that fathers can and should "mother" for the reasons cited above, the advocates of equal parenting have not sufficiently dealt with the Oedipal period. They have assumed a nuclear family structure in which women's mothering takes place, without facing the consequences of its structure for girls and women. As I have tried to show, male dominance is not the direct consequence of personality differences between men and women so much as it is of the asymmetrical structuring of heterosexual relationships. Any argument about equal parenting must deal with this fact. The role relationships reflected in the Oedipus complex do not derive directly from women's mothering but rather from the structure of the husband-wife relationship which ultimately makes mothers into wives subordinate to their husbands. Within a nuclear family, what the girl internalizes in the Oedipal period in interaction with the father is that she is "father's girl" until she becomes another man's wife. The boy, by contrast, learns vis-à-vis the father that he must give up being "mother's boy". He must become the dominant husband to another woman who will then mother him, but in a relationship in which he has control. The usefulness of the Freudian account of the Oedipus complex for feminists has been to tie into the structural fact of male dominance in heterosexual relationships and to show that the father-daughter relationship can be a debilitating one for women.

To the extent that marriages are male dominated, the influence of the father on the daughter may not be altogether helpful, and certainly to the extent that a father deals with his daughter as a sex object for himself, (with actual incest being the end point of this tendency) his influence on the daughter could hardly be considered salubrious. In such cases the male parent is not treating his daughter from the standpoint of a caring parent responsible for her growth as a total person. He is instead exercising his power over her to use or control her sexuality for his own benefit.

In the 1950's we worried about the dangers of seductive mothers to the psyches of males. The equal parenting argument needs to consider the issue of the dangers of seductive fathers to the psyches of females. In reality, it is fathers, not mothers, who are incestuous. This may be just the tip of the iceberg with regard to sexualized relationships between fathers and daughters and also between fathers and sons. It is significant in this connection that in overtly incestuous families, the mother is often found to be unusually powerless and dependent on the husband. In families where the mother's power tends to be equal to that of the father, incest is less likely to occur (Herman, 1981).

While interaction with the other sexed parent may provide a rehearsal for adult heterosexuality, the generational difference which gives superior power to the parent makes it inappropriate for children of either sex to remain in a sexualized relationship with either parent. This needs special emphasis with regard to the father-daughter relationship. In order to mitigate male dominance, the girl's tie to her father cannot continue to be viewed as wholly advantageous. It now has the effect of undergirding the female tendency to seek relationships in which the male is dominant.

The logic of my argument is that more involvement of the father in parenting cannot be a solution to male dominance as long as women and men are not equals in marriage and in heterosexual relationships. Without this, equal parenting would not change the father's being the central figure in the Oedipus complex for both sexes and would not prevent children's emerging from the Oedipus complex with the idea that heterosexuality means dominance for males, submission for women.

We may well be witnessing today a weakening of the hegemony of the male dominated heterosexual couple and a movement toward a more flexible system which allows either sex to parent and which (by virtue of a lessened emphasis on heterosexual couples) allows women greater opportunity to form relationships with women as well as men. An increase in singleness per se, however, by no means guarantees an end to male dominance unless economic equality can also be achieved. Male dominated heterosexuality, as it operates outside of marriage, in the workplace, and in informal living arrangements may be even less advantageous to women than marriage. The argument of this paper has been that one of the impediments to women acting on their own behalf has been not only their realistic dependency on men economically, but also the definition of femininity, itself, to mean being male oriented and playing up to men. The end of male dominance may then rest upon removing this link between male dominance and heterosexual interaction and eliminating the idea that male dominance is part of the very definition of heterosexuality.

NOTES

1. Actually Freud was more aware than most of the inadequacy of the terms "active" and "passive" to characterize masculinity and femininity (see Mitchell, 1974a:115–117, n.4). On the other hand, the active/passive usage is only the most general way in which he distinguished masculinity from femininity. My point can perhaps be made even more clearly because he also equated the following with the distinction: phallic-nonphallic, subject-object, dominant-submissive.

2. For example, in his 1931 article he says, "In this the complete iden-

tity of the pre-Oedipus phase in boys and girls is recognized, and the girl's sexual (phallic) activity toward her mother is affirmed and substantiated by observations" (Freud, 1974:53).

3. Nancy Chodorow (1978:154) makes this point briefly, saying that unwarranted assumptions on Freud's part have never been systematically refuted within the psychoanalytic tradition in a manner that presents a coherent alternative theory. In a footnote, she also states that Stoller's work is the basis for such a full substitute developmental account (1978:154).

4. The above analysis was suggested to me by Greenson's (1968) description of the case of a young "would be" transsexual male who thought of himself as a female and wanted very much to be a female like his mother, whom he adored. Greenson dissuaded the boy from this wish by getting the child to understand that he could love a female without being the same as a female. He could grow up to be a husband to a woman, just as Greenson was husband to his wife. At this stage, there were no overtones of dominance, just a simple identification with the idea of "husband."

5. In an article written after her book, Chodorow (1979) discusses how women's exclusive mothering accounts for men's greater interest in maintaining and emphasizing sex differences. This latter approach fits more closely with my own.

6. Marie N. Robinson's (1959), *The Power of Sexual Surrender*, which is used in "The Total Woman" and "Fascinating Womanhood" courses represents an extreme version of the belief that the wife's proper role is to fit in with her husband's inclinations, moods, and desires concerning sexual activity. Remarkably enough, on the first page of the book the author states that women today have, beyond the shadow of any doubt, achieved complete equality with men.

7. This relational/nonrelational difference need not in itself lead to dominance. There is no inherent reason why women's relational orientation could not be expressed outside of a domestic setting.

BIOGRAPHICAL NOTE

Miriam M. Johnson was born in Atlanta, and received her A.B. from the University of North Carolina at Chapel Hill in Sociology. She received her Ph.D. in Social Relations from Harvard. Professor Johnson teaches at the University of Oregon, where she is an affiliate of the Center for the Study of Women in Society. Her research interests in the past few years have been in sexual learning in the family. Her major published works are:. *Sex Roles: Sex Inequality and Sex Role Development*, with Jean

Stockard; and articles such as "Fathers, Mothers, and Sex Typing," "Androgyny and the Maternal Principle."

REFERENCES

BERNARD, J.
1981 "The Good-Provider Role: Its Rise and Fall." American Psychologist. 36: 1–12.
BURLINGHAM, D. T.
1973 "The Pre-Oedipal Infant-Father Relationship." Psychoanalytic Study of the Child. 28: 23–47.
CHERLIN, A.
1981 Marriage, Divorce, Remarriage. Cambridge: Harvard University Press.
CHODOROW, N.
1974 "Family Structure and Feminine Personality," pp. 43–66 in M. Z. Rosaldo and L. Lamphere (eds.), Woman, Culture and Society. Stanford: Stanford University Press.
1978 The Reproduction of Mothering. Berkeley: University of California Press.
1979 "Feminism and Difference: Gender, Relation and Difference in Psychoanalytic Perspective" Socialist Review 46: 51–69.
DINNERSTEIN, D.
1976 The Mermaid and the Minotaur. New York: Harper and Row.
FREUD, S.
1974 "Female Sexuality" (1931), p. 39–56 in J. Strouse (ed), Women and Analysis. New York: Grossman.
GREENSON, R.
1968 "Dis-identifying from Mother: Its Special Importance for the Boy." International Journal of Psychoanalysis 49: 370–374.
HERMAN, J.
1981 Father-Daughter Incest. Cambridge: Harvard University Press.
HORNEY, K.
1974 "The Flight from Womanhood: the Masculinity Complex in Women as Viewed by Men and by Women" (1926), pp. 171–186 in J. Strouse (ed.), Women and Analysis. New York: Grossman.
JOHNSON, M. M.
1975 "Fathers, Mothers and Sex Typing." Sociological Inquiry 45: 15–26.
1977 "Androgyny and the Maternal Principle." School Review 86: 50–69.
1981 "Heterosexuality, Male Dominance, and the Father Image." Sociological Inquiry 51: 129–139.
KAPLAN, A. G., AND BEAN, J. P., EDS.
1976 Beyond Sex-Role Stereotypes: Readings Toward a Psychology of Androgyny. Boston: LITTLE, BROWN.
LEVI-STRAUSS, C.
1969 The Elementary Structures of Kinship. Boston: Beacon Press.
MITCHELL, J.
1974a Psychoanalysis and Feminism. New York: Vintage.
1974b "On Freud and the Distinction between the Sexes," pp. 27–36 in J. Strouse (ed.), Women and Analysis. New York: Grossman.
MONEY, J., AND EHRHARDT A. A.
1972 Man and Woman, Boy and Girl. Baltimore: Johns Hopkins University Press.
ROBINSON, M. N.
1959 The Power of Sexual Surrender. New York: Doubleday.

Ross, H. L., AND Sawhill I. V.
1975 Time of Transition: The Growth of Families Headed by Women. Washington: The Urban Institute.
Rubin, G.
1975 "The Traffic in Women: Notes on the Political Economy of Sex," pp. 157–210 in R. R. Reiter (ed.), Toward an Anthropology Women. New York: Monthly Review Press.
Stockard, J., AND Johnson, M. M.
1979 "The Social Origins of Male Dominance." Sex Roles 5: 199–218.
Stoller, R. J.
1974 "Facts and Fancies: an Examination of Freud's Concept of Bisexuality," pp. 343–364 in J. Strouse (ed.), Women and Analysis. New York: Grossman.

Father Presence in Women's Psychological Development

SUSAN CONTRATTO

It was Christmas Eve afternoon. I was a small child of four or five. The glowing Christmas tree lights were reflected in the panels of our front door. The bell rang. I went to answer it. My father was at the door. He couldn't use his key because his arms were loaded with wrapped Christmas packages for us. I was delighted; he was Santa Claus, a big grin on his face! I remember it as the best Christmas we ever had. I was enraptured with him. He had a charm and excitement that my mother could not hold a candle to. Between my parents, there were some other differences, which at the time I scarcely knew. My mother was a full-time parent. She was a well-organized, thrifty woman from a very poor family of origin. As a result, she did her Christmas shopping far in advance of Christmas Eve, *and* she never relied on the store to gift wrap presents. My father, on the other hand, was a busy internist who rarely arrived home in time for dinner, let alone in the middle of the afternoon. He shopped at the last minute because other things took priority until that point. He was both forced and privileged to use store gift-wrapping services. My mother provided the daily, steady background which allowed him to make his charming, enticing, and dramatic entrance.[1]

INTRODUCTION

In this essay[2], I describe some of the learning that daughters do about fathers and go on to show some of the ways in which this learning neurotically affects their later relationships with men. What I will describe in the clinical section of this paper are the ways in which fathers are special for their daughters. They are often fun, imaginative, and clever, as well as frequently being powerful and important in the world outside the family. They come and go in contrast to mother, who is always around. They are, therefore, a scarce resource rather than one taken for granted. The relationship between mother and father in these families is unequal; within the family as without, father is more powerful.

Grown-up daughters rely on this early learning to make assumptions, often inaccurate, about the men in their lives. In these relationships they are preoccupied with controlling the presence of an overvalued man. Some of the ways they do this is by trying to become what they think he wants; by transforming anger into understanding; by hanging onto an internal image of an idealized man next to whom real men are found wanting. In my conclusion I extrapolate from clinical data to suggest other variables which we need to consider in understanding development in families. Finally, I address the theoretical implications of including others as psychologically meaningful family members.

Women form a sense of themselves, their self-worth, and their self-esteem as females in relationship with women and men through interacting in families. Mother, a woman; father, a man; and daughter, a woman are all people in relationship with one another. The mother-daughter relationship *and* the father-daughter relationship *and* the daughter's observations and experiences of the father-mother relationship all comprise the daughter's psychological legacy (Chodorow, 1978; Keller, 1978; Gilligan, 1982). Whether or not they are from intact nuclear families, almost all women in our society experience these relationships; sometimes in their absence through a caretaker's wishes and fantasies; sometimes through a comparison of what they have with the pervasive and well-articulated cultural expectation, sometimes through serial relationships with 'fathers'; and sometimes through designation of a brother as man of the house with the privilege that this entails.

Miriam Johnson's paper (this chapter) argues accurately, I believe, that the unequal structure of the male-female relationship in our culture is learned within the institution of heterosexual marriage through the unequal structuring of the husband-wife relationship. This essay suggests some of the ways in which daughters grow up to become women who participate in this inequality or fear that they will.

Family cannot be removed from culture; it is not a haven or a cushion or a safety valve. Family, far from being outside cultural and economic pressures, is enmeshed in them. Family functioning is informed by the culture and similarly, transforms and informs the culture (Brienes et al., 1978; Thorne, 1982). Male dominance in the culture at large is continuous with male dominance in families. Thus, we are exploring ways in which cultural dominance is translated into certain kinds of families.

Johnson proposes that income inequality, age inequality, and work status disparity are important extrafamilial components of this unbalanced husband-wife bond. In addition, in many families there is internal power and authority disparity. This is evident in communication between husbands and wives; men initiate topics more often than women, whereas women ask questions and make supportive statements. This dominance also includes nonverbal cues (Thorne, 1982:13). Decision making is controlled by men in both lower and middle class families (Rubin, 1976:106–113). In extreme forms, men dominate families through physical and sexual violence (Straus et al.,1980; Brienes and Gordon, 1983).

Psychologically, this pattern can be understood as a complicated system of intertwining needs and dependencies (Chodorow, 1978:191–198). The daughter's psychological development unfolds against a backdrop of paternal power in the family and in the culture, and that power necessarily has an impact on her own psychic structure.

The clinical material which follows suggests subtle ways in which daughters learn about and become a participant in a system of male domination within the family which they can carry unconsciously into adulthood. For example, the fathers who appear on these pages are fun, exciting, and playful. Their presence is a treat. They are catered to in large and small ways - sometimes because they are scary and insist on catering, sometimes because they are special and deserve it. The implication of these relational, rather private experiences is that changes in obvious structural inequities, for example income, may not have clear cut effects. This is a point which I treat at greater length in the end of this paper. I raise it now to alert the reader to the subtle and complicated nature of the inequity which emerges in these clinical examples.

Johnson makes an important theoretical distinction between gynocentric theorists, who concentrate on the relationship with the pre-Oedipal mother as key to the reproduction of male domination, and phallocentric theorists, who focus on the Oedipal father. Johnson rightly comments on the prevailing evidence for prephallic gender differentiation (Money and Ehrhardt, 1972; Blum, 1976; Galenson and Rolphe, 1976; Parens et al., 1976; Stoller, 1976). Theorists have two alternatives. They can push the Oedipal period to an earlier and earlier age, or they can assume that major learning for children of both sexes about their gender identity takes place through the mother, with the father a rather shadowy figure, idealized more than real. While the debate is an important one theoretically, neither position 'fits' the clinical picture as I will present it in the material that follows.

The father in these clinical vignettes is an important influence from early in the daughter's development. She experiences him directly, as an infant, as well as learning about him through her mother She also learns about mother and father in relationship with each other. He is both a person and a role, as of course is mother. An infant daughter becomes attached to him as an important person in her life. She understands at a later point that he is a male person, a member of that group with whom, if she follows the normative rules of our culture, she should have a heterosexual love relationship.

While the pre-Oedipal father is clearly not the same person as the pre-Oedipal mother for these clients, in part by virtue of role, in part because of their personalities, their presence for infant and toddler daughters leads to concerns in treatment of a wide range of separation and individuation issues. We are used to the mother being a multiplicity of internalized images which we (sometimes arbitrarily) sort into early (pre-Oedipal) or later Oedipal stages. This also happens with the father image. There is a continuum of paternal expectations ranging, in some instances, from deeply wished for and feared fantasies of merger to thinly veiled genital erotic thoughts and feelings about father. Sorting these out clinically is a complex and time consuming task. When, for example, a daughter talks about the feeling of specialness she has with father, this may have components of triangulation-competitiveness with mother— or it may involve identification with his power, prestige and competence—or it may involve both.

The fathers who stimulated all of the clinical material which follows participated very little in actual child care. As well as setting up a family situation in which they were a scarce but valued resource, one might also argue that their more limited presence allowed for heightened idealization. Certainly this is the case in some instances of paternal death, early desertion, or divorce (Wallerstein and Kelly, 1980). Chodorow (1978) makes the argument that because of relative paternal absence in early, caretaking, the norm in our culture is paternal idealization for the little girl and positional rather than relational identification for the boy. I would contend, however, that a result of developmental experience for both sexes is idealization and, often, its reverse for mothers, as well as fathers (Chodorow and Contratto, 1982). At a point in development, the dependent child relies on and internalizes an omnipotent and omniscient mother who only becomes a 'real' person at a later time and with some psychological struggle. A problem with sorting out paternal idealizations is that they often are based on actual power and control in the family, if not also in the world outside the family.

This issue leads to the question of what is real in client reporting. I believe the following: male privilege and the unequal relationship between mother and father that go with it are present in many families unless they have self-consciously gone against the grain of dominant socialization and culture. Further, that surrounded by the halo of male power, many of these fathers are unrealistically represented in the psychological lives of their grown-up daughters. Further, I believe that the daughter's perception of mother is distorted. Daughter has identified with the belittling and controlling stance of father towards mother. In fact, she has not seen aspects of mother's strength, competence, and complexity which father, himself, may appreciate though it is beyond the rather rigid, dichotomized thinking of the young child.

CLINICAL MATERIAL

To set the stage for the clinical material which follows, as well as interpretation of that material, I will describe who these women are, what the general goals of their therapy was, and the place of the following incidents in my work with them. I will conclude with some general statements about these families which contrast with the discussion about structural rearrangements in families.

The twenty-two women I am describing were all in their mid-twenties. through mid-forties. There were all white. Five came from working class backgrounds and the rest came from professional middle-class backgrounds. Three of them were in clerical occupations and the rest in professional ones. Though there was sometimes considerable marital strife in their family of origins, these families had nonetheless remained intact through the clients' adolescence.

While all of these women had relational difficulties sometimes with women and always with men, they fell into a variety of diagnostic categories: some were depressed, neurotically or more seriously. Some fluctuated between depression and debilitating anxiety. Several were borderline. One suffered from transient psychotic experiences. And some were women experiencing transient stress or confusion. Neither their fathers, mothers nor any particular pattern caused their presenting symptoms. There was no single cause for these women's difficulties.[3]

The objective of my work with them, as it is with all clients, was to bring adult comprehension and problem solving capacity to the remaining confusion of childhood, particularly as it concerns idealizations and abominations of mother, father, and significant others. We examine the emotional relationship of the client to these important other people and their complicated relationships with one another, as the client perceives them. With all of these women it was necessary to explore power relationships in their family of origins and examine the ways in which they were unconsciously bringing these past relationships to bear on present ones. In fact, it was essential to examine power relationships. Without this retrospective examination, I am convinced that these women could not have moved forward in their lives.

The clinical material that follows emerged in therapy and was the result of free association. Many of these early memories were previously forgotten. Some originally appeared in disguised form. It is not the task of this paper to describe the flow of the clinical process. Therefore, these vignettes sound like the answers to open-ended interview questions which they emphatically are not. While I refer to them as memories, it is important to remember that they became available to the client for analysis and understanding during the course of active therapeutic work.

These clients present a particular picture of their fathers, mothers and the relationships between them. Father is fascinating, fun, imaginative, and clever. He is powerful in the world outside the family as well as within the family. These grown-up daughters remember their mothers, on the other hand, as not fun or exciting and not powerful in father's charismatic way. They experience the father-mother relationship as unequal; he controls and belittles her and she caters to him. Each man had an impact on daughter's sense of herself, her feelings of self-worth, and her subsequent relational problems.

The fathers' family presence for the most part was 'normal'. They were present far less frequently than the mothers. None of them did any significant childcare, and all of the fathers worked full time outside of the home. (This tends, by the way, to continue to be the prevalent pattern. Equally shared childcare of small children is an extremely rare occurrence.) Many were out of the home more than eight or nine hours a day, either because they were ambitious and successful or, in some cases, because they needed to work more than one job to support the family. They did not sexually molest, torture, desert, or traumatize their daughters in any obvious ways. In short they were the model fathers of the '40s, '50s, and '60s.

Their relative absence made them both more salient to their daughters and less reliable. Their presence was an occasion, a break from the regular routine. A surprising number of the clinical vignettes that follow concern fathers' homecomings. These men were not absent fathers in the way we typically think of it. They were not fathers who were aloof and, therefore, psychologically absent or who were physically absent. They were present and very noticeably so, and their presence was an event in their daughters' lifes.

There is evidence that fathers are fun, exciting and imaginative and therefore special to daughters. For example, one woman, a professional in her mid-thirties, told the following early memory of her father:

He was just marvelous, he was wonderfully inventive. I remember once, (I must have been about four), he came up from the basement with wire, a battery, a socket, and a light bulb. He made a great, mysterious show of attaching them. First the wires to the socket, then the wires to the battery, then the lightbulb. Slowly and carefully, one then the other. I couldn't imagine what was going to happen. He pressed the switch. The light bulb turned on. I had no idea how he did that. I thought he could do anything.

Another client from a poor family described the excitement of being able to go to funerals with her father. These were major social events in the small town where she grew up, and she remembers them as frequent and great fun. She felt special when she went with her father. He also played an instrument in the community band. She has many happy, exciting memories of going with him when he played.

Other women had early memories of their fathers giving them something special—special in part because their families were poor, special also because the gift seemed perfect for the moment. One woman described how, on a very hot night when she and her brothers and sisters couldn't sleep because it was so sticky and still, her father arrived home from work. He moonlighted as a milkman and brought pints of ice-cold chocolate milk for them. In her words: "Nothing ever tasted so good."

Several clients described moments of particular warmth and understanding with their fathers. One woman told me: "My Dad and I really understood one another. From as long as I can remember, I could always talk with him. I could tell what kind of mood he was in when he got home and could always deal with him better than my Mom."

Another client, who also felt she had a special understanding, a private language, with her talented writer father, described an exciting game they used to play: "I wrote a few lines of poetry on the typewriter. It had a clue in it about where I was hiding. When he heard me stop typing, he waited, came in, and made a great play of trying to puzzle out my meaning and discover me!"

These memories show nurturing fathers. They are warm and make their daughters feel special, cosy, and cared for. What these memories also suggest is that these fathers were particularly exciting and fun for their daughters, especially, as it turns out, in comparison to their mothers. Virtually every one of these memories contrasted fathers to mothers who were unexciting and could do nothing marvelous (at least as the daughter experienced it). This was brought home to me dramatically by the same woman whose father was the wonderful magician. I asked her what her mother did when all the children were in school. Her answer - "Nothing." On probing, it turned out that her mother took care of an elderly relative, cleaned, shopped, canned and made preserves, cooked, washed, ironed, made clothes for the three children to save money and, when not exhausted, wrote poetry. The client whose father gave her the special milk, has never in our two years of working together, spontaneously associated to a memory of maternal giving. Similarly, the woman whose father played the exciting hiding game has never spontaneously described playing with her mother.

These grown-up daughters presented memory after memory of their fathers being powerful in the family and other family members catering to this power. What was consistently impressive in these memories was that grown-up daughters had internalized complex *interactive* patterns. Fathers did not act powerful for a passive audience. There was a response which acknowledged father's power, granted it, and allowed it to continue.

Sometimes the memory was relatively benign. For example, the father who came home after a day at work and had to have his papers and pipe just-so, to catch up on current events while dinner was being made. In this memory, the client remembers some apprehension and excitement around her father's homecoming and occasional irritation on his part if something were out of place.

Sometimes the memory is not so benign. A client vividly recalled a conspiracy between herself, her mother, and younger siblings over television watching. Her father did not allow it, as he thought it was a mindless activity. Because he believed that the client's mother could do without a car, this woman was home in the suburbs with three preschool children. Presumably by four in the afternoon she was hard pressed to have a little time for herself. The daughter remembers watching children's T.V. in the late afternoon while anxiously listening for the sound of the gravel crunching under the wheels of her father's car. At this moment, they would jump up, turn off the T.V. and rearrange themselves, praying he would not guess what they had been doing moments before. One client has vivid memories of her father's rages. This man, a highly successful lawyer, experienced extreme mood swings. Sometimes he would be warm, understanding, and loving. At other moments, he would be storming at one of the children or his wife, calling them obscene names, occasionally hitting one. She was afraid of her father from a very early age and then, later, remembers anticipating, dreading and trying to fend off his behavior, which could turn happy family times into terrible scenes.

Another client described a paradoxical paternal power. She became anxious and depressed when her boyfriend came down with the flu. It turned out that she was very upset by his passivity (he was not normally at all passive). Her associations were to her father who passively withdrew from her mother's attacks against him. The fights were about money, with mother accusing father of not being a go-getter and moving to a better paid factory job. The client recognized her father's passivity as power. She psychologically sided with her mother - he could have rescued the family from their unhappy economic position if he had chosen to.[4]

Some of the fathers brought explicit status power into the family. Their daughters learned early that they did 'important' work: they were doctors, lawyers, business men, professors. As a result, they were special people. Certain behaviors were allowed because of their status. For example, Daddy could take phone calls during supper, (a privilege denied children) because he had an important business deal. They were protected: "Don't disturb your father, he's working." Behaviors unacceptable for others were allowed them. A client recalled overhearing a fight between her parents in which her father was screaming names at her mother. Later, her mother explained to her that her father was a creative genius, that he was working on a book, and that he was overwrought. Correspondingly, the lawyer with the extreme mood swings described above was allowed these by his family because of the stress of his hard, important work.

A mark of status which daughters often recalled is space. Fathers not only had work space outside of the home but often had special space inside, too. A basement workshop for one father was private territory: as a treat, a daughter could be invited there to help. Another client described how her father found space in their crowded, chronically unfinished house: he worked under the family car on Saturdays. No one was allowed to disturb him in this dangerous place.

No client described a mother as having space of her own. Mothers were in kitchens or in their own bedrooms, where children felt free to walk in. In contrast, several clients remembered that when they were teenagers, they reacted very angrily if they felt their mothers were intruding on their privacy. These kinds of memories suggest an identification with father's space privilege.

All of these women psychologically know about their fathers' dominance and power in the family; most also are aware of their control. Sometimes this control was subtle. One woman described her parents as having the perfect marriage - they adored each other. In working with me, she recalled her panicky flight from an engagement. She remembered that her ex-fiance, in describing what he hoped their relationship would become, said, "And the husband and wife will be one." Sitting in my office, she said, "And, I thought to myself, that one will be the husband! And I broke off our engagement that day." Her reaction had been swift because her fiance inadvertently used the phrase which her parents had used in describing their relationship. She began to cry angrily while remembering that when she was a small child, her father had built a beautiful desk for her mother to use when writing her poetry. He then frequently teased her that she wasn't using it enough.

Another client was well aware of her father's control. In our first session together she said, "My mother is a marshmallow in the face of my father."

Clients described making unconscious choices to earn their fathers' respect. Part of the choice often meant, paradoxically, not being like the mother whom he belittled and, as far as the client could see, did not respect. Another example concerns a client who was talking about her difficulty, which became apparent in therapy, of asking for medical help when she needed it. Her first series of associations involved her mother and grandmother. Her mother twisted her foot while shopping with the client when she was a child of three or four. The grown daughter angrily described how her mother did this for attention. She then remembered that when she was younger, her beloved grandmother had broken a hip. She recalled her father angrily telling her mother that her own mother had done it on purpose. Finally, she remembered herself at puberty, sitting doubled over with bad cramps. Her father walked by and teased, "Can't take it, huh?" She resolved to tough it out and not let her female body play tricks on her.

These daughters felt more like effective, worthy persons themselves by being like, or gaining the respect of, this person—the admired, attractive, and powerful father. A good amount of a daughter's self-esteem, then, is tied to the relationship with him and becomes part and parcel of her problems in relationships with lovers.

The daughters' developmental stage, when much of this early and charged interaction takes place, is critical for understanding these later relationships. The very young child is egocentric; the world revolves around the self. Even after a sense of separateness and difference between the self and others and from one person to another has developed, the child still clings to the conviction that important happenings are caused by itself. Frequently, my clients recalled father-daughter incidents in which they believed they had created their fathers' responses to them, even when this was highly unlikely. For example, when an angry father came home from work, the daughter assumed that she was responsible for his anger, his good moods, his comings and goings. The father was not allowed to be a person in his own right with motivation, affect, and behavior independent of the daughter. While at this age it also true of mother, the consequences are different. Mother is more relationally familiar, reliably present, and not as interesting. There is less need and less motivation to figure her out in relationship to oneself. In particular, there is less need to figure out how to control the maternal presence.

These grown-up daughters are preoccupied with control in relationships with important men. If a woman can control the relationship she can, to some extent, regulate her sense of self-esteem by controlling the comings and goings of this overly valued man - overly valued precisely because he is the keeper of her self-esteem. These clients use methods of control in relationships prior to being vulnerable and within established relationships. A woman may be understanding and nonassertive within relationships. Both of these are traditionally feminine characteristics on the surface, and therefore are not dissonant with the clients' conscious sense of themselves as feminine people.

Several clients spent a great deal of energy trying to figure out what sort of woman the man she is interested in *really* wants so that she can be that kind of woman. These clients describe this activity as understanding. However, the internal process that goes on, in the words of one woman is, "always taking his pulse to see how you should feel and act." The same woman provided a good example of the way in which her 'understanding' was used in her family of origin to allow male privilege. During our work together she returned home for a holiday. At dinner, her father and older brothers were at one end of the table and she, her mother, and sisters at the other. During a lull in the conversation, she heard her older and much admired brother talking about his ex-fiance in derogatory and sexually explicit terms. She spoke up and said that as a woman she found his language insulting and could he clean up his act. He turned on her and said, "If you understood how much she hurt me, you would know why I talk about her in this way," and proceeded with his conversation. In working with me on this incident, my client was pleased with herself for speaking up but only realized at that point that he had effectively told her to shut up!

Speaking up in a relationship, even if only to acknowledge a difference, carries with it great fears. A woman in a relationship for some years experienced anxiety in recognizing, with me, that she is an intellectual who gets great excitement from working with ideas. Her lover, while not a dummy, didn't share the same excitement. Initially, she felt anxious and guilty over this secret pleasure. What emerged was the feeling that if she accepted this difference with pleasure, he might leave her. Her assumption was that independent pleasure and excitement was disloyal. Her assumption derives from a system of paternal power. A subordinate who wishes to maintain the good graces of a dominant person takes a risk when she says, "I don't totally need you. I am a person in my own right."

When the woman feels anger, disappointment, irritation in a relationship, she quickly denies it and often transforms it into understanding.[5] The potentially conflictual feelings are generally not conscious or are only vaguely felt. For example, a woman described her experience as follows: A male colleague with whom she was hoping to develop a relationship said he would help her with a new computer program. The date for the program presentation came and went and she ended up doing it herself. She was irritated and disappointed. On next seeing her, he apologized for having let her down but said he had been very busy. She graciously smiled and said, "That's perfectly all right." When reporting this to me, I inquired about her feelings on seeing him. She said she really did understand that he was busy, and they had had no definite plan for him to help her. I asked how she would have felt if the colleague had been a woman. She responded that she would have been annoyed and would have let a woman friend know it. I remarked that her understanding of him, then, was really too good to be true. She remembered at that point that upon walking away from her male colleague, she had thought of herself, "You jerk!" When it became clear to her that her denial of anger specifically concerned the fact that he was a desirable male, she realized why she could not tolerate feelings of anger toward him. Vulnerability leads to unacceptable anger which is turned into 'understanding' and a barely conscious diminishing of the important man.

There are problems for the woman in maintaining a relationship through these techniques. The benefit is that she believes she can regulate her self-esteem through keeping him close. The costs to her, however, are rather crippling. Each time she squelches an authentic reaction, either because it suggests difference or expresses actual conflict, she takes another little bite out of her self-confidence. The relationship always feels fragile to her because he doesn't really know her and might not like whom he saw if he really got to know her. She puts forward the false self she believes he wants, and consequently, feels that her real self is unappreciated and unnoticed. Paradoxically, then, controlling him as the guardian of her self-esteem leads to further diminishing of her self-esteem.

The grown-up daughters I have seen have many ways of controlling a relationship by not allowing it. While consciously they painfully yearn for relationships, without being aware of it, they sabotage possibilities. One way is to find men attractive who are unavailable; they are in other relationships, for example, or they are about to leave town. The possible rejection in this instance is controlled by the circumstances and cannot be taken personally. Another pattern is to reject the relationship as one begins to feel attracted to the man. A client described a recurring sequence in getting to know someone, beginning to like him, and then finding some piece of his personality that made him unacceptable. She began to feel vulnerable to him and quickly turned the tables. Only in retrospect did she see that she was searching for reasons to dismiss the relationship. Another variant is preoccupation with the aloof mystery man. A client described the experience this way. A genial co-worker asked her out for a beer and clearly wanted to get to know her. She could not take the time to develop a relationship with him because she was preoccupied with speculating about a relationship with another co-worker who barely gave her a second glance. This incident accomplished several psychological purposes for her. She rebuffed a possible relationship, again turning the tables and doing to another what she felt her father had done to her. She also imagined a gratifying relationship— again—one that was in her control because it existed primarily in her own head.

Incidently, as much as these women may unconsciously avoid love relationships with men as a way of controlling their vulnerability, they will be in situations with men where similar feelings are evoked. For example, a very competent professional woman who had chosen not to marry found that she was in a recurring pattern with male superiors. She felt extremely anxious and inadequate around them. Once she found herself unable to present a report of her work to her male superior. In discussing this with me she said, "I feel like all I've done all year is housekeeping!" This incidently was the same woman who said that her mother did nothing all day once the children were in school.

Her comment takes us full circle again, to mother, and helps us appreciate the bind that these women are in. As she, daughter, experienced father as controlling and belittling mother, she cannot allow any sameness between herself and her mother or she is guaranteed to lose his respect. In her lover relationship, then, she cannot allow any similarity between herself and her mother. She would lose her lover's respect, and worse still, she would become subjugated to his dominance. But of course, similarity between mother and daughter runs at very deep personality levels and requires enormous psychic energy to deny. As these identifications are not at all comfortable within the daughter, the shadowy suggestion of them feels overwhelming. To be at *all* like mother means to be totally like mother. An example will illustrate the intensity of this problem. A woman consulted me for a short term intervention around a decision she had been struggling with for over a year. This highly talented, attractive physician in her mid-thirties was faced with an unsolvable dilemma; her lover had an excellent professional position in one town and wanted to stay there. She had a good position (one which had some problems but was, on balance, suitable) in another town. She could work out a similarly good position in the same town as her lover. She felt, probably realistically, that the relationship would end if they did not live in the same town. She couldn't figure out why moving to the position in her lover's town made her feel literally sick at her stomach with anxiety. In sorting this out, what became clear was that she feared if she 'gave in' she would be just like her mother who had not taken an excellent job offer because her father did not want to relocate. She feared being swallowed up in a relationship in which she would be controlled by her lover as she believed her mother to be controlled by her father.

Not only does daughter not want to be like mother but, in addition, she has learned about father through mother (and vice versa). The psychological experience of the homecoming experiences of these women, and others I have talked with, suggests mother's anticipation, excitement, and apprehension conveyed itself in nonverbal ways to the very small child. These women remembered maternal behaviors which foretold their fathers' arrival home. These were often catering behaviors—making things nice for him, straightening the house, making dinner. Their mothers often explained their fathers' moods to them. They simultaneously were competitive with mother and devalued her; she knew more about this person, father, yet she was a bad teacher in that daughter didn't really learn to control him. Furthermore, mother's methods of being with father were self-effacing.

The therapeutic task with these women is to bring a new reality to paternal and maternal images by revealing their current rigid, polarized nature and reassessing them. These fathers have not said to their daughters, "I'm only human," and these mothers are not present in their daughter's minds with strengths as well as weaknesses. These clients overvalue masculine modes in thought and in relationships primarily because these modes are paternal, and secondarily and defensively, because they are not maternal. Holding firmly to an ethic of fairness and achievement, they rely extensively on logic and reason. At the same time, they feel the authentic appeal of caring and responsibility, intuition, creativity, and exchange. Yet, to 'give in' to these modes opens them to the self-accusation that they are just like their mothers. Therefore, it is absolutely necessary that esteem for the mother, as well as humanization of the father, be a goal of therapy. Perhaps I should say humanization of the mother, since it is not the therapist's job to idealize or glorify personality components of the mother. But all of the mothers of these clients had virtues and strengths which had been buried in the layers of the family myths.

CONCLUSIONS AND EXTENSIONS

Understanding is a problem for these women, and I believe, for many others as well. Understanding is a cognitive process which includes empathy, mental entering into the feeling or spirit of, gaining knowledge of, comprehending and becoming thoroughly familiar with a person. It becomes functional; we understand in order to act, not act, say, not say, feel or not feel. We all do this; we understand people and situations in order to place ourselves comfortably in relationship to them. These women, with their overvaluation of male and male-associated modes, 'understand' in order to give men the edge. They try to become what they believe the man wants in a relationship and, through understanding they allow male privilege. They have difficulty first understanding their own emotional, behavioral, and cognitive requirements and then, holding these up as equally worthy of understanding and attention from men.

There is predictable conflict when women insist on being understood. The power that men have in families and in the culture is comfortable for them. Why should men understand women's complaints, demands, and suggestions when such knowledge might lead, in fairness, to a change in their behavior. The individual woman might risk, as these clients did, intense and deeply felt anxiety over conflict with the over-valued man. She might lose this person who embodies her sense of self-worth. An individual is still vulnerable when she identifies with a group that speaks for womens' needs. The provoked reaction always contains personal attacks. Feminists, for example, are characterized as strident, selfish, and amoral.

The attractiveness of power is a recurrent theme in this essay. Children with their fascination for superheroes, dinasaurs, royalty, and monsters clearly love to be and are in awe of the king of the mountain. Boys grow up believing that they can be President, and according to some researchers, have a midlife crisis which signals, finally, the abandonment of this fantasy. Little girls, also, are fascinated by charismatic power, and for most of them, it becomes attached to gender - power is what father has; power is male. The girl does not envy the penis, she envies the charismatic power which the person with the penis has, apparently by right. The penis is not symbolic of power; it is attached to a person who has real, concrete, enviable power - a father in a family.[6]

These women learned in families that power has a gender: charismatic power with its excitement, visibility, and privilege is male. Maternal power, characterized by reliability, nurturance, and the capacity to comfort, is female. They are not necessarily public vs. private power or outside vs. inside power. Infants and children intimately experience these kinds of power and slowly begin to value them in relationships with people they care deeply about. As the female child becomes a person with a gender, she accepts, as part of her gender, entitlement to how she will have what kind of power.

Many women are deeply ambivalent about power. Pride easily shifts to shame, guilt, and anxiety at displays of power. Women do not want to be like men and yet want some of what they have and feel disenfranchised from it. Of course there are structural barriers which stand in the way of women seizing power, and there are massive structural supports for the maintenance of patriarchal power. Part of the problem is a deep-seated psychological ambivalence about entitlement to what women have learned is male power.

This essay also underlines the neurotic need for control that some women have in adult relationships. But control is by no means unidimensional or entirely negative. Parents control (protect) infants and small children. Responsiveness to the developing child's growing ability at self-control leads parents, often apprehensively, to step back and relinquish aspects of control. Parents who cannot do this are 'controlling': they do not allow or recognize the autonomous development of the child. Individuals learn to control themselves; physically they develop complex motor skills, communication ability, and bowel and bladder control: emotionally they inhibit immediate activity and become self-reflective, identifying a feeling or need and sorting out effective ways of expression. Children and parents take pride and delight in these accomplishments, all of which require self-control and lead to a sense of competence and mastery. Infants try to control the presence of important other people. The necessarily unsuccessful infant learns that other people are separate from itself. This separateness is learned with pain and difficulty. Feminist theoreticians have underlined the psychological issues in accepting maternal separateness (Chodorow, 1979). These clients illustrate difficulties in allowing paternal separateness; they are preoccupied with omnipotently controlling the presence and feelings of the overvalued man and are impotent to do so.

Recent psychoanalitic revisions alert us to the importance of pre-Oedipal relational reciprocal development. Feminists using this theory have followed its traditional psychoanalytic bias, mother first, father add-on. The women whom I have described had fathers who did not in any way 'share' parenting. They remind us that from early on, father is an equally important, though different relationship from mother. For these clients he represented excitement, competence, fun, and power. They felt special about themselves when they were with him, and they all felt a warmth in the relationship with him. In contrast, mother was always around. She did not do special things, and there was a security, a taking for granted about her. Deep-seated cognitive dichotomies developed; mothers/women were boring, fathers/men exciting; steady presence vs. coming and going; domestic power vs charismatic power; submission vs. dominance.

I believe that the mother, father, daughter pattern I have described is normative in our culture. It does not necessarily cause neurotic problems for large numbers of women. Nonetheless, it can create fertile psychological ground in daughters for their becoming grown-up participants in a male dominated culture.

When we propose changes in structural arrangements in families or when we speculate about the impact of existing arrangements, we need to pay careful attention to the emotional meaning of these for all of the persons involved in them. To illustrate how complicated this can become, I will briefly comment on two issues: equal parenting and single parenthood. While I completely support equal parenting, it is possible to see it as being relatively ineffective in changing the power dynamics I have described. A father, for example, might in a daughter's eyes take on some aspects of maternal power without giving up charismatic power. This could happen if family power relations between father and mother remained unchanged in important but subtle ways. It certainly would be likely if mother felt anxious and guilty about not being a full-time caretaker (Contratto, 1984). In fact, in such an instance, rather than feeling that femaleness gained power through work outside the home, a daughter might feel that she was deprived of the maternal presence.

It is difficult to argue that there will be specific psychological implications in the dramatic rise in female-headed households (81% increase from 1970 to 1979). Andrew Cherlin (1981:26–27) says that two-thirds of the rise was caused by the increase in divorced and separated mothers, while the remaining increase was due to never married mothers. Cherlin also points out that three out of four women remarry after divorce, and half do so within three years after divorce. For a good proportion of these female-headed households, then, the absence of a male is temporary. These mothers, for whatever reasons, do not choose single parenthood; they do not remain unmarried, and they do not form emotional bonds with other women to the exclusion of men. Therefore, one might speculate that the children in these families at some point would experience adult power relationships which differed for mother and father. Further, many of the women who do not remarry are older. Presumably, then, their children are older, and during the formative time I an describing, there was a father in the home. For those who did not remarry, moreover, there is no way of knowing if this was a chosen lifestyle. This also applies to those women who never married. Again, the mother's emotional evaluation of such a state is critical.

Not all women have experienced mothers and fathers of the types described by these clients. There is no single emotional family: mothers might be more or less present; they might have comings and goings;

they might be exciting, stimulating and provocative, love-inspiring, hate-inspiring or awe-inspiring. Fathers as well as siblings or other adults, might be present and absent in different ways. Nonetheless, women's early paternal experiences require that we revise our thinking about psychological development to put relational issues with father (or others) beside those with mother.

Since it is most often the case that men have charismatic power within the family, it is essential to look at early familial experiences as a likely source of women's ambivalence about power.

NOTES

1. This is an early memory of my own which I recalled when free associating to a dream which I had while I was immersed in preparing the above paper.

2. I am grateful to Nancy Chodorow, Evelyn Fox Keller, Sara Ruddick, and Marilyn Young for reading an earlier draft of this paper, expressing encouragement and enthusiasm, and making a number of suggestions, some of which I have been able to incorporate. In particular, Sara Ruddick made me clearly see the dichotomies enmeshed in the earlier draft. This version entitled "Fathers, Daughters and Lovers" was given March 3, 1983 at Claremont Colleges as part of their Women's Studies Colloquium Series. I want to thank members of the audience there for penetrating questions and useful comments.

3. There is no single cause, of course, to any psychological difficulty. I have found it useful to understand etiology of psychological difficulties within a framework provided by Evelyn Fox Keller (1985). Keller makes the distinction between laws of nature and order of nature in describing dominant scientific paradigms. In clinically useful psychological theory, there are not laws of development. However, there is an order to development - development is not anarchical or formless. Because of the urge to be 'scientific', however, and to discover developmental 'laws', theorists are still searching to describe the order of development.

4. This example illustrates a way in which unquestioned acceptance of paternal power short circuits a political analysis of the problem which might increase class consciousness and lead to political activity.

5. While this affective reversal is a relatively common defensive maneuver, it seems to me that defusing anger by transforming it into understanding may be particularly female.

6. This is clearly a controversial point. Theorists who believe that psychological development is fundamentally grounded in physical integrity and body attributes will not agree with it. I can only reiterate that

the emotional meaning of this early relationship with father is too complex and rich for me to believe that it can be reduced to fantasies about his penis.

BIOGRAPHICAL NOTE

Susan Contratto was born in Boston and grew up in Brookline, Mass. She went to Radcliffe and majored in Social Relations. After college, she did graduate work in Counseling Psychology. Dr. Contratto is primarily in private practice. Her research interests in the past few years have been in psychological development & family structure. Her major published works are: (1) "The Fantasy of the Perfect Mother," with Nancy Chodorow, (2) "Mother: Social Sculptor and Trustee of the Faith"; and (3) "Maternal Sexuality and Asexual Motherhood". She occasionally teaches at the University of Michigan, where she offers courses in "Group Process" and "Feminism and the American Family."

REFERENCES

BLUM, H. P.
1976 "Masochism, the Ego Ideal and the Psychology of Women." Journal of the American Psychoanalytic Association 5:157–93.
BRIENES, W., CERULLO M., AND STACEY, J.
1978 "Social Biology, Family Studies, and Antifeminist Backlash." Feminist Studies 4 (1): 43–67.
BREINES, W., AND GORDON, L.
1983 "The New Scholarship on Family Violence." Signs: Journal of Women in Culture and Society 8, (3): 490–531.
CHERLIN, A. J.
1981 Marriage, Divorce, Remarriage. Cambridge: Harvard University Press.
CHODOROW, N.
1978 The Reproduction of Mothering: Psychoanalysis and the Reproduction of Gender. Berkeley: University of California Press.
CHODOROW, N.
1979 "Feminism and Difference: Gender, Relation and Difference in Psychoanalytic Perspective." Socialist Review 9, (4): 51–69.
CHODOROW, N. AND CONTRATTO, S.
1982 "The Fantasy of the Perfect Mother," in B. Thorne (ed.), with Marilyn Yalom, Rethinking the Family: Some Feminist Questions. New York Longman.
CONTRATTO, S.
1984 "Mother: Social Sculptor and Trustee of the Faith," in M. Lewin (ed.), In the Shadow of the Past: Psychology Portrays the Sexes. New York: Columbia University Press.
KELLER, E. F.
1978 "Gender and Science." Psychoanalysis and Contemporary Thought 1:409.

KELLER, E. F.
1985 Reflections on Gender and Science. New Haven: Yale University Press.
GALENSON, E. AND ROLPHE, H.
1976 "Some Suggested Revisions concerning Early Female Development." Journal of the American Psychoanalytic Association 5:29–58.
GILLIGAN, C.
1982 In a Different Voice. Cambridge: Harvard University Press.
MONEY, J., AND EHRHARDT, A. A.
1972 Man Woman, Boy and Girl. Baltimore: Johns Hopkins University Press.
PARENS, H., et al.
1976 "On the Girl's Entry into the Oedipus Complex." Journal of the American Psychoanalytic Association 5:79–108.
RUBIN, L. B.
1976 Worlds of Pain. New York: Basic Books.
STOLLER, R. J.
1976 "Primary Femininity." Journal of the American Psychoanalytic Association 5:51–70.
STRAUS, M., GELLES, R., AND STEINMETZ, S.
1980 Behind Closed Doors: Violence in the American Family. Garden City: Anchor Books.
THORNE, B.
1982 "Feminist Rethinking of the Family: An Overview." pp. 1–24 in B. Thorne (ed.), with M. Yalom, Rethinking the family: Some Feminist Questions. New York: Longman.
WALLERSTEIN, J., AND KELLY, J.
1980 Surviving the Breakup. New York: Basic Books.

IV

THE PSYCHOANALYTIC SOCIOLOGY OF DEVIANCE

Introduction

Sociologists, in general, have always been sympathetic toward the poor and oppressed in American society and indeed have been accused of having a liberal bias. Certainly the founding fathers of American soci-ology in the 1920s and 1930s were concerned about the experiences that immigrant groups were having in our country, and they frequently de-scribed the social situations and inequalities engendered by discrimi-nation, sexism, and racism. Sociologists have continued to show how such processes operate in our courtrooms, prisons, and schools, and in other institutions of contemporary society. Such explanations are usually made from a structural perspective *or* an interactionist perspective. The former perspective focuses on how large-scale forces such as culture and the economy shape individual behavior. Wage and job discrimination may be the result of a large unemployed labor force, educational inequalities, or a tariff structure.

The interactional perspective, however, focuses more upon two types of individual interactions. One type assumes that the individual and the society are analytically inseparable. In this view, the society is the indi-vidual in interaction. Social order is created through interaction between persons, and the focus for students of this perspective is upon the mean-ings constructed by participants. The second school of interaction focuses the effects of the immediate situation upon the behavior of the indi-vidual. While such immediate situations involve structure and culture, these are not the larger structures studied under the structural per-spective. The situations could be a communication network (Leavitt, 1951), the courtroom (Emerson, 1969), the bar (Cavan, 1961), or the family at home (Laing & Esterson, 1964). The concern is with the im-mediate environment and the influence upon persons.

Included in the interaction perspective is the school of research known as labeling. In this perspective, agents of social control (the accusers and stigmatizers) are seen as the active social agents who define the rules governing 'normal behavior' as well as the behaviors that come to be defined as 'deviant'. The emphasis upon the *agents* of social control (teachers, parents, police, probation officers), and the *institutions* of control (family, courts, and schools) has tended to ignore the *psychology* of those being labeled as well as the psychology of the controllers. Standard studies of labeling theory, focussing on deviant behavior, have concentrated upon interaction and ignored the psychology of the controller and controllee.

The first article by Professor Robert Endleman, "Psychoanalytic Sociology and the Sociology of Deviance," argues for correcting this oversight by asking for an integrated psychoanalytic-sociological approach to the study of deviance. Endleman asserts that a psychological orientation is necessary for an adequate understanding of deviance and that the best psychology for supplementing a structural or interactionist approach, although imperfect, is psychoanalysis. In his article, Endleman takes us through the theoretical views of several sociologists who all approach deviance from a structural or interactionist perspective. He shows how each of these authors has neglected the psychology of the individuals who are considered 'deviant' or the psychology of other actors involved with the deviant. Endleman points out that it is not enough to probe only the sociological factors which may predispose the individual to deviant behavior, but that a fuller comprehension and understanding must also examine the person at a psychological level. Endleman states that a psychological orientation is *relevant* and *necessary* for understanding the sociology of deviance. He uses the writings of many well-known sociologists of deviance to illustrate how psychology is "implicit" in their analyses and how future work in deviance needs to make more explicit the psychology that is often taken for granted or assumed to be unimportant.

Examining, studying, and understanding the psychology of deviants does not mean that we need to look for psychopathology in individuals. Endleman makes a second and important contribution as he argues that deviance and pathology need not co-exist.

In the second article, "Prostitution, Economic Exchange, and the Unconscious," Professor Marion Goldman does exactly what Endleman calls for. She illustrates the problems with earlier sociological work on prostitutes and uses a psychoanalytic sociological approach to extend those earlier analyses of prostitution. She also goes beyond the usual approach of social scientists who have tended to focus exclusively on the psychology of the prostitute. In her work, Goldman argues against the consensus of sociologists, social reformers, and even prostitutes who believe that financial considerations related to sex segregation and discrimination in the labor force are major factors affecting the supply side of prostitution. Goldman contends that although economic reasons and social structure cannot be dismissed in explaining prostitution, they do not sufficiently explain the *reasons* women become prostitutes. For a comprehensive explanation of prostitution, theories of psychic structure *and* social organization are more useful.

In her article, Goldman shows how both the "psychic structure" of the female *prostitute* and of the client or *customer*, and social structural arrangements of *men* and *women* foster prostitution. Goldman's analysis is based in part on a reanalysis of some psychoanalytic studies. She shows how the careful reading of studies in the psychoanalytic literature may be a valuable source of data to those who wish to integrate disciplines. The Goldman article may be seen as a more specific application of Endleman's general concern, as well as our ongoing effort in this book, to show how unconscious social processes are linked with social organization. She describes the unconscious wishes and fears of female prostitutes and male customers, the social organization of gender, the social organization of parent-child relations and the economic realities and structures influencing women.

REFERENCES

Cavan, S.
  1966 Liquor License. Chicago: Aldine.
Emerson, R. M.
  1969 *Judging Delinquents.* Chicago: Aldine.
Laing, R. D., A. Esterson
  1964 *Sanity, Madness and the Family.* New York: Basic Books.
Leavitt, H. J.
  1951 "Some Effects of Certain Communication Patterns on Group Performance." *Journal of Abnormal and Sociological Psychology* 46: 38–50.

Psychoanalytic Sociology and the Sociology of Deviance

ROBERT ENDLEMAN

"Man is not a total abstainer from reason,
though he indulges in rationality with
fanatical moderation."
Robert Lowie, 1929

INTRODUCTION

ONE of the major areas of potential contribution of psychoanalytic sociology is to the study of deviant behavior, that is, behavior which varies from or runs counter to the norms of the society. Sociologists have for some time been interested, from a variety of angles, in the oddballs and misfits of society: people who don't fit into conventional molds. They have looked at eccentrics, prostitutes, alcohol and chemical adventurers, thieves, murderers, and rapists. Their scope has encompassed radicals and revolutionaries, both juvenile and adult, amateur and professional.

The sociological interest in deviance has had a variety of motives and modalities. In some cases it is journalistic, even sensationalist. In some it is reformistic, such as, let us clean up these horrors; or, in variation, let us clean up the horrors of the law and conventional society in their treatment of these poor outsiders. In some cases, it is human interest drama: violation is what points up the dramatic and critical in human life. Sometimes it is soberly "scientific", neither condoning nor condemning. Sometimes (but rarely) the interest is psychological.

Some sociologists of deviance have explicitly steered away from any psychological approaches to the deviant on the ground that such study amounts to reductionism. By reducing a sociological phenomenon and question to a psychological one, it is often said that the question is *irrelevant* to sociological analysis. In another version, sociologists object to a psychological view, thinking it always implies a judgment of sickness. In answer, some sociologists claim the deviant is *not* sick.

In reference to certain kinds of deviance, such as sexual variation and mental illness, some sociologists tend to regard questioning of the psychological status of the persons identified as deviants, as itself, part of the process of stigmatization, and in effect, punishment of the individuals involved. This tends to be the position of sociologists of the labeling persuasion (Becker, 1963; Scheff 1966; Perrucci 1974; Goode 1978).

Basically, the people of the world can be divided into two categories:

A. People who divide the world into two categories; and

B. Those who do not.

With respect to category (A), sociologists of deviance can be further sub-divided into two broad categories:

1. Those who believe there is a reality to deviant behavior.
2. Those who regard deviance as existing entirely in the eye of the beholder.

I shall briefly explain the difference.

Sociologists of category (1) believe the following: there are real people committing deviant acts, and the acts are authentically deviant; that is, acts that deviate from, violate, or otherwise depart from definite norms of the society (or of some subgroup of which the actor is a member). The *behavior* is deviant, whether or not it is detected by anyone, identified *as* deviant by onlookers, observers, or agents of officialdom of any kind; whether or not *labeled* as deviant; and whether or not the person committing such an act is officially or otherwise so designated, whatever consequences may flow from such labeling, and any official treatment of the person as a deviant. This may be dubbed the "deviance as reality" position. (Examples of sociologists who take this view are: Marshall Clinard, 1963; Richard Cloward and Lloyd Ohlin, 1961; Albert Cohen, 1955; Walter Gove, 1975; Travis Hirschi, 1969; Robert Merton, 1938; Walter Reckless, 1962, 1973; Edwin Sutherland, 1949.)

Other sociologists, in category (2), regard deviance as existing entirely in the eye of the beholder. For them, "deviance is not a quality of the act the person commits, but rather a consequence of the application by others of rules and sanctions to an 'offender.' The deviant is one to whom the label has successfully been applied. Deviant behavior is behavior that people so label" (Howard Becker, 1963). Deviance for these sociologists consists of the *attribution* of the quality of deviation to certain acts or persons. This may be called the "deviance as labeling" position. (Exponents of this view include: Howard Becker, 1963; Kai Erikson, 1962, 1966; Erich Goode, 1978; John Kitsuse, 1962; Robert Perrucci, 1974; Thomas Scheff, 1966; Edwin Schur, 1971.)

These two views are sharply contradictory. Sociologists of the deviance as reality may ask etiological questions such as, What is the *origin*—sociological or psychological or both—of the deviant behavior? Sociologists of the deviance as labeling view steer away from asking such questions:

their interest is in the *interaction process* that is set in motion when a person's action is labeled as deviant and what happens from there on. They ask such questions as Why are some labeled and not others?; How is labeling organized and accomplished?; What are the consequences of labeling?

While the first category of sociologists may leave some room for psychological questions, the second category does not. They are vehemently *not* interested in psychological questions, and in some cases, opposed to the raising of such questions, evidently on ideological grounds.

Clearly, my approach to the sociology of deviance belongs in the first category. I regard it as not only appropriate, but also as necessary to raise psychological questions about the *motivation* of the actors, in this case the persons who commit deviant acts.

Neither a psychological view, including the psychoanalytic one, which probes inner psychodynamics, nor a sociological view, which probes either the sociological conditions favoring the production of deviant behavior or the social interaction processes attending the relationship between persons defined as deviant and their onlookers and societal reactors, is able to provide all the answers to all the questions of importance about deviance. However, they *can* be seen as different and complementary approaches. We are all individual personalities with intrapsychic processes. We all play social roles, live in interaction with others, pay attention to or ignore or violate social norms. We all participate in, sometimes creatively expanding or modifying, an ongoing culture, or parts and segments of several different ongoing cultures and subcultures. No one part of these analytically distinguishable processes excludes the others. We need to know what on the individual psychological level makes the persons who are considered deviant act the way they do, think and feel as they do, be the kind of persons they are. We also need to ask: If the stigmatizers subject the deviant to stereotyping, discrimination, or any kind of victimization, how do they, the stigmatizers, come to be acting that way? By what intrapsychic processes, what projections, displacements, reaction-formations,? By what relationship to what prior intrapsychic experiences *they* have had, in relation to persons important in their lives, to other specific people in society?

SOCIOLOGY OF DEVIANCE NEEDS A PSYCHOANALYTIC SOCIOLOGY

A psychoanalytic-sociological approach maintains that the psychodynamics—of the deviants *and of the onlookers, accusers and stigmatizers, too*—are an essential part of the total picture. Our understanding of what is going on is defective and incomplete without inclusion of this element and its correct designation and analysis. In order to get to the point where we can do such work, we need first to clear up certain basic misunderstandings prevalent among sociologists (and many psychoanalysts). Let me address these as three main points:

    I.*Some* psychological orientation is necessary, alongside of and integrated with sociological approaches, for adequate understanding.

    II.Concern with psychological factors does *not* presuppose psychopathology.

    III.Deviance does not equal psychopathology.

    Let me elaborate on each of these.

I. A PSYCHOLOGICAL ORIENTATION IS NOT IRRELEVANT FOR UNDERSTANDING THE SOCIOLOGY OF DEVIANCE; IT IS NECESSARY

Far from being antagonistic to adequate sociological understanding of deviance and of reactions to deviance, psychoanalytic-psychological exploration of the subjective reactions of all the participants in the deviance and deviance-defining process, is essential. More generally, all social science needs an underlying psychology of human nature and of human reactions, and for my purposes, the best such psychology, imperfect as it may be, is psychoanalysis.

Sociological studies have all along included, usually implicitly, an assumed psychology of human responses. I will briefly show how nine well known theorists of delinquency, deviance, and crime explicitly or implicitly utilize psychology in their work.

Case 1. Durkheim on Suicide

Durkheim's most famous and most influential argument for a distinctively *sociological* approach, eschewing psychology (therefore psychological reductionism) is itself, on close inspection, built upon an unacknowledged but necessary set of psychological assumptions and propositions. His concept of *anomie* (ostensibly a preeminently sociological conception) in fact rests upon the assumption of inner subjective processes, without which there is no sense at all in positing a lack of integrative ties, or a lack of bondedness toward the norms of society. His celebrated formulation of the relationship between suicide and anomie (Durkheim, 1897), to be plausible, needs today to be reformulated as follows: Suicide results from unresolved conflicts, stresses, and anxieties in individuals for whom social cohesion would provide psychological support for people subjected to such stresses. In the situation of *anomie*: normlessness, such supports are lacking. To be sure, that was not Durkheim's own phrasing, but what is implied in his analysis. And it clearly refers to internal subjective states. So while Durkheim, the theoretician and methodologist (*Rules of the Sociological Method*, 1895), rejected using any psychology, it is there. In effect, it is smuggled in. Psychoanalytic sociology says, in answer: better explicitly to get the psychology in, and the best psychology is psychoanalysis.

Some deviance sociologists do in fact use some psychology, explicitly or implicitly, not necessarily formulated in terms of a particular psychological theory, such as psychoanalysis. The following eight cases also serve as exemplars.

Case 2. Merton on Social Structure and Anomie

Just as there is a good deal of implicit psychology in the anti-psychological work of Durkheim, so we find it again in the work of Merton. In "Social Structure and Anomie" (1938), a justly famous work, Merton's manifest intent is to present a sociological theory of the origins of deviance, as against psychological conceptions of its origin. The basic thrust of the paper is against attributing the malfunctioning of society to those of "man's imperious biological drives which are not adequately restrained by social control." But in his rebuttal, and his strong stand for a consistently *sociological* analysis, Merton nevertheless leaves a lot of psychology *in*. Like many polemicists, much influenced by the doctrines they fight against, Merton seems to have been heavily influenced by some psychoanalytic conceptions. These appear, for example, in his reference to internalized prohibitions (which operate, he says, in the individual heading toward the retreatist orientation, who is unable to adopt the illegitimate route, such as crime, because of *internalized prohibitions*). (Emphasis mine.) He notes that given a situation of anomie in his sense— disjuncture between goals and availability of legitimate means—the kind of deviant adaptation (innovation, ritualism, retreatism, or rebellion) a person turns to is determined by the particular *personality*. Elsewhere he writes that it is unlikely interiorized norms are completely eliminated. Thus, there is a good deal of psychology in this paper not systematically integrated with the basic sociological positions or systematically developed in terms of one consistent psychological theory.

We can point to a number of other recent deviance sociologists who, in one way or another, take psychological questions seriously and emphasize the psychological dimensions of their work. Being sociologists in good standing, each of these tends not to emphasize the psychological elements in his work and not to formulate them in terms of a particular psychological theory.

Case 3. Reckless et al., on the Non-Delinquents

Walter Reckless and a group of his colleagues did some research on how it is that some youngsters in a high delinquency area of the city, did *not* turn to delinquency (Reckless *et al.*, 1956: follow-up: Scarpitti *et al.*, 1960). They systematically compared the non-delinquents with the delinquents. What they found was this: the non-delinquents differed significantly in *self-concept*; that is, how they viewed themselves and the important people in their world. The non-delinquents saw themselves in positive terms; they saw themselves as law-abiding persons. They perceived good relationships between themselves and each of their parents. They saw the parents as fair-minded and interested in the sons' welfare. They defined themselves as boys who would not become entangled with the law. On each of these points they contrasted strikingly with the delinquent boys. These differences were maintained in the follow-up study done four years later.

Though this is not psychological at the depth-dynamic level such as we find in psychoanalytic studies, it does refer to the internal psychological subjective state of the persons involved and provides something of an answer to the psychological question: Why does a particular individual *not* become subject to neighborhood pressure to join a delinquent group that is eminently available in a high delinquency area?

Case 4. Cohen on Delinquent Subcultures

Albert Cohen, in *Delinquent Boys* (1955), posed the sociological question: How to account for the existence and features of the juvenile delinquent *subculture*? His answer is in effect a collective-*psychological* one: working class male juveniles face similar problems of adjustment, for which the gang subculture provides a kind of solution. They fail to come up to the "middle class measuring rod", therefore suffering affronts to their self-esteem and masculinity. Cohen clearly does take seriously the psychology of the deviants, and sees it as connected to the sociological question. These working class boys suffer from status frustrations, an internal psychological state that is negative and depriving. The context for this is indeed a *social* condition, i.e., that even working and lower class youngsters living in this society do not escape from the pressures of expectations that are often described as middle class. These pressures are essentially universal in this society, pushing the males, especially, to start early to work for achievement in some stable, respected, and respectable occupation. However, this social situation is relevant because it affects the internal subjective state of the boys under consideration. True, Cohen's psychology of what is going on in these boys does not take us very far into their intrapsychic experience, and does not explicitly use any systematic psychological theory. For fuller development of what Cohen touches on, we need to turn to work such as that of Fritz Redl (1945) and Redl and David Wineman (1951) on the inner-psychological dilemmas. But from the viewpoint of what I am asserting here, Cohen's work is a step in the right direction.

Case 5. Reckless on Containment Theory

Walter Reckless, does try to develop a general theory about deviance, and what he worked out is of interest here. He calls his approach "containment theory" (Reckless, 1962, 1973). For him, the basic question to be asked is not why persons deviate from the norms, but rather why they *conform* to the norms. Answer: each person has two kinds of controls upon him: one is external, the other is internal. These together *contain* his conduct. If they are both strong, he will basically conform to the dictates of his society. If both are weak, he is likely to deviate from the norms. The likelihood of deviation is a *probability*, not an all-or-nothing matter. That probability will be high if both containments are weak; moderately high if either external or internal control is weak while the other is strong; and very low if both controls are strong. Each individual is subject to pressures and pulls from both inside himself—the pleasure-seeking drives given in the personality, and other internally -generated forces pushing toward the attainment of optimal gratifications—and from outside himself—lures, enticements, opportunities, encouragements from the social environment. Containment that restrains an individual from moving with such pulls and pressures, possibly in the direction of deviant behavior, comes from both external and internal sources. The *external* comes from whatever supportive groups the individual has, principally family and other primary groups. In times past these included the clan, the neighborhood, the village, the caste, the tribe, the religious sect. In modern, urban, industrialized society, the latter are likely to be weaker, but one or more of the following may operate: a role structure providing scope for the individual; reasonable limits and responsibilities for members; opportunity to attain status; cohesion among members; sense of belongingness; identification with one or more persons within the group; provision of alternative means of satisfaction (when a desired means is closed). *Internal* containment consists of five "self" components:

1. Favorable self-image in relation to other persons, groups, institutions
2. Awareness of being an internally-directed, goal-oriented person

3. Relatively high frustration tolerance
4. Strong internalized morals and ethics
5. Well developed ego and superego (Reckless, 1962: 132–133)

This theory is a very promising approach. It is one of the rare ones that enables integration of sociological approaches with psychological approaches, focusing on society as well as the individual. It takes seriously the inner structure of the personality and succumbs neither to psychological determinism nor to sociological determinism. Unlike labeling theory, it does not wait to begin the analysis until *after* the deviant act has been committed or limit itself programmatically to societal reaction as the principal fact of deviance. It neither slights the thorny question of etiology—where does the deviant behavior come from?—nor neglects interaction processes, which are an essential aspect of what Reckless terms "external control" (or its absence) or whatever appears in its place. It assumes the actors involved, whether committers of deviant acts, their families and associates, those who define and label them or take (or do not take) official action, are all players of roles in interaction and are all personalities with intrapsychic structures. Though the psychological propositions here are rudimentary and sketchy, they are not inaccurate and can be filled out readily enough by a more psychoanalytic intrapsychic psychology. This is one theory in which interactionist sociology of deviance and dynamic psychology of the individual can be fruitfully integrated.

Case 6. Sykes and Matza on Neutralization Techniques

In this interesting paper, "Techniques of Neutralization" (1957), Gresham Sykes and David Matza take on the question of why delinquents, or anyone, violate laws or rules in which they believe. These authors challenge Cohen's assertion (in *Delinquent Boys*) that the boys, once enmeshed in the delinquent subculture, reject the validity of conventional norms and abide by their own moral code which in many ways is a reversal of the conventional ones. Sykes and Matza assert instead that the evidence of studies already made indicates that the boys engaging in delinquency do in fact still accept the conventional moral codes. They have in fact internalized these, and therefore are likely to feel guilt and shame about their misdeeds. Why then does such guilt or shame, anticipated, not stop them from committing delinquent acts? These authors contend that the delinquents, like many other people, have a somewhat *flexible* code. Any *absolute* power the norms might internally have is modified, or, as they put it, *neutralized* in a variety of ways. The paper is about five types of such techniques. These are rationalizations/justifications applied not only after the fact of commission of delinquent acts, but in advance as well, and in that case serve as facilitators for the commission of acts not fully acceptable, morally, to the participants. These five techniques are: denial of responsibility (it's not my fault, I come from a crummy environment); denial of injury (nobody got hurt by this, they can afford the loss); denial of the victim (he asked for it; these fags deserve to get beat up); condemning the condemners (the cops are all corrupt; teachers always play favorites) and appeal to high loyalties (I didn't do it for myself, but for my buddies; I couldn't let the gang down).

Much of this paper seems almost a rewrite in sociological or commonsensical terminology of psychoanalytic work on how a person can deal corruptly with his own conscience or superego. It remains for the intrapsychic dimension of this discussion to be strengthened and deepened for the leads in this paper to serve as an important integrating link between sociological and psychoanalytical forms of deviance.

The paper is coherent with Redl's work on how norm-violating kids use group support to circumvent superego pressures (Redl, 1945). It also fits with Bergler's discussion (1948) of how we bribe the superego and make alliances between the superego and the id. It can also be related to Adelaide Johnson's development of the concept of "superego lacunae", to refer to wavering and unreliable operation of the superego, derived from unconscious collusion by the parents who, in effect, have given the child a double message, one: don't do those bad things, and two: Mommy—or Daddy—will be fascinated with you if you do that risky, naughty thing, or Mommy—or Daddy—will admire your skill at getting away with things. (Johnson, 1949).

Case 7. LaMar T. Empey and J. Rabow on the Provo Experiment

In 1961, a description of a delinquency rehabilitation program appeared in the most prestigious American sociological journal, *The American Sociological Review* (Empey and Rabow, 1961). The program, known as the Provo Experiment, was built upon writings of many sociological theorists. Work by Thrasher (1936), Cohen (1935), Kobrin (1951), and Miller (1958) on the etiology of gang delinquency, and work done by Clemmer (1940), Sykes (1958), and Cloward (1960) on the inmate code provided the theoretical basis of the article. The program also had its applied roots in work developed by two sociologists who were trained at the University of Chicago: McCorkle and Elias, (McCorkle, Elias, and Bixby, 1958), as well as Rabow, who was trained by Elias at Highfields, a residential treatment center. The program was thus rooted in the Chicago-sociology delinquency-criminology traditions.

The Provo program provided a description of rehabilitative treatment that was quite anti-psychological. Indeed, the description of the program aroused the hostility of many social workers, psychologists, humanists, and directors of youth commissions, but it received very strong support from the sociological and correctional communities.

The support from within reflected the anti-psychological approach that existed among sociologists. Here was a program that described a treatment process and rehabilitation without talking about a defective superego, transference, and countertransference, and Oedipal resolution. Yet as Rabow, himself, was later to note:

In attempting to achieve distinctiveness, clarity, and sociological rigor, and in attempting to capture the significance of some important stirrings in the field of corrections, Provo excluded certain matters and methods of operation. The struggle to establish Provo with an exclusive identity and a significance of its own prevented discussions of Provo's similarities with other therapeutic practices and programs. These similarities were ignored in the paper (Rabow, 1971).

What is implied in this statement is that a more complex program description of the therapist's role and behavior and of the delinquents, themselves, would have made the program less appealing and attractive to sociologists; and perhaps less valuable to that constituency. Now sociologists could proudly point to their own program and could discuss rehabilitation and treatment in terms of role shifts (Rabow, 1965; Rabow and Elias, 1969) and not in psychological or psychoanalytic terms. Now sociologists had a program that discussed jobs and training without any focus on trauma and sibling rivalry. This oversight, however, was not without its consequence. The failure to specify clearly the complexities of treatment and issues of transference resulted in a program that, in emulating Provo, became a caricature (Rabow, 1971). The failure to describe accurately the importance of a supportive and therapeutic climate, to indicate unmistakably that more was going on than specifying alternatives and clear and direct threats (Rabow, 1965), helped alienate many practitioners. The Provo Experiment, in failing to specify the psychological aspects of a rehabilitative theory, did little to bring about the active participation and cooperation of the researcher-scientist and clinician practitioner. Ultimately, it contributed little to a more scientific appreciation of rehabilitation (Rabow, 1964).

Case 8. Matza on Bohemianism

As part of his seminal paper on "Subterranean Traditions of Youth" (1961) David Matza makes an illuminating characterization of bohemianism (with delinquency and radicalism, one of the three major "subterranean traditions"). He describes the concern in this life pattern for expressive authenticity: its romantic interest in primitives and other exotic peoples and cultures; its quest for transcendence; its acceptance (quest in fact) of voluntary poverty; its opposition to the commercialized life of bourgeois culture. While Matza's interest here is plainly at the level of *cultural* analysis, each of these characteristics involves certain definable *subjective* states, the full exploration of which would require a *psychological* analysis. Objective position in the class structure would not explain the bohemians' stance, so oppositional to that of the majority of people at their class level—at least upper middle class in the families of origin. (To be sure, having orientation families of affluence may be a precondition for the bohemians' development and cultivation of essentially neo-aristocratic values). Just as not all lower class youngsters become delinquents, not all upper-middle-class ones become bohemians (beats, at the time of Matza's essay, hippies, a few years later). Specific psychological-developmental factors differentiate them from class peers who do not turn in that direction, and these need to be explored by an in-depth psychological analysis.

Case 9. Lemert on Social Pathology

Though often considered a forerunner labeling theorist, Edwin Lemert does not at all share the labeling theorists' notion that all deviance is a matter of the labelers' so defining it. He is explicit that there are first deviant *acts* (primary deviation), and he is interested in the psychology of these acts, something the labeling theorists dismiss. Consider the following passage:

The importance of the person's conscious symbolic reactions to his or her own behavior cannot be overstressed in explaining the shift from normal to abnormal behavior, or from one type of pathological behavior into another (1951:74).

Lemert is interested in the *causes* of the original deviant acts (primary deviation), which he wisely concludes cannot be found in any one simple formula. Distinguishing original causes, which can be extremely variable, from effective causes, such as what happens when the deviation becomes a matter of social definition:

The deviations are not significant until they are organized *subjectively* (my emphasis—RE) and transformed into active roles and become the social criteria for assigning status. The deviant individuals must react symbolically to their own behavior aberrations and fix them in their sociopsychological patterns. The deviations remain primary deviations or symptomatic and situational as long as they are rationalized or otherwise dealt with as functions of a socially acceptable role. Under such conditions normal and pathological behaviors remain strange and somewhat tensional bedfellows in the same person. Undeniably a vast amount of such segmental and partially integrated pathological behavior exists in our society and has impressed many writers in the field of social pathology (p. 75).

This is a subtle and differentiated statement. By "abnormal" and "pathological" here Lemert means departing from the norms, or deviant; he does not intend psychopathology. Similarly, his usage of the term "sociopathic" in the title of the chapter in which those passages appear ("Sociopathic Individuation") simply means norm-violating. It is not equivalent to the meaning that term took on years later in sociological (and some psychological) parlance as a synonym for what had been called psychopath or psychopathic personality, or later still was called antisocial personality (meaning a personality syndrome). He uses sociopathic simply as a descriptive statement indicating that the person persistently broke mores and laws. Basically, the frame of reference for Lemert's use of normal and abnormal here is the *cultural* conception of normality, (in my tripartite division of conceptions: statistical, cultural, and transcultural) not implying an intrapsychic dimension.

The pattern of movement from primary deviation to a fullfledged secondary deviance (if it occurs at all) Lemert sees as involving contingencies both from outside the person and from within his personality. This view differs from the cruder versions of labeling theory which imply the person, once labeled, is thereafter entirely a pawn of those external outside oppressors, stigmatizers. For Lemert, "in the inner mental life of the person . . . there is continuous interplay between the external and internal limits" (p. 89); that is, outside forces limiting one's range of choices of action and inner psychological forces doing so.

Then on the matter of adjustment and maladjustment—by which Lemert seems to mean inner psychological stability and well-being, as against psychological disturbance or disorder—i.e., something close to what I call a transcultural or mental health standard of normality, Lemert wisely points out that:

Neither adjustment nor maladjustment are the inevitable consequences of departing from society's approved rules and regulations. . . . The degree to which a deviant is adjusted will be expressed by the amount of congruence between the societal definition and the individual's definition of the self. . . . Of course there is never a perfect convergence between these societal definitions and self-definitions, largely because there never can be perfect communication between society and the individual. Besides this, a complete and candid reception of society's evaluations would be too painful for most people, hence there is always a certain amount of misinterpretation of the societal self-defining stimuli and corresponding psychological subterfuge in even well-adjusted persons. It is here that the so-called dynamisms or mechanisms of the mind—dissociation, rationalization, projection and substitution—come into play to strike a working balance between the societal definitions and self-definitions, or to put it in completely subjective terms, between the "I" and the "me" (p. 91).

Though the psychological vocabulary here is an uneasy mixture of Meadian and Freudian, and rational-cognitive functions are given more emphasis over non-rational affective ones, there is assuredly a strong interest in the processes going on in the individual deviant and relating those in turn to the social processes of interaction with others who define, react, and stigmatize.

Those starting elements can certainly be expanded with the use of a more theoretically developed and systematically crafted psychology of the individual personality, such as we have in psychoanalysis.

Lemert's insistence that "neither adjustment nor maladjustment is the inevitable consequences of departing from society's rules" fits well with my propositions presented elsewhere in this paper: that is, the deviant is not necessarily sick, that deviance does not equate with psychopathology.

IMPLICATIONS OF THE NINE SOCIOLOGICAL WORKS

What is the main proposition to be drawn from these sketchy examples? Sociological studies of deviance need not be anti-psychological, or non-psychological, or exclusionary of psychological ideas. Good work in sociology recognizes that the actor, whether the deviant or the person reacting to the deviant, is a total personality. He has intrapsychic functions that connect with his deviant conduct and deviant self-concept or lack of one. Simultaneously he is a player of social roles, a participant in social interaction and in ongoing culture or transformations or denials of it.

To be aware of and pay careful attention to the internal psychological processes of the individuals involved does not mean that we are claiming that the intrapsychic is the *cause* of the deviance; it may or may not be. That is not to be prejudged but to be investigated by research. Neither does it exclude the social and cultural processes most sociologists of deviance attend.

While the classical Durkheim implicitly included a psychology underlying his analysis of anomie, the contemporary Merton included some ideas from psychoanalysis. Merton borrowed the concepts of manifest and latent from Freud's study of dreams and applied them to functions in sociological analysis (Merton, 1949). Sykes and Matza also seem to have borrowed from psychoanalytic ideas about superego functioning (without using Freudian vocabulary) in constructing their concept of "techniques of neutralization." Reckless' "inner controls" and Lemert's "inner limits" both point to phenomena similar to what is called, in psychoanalytic psychology, internalization. These psychological concerns are not inappropriate in sociological work. They need, rather, to be expanded, made more explicit, and be more explicitly connected with a definite psychology of personality. The connections between the intrapsychic processes are made in such a way as to show how the social-interactional, societal, and cultural ones are a combined process. For that we need both the sociology of deviance and a psychoanalytic-psychology of personality: neither the sociology nor the psychology should be reduced to the other.

What a psychoanalytic sociology of deviance proposes to do is to move from the kind of analysis begun by theorists like those just considered, and take it certain steps further, into the intrapsychic dimension of the subject, by an explicit application of psychoanalytic psychology.

II. CONCERN WITH PSYCHOLOGICAL FACTORS DOES NOT PRESUPPOSE PSYCHOPATHOLOGY

One of the prominent sources of resistance by many social scientists to psychoanalysis or to using it in dealing with social questions, is their assumption that if you ask psychological questions at all about any phenomenon, you are assuming that the persons involved are psychologically sick. To that, the psychoanalytic sociologist responds: NO! We are not assuming anything of the kind. To ask psychological questions simply means asking what makes someone tick, what makes him do what he does, regardless of whether there is anything sick about him or his behavior. A psychology of human conduct is concerned with normal (in the sense of healthy), abnormal (in the sense of sick), any kind of combination of the two, and anything in between. It is tedious to keep repeating this elementary point, but evidently necessary, because so many behavioral or social scientists, as well as ordinary laymen, seem to harbor this misconception.

Where did it come from? Possibly in part from the fact that psychoanalysis, as a practice, is a clinical psychology attempting to heal psychological malfunctioning such as psychopathology. Not too surprisingly, the clinician, on first encounter with a prospective client or patient, tends to be *looking for* the indicators of illness and to be less attuned to the indicators of psychic health. But psychoanalysis as a *theory* is concerned with understanding, psychologically, *all* aspects of human behavior, regardless of pathology. That in turn is what makes psychoanalysis amenable to integration with sociology and anthropology and any other social sciences, all of which may need to take into account the relationship between *subjective* personal experience and objective or supra-personal (social structural or interactional) aspects of people's lives in society, economy, and polity. (See Endleman, 1981, part I, for fuller development.)

III. DEVIANCE DOES NOT EQUAL PSYCHOPATHOLOGY

I want to ask here, How many times do we have to keep on repeating: the deviant is not necessarily sick; and the sick is not necessarily deviant? However, it is evident from published responses to my efforts at psychoanalytic-sociological understanding, especially on this topic, (Endleman 1981: Part V, and other psychoanalytic work on deviant behavior) that the point has not generally been understood. So it is necessary to repeat it again and develop it at length. *Deviant* is a concept in the sociology of normative order, meaning simply, varying from or violating the *norms* of the society. That is, those rules, regulations, and understandings which tell the people of the society how they *should* behave, act, conduct themselves, feel and think, and how they *should not*. Acts or stances toward the world that depart from such norms can be described, value-neutrally, by the objective social science observer using the adjective, "deviant." He refers to a person who acts, feels or believes in such a manner, using the noun, "deviant." (The whole analysis is full of problematics which do not concern us here, e.g., plural and ambiguous norms, central and peripheral norms, subsocietal differences.) The central point for now is that the concept means departing from the norms. It does *not* have an intrapsychic reference point. *Psychopathology*, by contrast, is a concept in the psychology of *intrapsychic* processes, referring to processes (or a total personality orientation) that are disordered in some important and identifiable manner. The norm referred to is a norm of psychological health or adequacy of functioning. To be sure, this is not a value-neutral concept, but one referring to the value of mental health, the idea that it is better to be healthy than to be sick, and to the fact (or assumption) that one can specify the basis of the standards of psychological health being referred to that are missed in the situation of psychopathology. A whole literature in clinical psychology and psychoanalysis addresses itself to these questions. It is not the same as society's norms for correct or conforming conduct that are the point of reference for deviance. Fulfillment of those norms may or may not lead to or constitute psychological health. I am fully aware that there are enormous problematics, even within one theoretical tradition such as classical psychoanalysis, about exactly how to formulate such standards of psychic health, and I have dealt with those questions at length elsewhere (Endleman, 1981: Part V). Here I am concerned only to assert that theoretically it can be done.

The deviant may or may not be psychologically sick. The psychologically sick may or may not be sociologically deviant. These are analytically independent variables. A tabulation of the combinations of deviance and sickness produces the classic four-fold table: Each of these cells will be considered.

		Sick?	
		Yes	No
Deviant?	Yes	(1)	(2)
	No	(3)	(4)

Occupants of Cell (1) and Cell (4) are easy to identify:

(Cell 4) Not Sick and Not Deviant.

Here we find persons who are healthy and conforming, demonstrably free of any kind of psychopathology (Maybe not ideally healthy but not clearly neurotic, psychotic, or otherwise psychologically impaired). They are conforming members of society, going about their business and not breaking any important rules: folkways, mores or laws. We don't know if there are any actual empirical cases, but it is a theoretical possibility, and where something approximating this exists, we tend to think of conformity and health as going together.

(Cell 1) Sick and Deviant.

An example is an extreme paranoid schizophrenic, with florid delusions and gross distortion of ego capacities, especially in reality testing. This person is deviant in that nearly everyone in society around him sees him as out of line with the norms—"right people don't think and act that way"—finds his delusions "crazy" (in layman's terms, certainly a stigma of deviance and someone about whom "something has to be done." By any clinical standard, this person is clearly pathological. This type of case will be further exemplified later.

It is cells (2) and (3) that give difficulty for laymen and sociologists. Can one be deviant and not sick? Can one be sick and not deviant? I answer YES on both counts. Let me cite brief examples.

(Cell 2) Deviant and Not Sick.

Example A. Non-Neurotic Criminals. Many criminals do not seem to be suffering from any identifiable psychopathology. They organize their life activities, including their law-breaking activities, in a reasonably rational manner; have an intact reality orientation (in some cases superior knowledge about how the law actually does function in society); have very little if any inner conflict about their criminal activities. They may be adept at using various rationalizations such as, "No one really gets hurt by this; I steal only from companies that can afford it, they're insured, anyway." These beliefs are hardly delusional. One could say about them that they have a weakly developed superego, but except in the extreme case of the psychopath, it is hard to count that as psychopathology, or is very problematical to do so. They are clearly deviant in that they regularly violate the laws, at least certain laws of the society, perfect qualification for the sociological concept, deviant. (For a variant psychoanalytic-sociological view on this, see Devereux, 1980: chs. 3,7.)

Example B. Exclusive Homosexuality. In other areas of deviance, for example, such sexual variations as exclusive homosexuality, it is more problematical whether psychopathology is clearly present or not. Certainly it has become part of the conventional wisdom in the sociology of deviance to claim of homosexuality either that it definitely does *not* indicate psychic sickness or that it may or may not be associated with such illness. (Compare almost any recent sociology of deviance text, e.g., Goode, 1978: pp. 371ff.) By contrast, classical psychoanalysts typically regard it as either a definite indicator of psychopathology or as being almost always associated with it. (Bieber *et al.*, 1962; Socarides, 1978; Stoller, 1975) However, it is also true that some clinicians, even psychoanalytic ones, take a more guarded view. They see it as *not necessarily* always associated with psychopathology (Person, 1983; Ovesey and Person, 1973; Eisenbud, 1982; Thompson, 1947; Mitchell, 1978). Still other clinicians (these are mostly *not* psychoanalysts) take a view very much in line with the gay liberation outlook: there is *no* psychopathology in homosexuality per se (Hoffman, 1968; Weinberg, 1972; Tripp, 1975). (See Endleman 1981: Ch. 12, for discussion of the whole range up to that date.) Although the non-neurotic criminal and the homosexual illustrate some of the problems in typology and classification, we can present a clearer and unquestionable case of deviance without pathology.

Example C. The Case of the Soviet Dissidents. In the Soviet Union at the present time, political dissidents against the regime face the prospect of being examined psychiatrically and being declared psychiatrically sick (largely on the basis of their dissidence) and, therefore, incarcerated in a mental hospital. Western psychiatrists question this diagnosis (Reich,

1983; Fireside, 1979). This is an excellent case for examining the relationship between deviance and psychopathology and the relevance, for serious understanding, of making a distinction between the two. Clearly, political dissidence is deviance simply by going against the rules of the society, at least of the regime in power. What is problematical is the designation of these individuals, not as traitors or enemies of the state (obviously possible), but as psychiatrically sick (a negative judgment from a very different arena of discourse). Objectors to this procedure argue that the designation as psychiatrically sick does not reflect an accurate appraisal of the dissidents' psychological state but is rather, an act of political persecution. In one case at least, Western psychiatrists found no evidence of psychiatric disorder in a person who had been hospitalized by the Soviet psychiatrists on such a diagnosis (Reich, 1983). Without an independent psychological evaluation by professionals not beholden to a particular political regime, we cannot concur in the judgment of psychiatric illness. Part of the process of arriving at their diagnosis of "illness" in these cases, the Soviet psychiatrists say themselves, involves the following consideration: in the political system of the Soviet Union, any overt opposition to the regime in power, or to the Soviet system is so exceedingly dangerous to one's job, one's security, even one's life, that one would *have* to be deranged (in some sense, to some degree) to dare to do this. Dead heroes are survived by live cowards. The better part of rationality, of circumspection, thus of sanity, would lead people not to dare to dissent, even with compelling, plausibly rational reasons. Doing so, therefore, the dissidents *must* be crazy (to put it as crudely as possible). Thus the very acts of dissidence are taken as the indicators of psychopathology. What Reich (an American psychiatrist) and his Western psychiatric colleagues found, on investigation of these cases, was that the Soviet psychiatrists tended to be sincere, and not simply craven toadies of an all-powerful political regime. In most cases, they really *believed* their diagnoses and believed that they were based on competent professional practice (Reich, 1983: 25).

Sociologists of deviance, particularly those working in the area of the sociology of mental illness, are likely to find this kind of case an apt confirmation of their view that typically psychiatric diagnosis of illness represents the application of a system of control over certain kinds of deviants, those who become labeled as mentally ill. Particularly, persons who are troublesome to society or its powerful segments, on political or social grounds, are more likely than others, psychologically similar, to be designated (diagnosed) as mentally ill and treated accordingly. The designation (labeling) and the consequent treatment—incarceration in a mental hospital—are instruments of *social control*. In the view of that kind of sociologist, the case of the Soviet dissidents provides only the most obvious and blatant example of that process. Such sociologists are likely to argue that the Soviet dissidents' case demonstrates that it is impossible to have a universal, transcendent set of criteria for assessment of mental health or mental illness that is not rooted in a particular culture and society—necessarily different from other cultures and societies.

(Cell 3) Sick but Not Deviant.

Cell (3) is probably the most problematical. While nearly all of the *seriously* mentally ill, that is, the psychotic, are sociologically deviant as well, in some less florid forms of psychopathology, the individual may be seen by others in society around him as basically conforming and adjusted.

Example D. The Compulsive Accountant. The illness I have in mind is a certain kind of expression of obsessive-compulsive character disorder in our society, manifested by punctilious performance of highly routinized duties in an occupation such as accounting or librarianship. In psychoanalytic terms, the obsessive-compulsive features, dealing with anxiety by extreme routinization of behavior, ego-syntonic rigidity in responsiveness, constrictiveness of life activities (still not experienced as conflictful), constitute a kind of psychopathology. The keynote is rigidity, disabling the individual to make new adaptations, by changing his behavior when necessary. Clinically, as long as the social and occupational setting continues, supporting the adjusted behavior patterns, the person has little inner sense of anything amiss. The good performance of work duties (within limits) and the lack of any deviation from folkways, mores, and laws, would qualify this individual as conforming and adjusted in sociological terms.

Example E. The Good Citizens of a Totalitarian Society. A more extreme example of Cell (3) (Sick but not Deviant), is the "good citizens" of a sick society submitting to the sadistic controls of a totalitarian regime. These people constitute the other side of the coin from the dissidents who are psychologically healthy. They, by contrast, may be adjusted and conforming, but it would take a collectively sanctioned psychological sickness to maintain this. Of course, in any such situation, the burden is on the psychoanalytically-minded social scientist to *demonstrate* the qualities of psychopathology involved. He cannot simply presuppose them *a priori* on the basis of his ideological disapproval of the totalitarian politics of the society—a difficult feat indeed.

The analytical independence of the categories of deviance and psychopathology rests on our recognition of the existence of different stan-

dards of judgment in reference to normality. Basically these derive from
two of the three conceptions of normality and abnormality analyzed in
previous publications (See Endleman, 1981: ch. 15; and 1967: ch. 7.)
These three are the statistical, the cultural, and the transcultural. In
brief outline:

a. *Statistical.* In this conception, normal is the average (mean, median,
or mode), the general run of what actually appears, while abnormal
refers to the unusual or rarely appearing, such as geniuses and idiots,
people of unusual or rare appearance or psychic experiences.

b. *Cultural.* Here normal equals conforming to the norms of one's
culture, adjusted to the expectations of living in that society; playing
one's expected roles; feeling "in line" with the people and the standards
around one. Abnormal means nonconforming or deviant, being malad-
justed, out of line with expectations; "marching to a different drummer."
One could be statistically abnormal while culturally normal, and vice
versa. The average person cheating on income tax, where that is widely
prevalent, would be statistically normal while culturally abnormal (breaking laws).

c. *Trans-cultural.* Most significantly to be differentiated from the other
two conceptions is the *trans-cultural* or *mental-health* standard. Here normal means psychologically healthy, functioning well, maintaining strong
ego capacities, adaptable, maintaining resilience, capable of withstanding
stress. Abnormal means psychopathological or psychologically sick in any
of a number of dimensions. The standard in the latter case is that of a
dynamic psychology of human functioning that is, theoretically, independent of any particular culture. It is not a relativistic standard, which
the cultural standard is. Health is not synonymous with adjustment (a
cultural conception), nor is sickness synonymous with maladjustment.
Rather, adjustment may be either healthy or sick, and maladjustment
either healthy or sick, or somewhere between the two. Health is not to
be equated with *statistical* normality: the healthy may be prevalent and
average, or unusual and rare; and so may the prevalent and average be
psychopathological.[1]

Thus, deviance is a category referring to *cultural* abnormality; psychopathology a category referring to *trans-cultural* abnormality. The standards and criteria for judgment, as well as the mode of assessment, in
each case, are different. The distinction is essential for clarity of analysis.

The stance of psychoanalytic sociology (my brand at least) is in opposition to those who automatically look for psychopathology in each
individual who is sociologically deviant and to those who make a blanket
denial that there is any psychopathology in the deviant.

An adequate psychoanalytic sociology of deviance needs to get beyond the inadequacies of most extant sociologists of deviance. It must exceed the limitations of psychoanalytic studies that deal only with the intrapsychic functioning of the deviant to forge a genuinely psychoanalytic sociology and apply it to this field.

There is no reason, in principle, why it could not feasibly be applied to each of the phenomena of deviance. Psychoanalysis is a set of psychological principles that apply to all human beings; sociology is applicable to interaction processes and group phenomena in any society. So the world of outsiders and oddballs, as well as the world of the conventionals that react to them with horror or fascination, is open to this fusion.

CONCLUSION

Is a psychoanalytic sociology of deviance feasible? Clearly my answer to that is yes. It is not just a psychoanalytic study of the psychology of the particular deviants, along with a study of the sociology of societal reaction to such deviance. It includes both of these but more. It integrates these two kinds of studies. It also includes a psychoanalytic study of the reactors, the stigmatizers, the official providers of treatment and punishment, and the rest of societal reactions. It looks for the identification of the kinds of collective fantasy involved in the interaction between intrapsychic processes (not only behavior) of the designated deviants and intrapsychic processes of the reactors, the putative (culturally) normal. It asks why the culturally normal "need" the deviant and how the two combine in an interactive process to play out a collective unconscious drama.

NOTE

1. See Endleman, 1981: 346–355, for elaboration of the eight possible combinations of normal-abnormal on these three dimensions. See also Devereux, 1980: Ch. 1 (originally 1956) for a major antecedent influence on my formulation.

BIOGRAPHICAL NOTE

Robert Endleman was born in Sudbury, Ontario, Canada and grew up there. He went to the University of Toronto and majored in Modern Languages and Sociology. After college, he did graduate work in Anthropology and Social Relations (Psychology/Sociology/Anthropology) for a Ph.D. at Harvard; later postdoctoral work in Psychoanalysis. Professor Endleman teaches at Adelphi University where he offers courses in psychoanalytic sociology, deviance, gender roles, mental illness. His research interests in the past few years have been integration of psychoanalysis with social science; Israeli Kibbutz. His major published works are: (1) Psyche and Society: Explorations in Psychoanalytic Sociology; (2) Personality and Social Life; and (3) "Psychoanalysis and Human Evolution."

REFERENCES

BECKER, H. S.
1963 Outsiders: Studies in the Sociology of Deviance. New York: Free Press.
BERGLER, B.
1948 The Battle of the Conscience. Washington: Washington Institute of Medicine.
BIEBER, I., ET AL.
1962 Homosexuality: A Psychoanalytic Study of Male Homosexuals. New York: Basic Books.
CLEMMER, D.
1940 The Prison Community. Boston: Christopher.
CLINARD, M.
1963 Sociology of Deviant Behavior. Rev. Ed. New York: Rinehart, Holt, Winston.
CLOWARD, R.
1960 "Social Control in the Prison," pp. 20–48 in Theoretical Studies in Social Organization of the Prison. Social Science Research Council: New York.
CLOWARD, R., AND OHLIN, L.
1961 Delinquency and Opportunity. New York: Free Press.
COHEN, A.
1955 Delinquent Boys. New York: Free Press.
DEVEREUX, G.
1980 Basic Problems of Ethnopsychiatry. Chicago: University of Chicago Press.
DURKHEIM, E.
1895 Rules of the Sociological Method. New York: Free Press. 1950.
1897. Suicide. New York: Free Press. 1951.
EISENBUD, R. J.
1982. "Early and Later Determinants of Lesbian Choice." Psychoanalytic Review 69: 85–109.
EMPEY, L.T., AND RABOW, J.
1961. "The Provo Experiment in Delinquency Rehabilitation." American Sociology Review 26: 679–695.
ENDLEMAN, R.
1967. Personality and Social Life. New York: Random House.
1981. Psyche and Society: Explorations in Psychoanalytic Sociology. New York: Columbia University Press.
1984. "Psychoanalysis and Human Evolution." Psychoanalytic Review, 71:27–46.
ERIKSON, K.
1962 "Notes on the Sociology of Deviance." Social Problems 9: 307–314.
1966. Wayward Puritans: A Study in the Sociology of Deviance. New York: Wiley.
FIRESIDE, H.
1979. Soviet Psychoprisons. New York: W. W. Norton.
GOODE, E.
1978. Deviant Behavior: An Interactionist Approach. Englewood Cliffs, N.J.: Prentice-Hall.

GOVE, W.
1975 "Labeling and Mental Illness: A Critique," in W. Gove (ed.), The Labeling of Deviance: Evaluating a Perspective. New York: Wiley (Sage).

HIRSCHI, T.
1969 Causes of Delinquency. Berkeley: University of California Press.

HOFFMAN, M.
1968. The Gay World. New York: Basic Books.

JOHNSON, A. M.
1949 "Sanctions for Superego Lacunae of Adolescents," in K. R. Eissler (ed.), Search-lights on Delinquency. New York: International Universities Press.

KITSUSE, J. I.
1962 "Societal Reaction to Deviant Behavior: Problems of Theory and Method." Social Problems 9: 247–256

KOBRIN, S.
1951 "The Conflict of Values in Delinquency Areas." American Sociological Review 16: 653–661

LEMERT, E. M.
1951 Social Pathology. New York: McGraw-Hill.

MATZA, D.
1961 "Subterranean Traditions of Youth." Annals of the American Academy of Political and Social Science 338: 102–118

McCORKLE, L., ELIAS, A., AND BIXBY, F. L.
1958 The Highfields Story. New York: Rinehart Holt & Winston.

MERTON, R. K.
1938 "Social Structure and Anomie." American Sociological Review. 3: 672
1949 "Manifest and Latent Functions," pp. 21–82 in Social Theory and Social Structure. New York: Free Press.

MILLER, W. B.
1958 "Lower Class Culture as a Generating Milieu of Gang Delinquency." Journal of Social Issues 14: 5–19

MITCHELL, S.
1978 "Psychodynamics, Homosexuality and the Question of Pathology." Psychiatry 41: 254–263

OVESEY, L., AND PERSON, E.
1973 "Gender Identity and Sexual Psychopathology in Men: A Psychodynamic Analysis of Homosexuality, Transsexualism and Transvestism." Journal of the American Academy of Psychoanalysis 1: 53–72.

PERRUCCI, R.
1974 Circle of Madness: On Being Insane and Institutionalized in America. Englewood Cliffs, N.J.: Prentice-Hall.

PERSON, E.
1983 Review of A. Bell and M. Weinberg, Homosexualities. Journal of the American Psychoanalytic Association 31: 306–315

RABOW, J., AND ELIAS, A.
1969 Organizational Boundaries, Inmate Roles and Rehabilitation. Journal of Research in Crime and Delinquency 6, (1): 8–16.

RABOW, J.
1964 "Research and Rehabilitation: The Conflict of Scientific and Treatment Roles in Corrections." Journal of Research in Crime and Delinquency 14 (1): 67–79.

1965 "Quantitative Aspects of the Group Psychotherapist's Role Behavior. A Methodological Note." Journal of Social Psychology 67: 31–37.
1971 "Displacement of Goals in Applied Social Science." Pacific Sociological Review, (1): 89–108.
RECKLESS, W.
1962 "A Non-Causal Explanation: Containment Theory." Excerpta Criminologica. 1 (2): 131–134.
1973 The Crime Problem. 5th ed. New York: Appleton-Century Crofts.
RECKLESS, W., DINITZ, S., AND MURRAY, E.
1956 "Self-Concept as an Insulator Against Delinquency." American Sociological Review. 21: 744–746.
REDL, F.
1945 "The Psychology of Gang Formation and the Treatment of Juvenile Delinquents." The Psychoanalytic Study of the Child. 1: 367–376.
REDL, F., AND WINEMAN, D.
1951 Children Who Hate. New York: Free Press.
REICH, W.
1983 "The World of Soviet Psychiatry." New York Times Magazine. Jan. 30, pp. 21 ff.
SCARPITTI, F. R., MURRAY, E., DINITZ, S., AND RECKLESS, W.
1960 "The 'Good Boy' in a High Delinquency Area: Four Years Later." American Sociological Review 25: 555–558.
SCHEFF, T.
1966 Being Mentally Ill. Chicago: Aldine.
SCHUR, E. M.
1971 Labeling Deviant Behavior. New York: Harper and Row.
SOCARIDES, C.
1978 Homosexuality. New York: Jason Aronson.
STOLLER, R. J.
1975 Perversion: The Erotic Form of Hatred. New York: Random House
SUTHERLAND, E.
1949 White Collar Crime. New York: Holt, Rinehart, & Winston.
SYKES, G.
1958 The Society of Captives. Princeton: Princeton University Press.
SYKES, G., AND MATZA, D.
1957 "Techniques of Neutralization: A Theory of Delinquency." American Sociological Review 22: 664–670.
THOMPSON, C.
1947 "Changing Concepts of Homosexuality in Psychoanalysis." Psychiatry. 10: 183–189.
THRASHER, F. M.
1936 The Gang. Chicago: University of Chicago Press.
TRIPP, C. A.
1975. The Homosexual Matrix. New York: McGraw-Hill.
WEINBERG, G.
1972. Society and the Healthy Homosexual. New York: St. Martins.

Prostitution, Economic Exchange, and the Unconscious

MARION S. GOLDMAN

IN winter of 1984 nation wide news media reported on two New Haven women prostitutes who had second stage Acquired Immune Deficiency Syndrome, the most feared, lethal, contagious disease of this century. AIDS is usually transmitted through .sexual contact or intravenous needles, and it wipes out the body's defenses against infections of all types. Both prostitutes, who are heroin addicts, are asymptomatic, and they will probably continue to walk the streets until they develop a fatal disease in three years or less. In the meantime they will have intercourse with hundreds to thousands of men, for the massive publicity surrounding the women has neither dented the rate of patronage in New Haven's vice district, nor diminished the number of addict-prostitutes on the streets ("Sixty Minutes," 1984).

Nothing demonstrates the fundamental irrationality underlying prostitution better than this case of undiminished, compulsive patronage. Furthermore, women who prostitute themselves may also risk contracting AIDS through multiple sexual contacts and intravenous drug use. Why can't men stay away? Why don't women do something else? Does grave physical risk make prostitution more exciting to men and women alike? Somehow, because widespread female prostitution is enmeshed in western social organization, it is usually taken for granted. This article will examine ways in which the everyday irrationalities of female prostitution mirror the interaction of social structure and psychodynamics in the cases of the prostitutes, themselves, and the men who patronize them.

Elements of danger have always been part of America's red light districts; as men faced muggings, brawls, or possibly being shanghaied to work aboard merchant ships, and women worried about violence from customers, pimps, and even madams (Gentry, 1964,; Goldman, 1981; Winick and Kinsie, 1971). Customers and prostitutes alike feared gonorrhea and syphilis; yet at the turn of the century (and sometimes even

today) women fought for positions in well-run brothels. Men flocked to
the teeming tenderloins despite the threat of epidemic venereal disease
(Haller and Haller, 1974:237–270). Men appeared eager to trade "a
night with Venus for a moon with mercury," although mercury treatments for venereal disease were both uncertain and risky—sometimes
producing side effects such as eroded jaws, gangrene, and strangulation
(Haller and Haller, 1974:265–270). Women in the trade were well aware
of disease, and high status prostitutes usually had the option of checking,
washing, and turning away obviously diseased men, although most prostitutes did not. The hazards of the game, however, could not then or
now be avoided by any of the players, no matter how careful or rational
they were.

The reasons why women become prostitutes and why men patronize
them, particularly as regulars, reflects an extraordinarily complex set of
interactions of structural, community, group, and individual variables.
The overall shape of the fast life, with women selling and men buying,
mirrors the shape of overall economic and political organization in which
women are subordinate to and dependent upon men. That subordina-
tion contributes to an exchange nexus in which almost all girls, from
their earliest years, learn to trade off affection or physical contact for
extrinsic considerations ranging from extra attention to special treats to
money. Neither economic need nor early exchange relationships, however, determines whether or not a woman will become a prostitute.
Experiences of real or relative deprivation, of various kinds of sexual
trade-offs, and of opportunities to become a prostitute must somehow
be filtered through a woman's own personality. Given the historical and
current poverty of lone women and the ubiquity of sexual trade-offs, it
is somewhat surprising that more women do not engage in commercial
sex. To be a prostitute in our society is a frightening choice, a bargain
in which personal shame and social stigma are traded for what is usually
a subsistence living, at best. The choice to be a prostitute, however, often
appears to be rational because there are so few alternatives for working
and lower-class women. In contrast, the choice to buy sex may actually
be somewhat less reasonable, less responsive to concrete material circumstances than the choice to sell it.

Customers range from men who visit prostitutes once or twice in their
lifetimes to occasional patrons seeking out sexual encounters on special
occasions—like a night out with the boys or a professional convention—
to regulars for whom prostitutes are an integral part of social life, to
compulsive customers who feel a need to see a prostitute several times
a week. Most early sociologists and psychologists (with the notable exception of Freud) defined prostitutes as deviant and, usually, irrational

as well, never considering the fact that patrons were equally bound to their own unfathomable unconscious wishes and drives. In his landmark 1937 article, "The Sociology of Prostitution," for example, Kingsley Davis simply assumed that men had naturally stronger sexual drives than women—drives that were satisfied most functionally to the overall society by prostitutes living outside the respectable community and its kinship networks. (Avoiding empirical data, Davis never noticed that most prostitutes' parents were respectable, and many, if not most prostitutes were married) (Davis, 1937; James and Meyerding, 1977).

Nowhere in their work did Davis or other early sociologists explore the possibility that gender-related differences in sexual drives and the ways in which those drives can be satisfied are intimately tied to family dynamics, family arrangements, and the overall organization of society rather than to biology alone. Instead, they assumed that demand for prostitution was an ongoing part of life based on the fact that women, unlike other primates, were always biologically available for sexual contact, and men would always desire more sexual contact than women. Thus, men would pay for women to perform sexually because women did not find as much intrinsic pleasure in sexual intercourse. Thinking about a social system with no motive for prostitution, Davis mused, ". . . we cannot imagine that system could ever come to pass" (Davis, 1937:753).

Men's general economic superiority, their simple ability to pay for sexual services, obviously contributes to their ability to demand commercial sex, as does their socialization to the perquisites of power in exchange relationships. Social structural phenomena, however, cannot explain how and why men turn to prostitutes for sexual satisfaction and adventure. Theories of unconscious processes and early childhood development offer the best insight into men's participation in sexual commerce. Of course, women who become prostitutes are usually more involved in the fast life and suffer the price of personal and social esteem and the daily risks of disease and violence. But prostitution is at least a two person transaction, involving both buyers and sellers.

Freud and his early followers had to think about prostitution, as it constituted an important element in the social life of Vienna and in their own and their patients' fantasy worlds (Janik and Toulman, 1973:70–80). Focusing on the Oedipal period from ages three to six, Freud saw the power of prostitution derived from a boy's necessary renunciation of his mother as a sexual object. If that renunciation were particularly painful and reintegration remained incomplete, he might continue through his life idealizing one set of women, upon whom he bestowed affection, and seeking sexual satisfaction from another kind, prostitutes

(Freud, 1963B:58–70). Adding to the attractiveness of fast women is the usually invisible presence of other men who also enjoy their sexual favors. Those men represent symbolic fathers with whom the customers share sexual access to a desired object. That sharing involves mixed rivalry and camaraderie, the elements present during the Oedipal period (Freud, 1963:49–58).

Also present on the demand side of prostitution are elements of men's earliest disappointments and frustrations. Most men (and women) are dependent upon the ways in which their caregivers experience and respond to their basic early needs. Mother figures' scornful responses to their childrens' undifferentiated natural impulses may lead to perversions or obsessions through which the adult acts out his early instinctual wishes. A report about St. Pauli, Hamburg's red light district, summed up the elements of narcissistic gratification that made prostitutes attractive to so many men:

You experience the masculine dream, as seductive as it is absurd, of being coddled by women like a baby and at the same time commanding them like a pascha . . . .(Miller, 1981:89).

Within that dream, the customer reenacts the pre-Oedipal fantasy of having every wish gratified and the Oedipal fantasy of having a woman who belongs to another man. The Oedipal conflict also appears in terms of splitting respectability and sexual satisfaction and the dichotomization of women into good and bad.

Let us explore the complex links between psyche and social structure that form the matrix in which prostitution flourishes. Neither social structural theory, nor theories of group interaction process, nor psychoanalytic theory in either clinical or structural contexts can alone explain why women become prostitutes or why men become their customers. Instead, a complex interaction and fusion of different forces leads some individuals to choose to participate in sexual commerce and others to choose against it. I emphasize the economic elements that influence the organization of prostitution and women's decisions to become prostitutes because empirical evidence overwhelmingly suggests that economic considerations are fundamental in shaping the readily available supplies of prostitutes. Very little research or theory has addressed the question of why men become customers, because social scientists, like almost everyone else, generally assume that it is simply the natural order of things. The demand for prostitution remains problematic, however, especially as it often involves perversions. Psychodynamic theories about the social structuring of male sexuality during the years from infancy through five or six are particularly useful in explaining why men continue to seek out prostitutes.

My basic assumption is that prostitution is a *social* phenomenon that cannot be explained by sociobiological concepts or by references to individual psychological trauma. While both of those may be small pieces in the puzzle, sexual commerce and its persistence through centuries of Western civilization can best be understood in terms of the intersection of sex discrimination and economic organization with the impact of family arrangements in which women almost singlehandedly mother the young.

PROSTITUTION, ECONOMICS, AND SOCIAL EXCHANGE

Assuming that the prostitute was deviant while the customer was not, social scientists have usually focused on women in the female-prostitute, male-customer dyad. The first major American sociological work on the traffic in women was W. I. Thomas's *Unadjusted Girl*, published in 1923. It was based on a series of case histories gathered more than a decade earlier for the Chicago Vice Commission's report on *The Social Evil in Chicago*. The report's central premise was that:

The honor of Chicago, the fathers and mothers of her children, the physical and moral integrity of the future generation demand that she repress public prostitution (Chicago Vice Commission, 1911:25).

Repression of prostitution primarily involved social control of women, although some note was taken of the need to instill young men with loyalty and honor toward the fair sex. Women, according to the report, became prostitutes because of social disorganization and economic exigency. The spread of the sporting life in Chicago, and for that matter across America, was caused by: (1) disintegration of strong family ties; (2) breakdown of religious institutions; (3) overemphasis on women's fashions and other forms of conspicuous consumption which led young women to enter lives of sin in order to obtain enough money for the clothes and grooming aids symbolic of feminine worth; (4) growth and spread of jobs characterized by bare subsistence wages for women; (5) development of seasonal industries leading women workers to seek other jobs during slack periods; (6) popularization of "low amusements," such as excursion steamers and dance halls where unattached women in search of mates were exposed to corrupting influences.

Thomas also considered these six structural reasons why women entered the fast life, but he added a social-psychological dimension in his discussion of the "four wishes," essential to human nature. They were desires for social response, recognition, new experience, and security. While the well-adjusted girl obtained gratification of the wishes by socially acceptable means, the unadjusted girl often had to violate sexual norms in order to achieve those fundamental goals, which, according to Thomas, were deeply embedded in the human spirit.

It is not difficult to read between the lines of the four wishes and discover how affluence can bring all of the them to fruition. Despite his social-psychology and concern with the breakdown of clear rules for sexual behavior, Thomas offered an almost radical critique of women's role in industrial capitalism. He asserted that most women became prostitutes because of the simple fact that they could not support themselves as factory workers. Those working as shop girls made even less money while facing temptation by the fine goods their establishments sold to ladies.

The economic theme in sociological analyses of prostitution extends to Kingsley Davis's previously mentioned article (Davis, 1937:744–755). Women, according to Davis, use sex to attain social status and power far more than men because they have fewer economic options. Sex for ulterior purposes, as a means to some other goal, is THE fundamental element in prostitution, although commercial sex is by no means the only social institution in which women trade sexual access for economic remuneration. The economic function of prostitution also affects customers, for men must work to obtain the money necessary to secure erotic gratification.

Despite these observations, however, Davis betrayed his ignorance of the economics of prostitution when he stated, "From a purely economic point of view, prostitution comes perilously near getting something for nothing" (Davis, 1937:750). No working prostitute could forget the obvious costs of her rent, police bribes, clothes, doctors' bills, contraceptives, and abortions, as well as the incalculable costs to her body and spirit (Hirschi, 1962). Prostitutes, themselves, usually mention economic rewards as the primary reason why they sell their bodies. Writing in *The Politics of Prostitution*, a monograph published in collaboration with the national prostitutes' organization, Coyote, Jennifer James asserted:

Today women are rarely forced into prostitution except by social and economic causes. If they were deprived as children, if they suffered economic need as an adult, or if they dream of financial success and status, women are more likely to enter prostitution. The lack of alternatives for women—especially for less educated women—are far more coercive than, say a pimp (James, et al., 1975:45).

Continuing studies at the University of Indiana's Institute for Sex Research indicated that ninety percent of 127 prostitutes interviewed mentioned money as their major reason for entering prostitution:

Some prostitutes have asked a simple question which may be paraphrased thus. As an unskilled, poorly educated female why should I scrimp along in a badly paid tedious job and live in unpleasant surroundings, when by prostituting a few days a week, I can earn several hundred dollars, have a nice apartment, frequent the better hotels, often meet interesting men of a higher socioeconomic level, and lead a life full of novelty? (Gebhard, 1968:29).

William Sanger's early study of New York City prostitutes and other research on nineteenth century prostitution indicated that almost all prostitutes were from the working or lower class (Sanger, 1937). Moreover, many of them were recent immigrants or women of color who faced racial discrimination as well as economic deprivation. This may have changed during the twentieth century, however, as women's families' economic position became less directly related to their own adult earning power. A mid-1970s study of Seattle prostitutes indicated that sixty-four percent of 136 women grew up in families with middle to upper-class incomes (James and Meyerding, 1977). Income, of course, is only one indicator of social class; but it may be that in the nineteenth and early twentieth centuries, women who had to work for a living were rarely, if ever, from middle-class families. Today women from all classes often must support themselves in the face of considerable economic discrimination.

Sociologists, social reformers, and prostitutes seem to agree that financial considerations tied to sex segregation and discrimination in the labor force are major structural factors affecting the supply side of sexuality. Economic reasons alone far from explain why women choose to become prostitutes. The two other major issues of individual choice and the fundamental commoditization of sex need additional explanation, for which theories of psyche and society are essential.

PROSTITUTION AND EMOTIONAL SURVIVAL

The historical and current position of women in the American labor force and the fact that a disproportionate number of people living below the poverty line are women would suggest that far more poor and working-class women might become prostitutes than actually do, if rational economic choice were the only motive for entering the fast life. Prostitution is one of a limited number of survival strategies for women facing real or relative material deprivation. For poor and marginal working-class women, the options may all be grim. More affluent, educated, women have some reasonably attractive alternatives, but none may offer the excitement or ostensibly easy money of prostitution. Some women enter prostitution because they believe they have no other alternatives to destitution, others because they seek companionship or thrills as part of the working life, and some drift into the fast life through the seduction of a pimp. Economic and social structure should not be dismissed in explaining prostitution, but it must be recognized that women who become prostitutes are usually by no means passive victims. They are, instead, active individuals who have made choices concerning their lives (Rosen and Davidson, 1977:xiii–xlviii).

The choices, however, may rest on experiences which are half-remembered, rooted in their early experience. Psychoanalytic theory emphasizes the importance of early childhood, generalized sexuality, and unconscious motivation. The individual women who become prostitutes make choices based on a culturally generalized set of sexual experiences interacting with their particular life histories. Real or relative economic deprivation is one element common to prostitutes' life histories, as are problematic experiences in early childhood. The nature of those experiences, however, is not unique or deviant, but is enmeshed in the general, difficult transition from infancy to childhood when girls and boys alike learn and internalize appropriate gender identities and gender roles.

According to Freud and later theorists, the process of becoming female is more subtle, more externally and internally complicated than that of becoming male. The successful outcome of the process, however, resembles the masculine model of the Oedipal crisis and its resolution, as girls learn to deflect the erotic impulses they feel toward their fathers and mothers onto appropriate adult love objects (Chodorow, 1978). Freud believed that forbidden love objects, such as men who were otherwise attached, were attractive to some women who had not fully resolved their intense desire for their fathers. Those women were satisfied only with sexual situations fraught with secrecy and intrigue. The forbidden male(s) and complicated procedures of concealment associated with adultery or prostitution reproduced some of the intense emotion associated with the feminine Oedipal conflict. The stigma and secrecy associated with the fast life may make prostitution fantasies or prostitution, itself, compelling to women seeking Freud's "necessary condition of forbiddeness" (Freud, 1963B).

Women are drawn to prostitution because of the implicit presence of others in the transaction, as customers represent men linked to other women. Freud remarked on the "need for an injured third party," as it developed in male customers. It also relates to prostitutes as they embody feminine Oedipal fantasies. Prostitutes symbolically compete with the respectable women who are legitimately related to their customers, and they also compete directly with other prostitutes in seeking customers. The general, invisible presence of third and fourth parties may replicate the intimate rivalry between mothers and daughters occurring in the relational triangle with fathers during the Oedipal period (Chodorow, 1978:200–202). Prostitution in American culture certainly holds a widespread fascination for women. It may be founded in earlier Oedipal fantasies, when they sought their fathers while they, at one and the same time, hated and wanted to identify with their mothers. Magazines like *Cosmopolitan*, songs like "Your Good Girl's Gonna Go Bad," and countless sensational-romantic novels about prostitutes and call girls all provide data to suggest that sexual commerce and promiscuity are attractive to far more women than actually ever become prostitutes. Those millions of women may indulge their need to compete sexually with others by identifying with high status prostitutes.

Some psychoanalytic theorists have tried to describe specific, unconscious patterns which lead women to become prostitutes. Karl Abraham saw frigidity as the *sine qua non of prostitution*. He believed that prostitutes were frigid because they had been frustrated in the Oedipal triangle, and this had led to a sense of hostility toward all men. Promiscuity was revenge against their fathers and also recreation of the earlier frustrating situation (Abraham, 1953).

Writing from a somewhat more sophisticated perspective, Helene Deutsch discussed the analysis of a prostitute and speculated about some of the psychodynamic causes of prostitution (Deutsch, 1976). Deutsch believed that the root of women's general fantasies about prostitution, as well as the decision to become a prostitute, could be found in the mother-daughter rivalry during adolescence, when sexuality and Oedipal desires once again come to consciousness. Young women, enraged by their mothers' relationships with their fathers and their fathers' sexual loyalty to their mothers, turn to promiscuity or promiscuous fantasies in order to demonstrate their independence and to become as "faithless" as their fathers. Prostitution can also be an ambivalent assertion of an adolescent sexuality—sexuality that is terribly threatening to everyone within the context of the nuclear family. A young woman's acknowledgement of her own sexuality and recognition of her mother's erotic tie to her father can prompt her to label herself a prostitute, a socially devalued being, and in a sense, to punish herself for her own eroticism by acting out her most extreme fantasies. Prostitution, real or imagined, involves a recognition of sexuality that is simply too hot to handle within the family.

Both Abraham's and Deutsch's hypotheses are potentially testable, yet neither has been examined in any detail in terms of empirical evidence. A number of small studies suggest that Abraham's discussion of frigidity does not reflect reality, and most prostitutes seem to be far from frigid.

A 1965 study of call girls, for example, found that only twenty-three percent of them had not experienced orgasms in private or working life, although many were frigid with customers most of the time (Pomeroy, 1965). Another, later set of case histories indicated less than ten percent of all prostitutes were anorgasmic, a percentage lower than married women (Gebhard, 1968:60). In prostitution, there is a general sharp dividing line between business and pleasure, and occupational ideology stresses their dichotomy. Thus a prostitute takes pride in noting:

> When I went into the business I had to learn to act. That was the most difficult thing for me to learn to handle. The game is an "illusion." . . . You must pretend to enjoy your work. The strain of pretending can be overwhelming (Symanski, 1981).

Pretending at work, however, by no means obliterates the possibility of pleasure at play. Some prostitutes may experience sexual difficulties outside their business hours because of antecedent conditions or because of drug abuse associated with prostitution. Frigidity, however, does not appear to have a causal connection to prostitution, and it may, in fact, have a negative relationship.

The issues of breaking away and sexual rebellion raised by Deutsch are more difficult to sort out. When interviewed, most prostitutes report strained relationships with their mothers; so do most adolescents and young adults (Gilligan, 1982). Separation, in fact is *the* key issue during that part of the life cycle. Certainly, family conflict leading to premature leaving home could set a young woman up to become a prostitute because she could support herself in few other ways. However, neither conflict nor running away is necessary or alone sufficient to create a personal choice in favor of prostitution. The issue of sexual conflict between young women and their mothers needs far more research for us to discover whether the quantity and quality of natural adolescent sexuality and fights for separation differ significantly between women who become prostitutes and those who do not.

Also working in the psychoanalytic tradition, Harold Greenwald attempted to develop a theoretical model of prostitution based on interviews and clinical studies of call girls. Greenwald has been criticized for using data from a small population of call girls who defined themselves as neurotic enough to seek professional help and generalizing from those cases to all prostitutes, from high status call girls to low status streetwalkers. His discussion of prostitutes' formative experiences, like Deutsch's, suffers not from being too narrow, however, but from being too broad and applicable to a much wider population.

He identifies the roots of prostitution in a girl's pre-Oedipal experience, in the narcissistic condition of a depriving mother whose lack of nurturance stimulates lifelong rage. Desiring to compensate for lack of appropriate love and the absence of a whole, intact sense of self, a young woman who becomes a call girl is attracted by the rebellious nature of the fast life and by the way in which it offers a sense of underworld "community," with its own argot, customs, and special identifications. Searching for a new, different way of life, call girls act out their rage at their depriving families. They maintain an illusion of being cared about by other people in the fast life and by the johns willing to spend money in order to have sexual contact with them (Greenwald, 1970).

The narcissistic or borderline personality which Greenwald identified, has more recently been defined as *the* dominant personality type of the seventies and eighties (Kernberg, 1975; Lasch, 1978). Writing in the immensely influential *Culture of Narcissism*, Christopher Lasch popularized a broad definition of narcissism and used his own description of a call girl's personality to illustrate that definition. According to Lasch, the typical call girl's personality now exemplifies the qualities necessary for success in American society:

She craves admiration but scorns those who provide it and thus derives little gratification from her social successes. She attempts to move others while remaining unmoved herself. The fact that she lives in a milieu of interpersonal relations does not make her a conformist or an "other-directed" type. She remains a loner, dependent on others only as a hawk depends on chickens. She exploits the ethic of pleasure that has replaced the ethic of achievement, but her career more than any other reminds us that contemporary hedonism, of which she is the supreme symbol, originates not in the pursuit of pleasure but in a war of all against all, in which even the most intimate encounters become a form of mutual exploitation (Lasch, 1975:64–65).

Lasch's generalizations have met with a great deal of skepticism, although most social scientists acknowledge that there is some truth, a sense of resonance in his sweeping statements describing the compensations for lack of initial love. These observations about prostitution or prostitute-like personalities, suggest that Greenwald may have perceived a developing social phenomenon before it became generally visible. Possibly from negativism toward women or lack of much warm, human contact with prostitutes, Lasch saw call girls as more cynical and manipulative than Greenwald. Both of their observations about the "call girl complex," however, indicate that decisions to enter the fast life may reflect early childhood experiences that are common to many, if not most women. The differentiating experiences involving the choice to become a prostitute may include some highly specific early childhood interactions.

Greenwald's most interesting observation about call girls' early lives was never integrated into his theoretical model. A number of his subjects volunteered information about exchanging sexual access or affection for material considerations before they were six years old. In one case, a foster father had bribed a girl with ball and jacks to perform fellatio (Greenwald, 1970:35). In two other instances the exchanges were far less explicit and threatening. They involved, respectively, an older male cousin, who exchanged caresses for toys and candy, and an elderly family friend, who offered a girl candy-money after she sat on his lap and allowed him to fondle her (Greenwald, 1970:49–50 and 168).

All information on sexual abuse of children indicates that these types of exchanges are relatively common, affecting far more of the female population than ever become prostitutes. The elements of exchange, power, and secrecy found in these early transactions occur as a matter of course in prostitution and are part of the basic sexual exchange for ulterior purposes. They are also linked to other ways in which women in American society relate to the world in situations ranging from dating and courtship, to marriage, to the occupational structure. In all of these cases, women often trade sexual favors for extrinsic considerations. As Emma Goldman noted nearly a century ago:

Nowhere is woman treated according to the merit of her work, but rather as a sex. It is therefore almost inevitable that she should pay for her right to exist, to keep her position in whatever line with sex favors. Thus it is merely a question of degree whether she sells herself to one man, in or out of marriage, or to many men (Goldman, 1970).

There is, of course, a vast difference between being a prostitute, a wife, or a corporate executive who experiences a bit of sexual harassment on her climb up the ladder. Nevertheless, sexual exchange involving women as sellers and men as buyers seems to be built into the social structure. If most women learn to bargain with their sexuality at an early age, it is somewhat surprising that more do not choose to be prostitutes, in spite of the stigma attached to sexual barter. The existence of a number of better alternatives and the psychic pain and exploitation attached to prostitution may explain why relatively few women enter the fast life.

The experiences of childhood sexual abuse discussed by the call girls in Greenwald's study are extremes of the sexual barter pattern, and those experiences also unfolded within badly disrupted family lives and relationships. It is probable that such interactions, particularly when they develop over a relatively long period of time, predispose women to enter prostitution. Those relatively explicit exchanges probably take place most frequently against the background of disruptive, narcissistic parenting;

but they are far more specifically defined and are most important during a far more limited time period than either Lasch or Greenwald consider in their theoretical discussions. Perceived economic need, combined with opportunity to prostitute and emotional receptivity based on general family climate and specific early childhood experiences must all be considered in explaining why women make the choice to engage in sexual commerce.

CUSTOMERS, THE OEDIPAL CONSTRUCT, AND NARCISSISM

The integration of sexual exchange into social structure and character is an extraordinarily complex phenomenon. Against a background of early childhood learning and economic incentives, we can begin to understand why women become prostitutes. Why, however, do men continue to demand prostitution when sexual contact appears to be available for most people in marriage or extramarital situations? We know relatively little about customers, especially those who have sporadic, casual encounters with prostitutes. Visibility in prostitution usually rests almost entirely on sellers because prostitutes must earn their livings and organize much of their lives around sexual commerce. Men, unless they are exceptionally compulsive customers, can compartmentalize their lives and rationalize their patronage as the fulfillment of a temporary need or whim.

According to all available research, at last seventy percent of American men have visited prostitutes at some time in their lives (Kinsey, Pomeroy, and Martin, 1948:597; Waksler and Douglas, 1982:176). They are especially likely to become steady customers when away from their families and/or in a situation with a badly imbalanced sex ratio, such as a military or mining camp (Goldman, 1981; Walkowitz, 1980). The majority of routine customers in big cities, however, are married and middle aged, being drawn from every walk of life from blue-collar workers to upper-class international executives (Waksler and Douglas, 1982:176; Stein, 1974). Some functionalist sociologists have attributed the ubiquity of prostitution to the socially important purposes it serves, including the sexual initiation of youth, protection of respectable women's virginity, and prevention of rape. Another functionalist argument, found earlier in the writings of St. Ambrose and St. Augustine, defines prostitution as a defense against marital instability and adultery. (As long as men alone engage in extramarital sex and their wives do not, these theorists do not define it as adulterous.) The sexual servicing of minority populations with an imbalanced sex ratio, such as Chinese and Filipino sojourners in the nineteenth and early twentieth centuries, was another function of prostitution (Cressey, 1932; Hirata, 1979). Also of note is the provision of sex to the physically and psychologically impaired.

Commercial sex does in fact serve those purposes, but they could also be served in ways other than prostitution. One other function often attributed to prostitution involves the satisfaction of sexual desires that are sometimes considered to be inappropriate. Prostitution provides clients with ritualized satisfactions they might find difficulty in asking for elsewhere; but then we are left with questions about why men desire those satisfactions with prostitutes or why they want them at all.

Both current and historical data suggest that most customers seek out or are willing to try types of sex not easily available to them in their marital relationships or with voluntary partners. In a long and sensitive discussion of what goes on in the marriage bed, Lillian Rubin points out that the "new sexual freedoms" of the last twenty years have left wives frustrated and confused. Despite changing customs and practices, men, for many complex reasons, often ask for what wives cannot give or else continue to explore only a limited number of sexual options with their mates (Rubin, 1976). I think it is also possible that however much a man increases his sexual repertoire at home, he will find new practices and sexual fantasies to explore with prostitutes—escalating the degree of deviance that provides him with satisfaction.

The satisfaction of many sexual perversions involves both extra money and extra time on the part of customers; yet prostitutes report widespread, growing demand for oral-genital contact, bondage and other sado-masochistic practices, fetishism, voyeurism, and elaborate combination-fantasies, including most of these practices. The desirability of these sexual styles is derived both from their scarcity and also from their association with half-remembered childhood eroticism.

The erotic magic of perversion is rooted in the pre-Oedipal period, when a male child's early expressions of sexual pleasure in tactile experiences, elimination, or masturbation genuinely shocked or disturbed his mother. The child internalized his mother's reactions and appropriated feelings of self-contempt and self-disgust. Unconsciously desiring to repeat that early humiliation, the narcissistic customer requests sexual activities which may involve actual punishment or which evoke a deep embarrassment and humiliation reminiscent of the feelings he once provoked in his mother (Miller, 1981:84–91).[1] Available research suggests that these activities are most often associated with high status call girls or brothel prostitutes, who are usually quite attractive. It is tempting to speculate that the acting out of perversion is most satisfactory with a woman who somehow resembles the lovely young mother of the remembered pre-Oedipal situation.

Other theorists, such as Lasch, have developed some general models of "narcissistic man," whose fundamental personality was primarily shaped not by specific humiliation, but rather by many early and ongoing frustrations at the hands of a depriving, non-nurturing mother. The father of the family is not the fearsome, potentially castrating patriarch of Freud's writings but is distant, removed, and relatively inconsequential (Lasch, 1978:173–189). The mother, on the other hand, is all too present, vacillating between seduction and anger, dominance and indifference (Lasch, 1978:171–176). The narcissistic male coming of age in this family arena is enraged at women; yet he displays a number of stereotypical feminine characteristics such as manipulation, exploitation, superficial charm, and desire for eternal youth (Lasch, 1978:31–51). These may sound familiar, since they are precisely the same characteristics psychoanalytic theorists have traditionally attributed to prostitutes. Despite his conflicts at a very early age, the narcissistic male necessarily experiences an Oedipal crisis which usually leads to heterosexual identification. Like the neurotic patients whom Freud described, he continues to split maternity from sexuality and good women from bad. This modern narcissist, however, combines the desire for a degraded sexual object with equally powerful wishes to avoid intimacy and experience unwavering admiration for his sexual prowess.

Many people have been surprised that current demand for prostitutes is as great as, if not greater than, that of the two previous decades, in spite of a pervasive, general loosening of sexual customs and expectations. In the 1970s, case studies and interviews with attractive, young, single men in the San Francisco Bay area revealed that they preferred to patronize call girls rather than become emotionally and sexually involved with women whom they were dating (Coleman, 1973:1–22 and 219:229; 1976). They explained their patronage on the grounds that prostitutes did not demand intimacy, commitment, or their own sexual fulfillment. This information beautifully illustrates a textbook pattern of narcissistic behavior. Moreover, the narcissistic flight from emotional closeness so beautifully described by Lasch could combine in many cases with the more specific, less common narcissistic perversions. The need for perversion and the fear of intimacy characteristic of "narcissistic man" may be amplified by the Oedipal division of women into sexual and maternal categories. That dichotomization will fuel demand for prostitution generating even more widespread patterns of patronage.

The desire for prostitutes, or the role of John, may be built into the social organization of male gender as it normally unfolds within the nuclear family. While there is questionable evidence that men's natural sexuality is stronger and more promiscuous than women's, it is obvious that male sexuality has been *socially* defined as greater (Symanski, 1981:239–273; Davis, 1937). Men and women alike learn to structure their sexual urges in terms of conscious recognition of pressure, the types of sexual satisfaction acceptable to them, and the appropriate people or objects with whom they may become sexually involved. Early childhood experiences and family dynamics shape those choices, and the conscious and unconscious drives toward prostitutes which men experience are tied to the normal achievement of masculinity in our society.

Prostitution is bound to patriarchy and to the structure of emotional life as we know it because of its connection to the male Oedipal crisis. Sexual commerce symbolizes the differentiation between sexuality and emotional intimacy that is both a difficult and a necessary part of early childhood socialization (Freud, 1927). Much of prostitution's fascination for men and for women, also, lies in this separation of erotic impulses from feelings of tenderness and trust. It is the only systematic interaction reducing sexuality to a pure exchange in which personal commitment has no place: the customer receives sex and the prostitute receives remuneration, while each isolates sexual contact from realistic emotional warmth.

Mature sexuality, according to Freud, is the fusion of affection and eroticism, but the path to maturity includes a number of barriers. All children's initial erotic feelings focus on their mothers, but they painfully learn to repress and deny those feelings as they come to identify with their sex-appropriate parent and assume a heterosexual object orientation outside the family. Unconscious, uncertain, sexual impulses continue to develop throughout childhood, however, and surface during adolescence when internalized incest barriers direct those impulses toward others with whom Freud said "a real sexual life may be carried on" (Freud, 1912). That whole lengthy process of sexual development forces men to focus their sexuality away from their mothers because they unconsciously fear their fathers' reprisals.

Prostitution vividly recalls for men the early situations in which it was necessary to separate sexuality and affection. It provides sexual outlets to individuals who have difficulty reconnecting sexuality and emotional warmth. Sexual barter is the ultimate extension of the mother-son incest barrier, ideotypically splitting sexuality and affection and involving partners who are by and large strangers to one another. Prostitution separates and specifies sex instead of making it a diffuse property of interpersonal relationships, and customers can compartmentalize sexuality, removing it from their affective attachments.

A great deal of prostitution's attraction for men is linked to "normal" heterosexual growth as it is revealed through the examination of neurotic development. Individuals making "that special type of object choice" of a woman of dubious virtue find that their jealousy of other men in a woman's life heightens their own intense erotic interest. They can at once express their anger toward other men by possessing a woman whom they desire and, at the same time, identify with those men.

The other men in prostitutes' lives, whether they are customers or pimps, represent symbolic fathers with whom patrons share sexual access to a desired object. There has been far to little scholarly note taken of the extent to which visits to brothels or individual prostitutes function to cement the bonds of men who actually visit prostitutes together or share tales of their adventures later on. Often men join together in search of different individual prostitutes, but some modern American rituals and rites de passage involve many friends enjoying the favors of a single woman. In sexual initiations or stag parties, for example, it is common for a boisterous group to listen at bedroom doors, shout out words of humorous encouragement, or actually watch the action, cheering particularly dexterous moves (Goldman, 1981,; Winick and Kinsie, 1971:885–209). Comradely prowess, mutual boosting and boasting, and stag entertainments have been integral to commercial sex in the United States at least since the formation of large, organized, brothel districts after the Civil War.

The incestuous Oedipal triangle, in which sons learn to restrict their sensual feelings toward their mothers, was also the key to Freud's discussion of impotence. Men unsuccessful in resolving the Oedipal conflict may actively seek sexual partners undeserving of the admiration which they consciously bestow upon their mothers. Some men are entirely impotent with any woman who elicits esteem or tenderness, and others only achieve potency when they have degraded those women. (Sometimes degradation takes the form of recently having sexual contact with a prostitute.) These are clearly neurotic impulses, but even men who have successfully resolved their Oedipal longings have some residue of unresolved sexual conflict encouraging them to dichotomize good and bad women.

In only a very few people of culture are the two strains of tenderness and sensuality duly fused into one; the man almost always feels his sexual activity hampered by his respect for the woman and only develops full sexual potency when he finds himself in the presence of a lower type of sexual object (Freud, 1963B).

Freud wrote that passage in post-Victorian Vienna where sexual ideology dividing good and bad women, and separating maternity from sexuality molded many people's emotions and behavior. That belief system still survives to some degree today. Although current ideology generally minimizes those dichotomies, the division of women as either sexual or maternal is nevertheless a powerful unconscious foundation for the traffic in women. Classical Freudian theory defines the Oedipus complex as the central force behind human health, including neurosis. While it may not be critical to all human experience, Oedipal conflict appears to be essential to people raised in nuclear families with a distinct sex-based division of labor—that is most people in the United States. The Oedipal crisis is crucial to the production of socially appropriate sex role identity in all cultures where women mother the young and fathers assume secondary roles in family organization.

I want to emphasize that the role of customer is a natural outcome of social arrangements in which women are the primary, if not the sole, nurturers of the young. Some extreme experiences of disappointment in the pre-Oedipal period or of frustration and fear in the Oedipal phase may generate perversion or compulsions to become a customer. But the basic narcissistic desires for humiliation and social distance and the Oedipal splitting of sexuality from nurturance are logical extensions of the most normal, successful socialization in contemporary America. Similarly, the experiences of real or relative economic deprivation, family conflict during adolescence, and early sexual exchange relationships are common to most women in any society. However, the quality of those experiences, the emotional depth at which they are experienced, and the range of realistic options for and against sexual commerce determine whether or not a woman decides to become a prostitute.

CONCLUSION

The relationships among prostitution, psychic structure, and social organization are so complex that it is tempting to label sexual commerce "the oldest profession" and dismiss it as an unchanging element of social experience. But prostitution can and does change over time, reflecting different definitions of human sexuality and different social arrangements. In the history of American prostitution, for example, demand for very young prostitutes has waxed and waned and then increased again, possibly reflecting different social patterns of parenting and social notions about when children can be exploited. More structurally, the advent of the telephone as a new technology drastically altered the pattern of brothel prostitution. It created two new groups of prostitutes, in "call houses" and as individual call girls (Symanski, 1980:77–78; Winick and Kinsie, 1971:52–54).

The psychodynamic foundations of supply and demand for prostitution reflect broad patterns of parenting. As long as children are raised in families in which mothers are *the* key objects in girls' and boys' early lives, the fundamental, unconscious structures supporting prostitution will remain in place. Girls, unlike boys, can successfully emerge from the Oedipal period without having to dichotomize nurturance and sexuality: boys must initially split off their sexual attraction to their mothers in order to come to terms, symbolically, with their fathers. That splitting off of sexuality from warmth and intimacy is, of course, one of the basic supports of demand for prostitution.

The organization of gender within the family also affects women's choices regarding sexual barter. The sexual and affectional exchanges for ulterior considerations that routinely occur between girls and their fathers or father-figures reflect the common family organization in which fathers have far more material and social power than mothers. Another facet of ordinary family organization that often underlies choices for prostitution is the family's inability to handle the violatility of adolescent girls sexuality and potential for pregnancy. As the boundaries of the nuclear family crash against a culture which increasingly hurries children toward premature adulthood, the normal tensions may become greater and greater, thus increasing the conflict leading to prostitution, which Deutsch took note of half a century ago.

The pervasiveness of female prostitution and male patronage is part of an intricate tapestry comprised of socially structured male-female differences in emotional needs, learned gender roles, family experience, and sex segregation and discrimination against women in the labor force. Prostitution is absolutely rooted in the organization of social life as we know it. The unusual and extreme family structures that encourage men's compulsive patronage, obsessions, or perversions, and the family circumstances and economic situations that compel women to choose to be prostitutes are extensions or extremes of normal patterns. They are emphatically not ultimate distortions or breaks with those patterns that we commonly regard as natural, if not ideal.[2]

The choice to become a prostitute reflects a number of individual experiences, but the central, conscious reason why women make that choice is real or relative economic need. However, economic deprivation must intersect with psychic vulnerability and opportunities to engage in sexual commerce before a woman will engage in prostitution. For both prostitutes and customers alike, partnership in sexual commerce rests on a whole matrix of intersecting life events and interpretations of those life events that occur on every level of social action, from abstract economic organization to highly individual unconscious needs. For example, an urban, middle-class woman who had an early history of sexual exchange (abuse) and left her family shortly before finishing high school would be less likely to become a prostitute than someone of similar experience who came from an urban working-class family. That working-class woman probably has more contact with prostitutes simply because she is likely to live in a neighborhood more proximate to red light districts. She is also more likely to move around the city on foot or with public transportation. Moreover, it is probable that her high school was less sheltered from visible crime—robbery, hard drug dealing, prostitution, and pimping—than was her middle-class counterpart's. The middle-class woman would probably have more access to private support systems, to counseling and other networks than does the working-class woman. All of these factors make a working-class woman more likely to choose prostitution, all other things being equal.[3] But, of course, they never are, and one of the most interesting intellectual aspects of female prostitution is the way it so obviously illustrates the diversity and complexity of social phenomena.

Women bear the majority of moral and legal stigma for prostitution because dominant sexual ideology and discrimination in the criminal justice system mirror our deep cultural belief that selling access to one's body involves selling oneself—something that should not be included in the market economy. Theories of psychosexual development and material structure are equally salient to a full understanding of sexual commerce, for prostitution reaches from the individual unconscious to international economic organization. Prostitution is scarcely a normal transaction—one that most people experience every day and take for granted as a natural part of the social world. Prostitution, however, does illuminate some of the emotional and social interrelationships hidden in more complex, ambiguous contexts. One last, hidden function of prostitution is that of a rather distorted magnifying mirror which ultimately clarifies part of the complex, vivid image of our everyday male-female relationships.

NOTES

1. I have referred to mothers, as does Miller, because it is mothers who have most contact with children and who *must*, by virtues of their social roles, nurture them from infancy through adolescence.

2. Please refer to Susan Contratto and Miriam M. Johnson in this volume. Johnson has consistently supplied supportive criticism to me and pointed out the need to consider the structural supports contributing to fathers' differential power within the family.

3. My thanks to Gerald M. Platt for suggesting this example to me.

BIOGRAPHICAL NOTE

Marion S. Goldman attended the University of California at Berkeley where she majored in Sociology. After college, she did graduate work in Sociology at the University of Chicago. Professor Goldman teaches at the University of Oregon and is an affiliate of the Center for the Study of Women in Society where she offers courses in the sociology of deviance and the sociology of gender. Her recent research interests have been on feminine achievement and ambivalence. Her major published works are *A Portrait of the Black Attorney in Chicago*; *Gold Diggers and Silver Miners: Prostitution and Social Life on the Comstock Lode*, which won the Hamilton Prize.

REFERENCES

ABRAHAM, K.
1953 Selected Papers on Psychoanalysis. New York: Basic Books.
CHICAGO VICE COMMISSION
1911 The Social Evil in Chicago. Chicago: Gunthrop-Warren Publishers.
CHODOROW, N.
1978 The Reproduction of Mothering. Berkeley: University of California Press.
COLEMAN, K.
1973 "A Portrait of Four Hookers." pp. 1–22 in George Csicesry (ed.), The Sex Industry. New York: New American Library.
1976 PERSONAL INTERVIEW
CRESSEY, P. G.
1932 The Taxi-Dance Hall. Chicago: University of Chicago Press.
DAVIS, K.
1937 "The Sociology of Prostitution." The American Sociological Review 5: 744–755.
DEUTSCH, H.
1945 The Psychology of Women. Vol. 1. New York: Grune and Stratton.
FREUD, S.
1933 "Femininity," pp. 112–135 in Freud, New Introductory Lectures on Psychoanalysis. New York: W. W. Norton.
1963a "Female Sexuality," pp. 194–211 in P. Reiff (ed.), Sexuality and the Psychology of Love. New York: Collier Books. 1931.
1963b "The Most Prevalent Form of Degradation in Erotic Love," pp. 58–70 in P. Reiff (ed.), Sexuality and the Psychology of Love. New York: Collier Books. 1912.
1963c "Some Psychological Consequences of the Anatomical Distinction between the Sexes," pp. 183–93 in P. Reiff (ed.), Sexuality and the Psychology of Love. New York: Collier Books. 1925.
1963d "The Taboo of Virginity," pp. 70–86 in P. Reiff (ed.), Sexuality and the Psychology of Love. New York: Collier Books. 1918.
1963e "A Special Type of Object Choice Made by Men," pp. 49–58 in P. Reiff (ed.), Sexuality and the Psychology of Love. New York: Collier Books. 1910.
1969 An Outline of Psycho-Analysis. New York: W. W. Norton. 1940.
GEBHARD, P.
1968 "Misconceptions about Female Prostitutes." Medical Aspects of Human Sexuality 3: 24–30.

GENTRY, C.
1964 The Madams of San Francisco. New York: Ballantine Books.
GILLIGAN, C.
1982 Psychological Theory and Women's Development. Cambridge: Harvard University Press.
GOLDMAN, E.
1970 The Traffic in Women and Other Essays on Feminism. New York: Times Change Press, 1900.
GOLDMAN, M. S.
1981 Gold Diggers and Silver Miners: Prostitution and Social Life on the Comstock Lode. Ann Arbor: University of Michigan Press.
GREENWALD, H.
1970 The Elegant Prostitute: A Social and Psychoanalytic Study. New York: Ballantine Books, 1958.
HALLER, J. S., AND HALLER, R. M.
1974 The Physician and Sexuality in Victorian America. Urbana: University of Illinois Press.
HIRATA, L. C.
1979 "Free, Indentured, Enslaved: Chinese Prostitutes in Nineteenth Century America." Signs: A Journal of Women in Culture and Society 5: 3–29.
HIRSCHI, T.
1962 "The Professional Prostitute." Berkeley Journal of Sociology 7: 33–49.
JAMES, J.
1975 "Answers to Twenty Questions Most Frequently Asked About Prostitution," pp. 36–45 in J. James, J. Withes, M. Haft, and S. Theiss (eds.), The Politics of Prostitution. Seattle: Coyote.
JAMES, J., AND MEYERDING, J.
1977 "Early Sexual Experiences and Prostitution." American Journal of Psychiatry 134: 381–390.
JANIK, A., AND TOULMAN, S.
1973 Wittgenstein's Vienna. New York: Simon & Schuster.
KERNBERG, O. F.
1975 Borderline Conditions and Pathological Narcissism. New York: Jason Aronson.
KINSEY, A. C., POMEROY, W. B., AND MARTIN, C. E.
1948 Sexual Behavior in the Human Male. Philadelphia: W. B. Saunders.
LASCH, C.
1978 The Culture of Narcissism: American Life in an Age of Diminishing Expectations. New York: W. W. Norton.
MILLER, A.
1981 The Drama of the Gifted Child. New York: Basic Books.
RATHER, D.
1984 "Sixty Minutes." CBS-TV, February.
ROSEN, R., AND DAVIDSON, S., EDS.
1977 The Maimie Papers. Old Westbury: The Feminist Press.
RUBIN, L.
1976 Worlds of Pain. New York: Basic Books.
SANGER, W.
1937 The History of Prostitution. New York: Eugenics Publishing Company, 1807.
STEIN, M.
1974 Lovers, Friends, Slaves: The Nine Male Sexual Types, Their Psycho-Sexual Transactions with Call Girls. New York: Berkeley.

SYMANSKI R.
   1981 The Immoral Landscape: Female Prostitution in Western Societies. Toronto: Nut-
   terworths.
THOMAS, W. I.
   1923 The Unadjusted Girl. Boston: Little, Brown.
WAKSLER, F. C., AND DOUGLAS, J. D.
   1982 The Sociology of Deviance. Boston: Little, Brown.
WALKOWITZ, J.
   1980 Prostitution and Victorian Society. New York: Cambridge University Press.
WINICK, C., AND KINSIE, P. M.
   1971 The Lively Commerce: Prostitution in the United States. Chicago: Quadrangle
   Books.

V

THE PSYCHOANALYTIC SOCIOLOGY
OF COLLECTIVE BEHAVIOR

Introduction

Collective behavior and social movements are the stuff that excites the imagination. For example, Boston Bruin fans rioting for playoff tickets, student fads, like those of spring break mania in Newport Beach or Fort Lauderdale, the French, Russian, and Chinese revolutions are interesting, exciting, even frightening events to read about but also wonderful to understand. And so too are the world leaders, such as the Roosevelts, Castros, and Maos exciting figures to fathom. They lead hundreds of thousands of people into better times from bad or out of bad times to movements for social change.

Collective behavior is the study of social arrangements that are neither mundane nor routine. Collective behavior studies have traditionally extended all the way from fads, riots, crowds, and panics to rebellions and revolutions. Recently, a distinction has been made in the field between collective behavior and social movements, the latter focused upon political, social, economic, and religious movements directed toward change or the reinforcement of already existing social arrangements.[1] The articles you are about to read by Gerald M. Platt ("The psychoanalytic Sociology of Collective Behavior: Material Interests, Cultural Factors and Emotional Responses in Revolution") and Charles Camic ("Charisma: Its Varieties, Preconditions, and Consequences") are focused primarily upon social movements. The complexity of the movements they deal with, however, suggests their remarks are also relevant to collective behavior.

What sparks a riot or a revolution? Who joins and why? Are events such as these brought about by rational, non-rational, irrational motives? Who becomes a leader, a follower, and why? These are the questions that guide studies of collective behavior and social movements.

The papers that follow address these issues. Both are innovative in the answers they present. But such a remark as the last demands justification; it must be placed in context to be understood. Both papers share a common theme: private and collective life are complex, incorporating realistic and non-rational factors simultaneously. Approaches to collective behavior must take account of the multidimensionality of collective actions. Platt and Camic do so and this is why their papers are innovative.

Previous approaches to collective behavior have been too simple, too narrowly focused. Platt and Camic want to rectify this simplicity because the reality of collective behavior demands it. Platt points to the diversity of conditions that motivate persons to participate in revolutions. Camic points to the diversity of types of charismatic leaders and the different needs they may serve for followers. Although social movements and movement followers may look alike from outside the movement, there is considerable variability among these, even when the reference is to a single phenomenon such as revolution.

In order to accomplish these analytic ends, Platt and Camic take a sympathetic but critical stance towards the "masters" and some contemporary writings on collective behavior. The authors begin their papers stimulated by the works of Karl Marx, Sigmund Freud, or Max Weber. Both of them go beyond the interpretations the masters have offered of collective behavior.

Platt suggests that Marx, Freud, and Weber took too specific an analytic stance on social movements. Therefore, no matter what they positively contributed in terms of understanding, these stances were too narrow, too reductionists, and treated too lightly the complexity of peoples' reasons for participation in collective actions. Camic suggests that while Weber made a remarkable breakthrough with his conception of charismatic leadership in collective action, he did not differentiate the types of charisma that have historically occurred. Thus, using Freud's conception of levels of personality innovatively, Camic develops a picture of charisma in its several forms, each serving different personality needs of followers.

Both articles were written independently of each other and yet they complement each other in the extreme. Together, the articles present an excellent introduction to the psychoanalytic sociology of collective action and social movements. This is an approach recognizing that social life is as diverse as personal life and is oriented by realistic and non-rational interests. Social behavior is attuned to the real world but unconsciously pressured by non-rational and irrational desires and values. The psychoanalytic sociology of collective behavior is an orientation that characterizes social life at a theoretical level of generality (consistent with the hopes among all the social sciences) but without violating the spirit and the complexities of the realities of social movements.

NOTE

1 Traugott, M. 1978 "Reconceiving Social Movements," *Social problems*, 26:38-49.

The Psychoanalytic Sociology of Collective Behavior: Material Interests, Cultural Factors, and Emotional Responses in Revolution[1]

GERALD M. PLATT

INTRODUCTION

STIMULATED by Gustave LeBon's *The Crowd* (1960), Freud published his only work directly addressed to collective behavior, *Group Psychology and the Analysis of the Ego* (1951, first published in 1922). This was Freud's attempt at explaining the psychology of men and women swept up into the apparent hysteria and violence of crowds. Despite Freud's usual brilliance, his *Group Psychology* is less than totally satisfying.

Some of Freud's shortcomings stem from LeBon's faulty description of crowds. But some of Freud's failure is the result of his own psychological categories which moved his analysis in the wrong direction—a direction inconsistent with his thinking on many other topics and inconsistent with later known facts about collective behavior.

Freud's thesis is that crowd behavior is regressive and infantile. In collective behavior, the masses give over their rational and conscious minds to the leader, and the leader harnesses the crowd's emotionality in the service of collective goals. Thus, the leader manipulates an infantilized crowd.

The archetype crowds for LeBon were the street masses of the French Revolution: they appalled him. The expressively violent street crowds, and especially the French Terror, became the model of all collective movements for LeBon and then for Freud.

At bottom, Freud was a positivist and scientist. He associated the highest form of civilization with scientific and rational thought—he associated mental health and maturity with these same attributes. For Freud, crowd behavior was antithetical to civilization and to everything he cherished in society. His analysis of crowds was, therefore, also a condemnation of collective behavior in so far as he suggested it to be something less than mature and rational or that it was irrational behavior analogous to childishness or mental illness.

By indirection Freud provided something of an analysis of the French Revolution. Karl Marx, too, wrote of the French Revolution (1935, 1964), though Freud took no note of Marx's work on the subject. The reasons are obvious. Marx had offered a rationalist interpretation of the same cataclysmic event.

Marx suggested that the French Revolution was provoked by successful bourgeois entrepreneurs who in prerevolutionary France were unable to establish a political position in society. Monarchical and aristocratic authority in prerevolutionary France excluded the bourgeoisie from political power, which was based upon birth and inheritance. The bourgeoisie warred against the king and aristocracy in order to secure power for themselves. The democratization of the French society ultimately served the interests of the bourgeois classes because the post-revolutionary constitution included them in a prominent way in society's political structure.

While Marx does not deny the violence and emotionality of the French revolutionary crowds, there was nothing irrational, neurotic, or infantile in the bourgeoisie's behavior. Indeed, the opposite is true. The bourgeoisie were acting rationally in terms of their class interests. They were economically on the rise in French society, they were vital to its operations, and yet they were excluded from the decisions which affected their lives—taxation, for example. The bourgeoisie fomented a revolution to redress this deprivation. In the language of Marxism, they acted rationally in terms of their material interests.

Max Weber also wrote of collective behavior and in passing remarked upon the French Revolution (1978). Weber offered a formulation which supplemented Marx's and implicitly supplemented Freud's. Weber axiomatically assumed that collective behavior grew out of material interests, but he also assumed that there must be an even more vital element involved than material interests for collective actions to occur. Weber suggested that collective behavior requires a charismatic leader who codified for the masses a plan of action, as Robespierre had done for the French. In describing someone possessing charisma, Weber meant a leader who was perceived by the masses as endued with divine grace, an elevated figure whose doctrinal revelations would lead followers out of chaos into a new society. In short, a charismatic leader, based on his own personal authority, would provide followers with a plan for social change.

In contemporary language, the charismatic leader's solution is referred to as ideology or cultural doctrine. It is the leaders and their solutions which harness the minds and emotions of the masses, giving them direction even in movements oriented to rational goals. Because

Weber stressed the role of ideology or culture doctrine in action, he is referred to as an idealist or cultural determinist.

The locus classicus of interpretive controversy in collective behavior is between Weberian cultural and Marxist material determinism. This controversy revolves about whether collective action is essentially the outgrowth of material interests, such as struggles over money, power, esteem; or whether collective action is fundamentally the product of cultural influences, such as moral or ideological doctrine, which give direction to action and change—for example, encouraging people to rebel against autocratic oppression and exclusion on behalf of inclusive liberal democratic doctrine, as occurred in the French Revolution.

Not in his *Group Psychology*, but in Freud's clinical case studies, there is direction for a solution to materialist-culturalist controversy. His clinical reports frequently intertwined both factors in a complex and multidimensional interpretation of individuals. These clinical case studies exhibit an awareness of the need to account for rational and irrational action, conscious and unconscious thought, emotional expressivity and emotional flatness, concrete material experiences and interests and culturally symbolic ones. In such subtle analyses we can find suggestions for our theorizing.

The failure of Freud, Marx, and Weber in their collective behavior studies is in their simplification, their tendency to reduce the complexity of mental and social life to a unity, the product of a single cause. This reductionism is exhibited in Freud's insistence upon the homogeneous and regressive mentality of crowds; in Marx's assertion regarding the unity of subjective consciousness stemming from shared class interests; and in Weber's suggestion of homogeneous mentality achieved through commitment to a charismatictic leader's ideology.

The theorists' reductionism is also inconsistent with known facts about collective behavior. The great revolutions, examples of political and labor unrest, mass movements of all kinds, have always been more complex than any of these theories can depict. Collective movements have been rational and irrational, emotional and disciplined, constructive and destructive. But most important, they have involved persons from different social classes, ages, religions, and with varying psychological dispositions and emotions on the same side, on different sides, on all sides of the conflict. Collective actions are complex, diverse, heterogeneous, and anything but simple, unified, and homogenous. Collective actions are as sociologically and psychologically subtle and diverse as any of the individuals described by Freud in his clinical studies.

The study of collective behavior demands a theory consistent with its complexity. A theory of collective behavior must capture and explain the multiplicity and multicausality of crowds, groups, and revolutionary parties. It must also preserve the reality of peoples' experiences in social movements, while offering a degree of generalization about them.

This is what I attempt to accomplish in my paper. And while I cannot offer, at this time, a definitive theory of collective behavior, I am convinced that the direction of the theorizing is correct.

I will illustrate the ways in which the complexity of collective action can be characterized by integrating classical sociological and psychological statements in an attempt to develop a theory encompassing the totality of responses in mass movements.

This paper is only one part of a larger body of work. I have, with my co-worker, Fred Weinstein, tried to develop a psychoanalytic sociology of collective action and social change (for example, see Weinstein and Platt, 1973; Weinstein and Platt, 1969; Weinstein, 1980; Platt, 1980). In doing so, we have been especially attentive to the materialist-culturalist controversy, trying to resolve this by assimilating these forms of analysis into each other. At the same time, we have tried to link these social and cultural levels to dynamic aspects of personality. In sum, we have attempted to emulate Freud's sensitivity to analytic complexity of individuals, but at the level of the mass movements.

The French Revolution and the Theory of Collective Behavior

This is a theoretical paper, not an empirical one. However, I have thus far illustrated concepts by reference to the French Revolution, and I will continue to do so. The reason is that the French Revolution became the archetypical revolution for all modern revolutions, not only in terms of form and organization, but also in terms of aspirations and expectations. The French Revolution, the first large-scale attempt at democratic revolution, shook the very foundations of European society. No other revolution prior to it had as great a democratizing impact upon the Western world.

By contrast, the English Civil War of 1642 was a democratizing revolution which culminated in the trial and execution of Charles I in 1649. As has been pointed out, the king's trial was not so much a personal indictment as it was a "bold exploration into the very nature of monarchy" (Walzer, 1969: 10). In so doing, the English critically examined aristocratic rule and significantly democratized their society. But by 1660, the English restored their king, placing Charles II on the throne. British society has never fully abandoned its cherished relationship to kingship.

The American Revolution of 1776 was the first historical movement to overthrow colonial rule (Lipset, 1963). To be sure, there was a war between the colonial and British armies. It ended in the defeat of the latter and the establishment of a centralized democratic government, but that war was restrained and its aftermath was relatively bloodless. Furthermore, the prerevolutionary colonies were democratically ruled, thus, their unification under a single constitution after the revolution was a continuation and extension of the politics that existed prior to the revolution. The American Revolution was significant but hardly as violent or as cataclysmic as the French.

The significance of the French Revolution is well recognized, and François Furet points out:

What the French brought into being at the end of the eighteen century was . . . democratic politics as a national ideology. The secret of the success of 1789, its message and lasting influence lie in that invention, which was unprecedented and whose legacy was to be so widespread. The English and French revolutions, though separated by more than a century, have many traits in common, none of which, however, was sufficient to bestow on the first the role of universal model that the second has played ever since it appeared on the stage of history. The reason is that Cromwell's Republic was too preoccupied with religious concerns and too intent upon its return to origins to develop the one notion that made Robespierre's language the prophecy of a new era: that democratic politics had come to decide the fate of individuals and peoples (Furet, 1981; 26, 44).

The French revolutionaries totally transformed French society. They attempted to destroy the very principle of kingship, as well as the aristocratic class, turning European societies upside-down. From 1789 through 1795, France, and Paris especially, were beset by a novel kind of mass street politics, violent and riotous. In the south, the Vendée was involved in a major counterrevolutionary movement (Tilly, 1964). Radical leaders like Robespierre and his colleages on the Committee of Public Safety had to cope with the real as well as imagined counterrevolutionary plots and intrigues (Weinstein and Platt, 1969:108–136; Furet, 1981:53–61). The gains of the French Revolution were threatened by nations outside its border from hostile European monarchies in collaboration with aristocrats and the Catholic hierarchy.

The Jacobin dictatorship of 1793–1794 and its Reign of Terror developed in response to these conditions. The Terror defined the modern experience of massive revolutionary violence, of the repression and execution of thousands and tens of thousands of real and imagined counterrevolutions. In the end, the French Revolution became not only the model for future revolutions of democratic aspiration but also for the methods of repression by which democratic revolutionaries attempt to secure their gains.

If one practical consequence of the revolution was that it serve as the model for future revolutionary attempts to democratize the world, another, though lesser, one is that the French Revolution became the object of incessant theorizing about revolutions, social movements and collective behavior. There has been no end to historical and social scientific studies attempting to make sense of the revolutionary turmoil, to understand the revolution's successes and failures, to explain its causes, and to depict the social positions and the psychodynamics of the people who participated in it.

To a degree, this essay is another such study, except that I will try here to demonstrate that the French Revolution was more complex, multilayered and overdetermined than has ever been depicted in theory that is currently available. This essay of course will not settle the historical or theoretical controversies that surround the subject, but it will demonstrate unequivocally that mono-causal, materialist conceptions of social class, or cultural-functionalist conceptions of the primacy of ideology or morality by themselves must fail to capture the complexity of collective movements in general. This is especially true of movements as complicated and disturbing as those that arose in the course of the French Revolution.

Interestingly, the paper that follows this one in the present volume, by Charles Camic, entitled, "Charisma: Its Varieties, Preconditions, and Consequences," takes up a similar theme from the point of view of leadership. Camic emphasizes that there is not one, but several types of charismatic leadership, each emerging in relation to the character, interests, and wishes of particular movements. Camic, among others (Geertz, 1983:121–146), realizes that social life, collective actions included, is obviously more complicated than people typically imagine and that social theory must provide a conception of leadership as diverse as are the complexities of social movements.

In these terms, my paper and Camic's are complementary, both describing social life in a manner consistent with my remarks about Freud's clinical studies in the introduction of this paper. Social life, like personal life, is constantly changing, involving real and imagined events, material and symbolic forces, rational and nonrational motives, all intertwined and serving to link conceptions of past, present and future. Social theory must provide for that kind of complex, multilayered, overdetermined reality. Attempts to squeeze this complexity into simple, comprehensible schemes, more for the sake of closure than for the sake of truth, violates this principle. It is important to stress, therefore, that my paper and Camic's are rooted in an alternative approach, one that attempts to preserve historical reality while providing theoretical coherence and to make better sense of the real complexities of social movements.

MATERIAL INTERESTS AND CULTURAL MANDATES IN COLLECTIVE BEHAVIOR

The works of Freud, Marx and Weber do not define the whole of the classics on collective behavior. Nor did the topic begin and end with their writings. Collective behavior and social change have preoccupied sociologists and psychologists from the nineteenth century to the present. I draw upon the classical writers already noted, upon other classical theorists such as de Tocqueville and Durkheim, and upon contemporary authors who have written on these and related topics.

Theories of collective behavior focus upon unstable and unacceptable material and cultural circumstances as the conditions out of which revolutions arise; it is nonsense to assume that conditions of stability and contentment produce revolutions. However, despite the general agreement upon the conditions for collective action there is much controversy regarding the specific character of the instability. At times the conditions are formulated as opposites of one another. I will begin by specifying some of the conditions for occurence of revolution.

Among the most frequently suggested sources of collective action have been those involving material interests. Within the Marxist tradition, interests refer to the possession of, or access to, economic resources. However, since the writings of Lukács, Lenin, Gramsci, and the Frankfurt School, interests in the Marxist tradition also have been defined as political resources, so interest theorists have been concerned with the possession of and access to political power. Marxists included among these interests concern with access to money, value, occupations, capital, land, political position, positions of esteem, titles. Consistent with contemporary Marxist theory, I will define interests as economic resources but also as political power and social esteem or, more simply, political and social resources.

Access to economic, political, and social resources may vary from extreme possession to extreme deprivation. This occurs through processes by which people have increasing access to those resources or are increasingly deprived of them. The Marxist tradition emphasized deprivation and the ways people became deprived of such resources. This is exemplified in Marx's emphasis upon the increasing immiseration of the working classes as the source of class consciousness and class warfare.

The assumptions behind this formulation are that classes deprived of resources experience increasing misery, starvation, political impotence, political and economic injustice, and blows to self-esteem, resulting in the conscious appreciation of their interests and action to rectify the situation. Those segments of the society most deprived—those with least access—will organize collectively to produce fundamental change. At the same time, those segments of society who possess the resources constitute the conservative elements struggling to maintain their advantages. The Marxist thesis is more complex than is expressed in this simple formulation; but this synopsis does capture its essence.

I refer to this Marxist position as the interest deprivation condition for collective action. Following the subjective language implied in Davies's (1962:5–18) classic article on revolution, I describe this interest dimension as one of blocked and decreasing access to economic, political, and social want satisfaction on the part of particular segments of society. In the Marxist tradition, this most readily refers to classes.[2]

By contrast, the process of interest satisfaction, or the condition of increasing access to resources as the precondition for revolution, is expressed in the writings of Alexis de Tocqueville (1856). It was de Tocqueville who suggested that prosperity, a rapid rise in affluence, and the weakening of the bonds of oppression and exclusion, fostered revolution. For de Tocqueville it was the dynamic economic growth of eighteenth century France, along with the availability of ennoblement, which encourage the French bourgeoisie to rebel in 1789.

De Tocqueville suggested that rapid social change unnerved people's sense of security, expanded their personal aspirations and expectations, and engendered in them a sense of discontent. The bourgeoisie as a class were undergoing such a change in eighteenth century French society. They accrued large amounts of wealth, they gained access to the peerage, and they were fast becoming the society's most important operatives. As Emmanuel Sieyes put it, the Third Estate was "everything." According to de Tocqueville, it was the bourgeoisie's rapid access to society's resources, the unprecedented increase in their want satisfactions, and not their exclusion, which radicalized them.

A quantitative analysis of social mobility in prerevolutionary France supports de Tocqueville's analysis. Shapiro and Dawson (1972:159–191) examined the relationship of radicalism and the opportunity for ennoblement in forty cities and towns. Using five indices of radicalism, they found that members of the Third Estate were more radical than nobility in the same localities and that these bourgeoisie were more radical in cities and towns, where the possibility for ennoblement was greatest. Shapiro and Dawson conclude that conservative, liberal, and radical historians who assumed that blocked mobility radicalized the French bourgeoisie were wrong. Rather, it was the Third Estate's political and economic successes that engendered in them a desire for even greater interest satisfaction and led them to attack kingship. Shapiro and Dawson conclude that increasing satisfaction of interests was crucial in the origins of the French Revolution.[3]

There is no reason to infer from these findings that de Tocqueville's formulation is superior to that of Marx's. Rather, I merely wish to underline that de Tocqueville's approach creates a different conception of reality; a conception that appears to have some validity. Therefore, I would prefer to put to one side the issue of theoretical correctness, instead suggesting that both Marx's and de Tocqueville's conceptions of interest satisfaction have value. I refer to their formulations as the Marx-de Tocqueville dimension of interests. And consistent with long-standing sociological tradition, I refer to this dimension as the social or interest dimension of analysis. I do so to distinguish it from that of the cultural or symbolic dimension of human existence. Further, I suggest that while the interest dimension is exceedingly important to an understanding of collective action, it is equally important to include a cultural dimension in the analysis of revolution. Therefore, I turn to a development of the cultural dimension in a manner similar to that accomplished for the Marx-de Tocqueville material interest dimension.

There is an excellent sociological literature that can be used to examine the cultural dimension of collective action. Max Weber's cultural analysis, especially one aspect of his concept of charisma may be employed for my work. In Weber's conceptualization of charisma, one function of leadership is to bring to society new moral principles, as new conditions or newly organized groups cannot be absorbed by the old morality. It is in the absence of a cultural doctrine legitimating and institutionalizing novel social activities that charismatic intervention occurs with the purpose of instituting new moral principles. For example, such a charismatic leadership role was played by Martin Luther in the protestant Reformation. Luther provided a morality that legitimated individualistic autonomy in the sphere of religion. This type of morality became characteristic of certain Western precapitalist societies and was codified in the religious doctrine that defined the private relation between man and God. At another and lower normative level, this morality became the means for an evaluation of personal worth in terms of performance rather than in terms of obeisance to the clergy and the sacraments.

The philosopher, Paul Schrecker, provides a language of cultural change that is consistent with my intended meaning for this Weberian dimension. Schrecker suggests that revolutions in any sphere of activity, be it political, artistic, economic, religious or scientific, involve a fundamental change in the most general constitutive norms or generative principles governing that area of endeavor. These generative principles give legitimacy to all lower level norms and principles within the scope of a particular institutional activity. Changes of this kind are revolutionary because they reorder the phenomenon itself; they change fundamentally the activities and practices of science, art, government, and religion. Institutions thus appear fundamentally different because the generative norms governing activities within them are fundamentally different (Schrecker, 1966:34–52).

This, then, is the Weberian condition of cultural change: it refers to unexpected or unaccounted for circumstances in which there are struggles to establish a new constitutive principle. More specifically, by this dimension I mean conditions of cultural change exist in the absence of a principle to organize novel social activities in a meaningful way. Thus, generative cultural principles are introduced (with political struggles among the advocates of contending potential principles) as moral doctrine to organize and give meaning to social activities (such as the distribution of resources, performance capacities, conceptions of self), which have evolved in a society in a given period.

In addition to Weber's conception of charisma, I also employ Durkheim's concept of anomie. Although Durkheim's concept of anomic culture is not typically related to social movements, disturbances of this type are also relevant to our studies. I formulate Durkheim's conception of anomie as cultural conditions in which social activities cannot be rendered meaningful in terms of extant and yet still valued moral principles; that is, valued cultural principles and expectations fail in their capacity to orient social action. For example, rapid inflation or deflation changes the worth of money precepitously, unsettling (valued) expectations regarding its purchasing power. In these inflationary and deflationary circumstances, individuals continue to want their money to have the same purchasing power it had prior to the economic chaos and are cognitively unsettled and emotionally disturbed that it does not. Such conditions characterized Germany in 1929, and Italy after 1945. These conditions of failed culture, which I refer to as the Durkheimian dimension, unsettle significant segments of a population and *can* set into motion collective action to resolve the failure of culture.

There is an important difference between the Weberian and Durkheimian dimensions of cultural failure, i.e., between absence and failure of culture. In the cultural conditions associated with the Weberian dimension, there are no legitimate principles by which to organize a course of action or to achieve a solution to novel social problems facing people; there is no doctrine in the extant culture to determine a morally legitimate and meaningful solution to such social conditions as, for example, the integration of a new urban working class into the political power structure. In these conditions, all suggestions for change are viewed from the perspective of the entrenched order as illegitimate (Schrecker, 1966). In the Durkheimian condition, moral courses of action exist but they are ineffective. An example of this at the cultural level is the inability to act as a good parent or family man in conditions of unemployment, particularly when certain jobs are no longer available as a result of industrial change. This example is especially consistent with Durkheim's conception of anomie, as the increasingly variegated nature of social life puts strains on the moral order to provide cohesive meaning to a differentiating social order.

In all of these conditions, the moral order fails to give cohesive meaning to social life. However, taking a lead from Habermas (1975), I can add another conceptual nuance: I am referring to *personally experienced* cultural failures, not to any theorists's superimpositions upon activity or experience derived from external observation. Of course, the imputation of objective conditions" is close to Durkheim's formulation of anomie because he approached the topics of *The Division of Labor in Society* (1933), *Suicide* (1951), with the hope of developing a positive science of sociology. But Durkheim's expectations notwithstanding, I must formulate moral failure from an interpretive, that is, experiential perspective.[4]

For our analysis I will treat the failure of culture and the absence of culture as separate conditions. However in reality they may impinge upon different segments of a population simultaneously in a particular historical circumstance. I will refer moreover to these cultural disturbances as the Weber-Durkheim cultural dimension.

Assuming the separateness of cultural and social levels of analysis, I have created two "orthogonal" dimensions effecting collective action. In turn each dimension is depicted as possessing two dichotomous categories of disturbing conditions. By employing both dimensions interactively I can establish a "formal" system of conditions for the occurrence of collective action. These interactive conditions are: cultural failure-increasing interest satisfaction; cultural failure-decreasing interest satisfaction; cultural absence-increasing interest satisfaction; cultural absence-decreasing interest satisfaction. I depict these interactive conditions in a four cell table suggesting four types of collective actions associated with each of the cultural-social conditions of disturbance. This typology is presented in Table 1.

Table 1. Typology of the Conditions for the Occurrence of Collective Movements

		Social or Interactive Level of Analysis	
		de Tocqueville Increasing want satisfaction or increasing satisfaction or interests	Marx Decreasing want satisfaction or decreasing satisfaction of interests
Cultural or Symbolic Level of Analysis	Durkheim Failure of a morality or failure of generative principles; morality or generative principles still valued	Utopian or Cultist Movements	Right wing or Fascist Movements
	Weber Absence of a morality or absence of generative principles	Democratic left movements, such as bourgeois revolutions, advocates of liberty, equality, brotherhood and legal justice.	Radical left movements, working class revolutions, interest in the redistribution of resources and advocates of distributive justice

COGNITIVE AND EMOTIVE RESPONSES TO MATERIAL AND CULTURAL CONDITIONS

The typology of collective action summarized in Table 1 is offered to readers who can in Erikson's phrase, "take it and leave it." However, at this juncture I want to use the Table to organize an analysis of personal reactions to typical material and cultural conditions of disturbance. The hypothetical actors experiencing the circumstances in the four cells will share some responses but also will demonstrate different reactions. Further, I want to suggest that while the cognitive and emotive experiences depicted do not determine the types of ideologies that develop in response to disturbing conditions, there is a certain affinity between personal reactions to conditions of disturbance and the types of formulations and practices adopted as solutions.

I begin the analysis with the conditions of the absence of a cultural morality (Weber) and increasing want satisfaction (de Tocqueville) among persons hitherto excluded from certain societal resources. Under these circumstances it is possible to expect that persons so affected will experience a sense of accomplishment, success, well-being, happiness, perhaps even euphoria. The increasing material achievement produces fantasies of unlimited potential; much, if not everything appears attainable and accomplishable.

However, these positive feelings will be tempered by a sense of frustration. Against the significant feelings of achievement there will be the experience of the absence of a cultural morality to legitimate, to perpetuate, perhaps even merely to acknowledge the success, leaving the people with a feeling of incompleteness. From the perspective of these people it becomes necessary to institutionalize their achievements.

Thus, such personal reactions encourage desires for methods and practices to justify, solidify and perpetuate accomplishments, that is, to legitimate and sustain accomplishments. There are desires for cultural and social forms to give credence to and to celebrate and sanctify the social arrangements that have developed. In short, there is the desire for a cultural morality that provides full inclusion for these people and their achievements.

By the same token, those who experience the absence of cultural morality to legitimate their integration (Weber) while suffering decreasing want satisfaction or declining interest satisfaction (Marx), undergo similar yet different cognitive and emotive experiences. The cultural-material circumstances they face produce in them the desire for recognition, legitimacy and sanctity, but also fright, anxiety and anger. Those segments of society undergoing decreasing want satisfaction in the absence of a cultural morality, are experiencing declining esteem, self-respect and power, while suffering a sense of incapacity to control their lives or circumstances. Though worthy and admirable in their own eyes, such people are faced with dire possible consequences, fears of starvation, exclusion, even extinction.

This discrepancy between a sense of worthiness and achievement and the absence of an organizing principle upon which to develop methods to rectify a situation which denies worthiness and achievement intensifies the negative emotions cited above; that is, people so affected do not have a method within the extant cultural framework to solve the dilemmas they face, their present is intolerable, they cannot see themselves in a viable future, and they are scared and angry.

Only a rapid and radical resolution to the problem can be meaningful for such people. There must be for them a morality that can legitimate activity directed to the *rapid reversal of the deprivation of fundamental needs,* while legitimating inclusion into the society's economic, political, and social processes. This integration cannot be accomplished either within the framework of the hitherto established moral order or through one which perpetuates current arrangements or justifies exclusion into the future. What is needed, from the point of view of those experiencing declining want satisfaction, is a moral principle that "reasonably" distributes the social resources, providing for a more equitable distribution of resources for the foreseeable future. There is a desire for a morality of distributive justice, one that guarantees the satisfaction of wants and interests, while preventing the recurrence of economic and political conditions engendering fear, anxiety, and a sense of failure and loss.

Up to now, I have described alternative conditions in abstract terms, which may appear vague without some explicit references and examples. So let me note quickly that the first set of conditions provoked and promoted the French Revolution from the standpoint of the bourgeoisie, while the second set provoked and promoted the Russian Revolution of October 1917, from the standpoint of the working classes in the major industrial capitals of the Russian empire. Keeping in mind, of course, that the workers and the leaders of the Bolshevik Party did not necessarily see eye to eye on the purposes and prospects of that revolution.

Similar feelings and cognitive styles occur in circumstances of decreasing interest satisfaction (Marx) when the extant and still valued morality appears to be failing or ineffective (Durkheim). Again segments of the population so affected, incapable of seeing themselves in a viable future, respond with fear, anxiety, and anger. In these circumstances, the typical response to the cultural dilemma is to suggest that the generative rules can be effective again if people would only behave according to the rules, or if society would only return to an idealized (i.e., retrospectively enhanced) past, when the rules were followed.

In short, conditions of moral failure and declining interest satisfaction lead to solutions which run in the opposite direction from those occurring in the absence of morality and in a period of declining interest satisfaction. There is, in circumstances of moral failure and decreasing interest satisfaction, the same sense of urgency, the need for rapid and radical resolution of the personal tensions and social difficulties. However, there is also in the society a considerable degree of continued loyalty to the extant morality (including an idealized past) and of resistance to moral change. Thus, the ideological and practical solutions are in the direction of the standardization and rigidification of moral practices, conditions we are familiar with from right wing ideologies and practices.

Finally, in materially improving conditions, or conditions of increasing want satisfaction (de Tocqueville), when the moral principles are perceived as failed (Durkheim), feelings of success, well-being, accomplishment, even euphoria, are threatened by the failure of the culture to give clear direction to these positive feelings (or clear recognition of the accomplishments); both feelings and accomplishments are affected by the ambiguous, hence threatening conditions. People experiencing these circumstances fear the loss of the positive feelings as well as the loss of their achieved position in society. The response to the interplay between positive feelings and accomplishments and the failed morality is to seek a secure position by idealizing the extant normative system and generating practices which reproduce the accomplishment. Religious doctrine typically plays an important role in creating an idealized conception of a perfect society in which people's places are guaranteed, recognized, and rewarded. The desire is for an idealized sacred community in which strict adherence to rules assures justice for all in this world and the next.

The moral failure of society or the incapacity to recognize the value of this successful segment of the society is also experienced by that segment as evidence of the world's moral corruption. This leads such people into a position of moral rigidity, resulting often in the isolation of the community from the contamination of the corrupting world (or in the hope for a future community from which such corruption is absent). This rigidity may take on a xenophobic character, separating the community from the general society even further. However, the fantasied or accomplished isolation serves the purpose of sustaining the hope for a community in which the achieved gains are perpetuated, while serving also to enhance a sense of superiority for their achievements and rectitude.

Once again I must note that these apparently abstract criteria have empirical references. The former set of conditions we recognize in right wing movements, the latter in one or another version of a utopian community of which Jonestown is an interesting example. I would argue in these terms that Jonestown collapsed with such catastrophic results because the community did not have the power to remain isolated and hence feared contamination and subversion. The mass suicide (with whatever degree of murder that was also involved) was a final declaration of their superiority, intactness, virtue and total isolation from mundane corruption.

IDEOLOGY AND PRACTICES IN RELATION TO MATERIAL AND CULTURAL CONDITIONS

Table 1 is best used only for heuristic purposes. It was developed, in part, to illustrate that interests and cultural doctrine are inseparable conditions of collective action. there is no way to deny the importance of interests and no concerted action unfolds in the absence of moral considerations that are codified into what is customarily referred to as ideology. Table 1 also was developed to illustrate the complexity of the potential personal responses to material and cultural conditions of disturbance. In short, no simple formulation, no single factor, material or cultural, can explain the multiplicity of responses to revolutionary conditions.

Take the French Revolution, for example: the bourgeoisie did perceive the world as progressive and perfectible, and they did seek to create a moral order and a political structure to legitimate their rule, to foster, as they saw it, that unlimited progress. They did see that the monarchical order could not absorb them, give them pride of place or a share of the political power without being fundamentally altered. At the same time, the sans-culottes, the artisan class in pre- and post-revolutionary France, did see themselves constantly in potentially or actually life-threatening situations. It was a novel situation, in historical terms, giving rise to claims for security and protection that were, from the viewpoint of both monarchical and bourgeois interests and moral perspectives, unacceptable. The sans-culottes did develop a particular kind of ad hoc politics to promote and foster their own interests against the rich and powerful. Thus, the bourgeoisie could have been the spokesmen for the sans-culottes only to a degree because the classes shared neither interests nor moral perspectives as to the solutions to the problems they faced. At the same time, however, the sans-culottes could not organize a unifying policy among themselves or develop a leadership that could represent and promote their interests under the given conditions. Neither class was unified and homogeneous. Indeed, the heterogeneous composition of the sans-culottes was particularly crucial for their inability to promote a unified policy in defense of their interests.

According to the typology described in Table 1, the French Revolution may be explained as happening in the *absence of a morality* for the integration of the bourgeoisie or the sans-culottes; however, their *interest circumstances were different*. The *former segment of of society enjoyed increasing societal resources while the latter were suffering from declining access to resources*. Their ideologies, independent of their accomplishments, could never be shared, although in the end, it was bourgeois ideology which prevailed, only partially integrating the sans-culottes.

More was involved in the French Revolution than the absence of a morality or rising or declining access to resources. The bourgeoisie and the sans-culottes can be separated in terms of material interests, though the shared the sense of needing a new morality. However, a formulation based on these elements alone cannot do justice to the reactions and ideologies of other classes in French society.

For example, once the revolution occurred, the French aristocracy experienced cultural and material conditions unique to them. They were, in general, suffering from severe attacks on their real interests while continuing to cherish the apparently failed morality that had formerly justified those interests. The aristocrats advocated a continuation of, or a return to, the traditional moral order, including the primacy of the monarchy. They became, in the familiar language of social science, the ideological right-wing of the French revolution. The French aristocracy could, therefore, be characterized as living through the cultural and material conditions depicted in the upper right box of Table 1.

I have explained basic social groupings in the French Revolution in terms of three of the possibilities established in Table 1. But what of the fourth possibility, the one characterized by increasing access and rising expectations in conditions of a failed or failing morality, leading to utopian or cultic movements? This condition describes in very consistent terms the political position and the situation of the political following of Robespierre and St. Just, who attempted to create, or at least gave expression to the vision of a republic of virtue; an ascetic, spartan, harmonious community that would have no place for pride, personal ambition, or self-interest and that would strive only to enhance the public good. They hoped to establish a correct network of laws and institutions to provide the objective basis upon which, in Robespierre's words, "to effect an entire regeneration and. . . create a new people" (Weinstein and Platt, 1969: 121–122). This is not to say that every one of their political allies and colleagues shared this vision or that they could over the long run sustain a mass following or that they had any chance to integrate successfully the sans-culottes in ways that other, more moderate proponents of bourgeois ideology could not. Obviously, Robespierre and St. Just failed: they were overthrown and executed in their turn. This is only to note that such a utopian and even cultic movement arose during the French revolution under the conditions I have described (see also Billington 1980:24–53).[5]

These four responses taken together represent alternative ideological postures in threatening or disrupted social conditions. They are indicative of the complexity and diversity of actual responses in a revolutionary setting, challenging and contradicting the possibility of any simple or reductive class, cultural or dynamic explanation of collective behavior. More important still, the complexity of the French Revolution goes beyond even this multifaceted depiction of collective action in response to rapid and violent social change.

It has often been observed, for example, that the wealthy and privileged strata in France "were complexly divided by estate memberships, degrees of nobility, types of property, regional ties, affiliations to towns or to country, occupational interests, and so forth." Some aristocratic wealthy were among those who opposed the traditional constitution of French society in 1789 and favored the bourgeois solutions to legal, political, and institutional problems. Thus, it has been noted that bourgeois sympathizers included "a hefty minority of the nobility–with a disproportionate number of nobles who were acclimated by birth and/or regular residence to urban life and culture. In fact, some of the key leaders of the 'revolutionary bourgeoisie/third estate' were aristocrats" (Skocpol, 1979:66). Obviously, a merely formal deduction (form Table 1, above) of the responses of these aristocrats from their objective social location, (i.e., material and cultural conditions) would lead to quite another—and wrong—conclusion. At the same time, suggesting that urban life as such had culturally "predisposed" these diverse aristocrats to bourgeois conclusions only violates or contradicts the data from another direction; i.e., those aristocrats with urban experience were only "disproportionately" represented and did not exclusively side with the bourgeoisie.

More specifically, the actions of the Parisian aristocracy create an additional problem for my analysis. A formal deduction from Table 1 suggests they should support ideologies that reinforced or reasserted the extant morality. While a portion of the urban aristocratic class did just that, a substantial number of the urban nobility fell in with the bourgeoisie and their ideology advocating a new morality. This portion of revolutionary French aristocracy contradicts an analysis derived solely from their objective material and cultural interests.

These rather familiar data, which always seem to be absorbed or reconciled by magic in interpretations of the French Revolution, compel a more fundamental conclusion: *while the disruption of objective material and cultural interests is a necessary condition for collective action, it is not sufficient to determine anything like the entire character of those reactions, nor does it give rise to anything like consistent numbers from one historical instance to the next. What is necessary to understand, in the final analysis, is the subjective experience of these material and cultural circumstances on both sides; that is, its affect on those who conform to logical expectations drawn from objective and material interests and those who do not.* This experience can only be interpreted and defined from the participants' point of view and not from a priori theories about objective conditions or subjective responses to such objective conditions.

Any theorist, in short, can take his analysis as far as suggesting potential reactions of classes of people to particular conditions in the light of objective material and cultural interests. It is the participants' perceptions of these conditions which ultimately define their meaning. Only when there is congruence between the theorist's suggested potential response to objective conditions and the participants' real, reported response does the theorist have the capacity to predict.

Put another way, there is only and inevitably a loose fit between a theorist's inferred influence of objective conditions on people and the meanings such conditions have for them; indeed, it is the looseness of fit that makes generalizing so perilous. This accounts for the inability of theorists consistently to apply their theories to particular instances. There may well be central tendencies in the ways people use their material and cultural interests to perceive and respond to different circumstances. These tendencies describe, at best, only some portion of the population defined by these interests. The segment so defined is forever changing, from one historical instance to the next, or even over a period of time within the same historical instance.

If we are to grasp collective actions in their totality—the goal of a social science, after all—theorists must not only provide for the ways in which people typically act, consistent with their objective conditions, but also for the ways in which people subjectively interpret any given situation— how they think, feel, and perceive unexpectedly and idiosyncratically in dynamic and clinical terms and function inconsistently in social or collective terms as well. This makes the development of theories about collective behavior more difficult, but it is the only way to account finally for the data or to get close to the lived experiences of people in real historical circumstances.

Some Concluding Remarks

These brief remarks of course do not cover all the issues, all the possible policies and practices, or all the personal reactions to unsettled conditions, even in the single case of the French Revolution. We may reasonably expect that any collective action *can* exhibit these four types of response, but there are even more possible types that I have not discussed—and perhaps not even thought of. The important thing to keep in mind is that social changes·are the accomplishment of complex struggles, compromises, and machinations among contending groups and factions developed before, during and after the action itself. In this context, we must always recall that in no sense can a theorist assume the explanation of a conflict can be formulated exclusively by the objective interests served as a consequence of that conflict. This evident complexity notwithstanding, there are still some important conclusions that must be drawn from the preceding discussion.

First, Table 1 is a formal fiction. At the moment of collective outbreak, real societies, real persons, populations, and revolutionary situations cannot be fit exclusively to any of the four cells. All four and perhaps more combinations of conditions and experiences characterize real revolutionary situations. We can conclude that normative perceptions of better times and worse times, or of a failed or absent morality, are not exclusively present on opposed sides in revolutionary situations. Rather those

perspectives occur at the same time among different groups and classes—
even among those on the same side of the struggle. These perceptions
are codified in ideological statements, which are expressed in abstract,
universal, and moral terms so that elements who do not share the interests of particular groups in an objective sense can nevertheless identify
with the codified principles and share the moral claims, as certain aristocrats identified with bourgeois ideology during the French Revolution.
This is why heterogeneous populations occur on all sides of a revolutionary or any other kind of conflict (Platt, 1980).

Second, the final definers of material and cultural conditions are the
people who live with them—never the theorists who impute different
objective or subjective effects on the basis of predetermined factors. Table 1 serves only to illustrate a point about the complexity of collective
movements; it suggests only an array of possible lived conditions. The
Table should be used in an attempt to understand the perspective of
participants in collective movements and the meaning of interacting
structural conditions as these impinged upon them. In developing this
typology I have assumed that no person or segment of a population
necessarily is always affected by either interests or culture in a manner
consistent with that described by the theorist. Obviously I have assumed,
too, that no individual lives solely in the world of mundane interests or
in the spirituality of cultural beliefs. Rather, both are simultaenously
operative in every act of every individual.

Third, as a result, Table 1 and typology it summarizes must be conceived of as heuristic and not some kind of structural-analytic scheme.
The table is best described in Blumer's phrase as a "sensitizing concept,"
that is, as a cognitive map by which we may orient ourselves to the
interpretive perspectives of different people, their various interests and
ideologies as these emerge in revolutionary situations. This means, that
I would not be surprised or dismayed if the typology did not hold up
or satisfactorily describe every instance of revolutionary change, or that
it would not have to be altered, or could not yet be further refined in
terms of other data.

There is always more that can be said, but the point is made. The
complexity is there; it is unavoidable. For example, it explains the
uniqueness of instances and, hence, the well-known difficulties of theories to particularize collective actions. The complexity is so unyielding
and regular that, in my opinion, it accounts for the different stances that
I have described in the introduction.

Each theorist focuses on a slice of the revolutionary reality in an effort
to get a handle upon the overwhelmingly complex social world. But by
proceeding in this manner, theorists distort the world, creating versions

of objective circumstances and subjective motives they wish to envision as occuring or having occured. The solution to the problems of social theory cannot come from arbitrary imposition of exclusive theoretical positions. Instead it must come from a frank confrontation with personally lived experiences of individuals in revolutionary circumstances. Adventures and romances, pretensions to exclusive insight on the basis of excessive simplification, will get us nowhere.

NOTES

1. This paper was first given as a talk sponsored by the Institute for the Advanced Study in the Humanities, the University of Massachusetts, Amherst, February 17, 1983. The talk was entitled, "Revolutions: Conditions for Their Occurrence," and was a shorter version of the present paper. Parts of this talk were previously published in a paper entitled "Conditions for Collective Action: Material and Cultural influences," in Michael Lewis and JoAnn Miller (eds.) *Social Problems and Public Policy, Vol. III.* Greenwich, Conn.; JAI Press, 1984. As always I want to thank my colleague Fred Weinstein for his comments, criticism, and editorial help with this paper.

2. Davies (1962:5-18) points out that there appears to be only one passage in Marx and Engel's writing where the deprivation formulation is couched in relative terms. Marx suggested that there are times of affluence when workers receive more economic resources but still their interests are less satisfied than those of the capitalists. They suffer an increasing relative deprivation because, as Marx points out, we measure our desires and pleasures against those of society in which we exist.

3. The best overview of de Tocqueville on revolution can be found in Melvin Richter's "Tocqueville's Contributions to the Theory of Revolution" (1966:75-121).

4. In a recent article, Charles Tilly suggests that Durkheim's formulations are useless for explaining collective actions. Tilly synopically presents findings to substantiate this point. However, he does not offer any detail regarding his methods for operationalizing his data. Should Tilly have derived his data from sources external to the experiences of the collective participants, it is not surprising that he found little relation between anomic culture and collective action (Tilly, 1981).

5. I have not taken the time or space in this article to discuss other types of charismatic leadership that arose during the French Revolution. Robespierre was only one example of such leadership, the most frequently referred to charismatic figure in the French Revolution. Charles Camic, in the following article, discusses several types of char-

ismatic leaders. Obviously, in my own conceptual terms, I would expect changing forms of charismatic leadership to occur with varying material and cultural conditions faced by different populations during crisis circumstances.

BIOGRAPHICAL NOTE

Gerald M. Platt was born in Brooklyn, New York, and grew up in Brooklyn and Manhattan. He went to Brooklyn College and majored in sociology and psychology. After college, he did graduate work in sociology at the University of California, Los Angeles. Professor Platt teaches at the University of Massachusetts, Amherst, where he offers courses in sociological theory. His research interests in the past few years have been in social change and collective behavior. Among his published works are: *The Wish to Be Free, Society, Psyche, and Value Change:* "Thoughts on a Theory of Collective Action: Language, Affect, and, Ideology in Revolution," in *New Directions in Psychohistory; The Adelphi Papers in Honor of Erik H. Erikson*, M. Albin (ed.).

REFERENCES

AYDELOTTE, W. O., BOGUE, A.G. FOGEL, R.W.
  1972 The Dimensions of Quantitative Research in History. Princeton: Princeton University Press.
BILLINGTON, J. H.
  1980 Fire in the Minds of Men: Origins of the Revolutionary Faith. New York: Basic Books.
DAVIES, J. C.
  1962 "Toward a Theory of Revolution." American Sociological Review 27: 5–18.
DURKHEIM, E.
  1933 The Division of Labor in Society. New York: Macmillan.
  1951 Suicide: A Study in Sociology. Glencoe, Ill: The Free Press.
FREUD, S.
  1951 Group Psychology and the Analysis of the Ego. New York: Liveright.
FURET, F.
  1981 Interpreting the French Revolution. New York: Cambridge University Press.
GEERTZ, C.
  1983 "Center, Kings, and Charisma: Reflections on the Symbolics of Power," pp. 121–146 in C. Geertz, Local Knowledge, Further Essays in Interpretive Anthropology. New York: Basic Books.
HABERMAS, J.
  1975 Legitimation Crisis. Boston: Beacon Press.
LEBON, G.
  1960 The Crowd, A Study of the Popular Mind. New York: Viking Press.
LIPSET, S. M.
  1963 The First New Nation, The United State in Historical and Comparative Perspective. New York: Basic Books.

MARX, K.
1935 The Class Struggles in France: 1848–1850. New York: International Publishers.
1964 The Eighteenth Brumaire of Louis Bonaparte. New York: International Publishers.

PLATT, G. M.
1980 "Thoughts on a Theory of Collective Action: Language, Affect, and Ideology in Revolution," pp. 69–94 in M. Albin (ed.), New Directions in Psychohistory, The Adelphi papers in Honor of Erik H. Erikson. Lexington, Mass. Lexington Books.

RICHTER, M.
1966 "Tocqueville's Contributions to the Theory of Revolution," pp. 75–121 in C. J. Friedrich (ed.), Revolution, Nomos VIII, Yearbook of the American Society for Politics and Legal Philosophy. New York: Atherton Press.

SCHRECKER, P.
1966 "Revolution as a Problem in the Philosophy of History," pp. 34–52 in C. J. Friedrich (ed.), Revolution, Nomos VIII, Yearbook of the American Society for Political and Legal Philosophy. New York: Atherton Press.

SHAPIRO, G., AND DAWSON, P.
1972 "Social Mobility and Political Radicalism: the Case of the French Revolution of 1789," pp. 159–191 in W. O. Aydelotte, A. G. Bogue, and R. W. Fogel (eds.), The Dimensions of Quantitative Research in History. Princeton: Princeton University Press.

SKOCPOL, T.
1979 States and Social Revolutions, A Comparative Analysis of France, Russia, and China. London and New York: Cambridge University Press.

TILLY, C.
1964 The Vendée. Cambridge: Harvard University Press.
1981 "Useless Durkheim," pp. 95–108 in C. Tilly, As Sociology Meets History. New York: Academic Press.

DE TOCQUEVILLE, A.
1856 The Old Regime and the French Revolution. Trans. J. Bonner. New York: Harper.

WALZER, M.
1969 The Revolution of the Saints, A Study in the Origins of Radical Politics. New York: Atheneum.

WEBER, M.
1978 "Charismatic Authority," pp. 241–246; "The Routinization of Charisma," pp. 246–254; "The Transformation of Charisma in a Democratic Direction," pp. 266–271 in G. Roth and C. Wittich (eds.) Max Weber Economy and Society. Berkeley: University of California Press.

WEINSTEIN, F.
1980 The Dynamic of Nazism, Leadership, Ideology and the Holocaust, New York: Academic Press.

WEINSTEIN, F., AND PLATT, G.M.
1969 "Robespierre: the Retreat to Authority." The Wish to be Free, Society, Psyche, and Value Change, pp. 108–136. Berkeley: University of California Press.
1969 The Wish to Be Free, Society, Psyche and Value Change, Berkeley: University of California Press.
1973 Psychoanalytic Sociology, An Essay on the Interpretation of Historical Data and the Phenomena of Collective Behavior. Baltimore: Johns Hopkins University Press.

Charisma: Its Varieties, Preconditions, and Consequences*

CHARLES CAMIC

SUMMARY

This paper explores the preconditions for, the nature of, and the consequences of charisma—factors that must be understood for charisma to be a useful empirical and theoretical concept. Unfortunately, as the first section of this essay demonstrates, due primarily to the influence of certain of Max Weber's discussions of charisma, sociological progress in these areas has been limited. However, drawing on two neglected hints by Weber—that the preconditions for the phenomenon of charisma are *extraordinary human needs* and that Freud's work can illuminate this field of inquiry—the second section of this essay attempts to correct this state of affairs through an application of the results of much psychoanalytic investigation. It argues that, because extraordinary needs (the preconditions for charisma) are of various types, charisma must be differentiated into four phenomena—omnipotence, excellence, sacredness, and the uncanny—and it then tentatively specifies both their variable immediate and long-range consequences. In so doing, it incorporates systematically many of the widely divergent findings reported in sociological research.

[O]ne difficulty . . . in theoretical sociology generally is that so much research proceeds upon the mistaken supposition that the linguistic repetition of concepts establishes their material identity to their contents or their logical constancy in use. Again and again sociologists continue to fall into a trap of treating the same word as though it necessarily included or comprised the same contents. [B. Nelson (1973:88–9).]

OVER a half century ago, Max Weber taught that the "formulation" and the "theoretical differentiation" of analytical concepts to capture aspects of the concrete social world are of central significance for the advance of sociology toward "a causal explanation of some historically and culturally important phenomena" (1922:19–20).[1] "Charisma",[2] Weber suggested, is one such differentiated and "relatively unambiguous" concept that promotes this goal (1922:216).

At one level, the logic of Weber's procedure seems to articulate well with analyses of the structure of scientific theories that have been offered by later philosophers of science, who argue that within a developed theoretical system certain basic and differentiated elements, known as primitives, are treated simply as given and all subsequent explanations are then stated in ways reducible to the irreducible basic terms. They insist, however, that before a term can be taken as a primitive, it must be antecedently clear to the relevant scientific community. Before this criterion is satisfied several other criteria must be met. Three of these are most important: The empirical referent of the term must be simple or homogeneous, the conditions under which it enters the theoretical system must be known, and its functions in that system must be specified in a consistent manner (that is, one must know specifically what it explains, see Rudner, 1966). Weber, when he insisted upon the relatively unambiguous conceptual status of the term "charisma," seems to have offered it as a primitive for subsequent sociological analysis.

An examination of the work of Weber and post-Weberian sociologists reveals that the empirical referent of the term "charisma" is anything but homogeneous and that the conditions under which charisma arises and the functions attributed to it are anything but antecedently clear to the sociological community. Given this situation, the process of "theoretical differentiation" that Weber advocated must be carried several steps further. This essay will attempt to do this while incorporating the diverse empirical evidence on the variety of empirical manifestations of charisma, their sources, and their consequences. It will be shown that some neglected hints by Weber on the conditions in which charisma emerges, when supplemented by the insights offered by Freud and subsequent psychoanalytic investigators, allow one not only to move beyond Weber's general formulation of the conditions in which charisma arises, but to differentiate several varieties of charisma and, thus, to comprehend its diverse consequences. Lest it be thought that such an undertaking violates the spirit of Weber, it is not inappropriate to recognize that Weber himself, after reading Freud, stressed the "altogether unconscious and seldom fully conscious" sources of charisma (1922:24) and wrote that "there can be no doubt that Freud's thought *can* become a very significant source for the interpretation of a whole series of phenomena in cultural history" (cited by Marianne Weber, 1926:376). This essay will attempt to show that here again the master was correct.

Here it should be stressed that throughout this essay only one of three possible perspectives on charisma will be employed. Charisma will be viewed in a relational context. It will be seen as the central content of a relationship between (1) certain persons or objects and (2) individuals or groups of individuals who attribute something special (that is, what is termed "charisma") to them. Though Weber was not fully consistent here, this approach to the analysis of charisma reflects, as Bendix (1960:313) has demonstrated, Weber's own considered approach to the topic. The relational perspective is also the one employed by Freud in the writings investigated below (see Rieff, 1954:204) and parallels what is termed the sociological perspective on charisma in contemporary sociological literature. While valuable, a second perspective (currently dubbed psychological), which examines the careers and personalities of selected charismatic leaders, will not be employed (on the sociological and psychological perspectives see, for example, Friedland, 1964; Jones and Anservitz, 1975). A third perspective, which could be called structural, because it examines either the organizational structure of groups headed by charismatic figures or the structure of interpersonal relations found among various followers of such figures or among the rank-and file members of charismatic communities, will likewise receive little attention.[3]

THE SOCIOLOGY OF CHARISMA

A concept in developed scientific theories is clear—it denotes simple or homogeneous phenomena in the empirical world whose sources and consequences are well specified. Before such development occurs, there is frequently a poor articulation between a concept and the phenomena it represents. At this stage, a concept is often too broadly conceived. Dissensus of necessity emerges concerning the sources and consequences of the phenomena denoted by the concept, for it represents not simple phenomena at all, but a variety of different phenomena with different sources and consequences. This stage in scientific development is not to be condemned—it is inevitable. It can become problematic for empirical research, however, when it is denied, when investigators prematurely assume that their concepts do capture, in a full and differentiated manner, the world out there. Broadly speaking, this has been the fate of "charisma."

Though Weber mentions the concept of "charisma" in *The Protestant Ethic* and in his specialized sociologies of religion, his most exhaustive analytical discussions of it appear in *Economy and Society*. Here he offers not one but three separate treatments of this topic, composed at different points in his career. Unfortunately, as the following examination of these three in chronological order will reveal, when taken together Weber's analyses of "charisma" reveal anything but that its empirical referent is homogeneous or that its sources and consequences are clearly specified (see Parsons, 1937:658–77; 1947:75–6; 1963:xxxii–xxxvi)—difficulties that have plagued most subsequent examinations of this topic and prevented the concept from playing the central explanatory role Weber anticipated.

Fortunately, Weber's work also reveals a way in which to surmount these difficulties.

The oldest section of *Economy and Society* in which "charisma" appears is *The Sociology of Religion.* At the beginning of this work, when Weber is investigating magical action—action that is "predominantly economic," oriented to the acquisition of certain earthly benefits (1922:399–400)— he observes that primitive people performing magical acts,

> . . . distinguish between the greater or lesser ordinariness of the phenomena in question. For example, not every stone can serve as a fetish, a source of magical power. Nor does every person have the capacity to achieve the ecstatic states which are viewed, in accordance with primitive experience, as the pre-conditions for producing certain effects in meteorology, healing, divination, and telepathy. It is primarily, though not exclusively, these extraordinary powers that have been designated by such *special* terms as "mana," "orenda" and. . . "maja". . . We shall henceforth employ the term "charisma" for such extraordinary powers (1922:400; emphasis added).

Though "charisma" here seems to denote simply extraordinary powers, closer scrutiny reveals something else about the phenomena represented by the term. Intrinsically, stones do not have extraordinary magical powers. Rather, these are imputed to certain stones by certain individuals. Their specialness is in the eyes of the beholders. That is, "charisma," for Weber, is a generic label for attributions of specialness, or extraordinary power, to certain persons or objects. This is how it will always be employed in this essay.

Three features of Weber's discussion here should be emphasized. First, he does not question whether these attributions of specialness are all of one kind. Within the context of this single example of primitive magic, this is not particularly troublesome. However, as will be shown, this becomes quite problematic when attributions of specialness are identified in a variety of other contexts and then treated as if they were homologous to one another.[5]

Second, and most significantly, Weber indicates at this point much about the sources of charisma. Attributions of specialness result from the extraordinary needs of the primitives. That is, desired material ends—rain, health, and birth—that cannot be accomplished, the primi- tives believe, directly by their ordinary, routine acts are the preconditions for imputations of specialness to stones or persons with the perceived capacity to satisfy such extraordinary needs. When this is no longer the case, such attributions cease. Weber notes, for example, that "In contrast to the ordinary person. . . the magician is permanently en- dowed with charisma. . . [However, i]n the event of failure the magician possibly paid with his life" (1922:401, 427). Here and throughout *The Sociology of Religion* charisma is viewed as fundamentally rooted in ex- traordinary human interests (cf. Parsons, 1937:667) (which are found, he here implies, in most social orders (see Parsons, 1963)). The prophet, because of his perceived ability to provide a system of meaning through which the discrepancies of the world can be explained, is deemed char- ismatic: He seems to resolve another extraordinary human need, the problem of meaning. The fundamental connection Weber discerns here between extraordinary human needs and charisma has often been ne- glected but is of immense empirical and theoretical significance.

Third, Weber in *The Sociology of Religion* also analyzes in some detail certain consequences of charisma. He implies that the immediate result of specialness is the formation of a relationship between the need- gratifying charismatic person or object and the needy individuals. The sociologically noteworthy feature of this relationship is that such indi- viduals unquestioningly obey the commands of those they deem char- ismatic. Weber says little about why this should be so. His chief concern is with the long-range, historical consequences for social systems wrought by those who have been deemed charismatic (and their obedient follow- ers). In general, Weber attributes two functions to them: They can con- tribute to the maintenance of a normative order (here his chief illustration is the charismatic magician) or they can contribute to major alterations in a normative order (here the principal example is the re- ligious prophet). Whether the long-range consequences of charisma will be to promote social stability or to promote social change seems largely to depend—though Weber is not explicit here—upon whether or not the charismatic figure must set himself in opposition to the established order to "prove" himself, to meet the extraordinary needs of his follow- ers. The magician, in order to convince his followers that he can provide rain, generally must work within (thereby enhancing the legitimacy of) the existing normative order; the religious prophet, in order to provide solutions to problems of meaning, typically must break with (thereby subverting the legitimacy of) that order (see Parsons, 1963:xxxiii–xxxiv). Despite these vastly different historical effects, Weber holds that both are, in the eyes of those whose needs they gratify, genuinely charismatic.

Though compressed in certain respects, Weber's analyses in *The Sociology of Religion* of the phenomena denoted by the term "charisma," their sources, and consequences raise no serious theoretical or empirical problems. When one examines Weber's second discussion of charisma, in his sociology of legitimate rule (1922:1111–57), it initially appears that his views are merely an amplification of these analyses. However, three discontinuities between the two sets of writings dwarf their similarities. The first of these becomes evident when Weber emphasizes the "entirely heterogeneous" (1922:1111) nature of charisma. Attributions of specialness, he suggests, are not found only (as in *The Sociology of Religion*) in the "religious realm." Rather, "these phenomena are universal" (1922:1112). In Weber's view, such diverse figures as the "Nordic berserk," the "legendary Irish folk hero Cuchulain" (1922:1112), Saint Francis (1922:1113), the robber capitalist Henry Villard (1922:1118), the Puritan self-made man (1922:1139), and Teddy Roosevelt (1922:1130) are all genuinely charismatic. Now, to be sure, there is some similarity between all such figures—they were all considered in some way special by certain individuals. But, it is certainly arguable that, having said this, there remain major sociological differences between the specialness of a saint and that of a legendary folk hero, between (as Weber himself noted elsewhere) that of a robber capitalist and a Puritan self-made man. Perhaps in another context Weber would have decomposed this undifferentiated and "entirely heterogeneous" lot. Here, however, as throughout the sociology of authority, Weber is primarily interested in differentiating bureaucratic, patriarchal, and charismatic authority from one another and in articulating the differences in the organizational structures[6] associated with each vis-à-vis the others. His concern is not with internally differentiating the phenomena denoted by the concept of "charisma" (nor those denoted by the concepts of bureaucracy and patriarchalism for that matter (see Blau, 1963)) so that it could serve as the relatively unambiguous concept Weber hoped it would be.

A second discontinuity between Weber's earlier writings and those under consideration is equally important in this respect. Though Weber again notes—and again leaves unexplained—the immediate consequences of charisma ("the surrender if the faithful [followers] to the extraordinary [leader]" (1922:1115)), his position on the long-range consequences of charisma has been subtantially modified. Time and again he insists that "charisma is indeed the specifically creative revolutionary force of history" (1922:1117), that it "transforms all values and breaks all traditional and rational norms" (1922:1115). Though Weber still offers examples of charismatic elements in stable social orders (as in his discussions of the charisma of lineage, of office, and of kingship), though he argues that, after it has receded as a "creative force," "charisma remains a very important element of the social structure," legitimizing the existing social order (1922:1146), he simultaneously emphasizes that in such cases "pure" charisma has been lost (1922:1121–2). He notes that, while charisma may be "found in all areas of life" (1922:1117), outside of a revolutionary context "its essence and mode of operation are significántly transformed" (1922:1136). To a large extent, this conclusion is an artifact of Weber's comparative analysis of the organizational properties of various authority structures. This concern leads him to compare charismatic *movements* (which, in key respects, are unorganized and unstructured) with, for example, bureaucracies (which are the reverse) and then to conclude that because these differ in structural properties, genuine charisma itself, genuine attribution of specialness to need-gratifying persons or objects, must have by and large disappeared throughout social orders that have bureaucratically (or traditionally) organized authority structures. Thus, when he locates charisma in stable social orders, he tends, as Shils concludes, "to think of such charismatic patterns as lacking the genuinely charismatic elements and as greatly supported by [utilitarian] 'interest' in guaranteeing stable succession and legitimacy" (1965:202)—a view hardly consistent with explanations of social stability found in *The Sociology of Religion* and thus hardly supportive of Weber's later assertion that his concept of "charisma" could provide sociology with an unambiguous explanatory tool.

Weber's extension of this concept to subsume a heterogeneous variety of extraordinary persons and his insistence on their revolutionary impact are bound up with a third—a more subtle and more important—departure from his earlier work. Though formally Weber still views extraordinary human needs as preconditions for imputations of specialness to need-gratifying persons (see especially 1922:1111), in practice, in this set of writings, these (and any other possible) sources of charisma are unexamined. Here Weber's comparative interests lead him to move facilely through human history, applying the term "charisma" to countless revolutionary figures. In the process, virtually no attention (or even mention) is given to the extraordinary needs (rain, birth, meaning, and so on) of the individuals who impute specialness to certain persons. This would be unobjectionable were the nature of their needs an obvious invariable, whose character could be inferred (if necessary) from Weber's earlier writings. But it is not obvious what extraordinary needs—let alone what invariable group of these—were met by members of his now greatly expanded list of illustrative charismatic figures, like the Nordic berserk, the robber capitalist Villard, and the Puritan self-made man. In other words, Weber is silènt concerning the preconditions for charisma, extraordinary human needs, in these and other examples. Indeed, unless one is alert, it is not even obvious that it is in the eyes of the needy, not in Weber's eyes, that these figures are charismatic, for his exposition tends inevitably to make one forget that they are the ones attributing specialness to those who gratify their, now unmentioned, extraordinary needs.

When Weber takes up "charisma" for a third time, in his famous discussion of the types of legitimate rule (1922:241–54), these difficulties concerning the homogeneity of its referents, their sources, and consequences become even more manifest, given the brevity of his remarks and the salience once again of the comparative analysis of different authority structures. First, as Weber's illustrations (1922:242) make clear, "charisma" again refers to any and all attributions of specialness. Weber himself remarks that for "present purposes it will be necessary to treat *a variety of different types* as being endowed with charisma in this sense" (1922:242; emphases added). Second, Weber gives virtually no attention to the sources of charisma. So long as individuals, "out of enthusiasm, or despair, and hope" (1922:242), recognize a person as powerful, this is enough for him to be genuinely charismatic. Why they should do so is a question Weber does not explicitly address. Indeed, beyond referring vaguely to some "miracle" and noting in passing that charismatic figures often "benefit. . . [their] followers" (1922:242), he gives no indication that such figures are regarded as special, are charismatic, *because* they gratify the extraordinary needs of others. In practice Weber's second formulation left unanalyzed the sources of charisma generally and extraordinary needs more specifically. Now these have disappeared even formally from his discussion. Third, Weber here again mentions without explaining the immediate consequence ("absolute trust in the leader" (1922:242)) of attributions of specialness by the needy to need-gratifying persons. Moreover, he is now completely unequivocal concerning long-run consequences: "Charisma is the great revolutionary force," opposing and repudiating existing social orders (1922:244–5). The attention Weber devotes to the order-maintaining consequences of charisma, so central in portions of *The Sociology of Religion*, is even less than in the sociology of authority. At one point, he does observe that charisma may become, through dissociation from particular revolutionary persons, "an objective transferable entity. . . [as in] the charisma of office" (1922:248), but even in such cases, he implies, "pure" charisma has given way "to the force of everyday routine" (1922:252). Perhaps had Weber not deleted those extraordinary human needs that are preconditions for genuine attributions of specialness from his formulation, he would have here recognized that (as he himself taught earlier) certain objects and persons within an established social order do meet extraordinary needs. As a result of this, the needy attribute specialness to them and obediently follow their dictates, thereby enhancing the legitimacy and stability of that order. Here, however, Weber takes a different route, one leading away from the evidence he supplied earlier and directly to the conclusion that the consequence of genuine charisma is necessarily revolutionary.

This third analysis of "charisma" by Weber constitutes part of "Conceptual Exposition," which is his synthesizing introduction to his earlier written analyses of it in *Economy and Society*. In an earlier section of this introduction Weber insists, as noted earlier, that "charisma" is a relatively unambiguous, or primitive, sociological concept, suitable for use in subsequent empirical analysis. That he advances this claim at this point it most remarkable, for it is at this very point that "charisma" satisfies none of the three criteria that must be met before a concept is acceptable as a primitive term. His final discussion of "charisma," especially when viewed in light of his previous work, indicates neither that the phenomena denoted by this term are simple or homogeneous, nor that their sources and consequences are consistently specified.

Nor, as the following three points will indicate, has this state of affairs been corrected in the half century since Weber. First, a brief glance at recent literature reveals that the undifferentiated term "charisma" is applied to a catalogue of personages even more variegated than Weber's own. Such diverse figures as Gandhi, Franklin Roosevelt (Willner and Willner, 1965), Sihanouk and Mao (Bendix, 1967), Saint-Simon (Jones and Anservitz, 1975), and professors, pimps, and pushers (Katz, 1975) are all charismatic. Edward Shils, perhaps the foremost analyst of charisma today, has gone further to argue that individuals impute charisma "to rules, norms, offices, institutions, and strata of any society" (1968:390), to certain central occupations, to wealth, to certain life styles, to education, to certain ethnic and religious group affiliations, and so on (1970), and even to "great occasions like the Coronation. . . Easter and Christmas" (1957:37). There has been no attempt to differentiate among all of these various attributions of specialness that "charisma" has been used to represent.

When one turns, secondly, to post-Weberian discussions of the sources of charisma, one discovers that *The Sociology of Religion* is rarely consulted and that Weber is accused, by those relying on his later remarks on charisma, of ignoring its antecedents (see, for example, Blau, 1963:304). To compensate for Weber's supposed neglect, contemporary sociologists have offered two, seemingly incompatible, interpretations of their own. One interpretation,[7] stated simply, suggests that social change is the precondition for charisma. More elaborately, it is argued that, whether it is viewed at the "macro" level (as in the widespread institutional collapse experienced in developing nations in the 50s and 60s) or at the "micro" level (as in the breakdown of old identities during adolescence), social change (which is variously conceptualized), the origins of which are attributed to a variety of non-charismatic factors, results in various types of cultural, social, and personal disruptions. Those persons who appear to end such disruptions by instituting a "new order," some different pattern of cultural, social, or personal arrangements, are, as a consequence, regarded as special or charismatic. The other interpretation, which explicitly objects to this one, suggests that the sources of charisma are located in the "inchoate sentiments" of individuals (Friedland, 1964), which exist, prior to social change, in "relatively ordered" social settings (Dow, 1969.:309; see also Berger, 1963; Dow, 1968). Those persons who can articulate and offer solutions for these sentiments are considered special (Friedland, 1964).

Of course, with the benefit of Weber's suggestions in *The Sociology of Religion* that extraordinary human needs are the preconditions for charisma and that such needs can exist in both changing and in "relatively ordered" social settings, one would have no difficulty integrating both of these interpretations, that is, in accounting systematically for attributions of specialness in both settings. Yet, a systematic analysis of extraordinary human needs as the preconditions for charisma is precisely what is lacking in sociological work on this question. Even when some opaque analysis of needs appears in this work (as in discussions of "inchoate sentiments"), they are introduced in an *ad hoc*, descriptive, and wholly incidental fashion. Never are they given the central attention Weber's earliest work demanded they be given and, thus, as in his own later work, the sources of charisma are nowhere consistently and comprehensively articulated.

It is now appropriate to turn, thirdly, to post-Weberian examinations of the consequences of charisma. Though it is everywhere implied that the immediate consequence of attributions of specialness is the formation of relationships where certain individuals automatically obey the dictates of those they deem special, nowhere has this outcome been explained. Moreover, rarely have sociologists sought to account for why charisma, the inherently revolutionary force in Weber's last writings, also prevented social change, according to this analysis in sections of *The Sociology of Religion*. Typically, Weber's inconsistent specification of the consequences of charisma is not noted and (as in the two interpretations of the sources of charisma just discussed) it is simply assumed that charisma does alter previous normative arrangements.

Despite appearances, this situation has scarcely been improved even by those few dissenting sociologists (notably Etzioni, 1961; Katz, 1975; and, above all, Shils, especially 1965; 1968) who emphasize the social stabilizing and legitimizing consequences of charisma. Shils, for example, argues that pure (rather than routinized) charisma is "an active and effective phenomenon essential to the maintenance of the routine order of society" (1968:390), that it "not only disrupts social order, it also maintains or conserves it" (1965:200). Yet, though Shils's argument serves as a valuable reminder of certain consequences of charisma that have generally been forgotten (even by Weber) since *The Sociology of Religion*, its result has not been to render the concept of "charisma" any more suitable as a primitive term in sociological analysis. If one argues that charisma can either "disrupt" or "conserve" a social order, it is necessary to specify in a consistent manner under what conditions charisma will produce one or the other consequence.[8]

Though one, at this juncture, might be tempted to endorse Ratman's claim that "the notion of 'charisma'. . . is not a useful one. . . it has not in any substantial way improved our understanding of the problems it touches on" (1964:341), the call to abandon "charisma" is premature. If the concept does not yet fulfill any of the criteria necessary before it can be accepted as the primitive term Weber took it for, his frequently neglected earliest work on the preconditions of these phenomena opens new possibilities.

PSYCHOANALYSIS AND THE SOCIOLOGY OF CHARISMA

"Writings that seek to apply the findings of psycho-analysis to topics" in the social sciences, Freud once observed, "have the inevitable defect of offering too little to readers of both classes,, (1912–13:75). Sadly, over sixty years later this situation still obtains. Doubtless to the concern of many sociologists, the preceding section treated certain concepts, like "social change" and "social order," as if they were everywhere accepted as unproblematic. Here, many psychoanalytic terms must be simplified and treated as also unproblematic, despite the conceptual chaos that currently reigns in psychoanalytic theory.

Even when psychoanalytic terms are treated as unproblematic, there remains the additional task of specifying which of the various, and disparate, viewpoints of psychoanalytic metapsychology (on these see Fenichel, 1945; Gedo and Goldberg, 1973; Rapaport and Gill, 1959) is most useful to sociological readers. Since the two fields may be, and have been, merged from a variety of perspectives (see Levine, 1977), it is necessary to stress that here the structural perspective of psychoanalytic theory, first articulated by Freud in *The Ego and The Id* (1923), will be primary, though, as will become clear, other perspectives will occasionally be used.[9] This choice is particularly convenient because it parallels that frequently made by Parsons (especially 1952; 1968) and his colleagues (especially Weinstein and Platt, 1973) in their efforts to integrate sociology and psychoanalysis (as will become apparent, much of their work has been incorporated herein), and thus its terminology should be reasonably familiar to the sociological community.

But why, in an essay on the problematics of "charisma," turn to Freud and psychoanalysis at all? The following three sections constitute the formal answers to this question. Here it may be put simply: The work of Freud and subsequent psychoanalytic investigators, in conjunction with the insights of Weber, permits one to begin to analyze systematically the preconditions of the phenomena denoted by the term "charisma," to differentiate these phenomena, and to specify consistently their various consequences.

THE PRECONDITIONS FOR CHARISMA

In *The Sociology of Religion*, Weber suggested that extraordinary human needs are the preconditions for attributions of specialness to those with the perceived capacity to satisfy such needs, but neither he nor later sociologists devoted systematic attention to these. The psychoanalytic structural model is particularly valuable at this juncture. This model, which conceptualizes the personality in terms of the ego, the id, and the superego, is a means "to group together mental processes and contents which are functionally related and to distinguish among these various groups on the basis of functional differences" (Brenner 1974:35).[10] Though the contents and processes associated with the ego, the id, and the superego have been conceptualized in a variety of ways (and occasionally reified) by Freud and others, following Schafer (1968a) the id, the superego, and the ego will here be taken as conceptual categories designating groups of functionally related motives or *needs*. Though this structural model has not yet been systematically validated in all cultural settings, the specific nature of the needs (and their salience and organization) associated with all three "structures" has been shown to vary substantially as a consequence of sociocultural learning and experience throughout the life cycle (see Erikson, 1950; Parsons, 1952; Schafer, 1967; 1968a; Weinstein and Platt, 1973).

Despite this variability, psychoanalytic research offers certain characterizations of the general contents typically associated with each component of the structural model. The individual needs designated in psychoanalysis by the term id are, on the one hand, "the full satisfaction of sexual and aggressive wishes" and, on the other hand, "a great variety of more or less infantile wishes and their close derivatives that have been rejected by ego and superego tendencies because it would be too dangerous to the persons to acknowledge and act on them" (Schafer, 1967:139–40). In certain sociocultural environments, the derivatives of libidinal and aggressive needs may assume such complex forms as the "wish to be free" (see Weinstein and Platt, 1969).

The needs referred to by the term superego are to fulfill the moral standards and to conform to the moral restrictions (including restrictions on id needs) of a given social order, which have been internalized as a consequence of identification with parents and other significant figures (see Freud, 1933:60–65; Rapaport, 1957a; Schafer, 1967).

The needs captured by the term ego are considerably more troublesome, given the problematic nature of psychoanalytic ego-psychology. What seems to be meant by expressions like "ego interests" is not one but two analytically distinct classes of needs, paralleling Freud's (1914) distinction between the "anaclitic" and "narcissistic" aspects of the ego. The first type, here termed dependency needs, includes the need for protection, for certainty, for physical security, and for meaning (see Slater, 1966:7–21; Parens and Saul, 1971). These seem to have been Weber's concern when he illustrated his notion of human needs in *The Sociology of Religion*. The second type of ego needs, here labeled ego-ideal needs,[11] are for achievement and attainment (in terms of prevailing cultural standards), for mastery, self-regard, and so on (see Lampl-de Groot, 1962; Schafer, 1967).

Even with this brief introduction, it becomes apparent that, by offering a systematic analysis of human needs, the psychoanalytic structural model supplies precisely what is absent in sociological discussions of the preconditions of charisma. Lacking such a model, these discussions have either neglected needs altogether or introduced them in a random and *ad hoc* manner (as in "inchoate sentiments"). The psychoanalytic model specifies, in a comprehensive, yet delimited, manner, what such needs (or "inchoate sentiments") are. It directs those investigating the preconditions for charisma not only to ungratified dependency needs (Weber's concern) but also to ungratified id needs, superego needs, and ego-ideal needs, for all such needs, *when extraordinary*, are the basis for attributions of specialness to need-gratifying persons or objects. Though this formulation may appear to render the array of preconditions for these attributions even broader than it is in the sociological literature, it will be argued below that the psychoanalytic perspective allows one to specify that a certain type of need is the precondition for a particular variety of charisma, while other types of needs are preconditions for different varieties.

Before turning to this, one other issue must be considered. Weber's expression when analyzing the preconditions for attributions of specialness was *extraordinary* needs. In his view, the satisfaction of ordinary needs does not lead to such attributions. Are the four generic types of needs discussed by psychoanalytic theory extraordinary? The answer is yes and no. Under certain conditions any need may become extraordinary, though none is extraordinary by definition. However, none is ordinary by definition either. Much like Weber, who, when discussing magical action among the primitives, argued that even what are conceived of as "economic" needs may, in certain sociocultural settings, be extraordinary for various individuals, one important line of psychoanalytic research suggests that it is not the nature of needs *per se*, but their dynamic condition within the socially-shaped human personality system that determines whether they are ordinary or extraordinary. This line of investigation deserves brief elaboration.

To provide this, one further psychoanalytic construct must be introduced—the Ego. Capitalized, this term will denote not a conceptual label for a system of needs (see above), but the supraordinate decision making, reality testing, regulatory agency (and its controls and apparatuses) of the personality system, which has been so thoroughly investigated by psychoanalytic ego (Ego) psychology since Freud (1923) and Hartmann (1939).[12] In relation to the various needs of the personality system (including ego that is, dependency and ego-ideal—needs) the Ego may, with some simplification, be characterized relatively as either active or passive (Rapaport, 1961; see also Fromm, 1972; Rapaport, 1951; 1957b; Schafer, 1968b).[13] The Ego is active with respect to certain needs to the extent that, by employing its own apparatuses and controls, it either attains direct or indirect satisfaction of the needs in question in a manner consonant with reality and other conflicting needs or institutes defensive measures (the "defense mechanisms" of Anna Freud (1936) and others) preventing ungratified needs from significantly subverting its functioning. The Ego is passive with respect to certain needs to the extent that it fails to so control them with its own apparatuses and structures, to the extent that it is overwhelmed (in whatever degree) by such needs (of whatever type), and is thus dynamically helpless vis-à-vis them (cf. Rapaport, 1961:539-40; see also Fromm, 1972:239). Ordinary needs will here be differentiated from extraordinary needs according to whether the Ego is active or passive with respect to them. Rapaport offers an observation that confirms this equation: When the Ego is passive, those persons and objects that gratify its "extreme needfulness", are endowed by the needy "with a power the effect of which amounts to slavery and surrender" (1957b:731). With only the most minor changes in wording, this psychoanalytic formulation is identical to Weber's earliest analysis of charisma.

Thus, it is possible to restate Weber's formula that extraordinary human needs are preconditions of charisma as follows: When the Ego is passive with respect to certain dependency, or ego-ideal, or superego, or id needs, those who gratify the ungratified needs in question are considered to be special. But this is more than a return to Weber's initial analysis via psychoanalytic terminology. As noted above, this psychoanalytic perspective, when coupled with the analysis to follow in the next section, allows one to specify consistently the preconditions for various types of attributions of specialness. Even without this further step, this perspective allows one to incorporate systematically both of the putatively incompatible post-Weberian interpretations of these preconditions within a single analytical framework, as will now become apparent.

In discussing Ego passivity, nothing has been said thus far concerning *when* this dynamic condition obtains. What renders the Ego passive with respect to various needs? That is, under what conditions do needs, of any of the above mentioned types, become extraordinary? Psychoanalytic research and particularly Rapaport's work provide two answers, though these are rarely stated explicitly.

The first suggests that Ego passivity is a product of socialization processes. To develop this argument fully would entail the introduction of the genetic perspective of psychoanalysis (especially Hartmann, Kris, and Loewenstein, 1946). Here, however, it is sufficient to recall that Ego activity with respect to various needs exists when the Ego, by employing its own structures and controls (on these, see Hartmann, 1939; Brenner, 1974), satisfies or defends against the ungratified needs in question. The intricate processes of interaction between the personality system and its environments that promote the solid formation of these structures and controls—and the processes that subvert it and thus foster Ego passivity—have been, of course, a central concern of psychoanalytic work on Ego development, Ego autonomy, Ego strength, and so on. Though there is no easy way to summarize such material here, its general thesis should be stressed: The structure of the Ego, of the apparatuses and controls that condition its degree of activity or passivity with respect to various needs, is a complex consequence of the patterns of experience and learning that are part of all sociocultural systems (see Rapaport 1957b; 1961, for his refined version of this argument).

The second answer suggests that object loss can produce Ego passivity.

To understand this, one must introduce the psychoanalytic notion of object relations—"the ties between and among individuals and who- or whatever they invest in their environment with emotional significance" (Weinstein and Platt, 1973:102). Generally, the Ego, to the extent that it is *active* with respect to dependency, or ego-ideal, or superego, or id needs forms, stable object relations with persons or things that in some way satisfy the needs in question. Unfortunately, this happy situation often changes (as, for example, through the death of a loved one) and an individual loses an object that had satisfied his or her needs. The various possible reactions by the Ego to this situation and their determiriants are treated elsewhere.[14] Here it is sufficient to note that, in one typical response to the loss of an emotionally significant object, the Ego is "overwhelmed" (Engel, 1961:95; Pollock, 1961:347) and becomes "helpless" (Freud, 1926:121) or passive (see Rapaport, 1957b:729) with respect to the need to restore the object lost to the gratification of id needs, or superego needs, or ego-ideal needs, or dependency needs (on the "need for restitution," see Rochlin, 1965:1–163; see also Weinstein and Platt, 1973).

At this point, it should be obvious that the psychoanalytic contention that Ego passivity with respect to various types of ungratified need is the precondition for attributions of specialness, is consistent with—and renders consistent—both sociological interpretations of the sources of charisma that were discussed in Section I. Since the socialization processes inherent in "relatively ordered" social settings render the Ego passive with respect to certain needs, it is not surprising that one sociological interpretation reports that charisma has emerged in such settings. since Ego passivity with respect to certain needs is also a typical response to object loss, it is also little wonder that the other sociological interpretation reports that periods of social change are preconditions for charisma. This is so because, as Marris (1973) and Weinstein and Platt (1973) have demonstrated, in times of social changes and disruptions discussed by those sociologists who advance this latter interpretation, individuals lose (depending on the level at which the change occurs) meaningful leaders, institutions, roles, identities, and so on. Freud observed long ago (1917:164) that humans react to losses such as these much as they do to the loss of other, significant and valued, need-gratifying objects. Thus, since Ego passivity with respect to various needs arises in both ordered and changing social settings, both, despite their sociological differences, contain the seed of attributions of specialness.[15]

However, to notice the obvious correspondence between psychoanalytic discussions of when Ego passivity develops and sociological interpretations of when charisma emerges is not to endorse the adequacy of the latter. The argument of this section, to repeat; states that when the Ego is passive, when individuals are helpless, *with respect to various needs*, those who gratify the ungratified needs in question are deemed special in various ways. If the two sociological interpretations together correspond to the psychoanalytic interpretation of when the Ego will be passive, they both fail to articulate the needs with respect to which the Ego is passive. Yet, unless one knows whether it is dependency, or ego-ideal, or superego, or id needs that are extraordinary,[16] it is not possible to specify satisfactorily the preconditions for various attributions of specialness. The psychoanalytic framework, by identifying both when needs are extraordinary and what these needs are (or may be), allows one to accomplish this—as will now become evident.

THE VARIETIES OF CHARISMA

By identifying four types of specialness that extraordinarily needy individuals—depending on whether they are dynamically helpless with respect to dependency, or ego-ideal, or superego, or id needs—attribute to those who in some way gratify their needs, Freud's work enables one to theoretically differentiate the concept of "charisma." Before examining these varieties of charisma, one comment is necessary: Throughout this discussion selected sociological illustrations will be provided in order to demonstrate that Freud's analysis allows one to differentiate systematically the vast array of charismatic phenomena. However, because empirical examples can rarely correspond perfectly to the pure strains isolated by psychoanalytic theory, these illustrations will, of necessity, not be apt in every respect.[17] This issue will be explicitly addressed at the end of this section. The examples are offered only as hypothesized approximations in this examination of Freud's discussions of the various phenomena called "charisma," the four varieties of attributed specialness.

The precondition for the first of these is extraordinary dependency needs. These had been Weber's starting point for his analysis of attributions of specialness in *The Sociology of Religion*. In *Totem and Taboo* (1912–13), Freud, investigating, as Weber had, the relationship between magic and such needs, also introduces his first variety of attributed specialness—*omnipotence*. Freud begins his analysis of magic at an earlier cultural stage than Weber had. He observes that at this stage magic and magical rituals are devices employed by the primitives to gratify certain great dependency needs: the need for rain and fertility (note the similarity with Weber), the need for protection from enemies, and so on

(1912–13:78–80). He comments that, "It is easy to perceive the motives which lead men to practice magic: they are [such] human wishes. All we need to suppose is that primitive man had an immense belief in the power of his wishes. The basic reason why what he sets about by magical means comes to pass is, after all, simply that he wills it" (1912–13:83). This belief in the power of will and thought to satisfy such dependency needs is termed by Freud the "omnipotence of thoughts." But, he continues, cultural development soon alters this pattern of thought, rendering individuals helpless with respect to such needs. At this point (where Weber takes up his analysis), when their own thoughts are no longer seen to satisfy their needs, individuals "transfer" omnipotence—"charisma" in Weber's language—to external objects, often to their gods (1912–13:88). At still later stages of cultural development (those of central concern to Weber), as fertility and rain become increasingly ordinary needs, the need for solutions to problems of meaning, Freud (1927) argues, emerges and leads, certain individuals, helpless with respect to this dependency need, to attribute to those objects who in some way gratify it, omnipotence (cf. Pruyser, 1973:253). This essay, when referring to attributions of specialness, to need-gratifying persons and objects, that result from extraordinary dependency needs, will substitute for Weber's general term "charisma" the term Freud employed when treating the same topics that led Weber to introduce his term—that is, omnipotence.

One may hypothesize that this phenomenon is represented both by certain Weberian examples of charismatic figures—the magician, the prophet, the "war-lord" (1922:1114), and certain "political heroes" (1922:1113), including his Teddy Roosevelt—and by much that is termed charismatic in contemporary social scientific discussions—modern political and military leaders, Franklin Roosevelt, Churchill, Washington, the young Mao, the young Sihanouk (on these last three, see Bendix, 1967), and by certain modern "secular, economic, governmental, and political" organizations (Shils, 1965:207 sees these as charismatic). In addition to these "macro" level examples, one should recall Bion's (1959:94) reports of attributions of omnipotence by members of small groups to those group members who seem to gratify their dependency needs. Slater (1966) records similar "micro" level illustrations of omnipotence.

Freud's analysis of omnipotence is but a fragment of his investigations of attributions of specialness. But, unlike Weber, Freud, when examining attributions of specialness whose precondition is not extraordinary dependency needs and whose object is, thus, not those who gratify these,

no longer uses the term omnipotence. For the related, but distinct, phenomenon, the attribution of specialness whose precondition is extraordinary ego-ideal needs, this essay follows Freud (1914; 1921) and
employs the term *excellence*. In his analysis of "narcissistic personalities"
(1914),[18] Freud observes that when "narcissistic gratification encounters
actual hindrances", or, to simplify somewhat, when an individual is helpless with respect to ego-ideal needs, he displaces onto those "whom he
once was and no longer is, or else someone who possesses excellences
he never had at all" (1914:81) the excellence he would otherwise attribute
to himself (1914; 74 1921:57; see also Kohut, 1971; Tartakoff, 1966).

One can suggest that many sociological examples of charisma are more
precisely instances of "excellence." Here one would include the charisma
that, according to Shils (1970), individuals attribute to certain prestigious
occupations and religious and ethnic affiliations, to certain lifestyles, to
wealth and education, the charisma that Katz (1975) sees imputed to
those with superior ability (like university professors), the charisma that,
according to Weber (1922), the puritans attributed to the self-made man,
and the charisma that the popular press suggests is imputed to the "beautiful people." Of course, in illustrations such as these, the excellent persons are not *directly* meeting ego-ideal needs. Much of the gratification
to the needy provided by those who have succeeded, who have "made
it," and who are thus regarded as excellent, is of a vicarious sort. However, though this element, as will be shown in the next section, affects
the *consequences* of relationships between the needy and those who gratify
their needs, it in no way denies that the attribution of specialness in such
cases is genuine. Having noted this, it is also essential to recognize that
gratification for those with extraordinary ego-ideal needs is not always
of this vicarious sort. Tartakoff (1966), drawing on a variety of psychoanalytic case studies, reports that relationships, nearly identical in
phenomenological description to Weber's description of charismatic relationships, have been formed between, on the one hand, college students, research workers, teachers, and members of many professions
(individuals, she notes, with great and frequently overwhelming ego-
ideal needs) and, on the other hand, those excellent persons who have
gratified their needs directly by recognizing and promoting their
successes and attainments. Sociological discussions of imputations of excellence and their consequences, which are central aspects of many task-
oriented social settings, have been surprisingly infrequent.

The opposite has been the case with the third type of attributed specialness, for which extraordinary superego needs are the preconditions.
To designate this phenomenon, the term *sacredness* will, following Freud
(1939:153–6), be employed. When the Ego, frequently as a result of

conflicting needs of other components of the personality system (especially id wishes), has become passive with respect to superego needs,
those persons or things that gratify these needs, that somehow fulfill or
reinforce internalized moral demands or perpetuate moral prohibitions,
are invested by the needy with sacredness (cf. Freud, 1939:156; Pruyser,
1973:263).

It was noted earlier (see fn. 4) that Parsons (1947:75–6) has compared
Weber's "charisma," with Durkheim's (1912:51–63) concept of the sacred, while Shils (1965:205) has identified it with Otto's (1917) parallel
notion of the holy. Given such comparisons, it has come about that those
listed in the sociological catalogue of sacred persons and things—religious rites, dogmas, and symbols, the pope, the church hierarchy, Jus-
tices of the Supreme Court, presidents, Gandhi, Moses, Queen Elizabeth,
ceremonial institutions like Christmas, Easter, and the Coronation, national flags and anthems, legal institutions, societal norms, even all that
is meant by "tradition"— have been taken as illustrations of charisma
(for convenience, many of these examples have been taken from Shils
(1957; 1958; 1965), who uses "charisma" and "sacred" almost inter-
changeably). To the extent that these objects are in fact deemed special
by those with extraordinary super ego needs, they can also be offered
here as relevant illustrations of Freud's concept of the sacred. Indeed,
Freud himself notes that, because, for some, they gratify extraordinary
superego needs by reinforcing certain internalized moral standards of
a society, "Everything connected with religion [its dogma, its rites, and
practices]. . . is sacred. . . [as are certain] persons, institutions, and procedures that have little to do with religion" (1939:154; see also Freud,
1907; Pruyser, 1973). But from Freud's work one gleans more than
illustrations of the sacred type of charisma. One also learns that equations
between Weber and Durkheim and Otto are misleading, for charisma
and the sacred are not equivalent. When imputations of specialness result
from extraordinary superego needs, and only then, do these imputations
represent the phenomenon of sacredness. When extraordinary needs
are of other types, Freud's work suggests, then the imputations to those
gratifying these needs, though genuine, are *not*, as should now be obvious, of the sacred variety.

Particularly neglected by those who fuse charisma with the sacred are
attributions of specialness for which extraordinary id needs are the preconditions. Though there are more evocative terms for this phenomenon
in English than the *uncanny*—the typical translation for Freud's *unheim-
lich*—this essay will employ this designation. It is a fourth variety of
charisma (cf. McIntosh, 1969:902). Indeed, Freud's description of the
uncanny sounds remarkably like Weber's description of charisma:

We... call... person[s] uncanny... when we ascribe... to... [their] intentions capacity to achieve their aim in virtue of certain special powers... The ordinary person sees in them the workings of forces hitherto unsuspected in his fellow-man but which at the same time he is dimly aware of in a remote corner of his own being. [1919:49]

The remote corner to which Freud refers in the last phrase designates, he explains, the id, those and aggressive wishes and their infantile derivatives, with respect to which the Ego is often powerless principally because they have been partially repressed by a variety of socializing agencies (1919:38, 47, 54). Those who in some way gratify these wishes are seen, by the needy, as uncanny.

Particularly interesting examples of this phenomenon are—or so one may hypothesize—the well-known instances of misbehavior, sexual promiscuity, and rebellion on the part of film stars (from James Dean and Brando to Belmondo and Nicholson), entertainers (Rolling stones, Alice Cooper, Janice Joplin, Lenny Bruce), criminals (Manson, Bonnie and Clyde, gangsters from the 30s), and so on, which the media make so much of in discussing charisma (for further illustrations, see Klapp, 1969; see also Freud, 1919). Certain of Weber's examples of charisma—the robber capitalist, the Irish folk hero, the Nordic berserk—seem relevant here, as do Katz's (1975:1386) examples of charismatic pimps and pushers. Based on his psychoanalytic observations, Redl (1942) supplies a charming account of this phenomenon in small learning groups.

The preceding paragraphs have employed Freud's work to argue that four separate phenomena have been masked by employing Weber's concept of "charisma" to denote all attributions of specialness. Now it again must be emphasized that omnipotence, excellence, sacredness, and the uncanny refer to imputations by individuals with differing extraordinary needs to those who in some manner gratify them—they are not just convenient classificatory categories to be employed without reference to the needs of the individuals who impute the specialness in question. Weber in *The Sociology of Religion* taught that no figure can be classified *a priori* as special. For him, the magician's specialness was in the eyes of those whose extraordinary needs he gratified. In social orders where individuals had different extraordinary needs, the magician was no longer regarded as special. Freud's analysis demands that one extend Weber's lesson: No figure can be classified *a priori* as omnipotent, excellent, sacred, or uncanny, even within the same social order. There are three interrelated reasons for this.

First, the very same figure to whom some impute specialness may be special in no way to others. Many of the above examples demonstrate this possibility: Certain persons in small task groups are at times considered omnipotent by those whose extraordinary dependency needs they gratify, but generally such persons are not special to those in the group with other needs, let alone to those outside of it. Second, the very same figure who is deemed special in one way by some individuals may be special in other ways to others. For some (those with extraordinary dependency needs) an American president may be omnipotent, while for others (those with extraordinary superego needs) he may be sacred; for some (those with extraordinary ego-ideal needs) a film star may be excellent, while for others (those with extraordinary id needs) he may be uncanny—possibilities that make life difficult for special persons, since they may lose the specialness they have for some through the very actions that meet the needs of others. Third, the very same figure may be regarded as special in a variety of ways by the same individuals, for individuals can have multiple extraordinary needs. For example, those who held Saint-Simon to be special (see Jones and Anservitz, 1975, whose excellent analysis is here put in the language of this essay) seem to have been a group with both extraordinary dependency and superego needs. since Saint Simon appeared to gratify both, they attributed, or so it seems, both omnipotence and sacredness to him—a situation that enhanced his initial appeal but rendered it highly unstable.

These three comments indicate that the extraordinary needs of the individuals who impute specialness to need-gratifying persons and objects introduce many empirical variations, making difficult any *a priori* attempts to utilize Freud's analyses of specialness for rigid classificatory purposes. But this is an advantage, not a limitation of these analyses. By focusing attention on the empirical variations in attributions of specialness—so long obscured behind Weber's undifferentiated term, "charisma"—they open sociologically significant areas of investigation, which thus far have been precluded. Extraordinary human needs (the preconditions for all attributions of specialness) are not randomly distributed, individual idiosyncracies. Rather, the variations in extraordinary needs in different times and places are socially structured, through both socialization processes and loss experiences. The sociologically obvious issue is what are the socially-patterned variations in resulting attributions of specialness? What, that is, is the social location of the phenomena of omnipotence, excellence, sacredness, and the uncanny? Where—in traditional or modern, capitalist or socialist societies, among what ethnic, religious, occupational, and educational groups, at what stages of the life cycle—will attributions of specialness to need-gratifying objects be of the sacred, or omnipotent, or excellent, or uncanny variety? Where will no attributions of specialness be found? Does the process of social differentiation reduce the likelihood that any one person or object can be regarded as special in multiple ways simultaneously, either by the same or different individuals? Sociologists have long enriched their understanding of other phenomena—alienation, crime, formal organization, social mobility, the community, urbanization, modernization—by differentiating these and exploring their socially-patterned vicissitudes. Freud's work allows one to do the same with the phenomena designated by the concept of "charisma."

THE CONSEQUENCES OF CHARISMA

Freud's analyses of attributions of specialness raise another question: What are the respective consequences of attributions of omnipotence, excellence, sacredness, and the uncanny to need gratifying persons and objects? This question can be answered satisfactorily only by empirical research designed to investigate the variable consequences of these various attributions. Because, as section I indicated, the tendency in sociological analyses of charisma, from Weber's later work onward, has been simply to posit, in advance of empirical investigation, what the consequences of attributions of specialness are, rather than to take them as empirically problematic and variable, this section cannot attempt an adequate answer to this question. Instead, it will employ psychoanalytic theory to examine sociological assumptions concerning the consequences of charisma and, in so doing, identify the factors that must be investigated before one can consistently specify the consequences of various attributions of specialness.

It will be convenient to begin by considering the immediate consequences of attributions of specialness. So that he could account for why charisma produces the long-range consequences he attributed to it, Weber, it will be recalled, noted first its immediate result: the formation of a relationship—with sociologically distinctive features—between the extraordinarily needy and those who in some way gratified their needs. Jones and Anservitz nicely summarize the two distinctive aspects of this relationship, as these have been posited, explicitly or implicitly, by both Weber and post-Weberian sociologists: first, the needy respond to the need-gratifying figure with attitudes of awe, devotion, reverence, and the like; second, the needy totally accept the figure's commands as morally binding and dutifully obey them (1975:1098).

What neither Weber nor others have explained is why either of these sets of responses obtain; their occurrence has simply been taken for granted. Now, no conceptual framework explains every thing; some things, insignificant or constant factors, must always be taken for granted. However, the responses under discussion are by no means insignificant—they are the crucial linkage between attributions of special-ness and their long-range consequences. Moreover, as psychoanalytic research, which has made the explanation of such responses a central concern, reveals, such responses are not constant results of attributions of specialness. The extent to which they obtain varies empirically and, thus, they cannot be taken for granted. The discussion of this psychoana-lytic research cannot be developed here in the full detail it deserves. Rather, two comments must suffice, one concerning each of the two sets of responses just described.

First, it is useful to outline the psychoanalytic explanation for why individuals respond to the need-gratifying figures they deem special with awe, reverence, and the like. The concept central to the explanation of these effects is transference,[19] which is usually described in the context of psychotherapy. Like the individuals discussed in this essay, the patient in therapy is extraordinarily needy, his Ego passive with respect to vari-ous needs, which the psychotherapist is frequently seen to gratify. In this situation, "The patient is not satisfied with regarding the ana-lyst. . . . as a helper and adviser who, moreover, is remunerated for the trouble he takes. . . . On the contrary, the patient sees in him the return, the reincarnation, of some important figure out of his childhood or past, and consequently transfers on to him feelings and reactions which un-doubtedly applied to this prototype" (Freud, 1949:31). The "prototype" Freud has in mind is the patient's idealized father—or mother, or brother (Freud, 1912:107). The extraordinarily needy patient responds to the analyst in a manner prefigured by early interaction with significant fam-ilial figures—with overidealization, blind belief, awe, reverence, self-sac-rifice, and so on (see Freud, 1912; 1915; 1921; 1940; Fenichel, 1945): Such responses sound much like those Weber and others have assumed to be consequences of attributions of specialness to need-gratifying fig-ures outside of psychotherapy, which is not surprising since Freud (es-pecially 1921) and others have demonstrated that transference does occur under such conditions. But psychoanalytic research on transfer-ence does more than supply an explanation for effects that Weber and others have merely assumed. It also reveals the limitations of their as-sumptions. Two points are necessary to develop this argument.

First, psychoanalytic research demonstrates that the degree to which the transference of childhood feelings and reactions onto need-gratify-ing figures occurs is variable. Transference is particularly marked in psychotherapy due to the form and content of social interaction between patient and analyst—its relatively constant and uniform character, the affective neutrality of the analyst, and so on (for fuller discussion of the variables promoting transference during analysis, see Fenichel, 1945:

especially 29–31). Variations in the form and content of social interaction outside of psychotherapy mitigate, in systematic ways, the transference of the responses under consideration (see Fenichel, 1945; Slater, 1966). For this reason, it is extremely misleading simply to posit that awe, devotion, and reverence are uniform and invariable consequences of attributions of specialness to need-gratifying figures. The extent to which such responses obtain is always a function of the social interaction between the extraordinarily needy and the figure they deem special. It must be determined empirically, not taken for granted.

Psychoanalytic research on transference qualifies sociological assumptions in a second way. This section has thus far focused on what is known as "positive transference," omitting mention of the concomitant process of "negative transference" (the classic discussion of this distinction is Freud, 1912). In psychotherapy, the patient transfers onto the analyst not only the affectionate attitudes that characterized his relationship with familial figures, but also the hostile feelings he felt toward them. In varying degrees, this occurs outside of analysis as well. Freud, for example, notes, in his discussion of responses to figures regarded as omnipotent, that "alongside of the veneration, and indeed the idolization, felt toward them there is the unconscious and opposing current of intense hostility" (1912–13:49). With few exceptions, this factor, hidden behind assumptions concerning positive responses like devotion and reverence, has been wholly neglected in sociological work on the consequences of attributions of specialness. Yet, if one is to understand these systematically, this factor is of central importance, as others have noted in different contexts. Otto argues that to comprehend at all the power of persons and objects deemed sacred, one must take account not only of the "feelings of gratitude, trust, love, reliance, humble submission, and dedication" (1917:8) with which individuals respond to them, but also of the fear, dread, terror, and unapproachability with which they are regarded (1917:12–24). Slater (1966:7–85) has shown that the negative feelings transferred onto figures seen as omnipotent in small groups are a major catalyst for later revolt against these figures—an observation that calls to mind Weber's observation that the same primitives who saw the magician as charismatic later took his life. The role of such feelings in the "routinization of charisma" could also be profitably explored, though this topic is outside the bounds of this essay. In any event, psychoanalytic research on negative transference—as well as that on positive transference—opens an array of critical empirical issues about certain of the immediate consequences of attributions of specialness that, following the example of Weber's work, have thus far been neglected.

It is now appropriate to consider, secondly, the other set of immediate responses to a special figure that has been assumed in sociological literature: that the needy individual accepts the figure's commands as morally binding and dutifully obeys them. That such effects obtain implies, in psychoanalytic terminology, that the content of the superego of the needy individual has changed through personal identification (on this process see Slater, 1961) with the special figure, that the figure's values and dictates have been internalized within the individual's personality as a set of moral standards he is compelled to fulfill. Though there are cases where extraordinarily needy adults do respond to the need gratifying persons they consider special in this way (see Freud, 1921), psychoanalytic research demonstrates that it would be incorrect to assert that this is the typical pattern of their response. Identification with a need-gratifying figure may, in degree, duration, and kind, fall far short of this form, which it is implicitly assumed to take in sociological literature (for a masterful discussion of these variations and their determinants, see Schafer, 1968a). A most interesting and relevant illustration here is what Weiss (1960:261–70) has aptly termed resonance identification,[20] a process that occurs when the gratification obtained from the need-gratifying figure is of a vicarious sort.[21] "In resonance identification," writes Weiss, the Ego "acknowledges that emotional contents which arise in another. . . [person] are only echoed within itself. . . Another person. . . enjoy[s] the satisfaction of these needs and desires which. . . [the Ego] cannot experience itself. Then it at least enjoys the other person's satisfactions vicariously through resonance identification" (1960:282, 264). A particularly noteworthy feature of this type of identification—which obtains quite frequently with respect to figures deemed special—is that, though it does lead to some temporary restructuralization of Ego apparatuses, it does *not* result in alterations of the contents of the superego (Weiss, 1960:269–70, 282). Thus, in cases of resonance identification with a need-gratifying figure, one would err in assuming that the needy accept his commands as morally binding and dutifully obey them.[22] The lesson of these remarks is clear: The nature of the identificational linkage between the needy and the figure they regard as special is variable and cannot be taken for granted.

With these remarks in view, the long-range consequences of charisma can at last be taken up. It has been observed that, after years under the influence of Weber's later work, which emphasized the revolutionary impact of charisma, certain sociologists have at last returned to the position he advanced in *The Sociology of Religion*, that, to use Shils's formula, charisma may either disrupt or conserve a social order. Such a formula was criticized for failing to specify under what conditions charisma will function in such divergent ways. Before detailing the direct bearing of the psychoanalytic framework of this essay on this question, two comments are in order.

First, it should again be observed that sociological discussions of such long-range consequences of charisma assume that its immediate consequences have already transpired in the manner that Weber postulated. One would not bother asking if a special figure and his obedient, reverent, and devoted followers disrupted or conserved a social order, if the figure had no obedient followers and those who regarded him as special felt more hostility than reverence toward him—though in such cases one might ask other questions about the ultimate consequences of attributions of specialness (see Katz, 1975, for an interesting beginning in this direction). To proceed with this discussion, it must here—but not in empirical investigations of the long-range consequences of charisma— be assumed that the immediate consequences of attributions of specialness have occurred in the way Weber assumed.

Second, it would be foolhardy in the extreme to suggest that the psychoanalytic considerations put forward in this essay can alone specify when special figures and their obedient followers will *succeed* in either conserving or disrupting a social order. *No* analysis of charisma could do this. Sociologies of charisma do not replace those of social movements, of social groups, of intergroup dynamics, of collective behavior, or of anything else. The ultimate effect of charisma depends on countless noncharismatic factors (cf. Oommen, 1967:99)—a point so obvious that it is often forgotten.

Within the limits set by these two qualifications, psychoanalytic considerations do enable one to move beyond the facile formula that charisma may either disrupt or conserve a social order to a preliminary specification (which awaits precise formulation in light of empirical research) of when special figures and the followers who have attributed specialness to them may produce these various consequences. As this essay has continually emphasized, the formation and maintenance of the relationship between such figures and their followers is predicated on the satisfaction of their extraordinary needs—and these are of various types. What satisfies one type of extraordinary need is often not what satisfies another type. In other words, the conditions under which special figures and their followers will potentially (see the second comment above on actuality) disrupt or conserve a given social order are implied by the nature of the need-satisfaction process in which their relationship is grounded. A precise determination of the stabilizing or dynamic potentiality of such a relationship requires an investigation of this process vis-á-vis the social matrix in which it transpires. Here it is possible only to speculate on this issue. The satisfaction of extraordinary superego

needs, which, by definition, are to fulfill the moral standards and conform to the moral restrictions of an existing order, entails, one might
hypothesize, less revolutionary consequences than the satisfaction of extraordinary id needs, which, again by definition, are repressed within
that order.[23] In other words, to prove themselves to their followers,
figures deemed sacred generally do not revolt against the moral standards of a social order; they are special because they uphold these standards. The reverse is the case for those considered uncanny. It is more
difficult to generate obvious hypotheses about the potential impact of
omnipotent and excellent figures and their followers, for the processes
whereby extraordinary dependency and egoideal needs are satisfied vary
in different socio-cultural settings. As Weber demonstrated in *The Sociology of Religion*, the potential consequences of satisfying extraordinary
dependency needs—and here this can be extended to egoideal needs—
are sometimes disruptive and, sometimes conserving of the existing social
order, depending on the extent to which special (omnipotent or excellent) figures and their followers operate within the boundaries of that
order to satisfy the specific variant of the needs in question.

One last complexity must be emphasized. This essay has implied, but
has given insufficient attention to, the dynamic interrelationships among
various human needs. Yet, it is a fundamental tenet of psychoanalytic
theory that the very processes that satisfy certain extraordinary needs
render individuals helpless with respect to other, very different, needs.
Freud argues (1912–13; 1939) that figures regarded as special are of
two ideal-types, "great men" and "heroes." The former are father figures
and potential agents of stability; the latter are son figures and potential
agents of change.[24] Though this essay, because it has found other of
Freud's analyses more useful for differentiating the concept of "charisma," has intentionally not developed the descriptive aspects of this
argument,[25] its dialectical implication is worth underscoring here. This
is well conveyed by Freud's otherwise curious remarks concerning the
primal horde (see especially 1912–13; 1921). To his sons, the primal
father was a special (omnipotent) figure, who gratified their dependency
needs. In so doing, he caused their id needs to be systematically ungratified. The next special (uncanny) figure was one of the "tumultuous
mob of brothers," who, to gratify such needs, revolted against the father.
This, in turn, generated other (especially superego) needs and the next
special (sacred) object was "the substitute for their father" (Freud, 1912–
13:143). Like other myths, this one of Freud's is not without "a rational
kernel" which can profitably be exploited. Analyses of the long-range
consequences of charisma do not stop at the point where a special figure
and his followers have, in gratifying their needs, succeeded in disrupting

or conserving a social order, for this process can render individuals helpless with respect to other needs,[26] which are preconditions for attributions of specialness to other need-gratifying figures who, with their followers, can produce, in the process of gratifying these, very different consequences.

CONCLUSION

By employing the conclusions of selected psychoanalytic researchers from Freud onward, this essay has sought to provide a framework for the systematic understanding of the phenomena (attributions of specialness to need-gratifying objects) to which Weber ascribed so much empirical and theoretical significance. It has suggested that the preconditions for these phenomena are various human needs (dependency, ego-ideal, superego, id) that are extraordinary (due to socialization or loss experiences), that these phenomena themselves are thus of different varieties (omnipotence, excellence, sacredness, and the uncanny), and that their immediate consequences (the formation of relationships with need-gratifying figures, characterized by awe, devotion, and obedience) and their potential long-range consequences (social stability or social change) are variable and various. The relation of this framework to past empirical research has been discussed, and its ultimate utility will be decided by future empirical research. One conclusion, however, is not premature: For "charisma" to become the powerful, unambiguous, primitive concept Weber hoped it would be, these variations of charisma must be systematically analyzed, not obfuscated, when the term "charisma" is employed.

NOTES

*I wish to thank Robert Bogart, Carol A. Heimer, Morris Janowitz, Donald N. Levine, Nina Camic, Carol Rahn, Barry Schwartz, Carol Stocking, and Mary C. Weber for their generous advice on this essay. This article was previously published in "Sociological Inquiry" 50(1) 5–23.

1. The text throughout will list only the original publication date for cited materials. Fuller information is available in the list of references.

2. The use of quotation marks is a tedious device. However, they are necessary in this essay to convey an important distinction between "charisma" as a concept to designate empirical phenomena and the phenomena themselves. Throughout this essay, charisma and its cognates will denote the empirical phenomena. When it is important to signify that the discussion is concerned with the concept *per se*, "charisma" will be used.

3. The second, or psychological, approach is best exemplified by certain psychohistorical studies—see, for example, Erikson (1942; 1968) and especially Freud (1939). Though not explicitly about leaders, Kris's work (1952) is of particular relevance here also. For pertinent sociological treatments utilizing the interpersonal variant of the third, or structural, perspective see Kanter (1972), Roth (1975), and Zablocki (1971). Psychoanalytic discussions along parallel lines are offered by Freud (1912–1913; 1921) and by Bion (1959), Mills (1959), McIntosh (1969), and Slater (1966). Discussions of the organizational variant of the structural approach are even more numerous. Work from Weber (1922) onward concerning the institutionalization and routinization of charisma exemplifies this approach. The analyses of Ake (1966), Runciman (1963), and especially Jones and Anservitz (1975) are particularly fine examples of it.

4. The review of the literature contained in this section is by no means complete. Only material that has employed perspectives compatible with the one utilized in this essay has been included (for other material, see fn. 3). Even from this perspective, there are two notable omissions. First, this essay has excluded all discussions that designate by different conceptual labels a referent similar or identical to that designated by "charisma." Parsons (1947:75–6) argues that Weber's "charisma" is "exactly equivalent to Durkheim's (1912:51–63) "sacred"; Shils (1965:205) finds a parallel between "charisma" and Otto's (1917) "idea of the holy." Though the extent to which these suggested equations are appropriate will be addressed below, little would be added to the argument by reviewing here these other discussion of charisma. Secondly, this essay has omitted, for reasons of space, the psychoanalytic interpretations of charisma offered by McIntosh, (1969) and Schiffer (1973).

5. One could even raise questions about whether attributions of specialness are all of one kind for the primitives. As Cassirer (1925:66), quoting Sonderblom, observes, the primitives' words for attributing specialness, such as mana, orenda, and so on, must be variously translated "as remarkable, very strong, very great, very old, strong in magic, wise in magic, supernatural, divine—or. . . as power, magic, sorcery, fortune, success, godhead, delight." Though Sonderblom's list refers to too many types of specialness to be very useful sociologically, one wonders if Weber, by offering "charisma" as the only translation of the various primitive words for attributing specialness, does not hide thereby the variety they represent.

6. Because social-organizational elements are not the concern of this paper, no discussion of the institutionalization and routinization of charisma is included here. It should be noted, however, that too many subsequent discussions of charisma, despite ample warning by Parsons

(1937:658–72), have been sidetracked from a discussion of the diversity of charisma *per se*, to a discussion of such elements.

7. For a mere sampling of the relevant literature here see Ake (1966), Apter (1968), Bain (1973), Barkun (1974), Burridge (1969), Dekmejian and Wyszominski (1972) Eisenstadt (1968), Fagen (1965), Oommen (1967), Parsons (1947), Smelser (1962), Tucker (1968), Willner and Willner (1965), Wolpe (1968), and Worsley (1968).

8. Shils (1965; 1968) offers a number of arguments either to answer or to circumvent this issue. However, to examine these here and explain why they are not convincing would consume space without altering the substance of this essay.

9. For the record, it should be noted that psychoanalysts stress both the limitations of employing any one of these perspectives alone and the analytical shortcomings of many of them in light of recent developments in the "theory of the self" (see Kohut 1971; Gedo and Goldberg, 1973).

10. It must be noted that this model is inapplicable to individuals whose development—sometimes termed "pathological" by psychoanalysis—has been so "arrested" that to characterize their personality needs in terms of it is to impute to them a type of personality organization they do not have (see, for example, Gedo and Goldberg. 1973).

11. There is much controversy about the ego-ideal. Lampl-de Groot (1962), for example, insists that it be distinguished from both the ego proper and the superego; Schafer (1967) argues that it really corresponds to part of the superego. Freud is also ambiguous on the matter. Wherever psychoanalytic theory decides to "locate" the ego-ideal is irrelevant for this discussion, which is not attempting to reify the ego-ideal and "locate" it within" the ego. It is merely attempting to identify a class of needs important in psychoanalytic research.

12. Using the same word in two different senses here is one way to avoid the present confusion over the ego in psychoanalytic theory. On this problem and for a different terminological solution, see Gedo and Goldberg (1973:53–69). A different alternative is implicit in Parsons (1968).

13. It is important to note that activity and passivity refer to dynamic conditions of the Ego, not to actual behavior (see Rapaport, 1961; Fromm, 1972).

14. The important works here are Bowlby (1961), Engel (1961), Fenichel (1945), Fleming and Altschul (1963), Freud (1917; 1926), Lehrman (1956), Loewald (1962), Pollock (1961), Parkes (1965), Peretz (1970a; 1970b), Rochlin (1965), and Siggens (1966). These have been helpful in composing the above remarks. The masterful sociological analysis of Weinstein and Platt (1973), which reviews much of this literature, is also fundamental.

15. The viewpoint advanced here is also compatible with (and indeed explains) the often reported sociological finding that in such changing situations (or, in the above language, situations of object loss), the "charisma-hunger" (to borrow Erikson's (1958; 1968) convenient expression) of needy individuals is so much greater than in "relatively ordered" social settings. Given the complex needs (and associated affects) generated by the loss-experience, Ego passivity is not confined to the inability to manage any one need of the personality system. In extremes, there is outright "annihilation" of Ego functioning (Fenichel, 1945:135). Often, the Ego, vacillating between attachments to lost objects and possible new object relations, simply submits, dependently, to external authority (Weinstein and Platt, 1973:107–8). No wonder then that situations of change are particularly characterized as preconditions for charisma.

16. The reader will notice that technically the foregoing comments are misleading in one important respect. In situations of object loss, the Ego is passive with respect to the "need for restitution," which has yet to be located in the structural model of needs, so basic to the argument in the text. Though, by various detours, one could translate the need to restore lost objects into the language of the structural model, I have avoided these here. They would lengthen, but not alter, the path followed in this paper. The reader troubled by this rather large omission is referred to Weinstein and Platt (1973: especially 105) where lost object relationships are differentiated in terms of the structural model. From here it is a short step, sociologically useful if psychoanalytically simplified, to the position implied in the text—conceptualizing needs in situations of loss in terms of the structural model, that is, seeing the need for restitution as the need to restore objects lost to the gratification of id, or superego, or ego-ideal, or dependency needs (or some combination thereof).

17. My sociological examples of Freud's varieties of attributed specialness suffer from a more serious limitation. Because sociologists have so rarely provided data on the extraordinary needs of those who are imputing specialness, I have no way of knowing what their needs were (dependency, ego-ideal, etc.) or if they were helpless with respect to these (that is, whether the condition of Ego passivity did obtain). I have assumed that latter and inferred the former, in order to offer relevant examples. Since my assumptions and inferences lack firm grounding in empirical research, my illustrations can be taken only as tentative hypotheses, which await confirmation in light of much-needed empirical research.

18. The remarks here could be profitably extended by employing Kohut's (1971) important work on this topic.

19. My remarks on this "almost inexhaustible subject" (Freud,

1912:105) also could be substantially refined using Kohut's (1971) work.

20. Weiss is cited here because his label for the process discussed is more illuminating than Anna Freud's term for the same process, "altruistic surrender." Her analysis of it (1936:122–34) is the more useful.

21. When is gratification of extraordinary needs obtained in a vicarious manner? An answer here would require both psychological and sociological considerations. For the former, the reader is referred to A. Freud (1936:122–34). Regarding the latter, one could hypothesize that needy individuals obtain vicarious gratification when figures are unavailable who might directly gratify extraordinary needs of various types, because of certain obvious "social-structural factors" (for a preliminary attempt to specify these, see Dekmejian and Wyszominski, 1972) and the absence of what Weber (1920:426) described as "charismatic education." This availability seems to differ with respect to different needs. For whatever reasons, in contemporary American society there seems to be a relative unavailability of figures to gratify directly extraordinary id and ego-ideal needs—a fact that would partially explain why figures deemed uncanny and excellent so frequently provide only vicarious gratification for those with such needs.

22. Some of Shils's work would seem particularly susceptible to this criticism. As hypothesized above, many of the charismatic objects discussed by Shils are considered special (or, more precisely, excellent) because, often vicariously, they gratify extraordinary ego-ideal needs. If this is correct, one would expect resonance identification with the object to occur and would not expect the result Shils (1965; 1968) postulates, that individuals automatically obey those they regard as charismatic.

23. Of course, this hypothesis about the revolutionary potentiality inherent in the satisfaction of extraordinary id needs must he modified when the Ego is passive with respect to these, not as an outcome of the socialization processes inherent in a given social order, but as a result of object loss and the need to restore an object that had gratified these. More detailed discussion of the disrupting and conserving consequences of satisfying the "need for restitution" is provided by Marris (1975) and Weinstein and Platt (1973).

24. Psychoanalysts now would speak of father or mother and son or daughter figures (see, for example, Schiffer, 1973).

25. It is interesting to note in this connection, however, that charismatic figures and their followers frequently use the imagery either of fathers (or uncles) or of rebellious sons (or brothers). The great, and well-studied, example of this is Hitler's use of oppressed son symbolism (see Erikson, 1942). The subtle interweaving of father and brother imagery among the Saint-Simonians, as described by Jones and Anservitz (1975), is also interesting in this regard.

26. The remarks on object loss and Ego passivity should be recalled here.

BIOGRAPHICAL NOTE

Charles Camic was born in New York, New York and grew up in Pittsburgh, Pennsylvania. He went to the University of Pittsburgh and majored in Sociology. After college, he did graduate work in Sociology at the University of Chicago. Professor Camic teaches at the University of Wisconsin, Madison, where he offers courses in sociological theory. His research interests in the past few years have concerned the development of modern social theory. His major published works are *Experience and Enlightenment*; "The Utilitarians Revisited"; and "The Enlightenment and Its Environment."

REFERENCES

AKE, C.
1966 "Charistmatic Legitimation and Political Integration". Comparative Studies in Society and History 9:1–13.
APTER, D.E.
1968 "Nkrumah, Charisma, and the Coup". Daedalus. 96:759–92.
BAIN, C. A.
1973 "Calculation and Charisma." Virginia Quarterly Review 49:346–56.
BARKUN, M.
1974 Disaster and the Millennium. New Haven: Yale University Press.
BENDIX, R.
1960 Max Weber: An Intellectual Portrait. New York: Doubleday, 1962.
1967 "Reflections on Charismatic Leadership", in D. Wrong (ed.), Max Weber. Englewood Cliffs N.J.: Prentice-Hall, 1970.
BERGER, P. L.
1963 "Charisma and Religious Innovation". American Sociological Review 28:940-50.
BION, W. R.
1959 Experiences in Groups. New York: Basic Books.
BLAU, P. M.
1963 "Critical Remarks on Weber's Theory of Authority". American Political Science Review 57:305–16.
BOWLBY, J.
1961 "Processes of Mourning". International Journal of Psychoanalysis 42:317–40.
BRENNER, C.
1974 An Elementary Textbook of Psychoanalysis. New York: Doubleday.
BURRIDGE, K.
1969 New Heaven, New Earth. New York: Schocken Books.
CASSIRER, E.
1925 Language and Myth. Trans. S. K. Langer. New York: Dover, 1946.
DEKMEJIAN, R., AND WYSZOMINSKI, M.J.
1972 "Charismatic Leadership in Islam". Comparative Studies in Society and History 14:193–214.

Dow, T. E., Jr.
  1968 "The Role of Charisma in Modern African Development". Social Forces 46:328–36.
  1969 "The Theory of Charisma". Sociological Quarterly 10:306–18.
Durkheim, E.
  1912 The Elementary Forms of the Religious Life. Trans. J. W. Swan. New York: Free Press, 1965.
Eisenstadt, S. N.
  1968 Introduction, in S. N. Eisenstadt (ed.), Max Weber: On Charisma and Institution Building. Chicago: University of Chicago Press.
Engel, G. L.
  1961 "Is Grief a Disease?" Psychosomatic Medicine 23:18–22.
Erikson, E. H.
  1942 "Hitler's Imagery and German Youth". Psychiatry 5:475–93.
  1950 Childhood and Society. New York: W. W. Norton, 1963.
  1958 Young Man Luther. New York: W. W. Norton.
Erikson, E. H.
  1968 On the Nature of Psycho-Historical Evidence. Daedalus 97:695–730.
Etzioni, A.
  1961 A Comparative Analysis of Complex Organizations. New York: Free Press.
Fagen, R. R.
  1965 "Charismatic Authority and the Leadership of Fidel Castro". Western Political Quarterly 18:275–84.
Fenichel, O.
  1945 The Psychoanalytic Theory of Neurosis. New York: W. W. Norton.
Fleming, J., and S. Altschul
  1963 "Activation of Mourning and Growth by Psycho-analysis". International Journal of Psychoanalysis 44:419–31.
Freud, A.
  1936 "The Ego and the Mechanisms of Defense". Trans. C. Baines. New York: International Universities Press, 1966.
Freud, S.
  1907 "Obsessive Acts and Religious practices". Trans. C. R. McWattes, in p. Rieff (ed.), Freud: Character and Culture.
  New-York: Collier, 1963.
  1912 The Dynamics of the Transference, Trans. J. Riviere, in P. Rieff (ed.), Freud: Therapy and Technique. New York: Collier, 1963.
  1912–13 Totem and Taboo. Trans. J. Strachey. New York: W. W. Norton, 1950.
  1914 "On Narcissism". Trans. C. Baines, in P. Rieff (ed.), Freud: General Psychological Theory. New York: Collier, 1963.
  1915 Further Recommendations in the Technique of Psychoanalysis. Trans. J. Riviere, in P. Rieff (ed.), Freud: Therapy and Technique. New York: Collier, 1963.
  1917 Mourning and Melancholia. Trans J. Riviere, in P. Rieff (ed.), Freud: General Psychological Theory. New York: Collier, 1963.
  1919 "The 'Uncanny'." Trans. A. Strachey, in P. Rieff (ed.), Freud: Studies in parapsychology. New York: Collier, 1963.
  1921 Group Psychology and the Analysis of the Ego. Trans. J. Strachey. New York: Bantam, 1960.
  1923 The Ego and the Id. Trans. J. Riviere. New York: W. W. Norton, 1960.
  1926 The Problem of Anxiety. Trans. H. A. Bunker. New York: W. W. Norton, 1936.

1927 The Future of an Illusion. Trans. W. D. Robson-Scott. New York: Doubleday, 1964.

1933 New Introductory Lectures on Psychoanalysis. Trans. J. Strachey. New York: W. W. Norton, 1965.

1939 Moses and Monotheism. Trans. K. Jones. New York: Vintage.

1940 An Outline of Psycho-Analysis. Trans. J. Strachey. New York: W. W. Norton, 1949.

FRIEDLAND, W. H.

1964 "For a Sociological Concept of Charisma". Social Forces 43:18–36.

FROMM, E.

1973 "Ego Activity and Ego Passivity in Hypnosis". International Journal of Clinical and Experimental Hypnosis 20:238–51.

GEDO, J. E., AND GOLDBERG, A.

1973 Models of the Mind. Chicago: University of Chicago Press.

HARTMANN, H.

1939 Ego Psychology and the Problem of Adaptation. Trans. D. Rapaport. New York: International Universities Press, 1958.

HARTMAN, H., KRIS, E., AND LOWENSTEIN, R. M.

1946 "Comments on the Formation of Psychic Structure". The Psychoanalytic Study of the Child 2:11–38.

JONES, R. A., AND ANSERVITZ, R. M.

1975 "Saint-Simon and Saint-Simonism: A Weberian View". American Journal of Sociology 80:1095–1123.

KANTER, R. M.

1972 Commitment and Community. Cambridge: Harvard University Press.

KATZ, J.

1975 "Essences as Moral Identities". American Journal of Sociology 80:1369–90.

KLAPP, O. E.

1969 Collective Search for Identity. New York: Holt.

KOHUT, H.

1971 The Analysis of the Self. New York: International Universities Press.

KRIS, E.

1952 "On Inspiration", in E. Kris, Psychoanalytic Explorations in Art. New York: Schocken Books.

LAMPL-DE GROOT, J.

1962 "Ego Ideal and Super-ego," The Psychoanalytic Study of the Child 17:94–106.

LEHRMAN, S. R.

1956 "Reactions to Untimely Death". Psychiatric Quarterly 30:564–78.

LEVINE, D. N.

1977 "Psychoanalysis and Sociology." Paper Presented at Annual Meeting of American Anthropological Association, Houston, Texas.

LOEWALD, H. W.

1962 "Internalization, Separation, Mourning, and the Superego". Psychoanalytic Quarterly 31:483–504.

MCINTOSH, D.

1969 "Weber and Freud: On the Nature and Sources of Authority". American Sociological Review 34:901–11.

MARRIS, P.

1975 Loss and Change. New York: Doubleday.

MILLS, T. M.
1959 "A Sociological Interpretation of Freud's 'Group Psychology and the Analysis of Ego,' " unpublished ms.
NELSON, B.
1973 "Weber's Protestant Ethic", in C. Y. Glock and P. E. Hammond (eds.), Beyond the Classics? New York: Harper.
OOMMEN, T. K.
1967 "Charisma, Structure and Social Change". Comparative Studies in Society and History 10:85–99.
OTTO, R.
1925 The Idea of the Holy. Trans. J. W. Harvey. London: Oxford. 1971.
PARENS, H., AND SAUL, L. J.
1971 Dependence in Man: A Psychoanalytic Study. New York: International Universities Press.
PARKES, C. M.
1965 "Bereavement and Mental Illness". British Journal of Medical Psychology 39:1–26.
PARSONS, T.
1937 The Structure of Social Action. New York: Free Press, 1968.
1947 "Introduction," in M. Weber, The Theory of Economic and Social Organization. New York: Free Press.
1952 "The Superego and the Theory of Social Systems", in T. Parsons, Social Structure and Personality. London: Free Press, 1964.
1963 "Introduction," in M. Weber, The Sociology of Religion. Boston: Beacon Press.
1968 "The Position of Identity in General Theory of Action", in C. Gordon and K. J. Gergen (eds.), The Self in Social Interaction. Vol. I. New York: Wiley.
PERETZ, D.
1970a "Development, Object-Relationships and Loss", in B. Schoenberg (ed.), Loss and Grief. New York: Columbia University Press.
1970b "Reactions to Loss", in B. Schoenberg (ed.), Loss and Grief. New York: Columbia University Press.
POLLOCK, G. H.
1961 "Mourning and Adaptation". International Journal of Psychoanalysis 42:341–60.
PRUYSER, P. W.
1973 "Sigmund Freud and His Legacy", in C. Y. Glock and P. E. Hammond (eds.), Beyond the Classics? New York: Harper.
RAPAPORT, D.
1951 "The Autonomy of the Ego", in M. M. Gill (ed.), The Collected papers of David Rapaport. New York: Basic Books, 1967.
1957a "A Theoretical Analysis of the Superego Concept", in M. M. Gill (ed.), The Collected Papers of David Rapaport. New York: Basic Books, 1967.
1957b "The Theory of Ego Autonomy", in M. M. Gill (ed.), The Collected, Papers of David Rapaport. New York: Basic Books, 1967.
1961 "Some Metapsychological Considerations Concerning Activity and Passivity", in M. M. Gill (ed.), The Collected Papers of David Rapaport. New York: Basic Books, 1961.
RAPAPORT, D., AND GILL, M. M.
1959 "The Points of View and Assumptions of Metapsychology". International Journal of Psychoanalysis 40:153–62.
RATMAN, K. J.
1964 "Charisma and Political Leadership". Political Studies 12:341–54.

REDL, F.
1942 "Group Emotion and Leadership", Psychiatry 5:573–96.
RIEFF, P.
1954 Freud's Contribution to Political Philosophy. Unpublished Ph.D. Dissertation, University of Chicago.
ROCHLIN, G.
1965 Griefs and Discontents. Boston: Little, Brown.
ROTH, G.
1975 "Socio-Historical Model and Developmental Theory". American Sociological Review 40:148–57.
RUDNER, R. S.
1966 Philosophy of Social Science. Englewood Cliffs N.J.: Prentice Hall.
RUNCIMAN, W. G.
1963 "Charismatic Legitimacy and One-Party Rule in Ghana". Archives Européennes de Sociologie 4:145–65.
SCHAFER, R.
1976 "Ideals, the Ego Ideal, and the Ideal Self", in R. R. Holt (ed.), Motives and Thought. Psychological Issues. Monograph 18/19. New York: International Universities Press.
1968a Aspects of Internalization. New York: International Universities press.
1968b "On the Theoretical and Technical Conceptualization of Activity and Passivity". Psychoanalytic Quarterly 37:173–98.
SCHIFFER, I.
1973 Charisma: A Psychoanalytic Look at Mass Society. Toronto: University of Toronto Press.
SHILS, E.
1957 "Primordial, Personal, Sacred, and Civil Ties", in E. Shils, Selected Essays. Chicago: Center for Social Organization Studies, 1970.
1958 "The Concentration and Dispersion of Charisma", in E. Shils, Selected Essays. Chicago: Center for Social Organization Studies, 1970.
1965 "Charisma, Order, and Status". American Sociological Review 30:199–213.
1968 "Charisma", in D. Sills (ed.), International Encyclopedia of the Social Sciences, Vol. 2. New York: Crowell.
1970 "Deference", in E. O. Laumann, P. M. Siegel, and R. W. Hodge (eds.), The Logic of Social Hierarchies. Chicago: Markham.
Siggens, L. D.
1966 "Mourning: A Critical Survey of the Literature". International Journal of Psychoanalysis 47:14–25.
SLATER, P. E.
1961 "Toward a Dualistic Theory of Identification". Merrill-Palmer Quarterly 7:113–26.
1966 Microcosm. New York: Wiley.
SMELSER, N. J.
1962 Theory of Collective Behavior. New York: Free Press.
TARTAKOFF, H. H.
1968 "The Normal Personality in Our Culture and the Nobel prize Complex", in R. M. Lowenstein, L. M. Newman, M. Schur, and A. J. Solnit (eds.), Psychoanalysis—A General Psychology. New York: International Universities Press.
TUCKER, R. T.
1968 The Theory of Charismatic Leadership, Daedalus 97:731–56.

WEBER, MARIANNE
1926 Max Weber: A Biography. Trans. H. Zohn. New York: Wiley, 1975.
WEBER, MAX
1920 "The Chinese Literati", in H. H. Gerth, and C. W. Mills (eds.), From Max Weber: Essays in Sociology. New York: Oxford, 1946.
WEBER, MAX
1922 "Economy and Society", in G. Roth and C. Wittich (eds.). New York: Bedminister, 1968.
WEINSTEIN, F., AND PLATT, G. M.
1969 The Wish to be Free. Berkeley: University of California press.
WEINSTEIN, F., AND PLATT, G. M.
1973 Psychoanalytic Sociology. Baltimore: John Hopkins University Press.
WEISS, E.
1960 The Structure and Dynamics of the Human Mind. New York: Grune.
WILLNER, A. R., AND WILLNER, D.
1965 "The Rise and Role of Charismatić Leaders". Annals of the American Academy 358:77–88.
WOLPE, H.
1968 "A Critical Analysis of Some Aspects of Charisma". Sociological Review 16:305–18.
WORSLEY, P.
1968 The Trumpet Shall Sound. New York: Schocken Books.
ZABLOCKI, B.
1971 The Joyful Community. Baltimore: Pelican.

VI

The Psychoanalytic Sociology of Science

Introduction

This chapter introduces the psychoanalytic-sociological study of science. The chapter contains two articles that complement each other. Professor Marion S. Goldman's "Science, Biography, and the Nonrational" complements and extends the article by Elizabeth Garber and Fred Weinstein, "The History of Science as Social History."

Garber and Weinstein's main point is that few theoretical or empirical links between social theory and personal ideas have been established. Their article is significant not for what it contributes by way of constructive theorizing but rather in their demonstration of the failure of traditional theories of science. Garber and Weinstein clear the decks so we can get on with the reconstruction of social theory. Goldman helps us land on these decks and shows us that they are composed of cultural and institutional processes, human subjectivity, and personal development. She uses these four processes to develop an argument that is substantive and rich. Her case study helps illustrate some of the complexities in this research arena and encourages us to pursue her insights and conclusions.

Garber and Weinstein argue that there is no adequate social history of science. They describe and dismiss the structural efforts of Marx and Marxists, the ideational efforts of Weber and Merton, and the cultural efforts of Turner and Geertz, as well as the contemporary effort by Kuhn.

Marx and his followers have always assumed that there is a relationship between ideational activity and structural and social relationships. However, they have failed to prove that this relationship exists.

Weber's sociology was used by Merton to develop an analysis of science during Puritanism. The glorification of God, the disciplined labor, the emphasis upon reason to control enthusiasm does not, in the authors' eyes, reflect the realities of the seventeenth century. The Weber-Mertonian thesis is thus challenged by heterogenity.

The cultural efforts which include Turner's concept of "liminality" and

Geertz's "thick description" are both unable to handle cognitive change.

Finally Kuhn, who did focus on nonrational elements in science, does not help us understand how new ideas are recognized, how they are made to fit in, and how they are interpreted. The role of values and evidence is not specified and clarified, and neither is the interaction between the rational and irrational.

Goldman and Garber and Weinstein share a common theme. They focus upon the importance of the unconscious and nonrational in apparently rational forms of thinking, that is, in science and in thought about society. Their common theme is the need for a social theory providing a level of analysis that includes a psychology of character, biography, values, the unconscious and irrational.

History of Science as Social History

ELIZABETH GARBER AND FRED WEINSTEIN

HISTORY as a discipline is distinguished by the diversity of its substantive branches; economic, social, political and cultural history, psychohistory, and history of science. These various branches, however, are
not equally mature or equally useful when measured by the criteria of
integration into the larger historical discipline: separation from their
distinct disciplinary origins, the sharing of common problems with other
branches of history, and the inclusion of their methods and findings in
the overall view of historical development. In terms of these criteria
psycho-history, for example, is still separate from mainstream history[1],
and ironically and unexpectedly so is the history of science.

The history of science remains separate because there is no adequate
or believable social history of science.[2] By that we mean there is no social
history of the distinctive attributes of science, the attributes from which
it derives its reputation and esteem, the ideas of science. There are of
course, objective, statistical, numerate studies of the scientific "establishment," studies devoted to the problems of funding, personnel levels and
recruitment, economic and social support, etc.; but all of these structural
analyses have no valid point for a social history of science unless they
can illuminate or help explain the ideas, purposes, actions and values of
scientists—all of those aspects of scientific disciplines that remain non-
numerate and subjective. These data may illuminate some other process,
the political, social or economic uses made of a science, for example, but
they cannot illuminate science in sociological terms, that is, as a socially
relevant, socially derived intellectual, dynamic and subjective vision of
nature, and as a common quest for understanding.[3]

Needless to say, there have been attempts at a history of science, even
a social history of science, but by the criteria enumerated above, they
are all revealed to be distorted in some sense or to serve the purpose of
closure. The intellectual history of science, the first kind of history of
science, is an easy example of what we are talking about. In this kind of
history there is an internal logic to the purpose of science, a rational
necessity that links scientific endeavor step by step. This history of science
tends to be technically correct, but whiggish, characterized by anach-

This essay appears in its unedited form at the request of Professors Garber and Weinstein

ronistic distortions, such as reading back from contemporary scientific opinion, or integrating examples in an argument only if they are consistent with rationalistic philosophical precepts. The history of science that emerges, then, is a history of progress, of the growth of scientific rationality, a vision of the unfolding of reason, unidirectional, linear, and purely intellectual.[4]

The problem is that science has a past which is as rich and complex as the history of the economic marketplace, of literature, or of political theory and political practise, so that as whig constitutional history is unsatisfactory as an explanation of English political development, so whiggish studies of scientific development are unsatisfactory as an explanation in the history of science. The view that scientific ideas have historical validity only as and when they flow into or lead up to ideas, ideals, and methods of the present state of science is short-sighted and leads, paradoxically, to an ahistorical image of scientific development.[5] Historians who approach the subject in this way merely gloss the data, denying the possibility of a comprehensive view that integrates all the aspects of science that root it in society; namely the scientists, themselves, their false starts and their failures, and the moral and wishful as well as cognitive components of their science. In the view of "rationalist" historians, for example, great men of science often seem doomed to carry a useless weight of wrong-headed ideas that undermine the essential purity of their "correct" views.[6] But such historians cannot integrate or explain the wrong-headed ideas in an overall or comprehensive historical view of the work of these scientists. The failures of genius are typically explained away as limitations of the human mind in the face of the difficult intellectual problems posed by science. On the one hand, the false starts, especially those that seemed initially respectable, the errors, the conflicting viewpoints, the unique or even bizarre beliefs, yearnings, or opinions of individuals would never become part of the historical account in these terms. On the other hand, the role of society in the formation of such beliefs and opinions, and in the formulations of scientific problems and their solutions, must similarly be ignored.

Among the major social histories of science, or sociological theories that seem pertinent to a social history of science, we must consider the contributions of Marx and Weber and their followers and the recent contributions of the cultural anthropologists, notably Victor Turner and Clifford Geertz, noting at the outset that we can treat them as briefly as we treated the whig interpretation of the history of science.

This is particularly true of Marx's and Marxist interpretations, whether the history of science is presented in terms of technological determinism, as occurs in some work of Friedrich Engels and in the work of J. D. Bernal,[7] or whether it is presented in terms of ideology, as also occurs in the work of Marx and Engels, elaborated by such writers as Georg Lukacs and Antonio Gramsci.[8] For what we are dealing with in either case is what Louis Althusser has referred to as "expressive causality," or what Gerald Platt has referred to as the theorist's exercise of "imperial dominion" over data, that is:

a vast interpretive allegory in which a sequence of historical events or texts and artifacts is rewritten in the terms of same deeper, underlying, and more 'fundamental' narrative, of a hidden master narrative which is the allegorical key or figural content of the first sequence of empirical materials.[9]

What Marx and Engels seemed to have provided and what the worst and best of Marxist historians have taken for granted ever since, is the mechanism, the process that links social location to individual and group mental activity, the way in which objective circumstances compel intellectual processes, independent of the conscious intentions and the conscious reporting of the people involved.[10] The fact is, however, that whether science or any other intellectual activity is conceived of as mechanically related to technological requirements or ideologically related to social arrangements (e.g., class)[11], Marx and Marxists have not provided any empirically valid scheme, any verifiable or even merely assessable depictions of the process by which social location determines cognitive and affective responses. They have only and routinely assumed the connection, arguing in the syllogistic terms we are familiar with from our experience with boojums and snarks. A description of bourgeois social relations and bourgeois ideology on the one side, and of scientific preconceptions and concerns on the other, is not a description of and does not give rise to a description of the process by which the one is transformed into the other.[12]

Moreover, if the "real" values, motives, and goals of the participants are hidden, actual accounts of their work are of no consequence and must be ignored as evidence. Thus, in Marxist historiography the cognitive processes of the participants are either distorted or channeled into terms and values that cannot be established through the actual historical evidence, while the authenticity of any account left by scientists of their experiences and the meaning of their lives becomes largely irrelevant. Reality is imposed for the outside, it is not revealed through the evidence, which is precisely what Althusser meant by "expressive causality," and Platt by "imperial dominion."

Thus, the question of appropriate evidence remains for Marxist historians. In the history of science we encounter participants who interpret the natural world, both idiosyncratically and collectively, in ways that are later revealed as false. That is, in the past there have been false starts, errors, wrong ideas, indeed whole theories that had been acceptable to scientists, investigated, researched, and then discarded as other theories were accepted in the light of further developments. And here we have the ultimate question for any social history of science: How do scientists organize their mental conceptions of the world, including values and ideals, including even fantasies which are also socially located, influenced, and bound so that they become refined as intellectual products, socially available, connected to the main body of contributions, and developed in the acceptable manner regardless of whether these products are subsequently revealed as false or less heuristic than some other product. This question in social psychology is the central question in the social history of science, the question that must be answered if there is to be a valid social history of science.

Perhaps the best known sociological alternative to Marxist theory is the theory of Max Weber, recalling always that Weber's sociology was developed in response to the challenge posed by Marx and that Weber did not himself extend his sociological analysis to the sciences. This task was accomplished by Robert Merton, who produced the first and most enduring examination of the implications of Weber's sociology for the history of science.

Merton's thesis is based on the concept of the ideal type—the Puritan as scientist. Puritanism with its emphasis on the glorification of God, social utility, diligence and constancy in labor, and the exercise of reason to control enthusiasm encouraged the rational investigation of nature as a study of "God in His Works" not emphasized in older theologies. Science was believed to lead to the spiritual as well as the material wellbeing of society.[13]

Even granting Merton's image of the Puritan, his categories do not reflect the realities of the seventeenth century, the range of backgrounds, philosophies, and theologies in the writings of seventeenth century English natural philosophers. Altogether they form too heterogeneous a group, theologically, socially, and psychologically to fit the mold of Merton's ideal type. Neither Weber's thesis nor Merton's interpretation of it leads to a satisfactory social history of science that can encompass the evidence, and their theories must be relegated to the realm of intellectual constructions or fictions.

The same kind of criticism can be levelled against other sociological positions, including Mannheim's functionalism[14] and role theory:[15] the process by which social location affects or determines mental activity cannot be specified. This criticism encompasses as well theories that stress cultural forms as distinct from social structural arrangements, particularly the more recent theories or the cultural anthropologists Victor Turner and Clifford Geertz. The theories of these authors attempt to explain mental activity or cognitive and emotional responses to situations marked by the loss of the routine and the familiar as a result of social or ideological change; in other words, they depict renewed efforts at coherence and closure, the development of a world view. But while loss[16] and change also occur in science, these anthropological theories do not explain scientific development even in those very instances where the familiar ideas and usual social arrangements seem to fail and all coherence disappears.

Turner's most important idea in this context is that of "liminality," a social and ideological situation of transition "betwixt and between" traditional and novel social structures and ideological constructs.[17] "Liminal" situations have historically offered people caught in disruptive circumstances, threatened by the potential or actual loss of familiar arrangement, a chance for renewed solidarity through the appearance of "liminal" thinkers and actors who legitimate the reorganization of structures and constructs, thereby restoring a sense of coherence to the world. Liminality is a useful concept, consistent with certain sociological and psychoanalytic concepts (e.g., charismatic leadership, transference). But it is not clear how the concept illuminates or serves a proper social history of science.

The point is that Turner's main idea does not facilitate our understanding of the process of change in science, the organization and reorganization of thought. Why is it that scientists tolerate data incompatible with theory for a long time, quickly reacting as the implications of these data "suddenly" become evident and compelling, making the incompatibilities intolerable and demanding immediate attention? Neither Turner nor any one else can or has spelled out the conditions, either internal to the disciplines, or external to them, derived from the wider community, that act as triggers, transforming science, moving the field and the community from one position to another. No one has been able to specify how the theory of choice of one individual, for that is how scientific endeavor begins and from whence it emerges, gets connected to the wider body of thought, how loyalties then shift, how something that might have been viewed as transgression is transformed into innovation, how social arrangements are affected as a result, not the least being the power structure and the resources.[18]

The fact that a theorist of Turner's stature cannot clarify how the dynamic states compelled by "liminality" work to produce a particular result in a sphere as culturally important as science stems primarily from the complexity of mental activity in general. This activity involves, to begin with, the fantasy responses to situations of stress or loss as change and novelty in science (as in politics or art) are affected by such unconscious and preconscious processes. The experience of scientists with such processes has been reported many times: we need only think of Pascal, Kekulé, Poincaré, or especially Einstein, who was always ready to acknowledge that importance in his imaginative thinking of the "softer," less cognitive, more affective or intuitive side of things.[19] As Freud once said, without the capacity for this kind of imaginative thinking, which especially in its origins is hardly distinguishable from fantasy thinking, there would be no progress.

This also involves at a level we discriminate only for analytic purposes—for practical purposes the processes under discussion are coterminous—the moral commitments of scientists to mentors and schools. These moral commitments, as much as cognitive commitments, account for the condition of "normal science," so well explained by Thomas Kuhn, in which experiments are reproduced to gain expected results while anomalous or contradictory data are and continue to be ignored. This is meant to underscore the observation that there is no such thing as a purely intellectual or cognitive mental process, and the cognitive orientations characteristic of scientific endeavor—no matter how successfully they have been exploited in different forms of technological mastery—remain as well, and perhaps at bottom, a moral phenomenon, that is, a superego standard which scientists employ without reflection to define their working world. Of course, there are primacies in the mental activity of scientists: there would be no progress either without cognitive discipline. But this does not preclude the moral basis of scientific activity nor does it preclude the possibility of shifting primacies away from the cognitive; that is, the domination of moral commitments which may lead and have led scientists to defend positions in ways and with a degree of unreasonableness or stubbornness that are later revealed to have been inappropriate from the standpoint of scientific endeavor.[20]

Ironically, perhaps the clearest example of shifting primacies, or of the penetration of wishful and moral content into a presumably scientific and hence controlled situation occurs in psychoanalysis, specifically in psychoanalytic training and in discourse among psychoanalysts where, as Maxwell Gitelson, Helen Tartakoff, Pinchas Noy, George Klein and many others have explained (and complained), distortions are fostered all the time. Important examples of these wishful and moral contents in psychoanalytic thought are easily adduced, including Freud's persistent and exaggerated adherence to his Lamarkian preconceptions, which even the faithful Ernest Jones at the last urged him to abandon, and including also (and we emphasize that this is a particularly crucial and indicative example) the failure of psychoanalysts to have developed a systematic theory of affects even to this day, which is a strange failure indeed, considering how central affective expression is in clinical as well as everyday social experience.[21] There is obviously something in the social arrangements of the psychoanalytic community which inhibits insight into crucial problems.

It is arguably the case that the development of psychoanalysis has occurred in the context of unexamined and unobserved wishful and moral contents and a powerful, authoritative figure. The evolution of the discipline into a "normal science" has been hindered by theoretical development as much as by its adherence to a particular focus. Clearly, the "schools" that persistently turn up in opposition to mainstream psychoanalysis stress aspects of mental activity that should have been systematically integrated in the first place and that were ultimately integrated in some useful if altered or attenuated form after an interim period of fruitless discord and vituperation. This was the case with certain ideas of Jung and Adler, of different Marxist critics (e.g., Reich, Fromm, and others who stressed the significance of social relationships), and very recently with ideas of Kohut and Schafer.[22]

The dynamic processes revealed by the history of psychoanalysis as a scientific endeavor—including the organization and promotion of certain ideas and the constriction of others, the suppression or repression of insight, the skewed modes of recruitment, training, and certification-as reported by psychoanalysts, themselves, in the context of issues of transference and countertransference, the effect of authority relationships, which obviously exist and which involve real interests as well as moral commitments and wishful expectations, are all themselves interesting features, not only of psychoanalysis as science, but of a general social history of science.[22a.] These problems have never really been explored as thoroughly as they should be.

But even beyond these problems there remains the paramount problem of how idiosyncratic fantasy responses to situations of social or cultural stress or loss (where radical change of every kind begins, as noted), and the systematic moral commitments of scientists to mentors and schools, are combined with disciplined cognitive capacities to produce an important or useful result. We have already noted, in our comments on Victor Turner, that no theorist of society or culture has come close to solving this problem. But we should also address in this context, and for a limited purpose, the work of another prominent anthropological theorist of culture, Clifford Geertz.

We can begin with Geertz's conception of "thick description," defining it as an ethnographer's constructed version of interpretive themes which the ethnographer uses to abstract and render coherent the diverse and variegated behavior of a community. Although unexamined by community members, these interpretive themes are used by them to allow a sense of shared meanings to emerge from shared, publically expressed behavior. An observer can infer the social significance of these themes, the ways in which they serve to sustain and bolster a community, both from subjective reporting (the "ideological" uses of language) and from competent displays of behavior. Thus, the elaboration of the themes ("thick description") provides a valid and assessable interpretive (semiotic) insight into the sources of social cohesion and solidarity—but from the inside, as it were, unlike Marxist, functionalist, and other perspectives which are derived from the outside. Geertz did this best, perhaps, in his "thick description" of cockfighting in Bali.

Now, according to Geertz, this approach can be operationalized with respect to any culture, including the culture of science. That is:

whatever their differences, both so-called cognitive and so-called expressive symbols or symbol systems have, then, at least one thing in common: they are extrinsic sources of information in terms of which human life can be patterned—extra-personal mechanisms for the perception, understanding, judgment and manipulation of the world. Culture patterns—religious, philosophical, esthetic, scientific, ideological—are "programs"; they provide a template or blueprint for the organization of social and psychological processes, as much as genetic systems provide a template for the organization of organic processes.[23]

However, not only are all the comments on the relationship of Turner's work to a social history of science true of Geertz's work, but there is one other notable factor in addition: Geertz denied any need to integrate in theory any process which captures or describes unique subjective mental activity within the collective net of culture. Geertz dismisses the need for a theory that integrates fantasy thinking or idiosyncratic wishful responses to social events which are, nevertheless, as we have stated, the source of innovative, novel, or revolutionary thinking. Thus, the individual, or in the case of science, the individual theorist, who can only have emerged from within a culture of shared meanings and behavior but who is, paradoxically, the indispensable source for change in that culture, is lost. We would claim as a result that even the most advanced anthropological theories of culture do not permit us to address the issue of a proper social history of science, and we are back to square one.[24]

Interestingly enough, this issue has only been confused by the work in the philosophy of science of Thomas Kuhn. For Kuhn, no matter what anyone might think and no matter how anyone might have used his work, had no intention of saving the history of science for social history or addressing what we have defined as the central problem of a social history of science: the relationship of social processes to the appearance, development, and acceptance of scientific ideas.

For our purposes Kuhn's most important contribution was to shift the attention of scholars from the empirical to the theoretical foundations of science. Philosophers, historians, and sociologists now discuss science in terms of theories and ideas, not in terms of "the facts of nature." And because of Kuhn's work, they are concerned with the processes by which ideas and theories appear, develop, and change.[25]

However, this shift does not constitute a foundation for a social history of science. To be sure, Kuhn disturbed the philosophers by introducing nonrational elements into science, and he clearly went beyond any purely rational image of science. Moreover, he saw the need for a psychological description of the way that new theoretical forms emerge, choosing the ideas of gestalt psychology,[26] characterizing the process on the level of the individual as a "conversion process."[27] This is a nonrational process that requires the scientist to "see" the problem in a new way, illustrating how individuals perceive problems. But the depiction of this rather idiosyncratic, dynamic process cannot serve to explain how the ideas of the individual scientist are fit into a discipline. Kuhn's psychology, which deals only with the moment of an individual's initial recognition of pattern change, addresses certain issues in puzzle solving, esthetics, and theory choice, but not in ways that create a social history of science in the terms employed here.[28]

Even at the individual level pattern recognition is only the first step in the construction of new theories, methods, and language. There are other processes which are as important as the reorientation of ideas. Indeed the interpretation of the meaning of a new vision of nature— confronting its implications in concrete examples—is at the center of even the initial examination of a new paradigm.[29] Further, the psychological process, the role of values versus the use of logic, the role of evidence, the interaction of rational and nonrational elements in the construction of scientific theories, the making of choices in science, cannot be understood in the categories available in Kuhn. For example, aesthetic choice plays an important role in theory determination and interpretation, but Kuhn's categories cannot tell us why certain choices are made, how the social location of the scientists affects these choices, or how these values get transformed into conceptions useful for understanding nature.[30]

Indeed for Kuhn the social and external cultural contexts are truly peripheral to the actual conduct of science and remote from the cognitive processes of the scientific community and the individual scientist. It is only at one point, during a revolution in scientific ideas, that Kuhn joins science to its cultural context, or hints at any external source for the values on which science is built.[31] He implies that during a period when there is no commonly held image of nature embodying values and methods integrated in appropriate language and behavior within a discipline, scientific ideas themselves are open to notions from other areas of culture. Thus, the interaction of science and its context is minimal and unspecified, the life history of science is not rooted in the larger society. The general culture is a stimulus only under extraordinary circumstances occurring within science and not an inherent aspect of the very development of scientific ideas. In general, while scientists live in a general culture, as scientists, the specialized context of science alone serves as the source of their problems and offers the means for their solution, particularly as their science becomes technically more remote from ordinary discourse.[32]

Thus, Kuhn cannot even address the problem of how ideas from one cultural domain are transformed into the basis for a scientific theory. He has no terms with which to explore, for example, how Malthus's ideas on population were transformed by Charles Darwin into a key idea in his mechanism for evolution. Nor can he examine the changes of meaning necessary to obtain heuristic, scientific results from an extrascientific idea. Darwin fundamentally changed the meaning of Malthus's thesis from a social process that preserved Christian morals into a description of a basic biological process of nature. Appropriation, transformation, and the technical development of ideas within a scientific context are all important historical processes. They root science in culture, yet spotlight the differences in the use of ideas and methods in diverse cultural domains. In Kuhn, however, science remains isolated from any links with its cultural context under normal circumstances. Moreover, Kuhn has not spelled out criteria which allow us to identify where and when conditions internal to the various disciplines of science trigger the transformation from the stage of tolerance to one of crisis. In this context Kuhn has similarly neglected to explain how differing social or cultural conditions may affect the visibility of anomalies and whether they can be tolerated or not.

Kuhn's work cannot be used to transcend Marxist social theory or sociological or anthropological analysis because he chose to concentrate on changes in scientific perceptions of nature, intending to construct an epistemology, not a social history of science. In addition, Kuhn claims in these terms a special place for science and its history because of its technical nature and because the objects of its study set it apart from other forms of knowledge.[32] But he offers no reasons for the uniqueness of scientific knowledge in comparison with other forms of knowledge that historians routinely argue are rooted in particular social arrangements at particular times. Thus, to view Kuhn's work as a basis for a social history of science is to misjudge the focus of his attention and to misunderstand the requirements of a social history of science.

To be sure, through the very force of his argument, Kuhn has made us accept that science in its ideas and theories is built upon a system of values and articulated through a series of choices based on those values. Still, he has not tried to develop any theory of the social and cultural origins of those ideas and values and, consequently, no method for linking science to social arrangements.

Darwin's theory again provides us with an interesting example of the problem we are discussing. The evolutionary mechanism Darwin described was seen by himself and his contemporaries, both inside and outside of science, as heralding a new order of nature and man, replete with challenges to the established balance between science and religion. But it was Darwin's special uses of an already available language, Malthus's language of "struggle,"[33] as well as his ability to emphasize the uniqueness of his theory and to minimize what he recognized as theoretical lacunae,[34] that distinguish the work that made him famous. Clearly, the language of "struggle" was crucial; yet "struggle" has various meanings, and the several that Darwin attached to the concept were explicitly different from those of his cultural source, Malthus.[35] At the same time, we have no idea what Darwin picked up from the common culture that allowed him to choose and shape to his own purposes this particular language, nor is it all that clear either why Darwin's completed treatise became so compelling that it served to redefine natural history and change the research direction of the discipline.

The point is, in short, that what we have at the moment is the illusion of a social history of science; a real one does not exist. Certainly, the cognitive and affective processes involved in scientists' choices of theory or in the development of scientific ideas cannot be accounted for by a social history rooted exclusively in social categories. It is also certain that there is no established social theory that can provide empirically warranted links between social relationships and mental or ideational activity. It cannot be repeated often enough, or stressed heavily enough, that Marx and the Marxists assumed what they had to prove from the beginning: that the Merton thesis is refutable by reference to the data and that anthropological, or for that matter, psychoanalytic propositions (concerning Oedipal rivalry, an "instinct" for mastery, the termination of idealizing transferences, the recovery of an "oceanic feeling," or different types of object loss, etc.) are themselves either refutable by reference to the obviously heterogeneous data or are so amorphous and vaguely cast as to become empirically negligible because it is impossible to discriminate among instances of scientific discovery or to account for different and changing ideas of science. Moreover, the version of a history of science that Kuhn offered does try to assimilate the psychological, cultural, and social aspects of science, but in the context of intellectual history, a form of history which isolates science as practise—or scientists as practitioners—from the social relationships, conflictual or integrative, that all agree affect other mental contents.

The principle reason that it is so difficult to tie science and society together is that we have no social theory capable of establishing substantive links between social relationships and scientific endeavor. Until we have such a theory, one which can address the question of how scientists organize their conceptions of the world in ways that make them socially compelling, science will necessarily continue to appear as an insular activity, detached from the everyday social world, and the history of science will remain detached from the history of that everyday social world.

Finally, it is necessary to emphasize that if there is no social theory adequate to the social history of science, if there is no empirically warranted or assessable way to link social relationships to the different ideas that have oriented scientific activity over time, then we might well wonder whether we have a social history of any network of ideas or any body of theory—political, economic, religious, or familial—or whether what we really have are fictional or ideological constructs that more readily serve the function of closure than the search for truth. What one should learn primarily from this brief review of the dilemmas of a proper social history of science is that the problems involved in understanding the source and elaboration of scientific ideas are not unique to science; they are only instances of quite common problems, so common in fact that they have threatened to undermine the social sciences generally, as they have also given rise to an interpretive crisis in history, a crisis which accounts, in our opinion, for the current "retreat to narrative." This retreat is tantamount to a confession that the constitutive or regulative constructs which have guided sociological and historical interpretation over the past century and a half may well have played themselves out, and there seems to be at the moment no place else to go.

NOTES

1. See Lawrence Stone, "History and the Social Sciences in the Twentieth Century," in *The Past and the Present*, Boston, Mass.: 1981, 3–44.
2. In this paper we will be dealing with scientists engaged in research,

not as teachers, advisors, or popularisers. The process of trying to understand natural phenomena is not the same as the teaching process. In the latter case, unless the scientist is teaching an advanced graduate course, science is typically presented as a closed, logical, empirically based body of knowledge.

3. Derek Price's pioneering first piece on the growth of science is a case in point. He does, indeed, map the phenomenal, continuous growth of science from the seventeenth century up through 1960, but cannot inform us about the content of that growth; whether it was due to reinterpretation or new, more successful theories replacing older ones. Derek Price, *Little Science, Big Science* (New York: Columbia, 1963).

4. This view of the history of science ultimately meshed neatly with the typical twentieth century philosopher's view of science as a finished, logical structure. Indeed, the philosopher's methods, ideas, and language were uniquely suited to dealing with problems of structure, though at the expense of "thick description." Unwittingly, the philosophers reinforced an incorrect view of the history of science.

5. Such a rationalist view is reflected in George Sarton's history of science. His dependence on the current philosophy of science derived from early twentieth century French philosophers. However much they differed amongst themselves they all saw history in terms of the gradual rationalization of man's existence through the action of Mind. Ideas can change history. The history of science became, therefore, a model for this rationalization of man's existence, because science was the rational investigation of nature. See Sarton, *Introduction to the History of Science*, reprint (Malabar, Fla.: Krieger Publishing Co.) 3 vols.

6. See Sarton's "Judgement of Aristotle's Natural Philosophy and Its Influence on Ideas in the Sciences into the Seventeenth Century." George Sarton, *A History of Science*, vol. 1, Ancient Science through the Golden Age of Greece. (Cambridge, Mass.: Harvard University Press, 1952), pp. 467–500, p. 499, and his definition of the history of science in Sarton, *A Study of the History of Science*, pp, 4–5, bound together with *A Study of the History of Mathematics*, reprint (New York: Dover, 1957).

7. "Engels to Starkenberg", in Marx and Engels, *Selected Correspondence*, p. 517, quoted in J. D. Bernal, *Marx and Science* (London: Lawrence and Wishart Ltd., 1952), p. 30. J. D. Bernal, *Science in History* (Cambridge, Mass.; M.I.T. Press, 1971) 4 vols., and *The Social Function of Science* (Cambridge, Mass.: M.I.T. Press, 1969).

8. See Karl Marx and Friedrich Engels, *Selected Correspondence* (Moscow: 1954), p. 541.

9. Jameson, *The Political Unconscious* (Ithaca; Cornell University Press, 1981), pp. 28–29.

10. To see the convolutions of language and the ambiguities of inter-

pretation this leads to, see Phillip T. Kain, "Marx's Theory of Ideas," *History and Theory* (1981), pp. 357–378. A more convincing case for the scientific character of Marxist historiography, if one accepts the notion of a 'research program,' is Howard Bernstein, "Marxist Historiography and the Methodology of Research Programs," *ibid*, pp. 424–449.

11. The problems of this approach to the history of science can be seen in James R. Jacob, *Robert Boyle and the English Revolution* (New York: Burt Franklin, 1977). Jacob's argues that Boyle's science inherently contains values from the governing elite of the 1650s and that his natural philosophy 'constitutes his response to revolution.' However, if that is so, Boyle has left us with no record of this connection. No data appropriate to this conclusion exists. Yet Boyle has left us with an account of his life and its meaning to him in this critical period. To transform this meaning into ideology denies the authenticity of all this evidence. See Robert Boyle, "An Account of Philaretus, during his Minority," in *The Works of Robert Boyle*, (ed.) Thomas Birch (London: 1772), 6 vols., vol. 1. Similar pitfalls for the ideological interpretation of science are evident in Morris Bermann, *Social Change and Scientific Organisation: The Royal Institution*, 1799–1844 (Ithaca: 1977). While Bermann can establish that the research and functioning of the Institution followed from those of its founders in its early years, improving landlords, he is less successful at linking social values and research. When the institution was revived it was in the hands of professionals who believed that science was the key to understanding social problems. However, Bermann reverses this to see them, and Michael Faraday, as advocates of solving society's problems with the "technical fix," that is, as an adjunct to the scientific method, and seeing science as an instrument of social control—for which he has no evidence.

12. The problems of this lacuna are illustrated by the literature on the role of puritanism in the origins of modern science. In particular see Christopher Hill, *The Intellectual Origins of the English Revolution* (Oxford: 1963). While his argument is complicated by his insistence that science is rational and progressive, Hill's basic problem is that the data and the scientists involved in early seventeenth century England just do not fit into the narrow categories he has available. For instance, John Dee certainly does not measure up to any criteria of rationality of the twentieth century in much of his work into the structure of nature; he was an important astrologer and numerologist as well as a mathematician. Charles Webster, *The Great Instauration: Science, Medicine and Reform*, 1626–1662 (London: 1975) suffers from the same dilemma even though his net is more widely cast than Hill's. As T. K. Rabb has stated in his review of Webster, we do learn a great deal about the reform movements

in England of the early seventeenth century and English Puritanism, but not much about science in the same era. Both Hill and Webster omit any consideration of the actual problems investigated by the scientists they consider and their solutions to these scientific problems. Thus the ideology remains unconnected to any specific scientific result as neither the work nor a process to link those results to the ideology is detailed. The literature on the role of Puritanism in the scientific revolution in England and the founding of the Royal Society is extensive. The relationship between science and religion revealed by these studies is complex, and scientists were of all faiths. See Richard S. Westfall, *Science and Religion in Seventeenth Century England*, reprint (New York: Archon Books, 1970). See also, the collection of papers on this subject in *Past and Present*, edited by Charles Webster, *The Intellectual Revolution of the Seventeenth Century* (Boston: Routledge and Kegan Paul, 1974). Webster's own case for the puritan origins of both modern science and the Royal Society is in *The Great Instauration* (London: Duckworth, 1975). Webster's scholarship is very impressive but his thesis has recently been challenged; see, Lotte Mulligan, "Puritans and Science: A Critique of Webster," *Isis*, *71* (1980), 456–469, and, "Civil War Politics, Religion and the Royal Society," *Past and Present* (1973) pp. 92–116, and "Anglicanism, Latitudinarianism and Science in Seventeenth-Century England," *Past and Present* (1968), *40*, pp. 16–41. In this connection, see also, M. Theodore Hoppen, "The Nature of the Early Royal Society," *British Journal for the History of Science* (1976), *16*, pp. 1–23, 243–273.

13. Robert K. Merton, *Science, Technology and Society in Seventeenth Century England*, reprint (New York: Harper and Row, 1970). Merton's image of the Puritan, however, omits basic aspects of Weber's characterization.

14. Karl Mannheim, *Ideology and Utopia* (trans,) L. Wirth and E. Shils (London: Routledge and Kegan Paul, 1936), and *Essays on the Sociology of Knowledge* (London: Routledge and Kegan Paul, 1952). For the application of sociology of knowledge to science, see Barry Barnes, *Scientific Knowledge and Sociological Theory* (Boston: Routledge and Kegan Paul, 1974). For the sociology of scientific knowledge see Barnes, *Interests and the Growth of Knowledge* (Boston: Routledge and Kegan Paul, 1978) and Barnes and Stephen Shapin (eds.) *Natural Order: Historical Studies of Scientific Culture* (London: Sage, 1979). See also Paul Forman, "Weimar Culture, Causality and Quantum Theory, 1919–1927; Adaptation by German Physicists to a Hostile Intellectual Environment," *Historical Studies in the Physical Sciences* (1971), *3*, pp. 1–118. See also David Bloor, "Polyhedra and the Abominations of Leviticus," *British Journal for the History of Science* (1978), 11, pp. 245–272. However, both Forman and

Bloor discuss issues in the philosophy of science rather than its research content or development. Causality was no longer an issue in physics even before the first world war, and Bloor misinterprets Imre Lakatos's philosophy of mathematics; see John Worrall, "Reply to David Bloor," *Ibid*, (1979), *12*, pp. 71–81. The confusion of philosophy of science with research is common in the social history of science.

15. For role theory applied to science, see Joseph Ben-David, *The Scientists' Role in Society* (New York; 1971). For a discussion of role theory, see Peter L. Berger and Thomas Lackmann, *The Social Construction of Reality* (Garden City, New York; 1966) pp. 72–92, and for a recent critique, see Anthony Giddens, *New Rules of Sociological Method* (New York; Basic Books, 1976), passim.

16. Loss is expressed by scientists in periods where the old cognitive structures fail and no new ones are yet in place. The most graphic are seen in those physicists involved in the development of quantum mechanics, especially during the years 1925 to 1927, when coherence in theoretical atomic physics had completely disappeared.

17. Victor Turner has developed the notion of liminality in several books; the most convenient discussion is in Turner, *Dramas, Fields and Metaphors*: Symbolic Action in Human Society (Ithaca: Cornell, 1974) pps. 231–270.

18. In science, new ideas are often so compelling that as they are incorporated into the body of thought, the culture of science itself may change; that is, the acceptance of a new theory may well involve the restructuring of a community, as is revealed particularly in the history of psychoanalysis. For science in general, see Thomas S. Kuhn *The Structure of Scientific Revolutions* (Chicago, 1962).

19. For dreams and fantasy in science see R. A. Brown and R. G. Luchcock, "Dreams, Daydreams and Discovery," *Journal of Chemical Education* (1978), *55*, pp. 694–696, Cackowoski, "A Creative Problem-solving Process," *Journal of Creative Behavior* (1969), *3* pp. 185–195, Howard Gruber, *Darwin on Man* (Chicago, 1981) second edition, see chapter 12, A. Koestler and J. R. Sythies *Beyond Reductionism* (Boston: 1971) and Koestler's *The Sleepwalkers*. While the latter reveals acute math anxiety and an inability to see mathematics, or anyone other than Kepler as creative its emphasis on the nonrational is a salutary reminder of how few scientists are able to accept the idea of irrationality and science; the two are usually seen as mutually exclusive. See Byron Vanderbilt, "Kekulé's Whirling Snake," *Journal of Chemical Education* (1975) *52*, p. 709. Or scientists simply cannot pinpoint the break in the supposedly logical development of their ideas, nor can many historians, while they can describe the particularly revealing experiment or theoretical develop-

ment. See Aris et al (eds,) *The Springs of Scientific Creativity* (Minneapolis: 1983). However, some scientists have tried to explore this aspect of their science. See Henri Poincaré, *Science and Method* (London: trans. of 1908 edition, 1914) and Arthur Miller, "Albert Einstein and Max Wertheimer," *History of Science* (1975), *13*, pp. 75–103.

20. Stanley Goldberg, "In Defense of Ether: The British Response to Einstein's Special Theory of Relativity," *Historical Studies in the Physical Sciences* (197) 2 pp. 89–126. Seymour Mauskopf (ed.) *The Reception of Unconventional Science* (Washington: AAAS, 1979)

21. Maxwell Gitelson, "Therapeutic Problems in the Analysis of the 'Normal Candidate,'" *International Journal of Psychoanalysis* (1954) *35*, pp. 174–183; Helen Tartakoff, "The Normal Personality in Our Culture and the Nobel Prize Complex," in *Psychoanalysis, a General Psychology*, Rudolph M. Loewenstein, et. al., eds., (New York: 1966); Pinchas Noy, "Metapsychology as Multi-Model System," *International Review of Psychoanalysis* (1977), *4*, 10; George S. Klein, "Freud's Two Theories of Sexuality," in *Clinical-Cognitive Psychology: Modes and Integration* (ed.) Louis Breger (Englewood Cliffs, New Jersey: 1969), 136–137; see also Heinz Kohut's statement in "Thoughts on Narcissism and Narcissistic Rage," in *Psychoanalytic Study of the Child* (1972) *27*, pp. 366–367; comments on the work of Erik Erikson by Daniel Yankelovich and William Barrett, *Ego and Instinct: The Psychoanalytic View of Human Nature Revised* (New York: 1970), p. 120. p. 153. On Ernest Jones and Freud see, Henry Edelheit, "On the Biology of Language," in *Psychiatry and the Humanities* (ed.) Joseph H. Smith (New Haven, Conn.: 1978), vol. III, p. 62.

22. On Jung, see Erik Erikson's comments in *Identity and the Life Cycle* (New York: 1959) Psychological Issues, Monograph 1, vol. 1, p. 31n. On Adler, see the more grudging statements by Roy Schafer, "Action Language and the Psychology of Self," *The Annual of Psychoanalysis* (1981), VIII, 86–87, Kohut went the other way, posing his work as complementary to mainstream psychoanalysis; Schafer pointed out that in fact it is an independent form of psychoanalysis and the kind of tie Kohut was seeking to maintain is not in fact necessary.

22a. These mechanisms have appeared in other sciences. After the publication of Lavoisier's new chemistry (1789), a propaganda campaign was launched to win over the chemists of Europe and included the establishment of their own journal, *Annales de chimie*. See Carleton E. Perrin, "The triumph of the antiphlogistians," in *The Analytic Spirit* (ed.) Harry Woolf (Ithaca; Cornell, 1981) pp. 40–63. For the role of authority figures, Anton Lorentz is seen as crucial in the acceptance of the new quantum theory about 1908. He has, however, been criticised for being too cautious and retarding its development. See A. Hermann, *The Genesis of Quantum Theory* (Cam. Mass.: 1971). See Max Dresden *H. A. Kramers* (1984) on the supression of key solutions to important problems in quantum physics by the criticism of a key authority figure in physics in the 1920s, Niels Bohr. Einstein was well aware of the political structure of German physics, and despite his public persona of the loner, assiduously cultivated his career early within the establishment structure of the German university system. See Allen Wedell and Martin J. Kelin, "Some Unnoticed Publications by Einstein," *Isis* (1977), *68* pp. 601–604.

23. Clifford Geertz, "Deep Play: Notes on the Balinese Cockfight," in *The Interpretation of Culture* (New York: 1973), pp. 412–454. The quotation is in *Ibid*, p. 216.

24. The problem of charismatic leadership is a constant reproach to conventional social theorists who are always reluctant to address themselves to single individuals. In the field of science and in the social history of science, the individual is unavoidable.

25. Thomas S. Kuhn, *The Structure of Scientific Revolutions* (Chicago; University of Chicago Press, 1961), second edition with "Postcript," (1970).

26. *Ibid*., first edition, pp. 110–134.

27. Sociologists of science and social historians ignore this aspect of Kuhn's ideas. Philosophers concentrate upon it because it is here that Kuhn directly attacks the old epistomology. The quarrel is whether the process of creativity in science is "the psychology of invention" or "the logic of scientific discovery." Kuhn's most persistent critic on this point has been Dudley Shapere, "Plausibility and Justification in the Development of Science," *Journal of Philosophy*, (1966), *63* pp. 611–621, to the development of an alternative in, "Notes towards a Post-Positivistic Interpretation of Science," in (eds.) Peter Achinstein and Stephen F. Barker, *The Legacy of Logical Positivism* (Baltimore: 1969), pp. 115–160, and *Galileo: a Philosophical Study* (Chicago: University of Chicago Press, 1974). See also his review of Kuhn's *Structure of Scientific Revolutions*, Shapere, "The Structure of Scientific Revolutions," *Philosophical Review, 73* (1964), pp. 383–394. Several other philosophers have developed alternatives to Kuhn. See Ian Musgrave and Imre Lakatos (eds.) *Criticism and the Growth of Knowledge* (Cambridge: Cambridge University Press, 1970), especially the essay by Imre Lakatos, "Falsification and the Methodology of Scientific Research Programs," pp. 91–196. Lakatos developed the most detailed alternative to Kuhn's philosophy of science. See Lakatos, *Proofs and Refutations* (Cambridge: 1976), and, *Philosophical Papers* (Cambridge, 1978) 2 vols., and Mary Hesse, *The Structure of Scientific Inference* (Berkeley, Calif.: University of California Press, 1974). See Frederick Suppes (ed.) *The Structure of Scientific Theories* (Urbana, Ill.: University of Illinois

Press, 1977), pp. 6–232, for an excellent account of the state of affairs in the philosophy of science since Kuhn. Stephen Toulmin, *Human Understanding* (Princeton: Princeton University Press, 1972) is the culmination of an evolutionary theory of development of science begun before Kuhn's *Structures* appeared. The most developed philosophy of science to take history into account before Kuhn was Karl Popper, *The Logic of Scientific Discovery* (London: Hutchinson, 1959) and *Conjectures and Refutations* (New York: Basic Books, 1965). The common problem of philosophers who insist that science is a purely intellectual endeavor, while refuting the old positivist epistemology, is to redefine rational. If they accept that science develops over time through the activity of men, that theories of science guide experiment and are the means through which experiment gains any meaning, they must develop new criteria for determining the rationality of acts of choice made in Science between competing interpretations or theories. No such criteria have surfaced as yet. Philosophers have largely been unsuccessful in these attempts. See Larry Laudans, *Progress and Its Problems* (Berkeley: University of California Press, 1977) for a recent attempt. The problem of trying to force scientific research into a purely rational mold is illustrated in Mary Hesse, "Reason and Evaluation in the History of Science," in Mickulaus Teich and Robert Young (eds.) *Changing Perspectives in the History of Science* (London: Heinemann, 1973), pp. 127–148 and P. M. Rattansi's commentary, pps. 148–166.

28. Kuhn's psychology cannot account for the protracted struggles in the eighteenth and early nineteenth centuries to construct a complete mechanics. Certainly Newton's *Principia* was called upon, but more symbolically than actually, for its content or method in constructing that new science. A language, differential and integral calculus, had to be created and then developed. The calculus was used to express new concepts, not contained in the work of Newton or Descartes, then to understand them in their mathematical form and then to interpret them physically. See Clifford Truesdell, "Reactions of Late Baroque Mechanics to Success, Conjecture, Error and Failure in Newton's *Principia*," *Texas Quarterly*, (1967), *10* pp. 239–259. Nor does Kuhn's psychology capture the struggles of a scientist trying to express precisely his meaning and new ideas. See Westfall, *Force in Newton's Physics*, pp. 360–363, and chap. 9, as Newton tried to capture the meaning of his new concept of force and framed and reframed his ideas.

29. This is common to science and any other creative field. Reorientation must be followed by interpretation. This is done by pursuing its implications in particular cases or circumstances to reach concrete results or particular artistic forms. Some of these problems for science have

been examined by Robert Westman, "The Melancthon Circle, Rheticus and the Wittenburg Interpretation of the Copernican Theory," *Isis*, *66* (1975), pp. 165–193.

30. There are few scholars who have tried to investigate the creative process in science. One of the most consistent in trying to understand the history of science through an understanding of genius is Gerald Holton, *The Scientific Imagination* (New York: Cambridge University Press, 1978). See also Jacques Hadamard, *The Psychology of Invention in the Mathematical Field* (Princeton: Princeton University Press, 1945).

31. Kuhn, *op cit.*, (note 25), first edition, pp. 151–152. In revolutions Kuhn also neglects the role of experimental evidence, which has in important instances, (the quantum revolution) materially altered theoreticians' conceptions of the key problems they were examining. Here enters the vexed issue of the dependence of science and its ideas on available technology, a problem we will consider in a later paper.

32. Kuhn, "The Relationship between History and History of Science," *Daedalus*, *100* (1971), pp. 271–304, reprinted in *The Essential Tension: Selected Studies in Scientific Tradition and Change* (Chicago: University Press)

33. Gavin de Beer, Charles Darwin (London: Nelson, 1963).

34. A similar discussion is possible for Newton's *Mathematical Principles of Natural Philosophy*, and for his *Opticks*.

35. Edward Manier, *Young Darwin and His Cultural Circle* (Boston: Roidel, 1978), pp. 75–85, especially 82–83.

Science, Biography, and the Nonrational:
Some Issues in the Social Psychology of Science

MARION S. GOLDMAN.[1]

INTRODUCTION

T HIS discussion complements and goes beyond that of Elizabeth Garber and Fred Weinstein's "The History of Science and Social History."[2] Garber and Weinstein's main point is that few theoretical or empirical links between social theory and personal ideas have been established. Sociologies of science, whether Marxist, functionalist, anthropological, or historical, have not proven their contention that social and cultural circumstances shape scientific ideas. By contrast, I will show that a sociology of science should integrate a conception of cultural and institutional effects, a social psychology of creative processes, and an analysis of personal development and human subjectivity with the ways in which scientific views of the natural and physical worlds are achieved. This will be illustrative rather than definitive, however, because a theory of science as complex as we envision cannot, at this point, be fully derived.

In a society so dependent upon scientific innovation for economic growth and improvement of our daily lives, scientists have become, perhaps inadvertently, moral philosophers, shaping our existence. Yet the social sciences and the public, ironically, know less about the "hard" sciences than they do about middle-class housewives and factory workers.[3]

IRRATIONALITY IN SCIENTIFIC DISCOVERY

The popular, and often social scientific, view of "hard" scientists is that they develop knowledge in an orderly and rational manner (Streisinger, 1981:41).[4] This "outsider's" view of the sciences makes them appear more rational than they really are. Actually, the sciences proceed erratically, frequently moving in spurts and stops, in misdirections, and with faulty methodologies. The only self-correcting mechanism in the sciences is the prescription to scientists that "an idea in science is useful only if it leads to further experiments, even if those experiments disprove the idea that generated them" (Streisinger, 1981:42). It is the continuous return to examine the same scientific idea that acts as a corrective to the error and irrationality often intrinsic to science.

Irrationality in science does not always have to be disfunctional. Extraordinarily irrational commitment is essential to the creative process. Science at the cutting edge proceeds in a knowledge void. Only irrationally committed individuals can overcome the anxiety that void engenders and continue their pursuit of knowledge. Tenacious personal investment and irrational attachment to an idea, therefore, can lead to creative scientific innovation and new scientific knowledge.

Irrational commitment to a particular line of thought or to a particular scientific methodological strategy can have the opposite effect. Scientists can dedicate their lives to an idea or an approach which, in the long run, proves to be useless. The discovery of the structure of DNA is one of the greatest chapters in the history of science, yet it is strewn with illustrations of irrational commitments, irrational grounds for action, and misdirected ideas. It is also filled with obsessions that generated the greatest biological discovery of the twentieth century.

For example, Fredrick Twort, a British bacteriologist, spent twenty years trying to determine how tiny bacteriophage multiplied, a problem occupying many biologists interested in cellular development. He set out to find the proper nutrient culture in which phage would grow in the laboratory. Once phage could be produced in large numbers in an environment that could be examined through microscopic observation, Twort assumed he could describe their multiplying process. Twort's theory appeared simple and logical and he continued, apparently without end, to search for a laboratory substance that would grow bacteriophage. Later it was discovered that phage could only grow inside other bacteria, and there was no external culture that would nurture them. Twort's failure resided in his irrational commitment to a line of inquiry that just could not work.

Similarly, in the early 1950s, an x-ray crystallographer, Rosalind Franklin, through a process of x-ray refraction, worked to discover the structure of DNA. By shooting x-rays through a cell and then observing the ways they refracted upon an x-ray plate, Franklin made "pictures" of cells' structure. One accidental, unique x-ray picture of a wet cell sent Franklin off looking for a new fundamental chemical law and convinced her that DNA was not helixical in shape, although it was commonly believed to be so.

Throughout her research, Franklin shared her x-ray pictures with James Watson, who, with Francis Crick, later discovered the structure of DNA. Watson, however, never fully befriended Franklin and admittedly treated her badly because she was a woman scientist (Watson, 1968:

Epilogue). Franklin never had a colleague to dissuade her from a misguided belief. To be sure, Franklin's irrational commitment to a particular idea was her own doing, but she was isolated in the scientific community because she was a female in a male world. Franklin's work was also the victim of irrational gender discrimination (Judson, 1979; Platt, 1983; Sayre, 1975).

Before World War II, relatively few scientists believed that DNA was the material of heredity. However, in 1952, A. D. Hershey and Martha Chase demonstrated that the same phage Frederick Twort had been trying to nurture *in vitro* grew inside bacteria by means of a complex process—the phage first attached to the host's outside by the tip of its tail. The phage then injected DNA into the bacterium while the protein "package" of the phage, that is its outer body, remained on the outside of the bacterium host. The DNA inside the bacterium then reproduced all of the phage, both the outer protein package and the inner DNA. This experiment demonstrated to Hershey and Chase that not only could they reproduce phage through this method but that DNA was the material critical for the reproduction of cellular life. Many other scientists had to discard their own theories.

It was about this time that the competition involved in the discovery of the structure of DNA began in earnest. In science, where priority of discovery is often of utmost importance to individuals in competition, the struggle was on. Franklin had been close as noted, but she became misdirected. Linus Pauling, the winner of two Nobel Prizes, entered the race. He was Watson's most feared competitor. However, Pauling suggested a three-strand model of DNA, which proved incorrect and finally discouraged his involvement.

James Watson, the young, and by his own description, single-minded scientist, with his co-worker Francis Crick, working day and night to keep ahead of the competition, finally offered the correct ideas. It was not through experimentation but by constructing paper and wire models that they broke the DNA code and established its structure. The night before the discovery, Watson, while speaking to a chemist friend, by chance, acquired some new chemical information which put into place the final pieces of the puzzle (Watson, 1968). The next day Watson and Crick designed a model that represented four base pairs and the intertwined double helix. This was their break-through structural model, described in a 900-word paper and published in *Nature*.

In the cases of Twort and Franklin, irrational single-mindedness in the search of scientific truth produced failures. Watson and Crick were no less irrationally committed to their ideas and to a desire to discover the structure of DNA than were the former two. However, in their case

the commitment culminated in the correct solution and the most significant biological breakthrough of the twentieth century. The most important point to draw from their achievement for a sociology of science
is not their success, but that they could not know when they set out to
discover DNA that they would do so. It is that point alone that substan-
tiates the need to recognize and theorize about personal, irrational commitments in an adequate sociology of science.

We can conclude that irrationality, as well as rationality, chance, and
good luck are as important in scientific discovery as are the years of
training and carefully planned research. Science is not a smooth road
to discovery dominated by the rational accumulation of knowledge
through rational contemplation and research. To understand the scientific process as a sociological phenomenon, science must be characterized in all its complexity. To describe it solely as a rational social
process is not to characterize it but to caricature it and, thus, to remove
it from the natural order of social life.

Institutional Influences upon Scientific Discovery

A myth surrounding scientific discovery is that it is pure and objective,
untainted by the interests of governments, the marketplace, or personal
aggrandizement. Like all myths, this one is only partially true. The great
European explorers of the fifteenth century, precursors to modern scientists, were driven by the intellectual curiosity of discovery but were
financially supported by the crowns of Europe interested in acquiring
new lands to own and exploit. The early celestial observers of the six-
teenth century were interested in objective knowledge about the movement of heavenly bodies and the place of earth in the universe, but they
were also involved in improving navigational laws for European
explorers. The scientific explosion of the seventeenth century, while
stimulated by religious motives to understand God's workings, simultaneously served the interests of the developing capitalist industrial revolution.

Scientific discovery is always a blend of the influences of pure and
practical motives. Scientists want to know the truth, but they also are
influenced by those who fund their work and by personal desires to be
rich and famous.

Nowhere is this pattern better evidenced than in contemporary molecular biological research. For example, in the health sciences, research
on human cells and their mutation involves the use of human blood,
tissues, or organs in the production of cell lines. There is now a struggle
over who owns and can market what is developed. A cell line is a culture

of living cells that can be grown indefinitely in a laboratory environment. Scientific supply houses routinely sell common cell lines for use in science classes, and for years researchers working on the same problems have shared cell lines with one another. Some new biological technologies involving *in vitro* synthesis of substances like insulin or interferon have been developed from cell lines. These potentially immensely profitable treatments of cell lines have raised a number of legal questions and financial struggles that threaten and influence scientific research and the scientific community, itself.

When researchers share cell lines they have developed, who has title to them? What if a cell line with some slight alteration yields an unexpected, but extremely lucrative product—such as a safe, highly controllable protein that destroys unnecessary human body fat? Battles over patents and prerogatives among researchers, universities, government agencies, and corporations are finding their ways into the courts, and more will come.

Some recent litigation involves the rights of blood or tissue donors to the ultimate products scientists derive from their cells. At major research centers in the health sciences, blood or organs removed in the course of treatment regularly become used in research. In a recent lawsuit, a former patient claimed that researchers used his blood and spleen to generate discoveries of sufficient financial promise to merit the scientists' and their university's application for a patent. The plaintiff asserted that his blood was "unique," and he had therefore been cheated out of the right to share in profits derived from his body (Clark and Tibbetts, 1984). At this point, no usable products have been developed from the plaintiff's tissues, and the patent, itself, represented an attempt upon the part of the researchers and the university to safeguard against later litigation if a promising set of treatments were derived from the tissue cell line.

The legal issues of who owns what and the implications of that ownership will undoubtedly take decades to interpret. In the meantime, the vague possibilities of immense profits from basic research in the health and biological sciences introduce nonrational, extraneous elements into the process of scientific discovery. The resolution of legal conflicts takes time and financial support away from the research enterprise itself and undermines some of the social-psychological cornerstones associated with scientific discovery. The increasingly necessary consideration of the legal and financial consequences of sharing cell lines throughout a research community erodes the fragile cooperation that is also part of science. Modern science, despite the tenacious individualism of a James Watson and others, is also based on collective efforts within research teams and throughout national and international research networks.

Technicians, as well as principal investigators, can be brought into devastating litigation by merely performing everyday laboratory tasks on disputed materials. Questions of ownership could extend from cell lines to experimental procedures to scientific results themselves. The confidence that is a part of science is shaken unduly by the possibilities of stringent patent regulations and a tangle of new litigation that is almost a comic replica of the struggles over mineral rights that occurred a century earlier in the United States.

We have noted only the financial and legal struggles over cell lines. Similar and perhaps even more intense struggles are going on in the areas of electrical engineering, laser technology, the investigation of space, and space technology. The case of cell lines is illustrative of external influences in molecular biology, but even in this domain of science, it is only a small part of the governmental and corporate intervention in research developments in the discipline. Cures for cancer, burn treatment, skin grafting, methods of contraception, organ transplants, the development of "artificial" or "new" cell strains for industry, government, or military use are all areas of research influenced by the discovery of DNA. These areas of research are under extreme pressure from external institutions to follow paths of development serving profit and power interests of one or another form.

We have noted that science was never entirely pure or objective, but the stakes over the direction of scientific development have never been as high as they are today in modern societies. The nonrational factors now influencing science from institutional interests external to it have never been greater.

GENDER AND SCIENCE

Science, similar to any institutionally defined occupation, favors particular personal cognitive and emotive styles. Cognitive and emotive styles tend to be unconscious and, thus, removed from conscious examination, reflection, manipulation, and change. Scientists who do not publicly exhibit cognitive and emotive styles familarly associated with the occupation of science tend to be punished by other scientists, even when such punishment is irrational, because it is related to personal styles and not the significance of the individuals' scientific contributions (Keller, 1978:409–411; and 1982:559–595).

Despite this, studies of cognitive and emotive styles among scientists indicates that there are considerable differences and variations among scientists in their personal styles depending upon their gender, ethnic and cultural background, scientific disciplines (and even subdisciplines), degrees of professional accomplishment, and recognition within the sciences (Keller, 1975:428). Nevertheless, certain themes in the life histories and self-perceptions of scientists appear to emerge consistently.

Physical scientists tend to rank high on personality measures of autonomy and of masculinity (in which masculine responses are defined as the opposite of those usually given by women). Scientists are characterized as having high needs for separation and individuation (Keller, 1982:599–600). David McClelland found that ninety percent of his sample responded to the "mother-son" picture in the Thematic Apperception Test by suggesting parents and children should go their separate ways. This response sharply contrasts with the story given to the same picture by a general sample of people who were not scientists (McClelland, 1962:309–341).

Evelyn Fox Keller, a mathematical biologist, physicist, and scientific biographer, has examined the interdependence of masculinity and culture in American society in terms of the earliest relationships of sons and mothers. Keller argues that the majority of men who shape and are in turn shaped by the structure of scientific research share a particular stance toward other people which developed in their early years when they were dependent upon their mothers for nurturance and emotional support. Using a psychoanalytic object-relations approach,[5] she sought to account for the "scientific personality" in terms of innate drives and in terms of early relationships with significant individuals, such as the relationship of sons to mothers.

Infant boys are faced with an early maternal environment that is deeply at odds with cultural definitions of masculinity. Maleness in our culture is defined in opposition to femaleness. As boys develop in our society, they are asked and forced to give up from their personalities everything that reflects expressions of culturally defined femaleness.

The early and essential mothering of boys creates an environmental circumstance that is contradictory to the ideal of masculine independence and autonomy. Among boys whose inborn traits and/or interactions with their mothers make their early struggles for independence more conflictual than is usually the case, this contradiction between the needs for nurturance and those for autonomy creates an intense anxiety about self-identity and maleness. As men, these boys try to alleviate their anxiety by striving for autonomy through social and public expressions of power, rationality, and objectivity. This extreme autonomy comes at a cost: it carries with it not only the satisfaction of independence and masculinity but also negative and frightening feelings of isolation and unconscious fantasies of aggression toward the mother. Men so conflicted as boys enter into a never ending cycle of striving for greater autonomy and mastery. This provokes anxiety over feelings of loss and aggression and, in turn, leads to intensified striving for independence and mastery to quell the unconscious anxiety (Keller, 1982:595–598).

Keller suggests these extreme, stereotypically masculine types gravitate toward the sciences. The culture of masculinity not only dominates the cognitive and emotive styles of these professions but also shapes the ontologies found in scientific theories, the definition of problems and their methodologies (Keller, 1982:590–591). Keller points out that the sciences, organizationally and theoretically, consistently reiterate masculine cultural themes of hierarchy, dominance, and independence. An understanding of the origins of scientific theory must also include an understanding of psychological origins and cultural supports for maleness in our society.

Keller illustrates this last point through a discussion of Barbara McClintock, the Nobel Laureate geneticist, virtually unknown outside the scientific community when Keller began to write about her. McClintock's theorizing is opposed to a male cultural conception of hierarchy and domination. Her "feeling for the organism" led her to describe DNA in constant, delicate interaction with its environment. McClintock suggests the program encoded by DNA is itself subject to change, because cellular development is complex and systemic (McClintock, 1980). This perspective assumes an interdependence rather than domination, and Keller suggests it reflects a female worldview focusing on interaction rather than a male culture stressing hierarchy and domination.

Keller's work can function as a starting point for a psychoanalytic model to investigate the development of the sciences. There are, of course, a number of other psychoanalytic approaches that could be used besides the object-relations model. They could be applied to systems of thought and interpersonal relationships, rather than solely focused upon individual dynamics.

Science has become so mythologized in our culture that it is often difficult to think of it as an object of study open to question. Many of the studies discussed in this chapter and in Garber and Weinstein, "The History of Science as Social History," are several decades old. We do not know what the effects of new technologies, discoveries, or institutional influences have been on science. However, science is part of society, as are scientists, and both, therefore, are open to sociological investigation and to understanding as social and psychological phenomena.

Perhaps the great scientists such as Einstein or McClintock are by definition unique, since they offered new ways of looking at scientific "realities." Most other scientists, seem to share the worldviews, backgrounds, and traits of those described by McClelland and Keller. The history, sociology, and psychology of science must, therefore, account for ways in which the very fibers of science are affected by the dominating cognitive and emotive styles. The ultimate goal is to make the processes of science, in all their nuances, accessible and understandable from a sociological perspective.

A PERSONAL REMINISCENCE OF A MOLECULAR BIOLOGIST: GEORGE STREISINGER

A good way to illustrate the issues involved in a sociology of science is to highlight some observations on a scientist and colleague from the University of Oregon. George Streisinger was a molecular biologist and development geneticist. He used to introduce his beginning level classes to science by showing them slides of Nobel Prize winners hiking, having picnics, or playing with their kids in order to indicate that "scientists are people too." I hope this portrait of his career will put a more "human element" into the preceding discussion of science and society.[6]

Streisinger's personality was markedly different from the popular stereotype of a cold, competitive, introverted researcher. One of his teachers, Nobel Prize winner Salvador E. Luria, described him as buoyant and dynamic. His colleagues appreciated his personal warmth, interest in others' ideas, and political commitment to a just and equalitarian society (Luria, 1984:131). The Institute of Molecular Biology, which he helped build, is well known for its unusual emphasis on cooperation, and its members' collective vision of science as an intensely human enterprise (Hager, 1984). The scientist's work and the Institute are nonetheless very much part of the mainstream of national and international molecular biology. Streisinger's professional biography illuminates many of the questions that must be examined in order to develop a social psychological theory of science.

Streisinger was born in Budapest between the World Wars, in a city torn by the fall of an empire and soon to partake of worldwide depression (Stahl, 1985). His early curiosity and interest in nature led him to the wave machine at the Hotel Gellert and the lizards sunning on the hills above it. In 1939, he left them behind, emigrating from Hungary to the United States with his mother and brother. They settled in New York City, where Streisinger attended the Bronx High School of Science. His continuing interest in herpetology filled the family flat with salamanders.[7]

Although he seldom spoke of the past, Streisinger sometimes speculated with his students and colleagues about the impact of the Nazi terror on the current state of science in the United States and the world as a whole. By the end of World War II, the ultimate irrationality of Nazi ideology led to the extermination of many millions of European Jews, other "non-Aryans," and progressives—some of them were scientists, and some of them may have become scientists. A surprising number of scientists managed to escape and many of them, like Streisinger, came to the United States. During and after the war the close cooperation and interaction of scientists from every European nation led to an extraordinary growth of research and discovery in a number of scientific disciplines. The irrational horror surrounding World War II created, according to Streisinger, a strange and startling opportunity for collegial cooperation.

Little research has addressed the full impact of the War on the scientific community and its composition; those remain critical areas for a full understanding of American science. We can say, as Streisinger did, that policies of extraordinary irrationality influenced science and scientists and that the effects of those policies need to be further understood.

At the age of sixteen, Streisinger co-authored his first publication, "Experiments on Sexual Isolation in *Drosophila*" (1944), with the noted geneticist, Theodosius Dobzhansky. He was the sole author of two more papers on fruit flies in 1946 and 1948. His undergraduate years at Cornell, however, were not entirely distinguished. According to his own accounts, Streisinger nearly flunked out of the College of Agriculture because he was not particularly interested in subjects other than science and because he had recurring troubles with requirements in physical education and R.O.T.C.

These biographical notes raise additional questions concerning the psychology and sociology of science. Streisinger exhibited a consuming interest and extraordinary talent for science at an early age, as have many other noted researchers. What are the relationships between early predispositions and later achievements? How do social support and academic encouragement facilitate the development of scientists, and how does their absence, as Keller has asserted is often the case for women, mitigate against scientific achievement? Finally, how do unique personality traits and life histories affect career outcomes?

In 1953 Streisinger completed his doctorate with Luria at the University of Illinois and published a series of papers in genetics while concluding postdoctoral research at Cal Tech. Working at the famous Cold Spring Harbor Laboratory and at the MRC at Cambridge, he did work on the biology of phage T4 proteins and their genes and on the phage T4 chromosome structure. Moving to the University of Oregon, he continued his research on phage, broadening scientific knowledge of the structure of proteins and their mutation. Through his work on T4 phage,

Streisinger discovered that circular linkage in chromosome structure was widespread and not limited to *E. coli*, as was once believed. This was a real breakthrough for research in molecular biology that "had a liberalizing effect on everyone's notions about chromosomes" (Stahl, 1985).

By 1970, Streisinger had moved back to the cold-blooded vertebrates that interested him in his childhood. He set about developing a method to study vertebrate genetics with the same relative ease and rigor that scientists used to study far simpler phage genetics. He developed a method of causing parthenogenesis of mutant female zebra fish. With this work he created a sophisticated method of cloning and an extraordinary new resource for the study of vertebrate genetics. His method allowed for the immediate expression of recessive mutations in a large, rapidly maturing population. Streisinger had, in essence, created "a phage with backbone," a vital, new source of information for biologists throughout the world.

He published four papers on zebra fish, the earliest of which earned Streisinger recognition on the cover of *Nature* in the spring of 1981. He was preparing two new papers when he died suddenly of heart failure in the summer of 1984. Streisinger's distinguished scientific career will probably have little direct impact on a large popular audience, and his name will not be a household word like those of a handful of modern researchers. Yet his career and those of other significant, relatively unknown researchers are the stuff that science is made of. This is material for understanding the intricate, complex interactions between character and culture as they affect the science and technology that have such a vast impact on social organization.

Streisinger's scientific career also raises a number of issues concerning mentorship, colleagueship, and our understanding of the interaction among scientific disciplines. His postgraduate career at Cold Spring Harbor, Cal Tech, and Cambridge follows the general pattern of distinguished science as it is practiced at distinguished institutions. The bulk of Streisinger's contributions were made while he was on the faculty of the University of Oregon, an historically underfunded and geographically isolated institution. That university, however, has managed to sustain important research institutes in both molecular biology and theoretical physics. The existence of a major, internationally recognized Institute of Molecular Biology in Eugene, Oregon, suggests the need to study patterns of collegial support and communication among scientists as they build through everyday interaction and as they can be sustained at long distance.

Streisinger's scientific career also indicates a need to view formal disciplinary boundaries with some skepticism. His thinking and research crossed between developmental genetics and molecular biology. It was sometimes hard to tell where one left off and the other began. Much of the best science does not stay within the boundaries of one discipline, and many categories have been artificially imposed. Some of the best science also does not stay within universities. Streisinger's findings on chemically induced mutations in phage T4 led him to become a student of chemically induced mutagenesis. He was actively involved with understanding and preventing the potentially mutagenic consequences of herbicides applied to Oregon forests in the process of regeneration.

He brought his scientific creativity and meticulousness into other areas of general concern. Streisinger was a gourmet cook, and shortly after the first of his pathbreaking zebra fish articles appeared, he was a guest chef at a nouvelle haute quisine restaurant. (The menu, however, was not fish.) A number of other scientists are excellent cooks, and this aspect of masculine nurturance contradicts some of Keller and McClelland's notions of the nonnurturing "male scientific personality." The relationship between science and cooking deserves further investigation on its own terms, since it may tell us something general about creativity and ways in which very different kinds of work are more similar than we think.

Perhaps nothing brings use closer to the heart of science than the day-to-day relations among colleagues and co-workers. The process of creativity is both isolated and collective. Streisinger's impact on his fellow scientists is best summed up by the statement made at his funeral by another distinguished molecular biologist, Frank Stahl:

> I depended on George. No matter that he was sometimes late. For the really important things, I depended on him. I depended on George as my standard of excellence in science. Not only was he always supportive, but his intuition, his industry, and his courage lighted my way. I learned a lot from George. On the other hand, I never managed to teach him to write his papers on time. And energy—I could count on George's energy and enthusiasm to warm and refuel me. And indignation—like right now I'm mad that George is gone! And I feel lost that he's not here to wax indignant over the unfairness of it. And I depended on George for sweet things—like the July sun at Indian Creek, and the flower baskets that appeared magically on May Day. This summer was a sweet one for George. He'd loved his work and his colleagues, and his friends, and his family—and it showed. And that made our summer sweet, too.

Some Concluding Remarks

It is clear that the social sciences do not understand the hard sciences well enough. There is something important and profound in this failure. The social sciences are undergoing a general crisis. Quantitative and structural sociologies, those found in the various versions of positivism, Marxism, or functionalism cannot provide the understanding of social behavior equal to their original promise. This volume on forms of psychoanalytic sociology is a reflection of this crisis. A group of sociologists is looking to another discipline to find the intellectual stimulation and new lines of thought to revitalize sociology: that is, to develop better social theory.

Underlying all of this is the realization that social life is more complex, more multilayered than we ever thought—if that point needs to be underlined one more time after all that has been said. This group of psychoanalytically oriented sociologists has come to realize that traditional social theories just will not do. Sociology must develop theory adequate to the task of explaining the complexity, the multidimensionality of social life. Such theorizing needs to provide for cultural and institutional influences, for personal development, and for conscious, unconscious, rational, nonrational, and irrational subjective thought. Traditional approaches just cannot account for the unpredictability, the capriciousness, the plain reality of social life.

NOTES

1. Although I bear responsibility for this article, it is really a collective effort. In the best tradition of science, Gerald Platt helped order and refine the ideas in my original draft, improving it beyond measure.

2. Garber and Weinstein have provided a thorough overview of social science literature on the organization and development of sciences, and the reader is referred to their article for additional bibliographic materials.

3. I have mentioned these two populations because a number of extremely popular books in the social sciences published over the past decade dealt with them (Aaronowitz, 1973 and Friedan, 1962).

4. Many of the examples used in this paper are derived from George Streisinger's "Notes on Growth, Reproduction and Heredity" (1981). These, in turn, are related to an earlier series of class notes printed from the introduction to molecular biology given by Salvador E. Luria at the University of Illinois.

5. That is, the study of intense, emotionally charged relationships with significant others.

6. In an attempt to make science more accessible to the general public, the Alfred P. Sloan Foundation supports the writing and publication of the autobiographies, reminiscences, and personal essays of accomplished scientists. This brief discussion reflects the general direction of the development of a widely read, general history of science.

7. The biographical information in this section was derived from an obituary written by Franklin Stahl. The interpretations are the author's and do not reflect Professor Stahl's opinions.

REFERENCES

AARONOWITZ, S.
 1977 False Promises. New York: McGraw Hill.
CLARK, M., AND TIBBETTS, L.
 1984 "Research Issue: Who Owns Patients' Cell Lines?" Newsweek Magazine, September 24, p. 61.
FRIEDAN, B.
 1962 The Feminine Mystique. New York: W. W. Norton.
HAGER, T.
 1984 "The Making of an Institute," pp. 22–27 in Old Oregon. December.
JUDSON, H. F.
 1979 The Eighth Day of Creation. New York: Simon & Schuster.
KELLER, E. F.
 1978 "Gender and Science." Psychoanalysis and Contemporary Thought 1: 409–433.
 1982 "Feminism and Science." Signs: A Journal of Women in Culture and Society 7: 589–602.
LURIA, S. E.
 1984 A Slot Machine, A Broken Test Tube. New York: Harper & Row.
McCLELLAND, D. C.
 1962 "On the Dynamics of Creative Physical Scientists," pp. 309–341 in L. Hudson (ed.), The Ecology of Human Intelligence. London: Penguin Books.
McCLINTOCK, B.
 1980 "Modified Gene Expression Induced by Transposable Elements," in W. A. Scott, R. Werner, and J. Schultz (eds.), Mobilization and Reassembly of Genetic Information. New York: Academic Press.
PLATT, L.
 1983 "The Discovery of DNA and the Failure of Rosalind Franklin." Unpublished paper.
SAYRE, A.
 1975 Rosalind Franklin and DNA. New York: W. W. Norton.
STAHL, F.
 1985 "Obituary of George Streisinger," Genetics (forthcoming).
STREISINGER, G.
 1981 "Notes on Growth, Reproduction, and Heredity: the Molecular Basis of Some Biological Processes." Class Notes for Biology 105 Reproduced at the University of Oregon.

VII

Five Perspectives on the Psychoanalytic Sociology of Society

Introduction

The student-reader now has a good conception of the relation of sociology to psychoanalysis. He or she also has a good conception of the ways these approaches have been applied to the study of topics such as gender, deviance, science, and collective behavior. In this section, we take the time to summarize ways in which the two disciplines have been associated with each other over the years. Such a review will help the student understand past successes and failures in attempting to integrate the two disciplines.

Simultaneously, we present a paper by Neil Smelser that suggests that cultural values, such as individualism and rationality, that characterize our society are nonrational myths to which Americans adhere. In his paper, "Collective Myths and Fantasies" Smelser suggests that the "good life in California" is just more of the same good life that has always existed in America; it is "competitive individualism," and California is hardly a laid-back society. In analyzing American myths, Smelser reports that while they may exhibit paradox, reversal, irony, and even ambivalence, in the end, they serve the function of supporting traditional American commercial and political values.

Myths, of course, are not only found among societal members; occupations and professions also have myths about their origins and importance. In the following little fairy tale, Jerome Rabow captures the mythic history of the relation between sociology and psychoanalysis.

A Fairy Tale

When we sociologists were introduced to sociology we learned that it was the queen of the social sciences. As queen she and she alone was concerned with the social, political and economic realities that profoundly affected people's lives. She was respected for the bold and daring generalizations she pronounced, generalizations that seemed to outflank and outrank the other and lesser social sciences. Many knights were eager to enter this kingdom and become subjects of the queen. Others, unhappy with the queen's grandiosity, searched for and found a realm where psychoanalysis was king. In this kingdom, the subjects burrowed and tunneled into the depths of the human mind to discover the realities of Oedipal battles and their resolutions and the repressed libidinal and aggressive drives. These subjects were convinced that civilization rested upon the covered discontents of mankind. It was a matter of time before the growing and expanding kingdoms encountered one another. There was immediate initial attraction. Differences between the two seemed minor and paled when considered in the light of their overall concern for truth and scientific discovery. There were moments of rapture and delight as each found the other's view supplemental and unthreatening. They began to share deep secrets and assumptions, and it seemed that the courtship would ripen into a mature union. A closer examination would have revealed that such excitement was premature. Envy operated below the surface and the public pronouncements of appreciation were countered by private utterings that the knights from the other kingdom were not wanted in the realm. Each group felt it was sufficient unto itself. The unification efforts ceased and the subjects and disciples of the queen retreated into their lofty, ivory towers removed from primary process, while the disciples and subjects of the king burrowed into training institutes and away from empirical and temporal investigation. Having parted they each prospered. The training and recruitment of new subjects was not difficult for either of the groups. Stereotypes about each other's deficiencies were perpetuated at annual meetings and in professional journals. Knights of the queen were seen as deceivers of youth who perpetuated illusions of utopian societies. Knights of psychoanalysis were seen as too introspective and politically insensitive. Gradually, with time and the passing away of the elders, the subjects of the two realms became less harsh in their judgments of each other. Brave individuals attempted a reapproachment. A man of heart and a devout parson were instrumental leaders in this movement. The hearty man established the adaptive functions of the ego in contrast to a repressed functioning ego. The devout parson articulated the organizing and symbolic functions of culture in relation to the id or primary process, and argued for a non-antagonistic relationship between the individual and society. A son of Erik, a child from another kingdom, and oriented toward art during his youth, did much for establishing the legitimacy of the king and queen's interests. Erik recognized new stages of development and translated the discoveries of each into recognizable objects and processes. The journals of the king began making references to the value of studying object relations, while the queen's journals had references to regression in groups and oedipal struggles. New kingdoms in cybernetics and information theory were cited by both. With the growth and increasing security of each of the two realms, a reconciliation between the two is being considered. Will it occur? (Rabow, 1981. p. 119–18).

The question posed at the end of the fairy tale is similar to one posed by Smelser at the close of his article but of less significance. Smelser asks: Will the future bring positive change to American values? Rabow asks:

Will the relation between the two disciplines improve? Whether new myths will develop for both America and sociology's relation to psychoanalysis depends upon how inappropriate the present myths are viewed to be for the development of both. In this sense, the process of myth-making is similar for societies and disciplines.

In his article about the discipline of psychoanalytic sociology, Rabow summarizes the different ways sociology and psychoanalysis have been connected recently and in the past. Rabow argues that these various integrations are based on the degree of emphasis given to one or another of the disciplines. His essay brings together a large body of work in an emerging discipline. It succeeds by simplifying an exceedingly complex literature. Rabow ends the piece by offering fruitful directions in which the integrations may proceed.

Rabow presents five categories of integration which he entitles "acknowledging," "gauntlet," "suggestive," "integrative," and the "sociology of knowledge." The discussions in each of the sections elaborately speak for themselves. However, it should be pointed out that each of these five forms of integration can be used to understand the approaches of specific articles, monographs, and discourses in the area of psychoanalytic sociology.

The future of the social sciences, as with all disciplines, rests on the generations of students who pursue careers within them. The future of social scientific disciplines rests, in turn, on the education of students as researchers, theorists, and critics. It is our wish that this will mean students who recognize and appreciate the complexity and multidimensionality of social life, the importance of conscious rational action, and non-conscious, irrational and nonrational behavior. It is the intention of psychoanalytic sociology to educate students in the social sciences about these complexities and levels of analysis.

REFERENCES

RABOW, J.
1981 "Psychoanalysis and Sociology: A Selective Review." *Sociology and Social Research* 65 (2);117–28.

Collective Myths and Fantasies

NEIL J. SMELSER

INTRODUCTION

IN entering the study of collective myths and fantasies, I note first that I am aware of—and humbled by—the really noble tradition of studies in the fields of psychoanalysis and anthropology. In the former, the heritage includes the names of Freud, himself, Rank, Jung, Roheim, and Erikson; in the latter we find Westermarck, Fraser, Malinowski, Levi-Strauss, and Eliade. While these scholars have relied more or less on the special assumptions of their own disciplines, in both cases they have acknowledged that collective myths and fantasies provide a special and important link between the psychological and social sides of life. Freud regarded the formation of neuroses, the dynamics of fantasies and dreams, and "the creations of the popular mind in religion, myths, and fairy tales as manifesting the same forces in mental life" (Freud, 1959a:252). In one place he referred to myths as "distorted vestiges of the wishful phantasies of whole nations" (1959b:152). In a perhaps over-enthusiastic moment, he characterized mythology as *"nothing but psychology projected into the external world"* (1959c:258), but his writings consistently stressed the infusion of collective myths into the religious, legal, and other institutions of humankind. On the other side of the disciplinary boundary, Bronislaw Malinowski stressed the social functions of the myth—"it expresses, enhances, and codifies belief; it safeguards and enforces morality; it vouches for the efficiency of ritual and contains practical rules for the guidance of man" (1971:19). At the same time, and consistent with Freud's psychological emphasis, he noted that the telling of myths is "in satisfaction of deep religious wants, moral cravings, social submissions, assertions, even practical requirements" (1971:19).

In this essay I want to continue the stress on both the psychological and the social significances of collective myths and fantasies. I hope to open up a few new avenues of exploration of these phenomena; and unlike many past traditions of emphasizing classical, primitive, and folk myths far from our own civilization in time and place, I am going to concentrate—for illustrative purposes—on a myth which is close at hand: the myth of the good life in California.

Definition of Myth

Early in my explorations, I decided to consult the *Oxford English Dictionary*, which told me that a myth is "a purely fictitious narrative usually involving supernatural persons, actions, or events, and embodying some popular idea concerning natural or historical phenomena." Upon reflection, I found this definition a letdown. It is a mistake to regard myths as "purely fictitious." I also found the stress on the supernatural to be constricting. So I turned elsewhere and sought the assistance of a competitor, *Webster's Unabridged*. Among its six or seven meanings for myth, one especially caught my eye: "a belief or concept that embodies a visionary ideal (as of some future utopian state or condition), for example, the Marxian fostered myth of a classless society." I liked this one better, partly because of its reference to fantasy, and partly because the myth of California seemed to be a clear instance of this meaning. In the end, however, and on the basis of my explorations, I came to regard this meaning as only half-correct; my reasons for so regarding it will constitute a large part of my analysis.

The Structure of Myth: First Approximation

To begin, let us consider two simple classical myths, both dealing with gold and greed, which will prove to be important California themes: the myth of King Midas and the myth of the goose and the golden eggs. In the first, Midas had showed generous hospitality to Silenus, and Bacchus permitted him to ask any recompense he wished. Midas asked that whatever he touched would turn to gold. The very wish proved his undoing, however, since even the food he touched turned to gold, and he could not eat. So he had to ask Bacchus to revoke the favor. The second, equally familiar, involves a man who owned the goose that laid one golden egg a day. Not satisfied with the riches being accumulated, the man killed and cut open the goose, thus stopping the supply. In both myths there is desire and punishment, wish and renunciation. In both cases, moreover, there is a certain correspondence between the punishment and the crime—greed ends in the threat of starvation, and insatiability ends in deprivation. Even these simple fables offer a *number* of possibilities for identification and affective reactions on the part of the hearer. In the Midas myth, the hearer may identify with the generous Midas, the greedy Midas, the starving Midas, the penitent Midas, the generous Bacchus, or the mischievous Bacchus and may take a positive or negative posture toward any or all of these representations. Incidentally, these simple myths also reveal a social use made of them: social control. In this process *one* facet or ingredient is highlighted and made a mandate. In my daughter's literature book, where I turned to refresh my memory on the goose and the golden eggs, the story was followed up by the moral: "Beware of being greedy. It doesn't pay to be impatient." But the rest of the ingredients—the greedy wish, for example—are there to be heard as well.

As a first approximation, then, we may say that a myth has a structure that is ambivalent in at least two senses: it contains a wish and its appropriate negation; on the part of the hearer, it permits an ambivalent orientation to each of those two elements. A myth, like a dream, is full of opportunities for psychodynamic play. It is a playground for reversals, condensations, undoing, and the rest of the possibilities. A myth might be regarded as lying on a continuum of mental productions. At one end is the dream, next the daydream, next the myth, next the ideology, and, finally, formal theoretical-empirical thought. The related dimensions running along this continuum are: the relative dominance of primary or secondary process; the degree of formal structure; the self-conscious application of rules, logic, and inference to the mental production, itself.

THE HISTORICAL ELABORATION OF MYTH IN CULTURAL CONTEXT: THE CALIFORNIA MYTH

From its inception, the name, "California," has brought to mind a kind of utopia. Appearing in Spanish fiction in the late fifteenth century, it was an invented word, referring to a mythical island, and was one of a family of visions—including the Seven Cities of Cibola and El Dorado—of "an early paradise, with unbounded productiveness without labor, with beautiful women, gold and pearls" (Gudde, 1969:48). From the beginning, the myth made reference to "productiveness without labor"," and to gold and women. The land of California was thought to be located "at the right end of the Indes" and inhabited by "handsome black women like Amazons." Apparently these fantasies were closely associated with the hopes of the Spanish explorers of the time. When explorers did reach the western shores of what is now the North American continent, they applied the name of "California" to the coastland. Some time later, Sir Francis Drake named the same area "New Albion." For almost a century, there was a kind of linguistic war between the Spanish and the British over the correct name, a war symbolically representing the prior discovery and claim to the land (Gudde, 1969:49). The Spanish finally won this verbal battle; ultimately, the British acknowledged that victory. In fact, in the 1850s, London"s "fast young men" adopted the name "California" as a slangy synonym for "money," no doubt in response to the recent drama of the California Gold Rush. I am, personally, pleased that "California" won out, since "New Albion" seems a drearier name (try to think of San Francisco, New Albion). It has fewer of the fantastic and utopian connotations of the original version of "California" and would not fit so neatly into my analysis today.

Be it noted, then, that "California" as a vision predated the establishment of the American nation by several centuries, It connoted plenty, ease, and we might say, the good life. But in the nineteenth century, when that myth was revived and supercharged by the discovery of gold and the frantic migrations of the mid-century, its *cultural context* was very different from that of the Spanish context in which it was invented. What were the main features of that cultural context? I turn first to Max Weber's famous thesis concerning the religious origins of the capitalist economic spirit in the seventeenth and eighteenth centuries. You will recall that Weber especially stressed the psychological tensions in ascetic Calvinism, a dominant force in colonial America, as well as in northwest Europe. The religion of Calvin was, in the first instance, one of complete predestination of human affairs by God. Weber summarized the implications in the following way:

We know only that a part of humanity is saved, the rest damned. To assume that human merit or guilt play a part in determining this destiny would be to think of God"s absolutely free decrees, which have been settled from eternity, as subject to change by human influence, an impossible contradiction. The [human and understanding] God of the New Testament [has been replaced] by a transcendental being, beyond the reach of human understanding, who with His quite incomprehensible decrees has decided the fate of every individual and regulated the tiniest details of the cosmos from eternity (Weber, 1958:103–4).

Weber regarded this doctrine as one of "extreme inhumanity." He argued that it "must above all have had one consequence for its adherents: a feeling of unprecedented inner loneliness of the single individual." The doctrine also generated a haunting sense of uncertainty. "The question, Am I one of the elect? must sooner or later have arisen from every believer and have forced all other interests into the background" (Weber, 1958:110). It was in the context of this intense religious anxiety that the Calvinistic emphasis on worldly activity arose as the most suitable means of "counteracting feelings of religious anxiety" (Weber, 1958:112) and the surest sign of salvation. In Calvinism, this worldly activity took the form of sober self-denial and systematic self-control. Predictably then, the Calvinistic ethic contained the following elements:
- "the avoidance of all erotic pleasure . . . "
- "the elimination of all ideal and exploitative enjoyment of unearned wealth and income . . . "

- "the avoidance of all feudalistic, sensuous ostentation of wealth . . . "
- "the avoidance of all surrender to the beauty of the world, to art, or to one's own moods and emotions . . . " (Weber, 1968:556).

The ethic is renunciatory, ascetic, and joyless in the extreme and calls for a rationally controlled pattern of life; and "when success crowns rational, sober, purposive behavior, . . . such success is construed as a sign that God's blessing rests upon such behavior" (1968:556).

What concrete form did this rationally controlled pattern of life take? To illustrate this Weber turned to the homilies of Benjamin Franklin, who, more than anyone, symbolizes the secular American manifestation of Puritanism in the eighteenth century. It was Franklin's assault on idleness of any kind—of time, of hands, of money—and his exaltation of the values of prudence, industry, frugality, punctuality, and honesty that caught Weber's attention (Weber, 1958). These attributes, he argued, were the very ones that were so important in building the rational organization of economic activity that contributed to the institutional success of capitalism.

The paradox, of course, in this analysis is that those very qualities, bred of anti-materialism, end in the accumulation of tremendous material rewards. In the end, Weber saw this as undermining asceticism. He encapsulated the problem in a famous quotation from John Wesley, the founder of Methodism:

I fear, wherever riches have increased, the essence of religion has decreased in the same proportion. Therefore I do not see how it is possible in the nature of things, for any revival of true religion to continue long. . . . For the Methodists in every place grow diligent and frugal; consequently they increase in goods. Hence they proportionately increase in pride, in anger, in the desire of the flesh, the desire of the eyes, and the pride of life (Weber, 1958:175).

Catholic writers and other scholars such as Pitirim Sorokin (1937) have challenged Weber's interpretations by claiming that from the beginning the driving force behind Protestantism was not asceticism but, rather, material desire (Weber, 1958). This line of criticism is consistent with their belief that Protestantism was essentially a secular development. It is not necessary, however, to take a stand here on first causes. Ascetic Protestantism contained the themes of renunciation, asceticism, and labor on one side and worldly success, impulse gratification, and happiness on the other. It portrayed these as locked in powerful tension with one another. This world view contained the ingredients *and* the structure of a myth and permitted the possibility of psychological ambivalence toward any one or all of these ingredients.

The Puritan background is one important element of the cultural context in which the myth of California must be assessed. A second and closely related part of that context is the complex of myths created over a series of decades in the late nineteenth century by that master maker of myths, Horatio Alger, Jr. Beginning with the publication of *Ragged Dick* in 1867, Alger supplied America's booming, high capitalist period with some of its principal myths. As Franklin had taken a step away from the joylessness and asceticism of Calvin—especially in his own personal life—so Alger took another worldly step. For it was the wealth that counted, and there was luck as well as hard work involved. Or, in John Seelye's words:

It was for Alger's boys to work hard, honor your parents (excepting wicked stepparents), save your money, aim high, don't smoke, gamble, or drink hard liquor, and some day you will stop a runaway horse, behind which will be a carriage containing a rich man's daughter whose father will reward you with a good job and a chance to get ahead in the world, all of which will have been sent to you by God for having worked hard, honored your parents, saved your money, aimed high, and not smoked, gambled, or drunk hard liquor (Seelye, 1965: ix).

With this preoccupation with wealth, it seemed inevitable that Alger would turn to California; indeed, six California novels appeared between 1878 and 1891. All were on the "get rich" theme, but Alger made some concessions to discipline and renunciation; his boys stayed away from the saloons and gambling halls, and they worked hard. Lest the readers suspect Alger had strayed too far from the ghost of Calvin, he explained his recipe for success in the preface to *The Young Miner; or, Tom Nelson in California*:

Though [Tom's] prosperity was chiefly due to his own energy and industry, it is also true that he was exceptionally lucky. Yet his good fortune has been far succeeded by that of numerous spirits in Colorado, within the past twelve months. Some measure of prosperity generally awaits the patient and energetic worker and seldom comes to those who idly wait for something to turn up (Alger Jr., 1879).

The California myth, itself, locked inextricably with the mythology of gold in general, went the rest of the way. Wealth was for the finding, women were loose, whiskey was plenty, and public disorder prevailed. The California myth in the context of nineteenth-century culture was one of a *family* of myths, all struggling with the same tension between renunciation and reward. The California myth is the negation of Calvin—or its natural culmination, if you follow the Catholics and Sorokin—for it renounces work and discipline and revels in worldly pleasures.

The theme of gold-for-the-finding was only one phase in the development of the California myth. In the past century it has been elaborated along a variety of different lines. The content became more diverse. The myth of mastery and conquest of the West, which had pre-dated even the Gold Rush with James Polk's mission of "manifest destiny," continued to be prominent throughout the frontier period. Toward the later part of the century, the themes of natural beauty joined those of abundance as the rhapsodies of John Muir caught the public imagination. Oil, automobiles, and other industries "took off," and the myth of opportunity and plenty was renewed again and again. Perhaps the most dramatic elaboration was that of the Hollywood myth, which added the element of instant exhibitionism to that of instant narcissism—the magical rise to stardom with the world at one's feet. The magic includes also the notion of being "discovered" and plucked from obscurity by a powerful director—much like the Alger boys' sponsors and Little Orphan Annie's Daddy Warbucks. A later phase was that of the good life, as symbolized in the pages of *Sunset Magazine*, with the outdoor architecture, the barbecue, the sun, the green and the ease. As if driven by some repetitive compulsion, Californians have endowed Marin County and some aspects of life in Silicon Valley with the principal ingredients of the California myth. Whatever variations, the theme remained the same—what Mark Juergensmeyer has described as "a blending of grace and works that would have pleased John Calvin." He hastened to add that while it had the ingredients of Calvinism, those ingredients were surely rearranged: "the work for Californians was fairly easy and the rewards of grace were bountifully immediate" (1980).

Juergensmeyer went even further. He saw in the myth of California a kind of religion, which he defined as a "symbolic gesture toward ultimate restoration and transformation" (1980). What were the ingredients of this religion: Juergensmeyer mentioned three:

- "Freedom from guilt." If one starts over again, one is free from the burdens of the past, ghosts, and former actions.
- "Freedom from obligations." For those who migrated to California this meant to sever ties with the past, friends, and community. California connoted a vague, happy association of the free, an anonymous congregation of souls, united by their commitment not to intrude on one another.
- "The purifying powers of change." This is the counterpart of redemption and rebirth, not in the future, as many ideologies have it, but in the present.

Religion perhaps, but to the fundamentalist churches, the easy life in California has proved to be anti-religion, voiced first from the pulpit, and more recently, from television evangelists, who in their messages restore what the myth of California has denied—guilt, responsibility, and certainty.

The antagonism between California's religion and evangelistic, often Calvinistic, churches suggests that, upon reflection, we could not seriously believe that the California myth could remain in isolation from these elements in the American tradition and that to embrace that myth means sooner or later and in some way, we must pay a price for it. As we explore further what the myth of California connotes, we find a seamier aspect, which exists side by side with utopia and permits us, in our inner psychological dialogues, to pay that price. One part of the price is that which accompanies *any* utopia sired by discontent with one's circumstances: disillusionment and depression. Those who experienced the guilt, the obligations, and the staleness in their home communities and sought liberation by migrating to California were bound later to discover a fundamental truth: an irreducible amount of an apparent alienation from one's external environment is *internal* in character; to pin one's hopes for happiness on a change of circumstances is to invite an ultimate return of that alienation, *whatever* the new circumstances.

There is also a more dire and direct set of retributions in the California myth. A mountain pass between Reno and Sacramento is named Donner Pass. The referent, indeed the occasion for its bearing that name, is a party of migrants led by George Donner, one of the many parties that joined the Great Migration of 1846, when it was believed that the route to California was passable. The Donner story is simple and tragic: the party became stranded in the Sierras in November, 1846, by heavy snows. Despite heroic escape efforts, many of them perished. The reason the story has not joined the dozens of unremembered stories of its kind, however, is that the surviving members of the Donner party cannibalized their dead in order to gain strength to move forward (Stewart, 1960). What better retribution for greed than to die and be devoured? What better reason for the story to become part of the California myth of plenty and passivity?

The famous earthquake is another part of the California myth dramatized by the great San Francisco tragedy of 1906. The precise symbolism of the earthquake in the the popular mind is difficult to discern, but two recurrent fantasies are: the earth will open and swallow people; and as a kind of variant, California will break away from the continent and either be swallowed by the Pacific Ocean or will again become an isolated island, as it was drawn on the imaginary maps of the Spanish dreamers. Once noted, the symbolism of oral destruction is, perhaps, too obvious to call to attention. It is, nonetheless, consistent with the notion that the California myth has a precise retributional counterpart.

The reason for my impatience with the dictionary definitions of "myth" must now be clear. A myth need not be a purely fictional account; the fate of the Donner party is a documented historical episode. The threat of earthquakes is clearly real to this day, though perhaps not in the precise sense called forth by the fantasies. The point is not fiction versus fact; it is, rather, the psychodynamic blending of fiction and fact to complete the inevitable logic of ambivalence in myth. My impatience with the exclusively positive and visionary definition of myth stems from the same considerations; there is no happy myth without its unhappy side and no dark myth without its light side.

The dismal, negating side of the California myth goes further. Consider the following themes:

- On material plenty: The words of a recent popular song, played to the point of tedium on California country and Western radio stations, run as follows: "All the gold in California / Is in a bank / In the middle of Beverly Hills / In somebody else's name."

- On stardom: As a matter of fact, Hollywood actors and actresses have a variety of lifestyles, some very humdrum. As a matter of collective fantasy, however, the stars of Hollywood, in addition to receiving the earthly gratifications due to the gods, drink themselves to death, pop overdoses of drugs and sleeping pills, and generally live ruined, dissolute, and miserable lives. Such is the power of myth to select and distort.

- On social relations: Californians may be guiltless and freed from social obligations, but by the same token, their lives are believed to be anomic, plagued by divorce and separation, isolation, and loneliness. Such are the themes extracted by James Hughes in his survey of post-industrial California novelists (1980).

- On craziness: Californians may be liberated, but the mythological cost is the danger of going berserk: both Los Angeles and San Francisco are known as places of refuge for the wild, the cultish, and the bizarre.

- On ultimate retribution: The bridge connecting San Francisco and Marin County may be Golden, crossing the gate to the Golden State, but it is one of the most well-known symbols of violent suicide in the world.

All these blended elements of the California myth are rooted in a certain social reality—a reality perhaps engendered in part by the myth itself—but I am stressing another dimension of that myth. Its elements manifest themselves as a series of dialogues with the Puritan past; the common theme of this dialogue is that in our revelries in California's paradise we have, in fact, perpetrated a betrayal and must ultimately pay the terrible cost.

FURTHER SOCIAL AND POLITICAL SIGNIFICANCE OF MYTH

Up to this point I have stressed what might be called the cultural and psychological dimensions of myths, their tensions and ambivalences. Myths have their place in the drama of social interaction as well; and to close my exploration, I will note a few of the social uses and significances of myths, staying with the illustrative example I have been following.

To choose the most obvious social significance first, a myth may have a certain commercial value: people will pay to see fantasies enacted on stage and screen or to read them in literary representations. Our illustrative myth of California lends itself well to commercial use, if not exploitation. Generations of real estate brokers, surfboard manufacturers, and sellers of bathing suits and suntan lotions have made free use of elements of the myth to vend their wares. So myths are, in one capacity, a free resource to advertisers.

There is a more subtle function of myth that appears in the fabric of daily, informal intercourse among people. We use myths to express our normative postures and to secure the same from others, thereby binding ourselves in a kind of momentary solidarity. Permit a biographical example. In the late 1970s, I served as a director of a student exchange program in the United Kingdom, supervising the work of about 130 University of California undergraduates as they spent their junior year abroad. They were scattered around the British Isles: from time to time they came through London on their way to Paris, Rome, Athens, or other places with distinctive myths of their own. When they visited my office in London, I asked them, in the course of conversation, where they were going, and if they said Paris, for example, I immediately conspired with them in their romance and euphoria, told them of experiences to have, food to eat, atmosphere to absorb, and generally envied them. As often as not, however, when they went to Paris, they froze while standing outside American Express waiting to check their mail, slept in fleabags, were unable to afford the Parisian cuisine, and perhaps were accosted by abusive people. Yet when they returned to London and I asked them how it was, they said "fantastic;" and I envied them again. In this way we conspired to deny reality and shared in that denial, thereby doing our bit to perpetuate the myth of Paris. These kinds of episodes are daily and repeated occurrences, and taken as an accumulation, they constitute a mechanism for building and reproducing myths. We Californians in England did the same with our myth as well, maintaining our suntans as long as can be done in Britain, romanticizing California to the natives and to one another. The main social significance of these thousands of collective little crimes of distortion, I believe, lies in sustaining solidarity with our fellow humans. Our own inner realities are so idiosyncratic and complex at any given moment that comparison or relation to another inner reality is almost impossible. Sharing in a myth for a moment is a way to unify two selves in a kind of regressive solidarity, to orient to the same object, to evoke the same affect, and to become temporarily one.

In addition to being an economic and social resource, the myth may be a political resource, constituting the framework within which political dialogue occurs and permits politicians to seize one ingredient of a myth, mobilize support in its name, and use it as a weapon to discredit others. To illustrate this significance, we might turn to the political rhetoric of two of California's recent governors, Ronald Reagan and Jerry Brown. During the campaign of 1966, when the Great Society was reaching its full expression and when California higher education was in full turmoil, Reagan hammered home two primary themes: high welfare costs and the mess in higher education, both of which he promised to clean up. On welfare his campaign was a positively Franklinian attack on sloth and ideas: "It's hard to figure," he said, "how welfare costs are going up while need and unemployment are going down" (L.A. Times, 1966a). When the Los Angeles Times (1966b) endorsed him for governor, it predicted he would "rescue discouraged men from the economic junkheap, and get them into gainful employment." In a variation on that theme, Reagan described welfare as "prepaid vacations for a segment of our society which has made this a way of life" (1966c). Was not this an assault on one central ingredient of the myth of California—getting something for nothing? It was; and in part, it was a play on our guilt for having entertained that desire ourselves and an invitation to displace that guilt on others. On the student front, Reagan's attack was more complex, but the same theme emerged: the students were privileged to receive an education from the state of California, and they should work to justify it instead of assaulting University authorities and engaging in what Reagan referred vaguely to as "sex orgies on the Berkeley campus." These themes show Reagan maneuvering in, and exploiting that family of myths I have ranged from the Calvinist to the Californian. They reveal him as adopting not only a politically but also a morally reactionary stance.

We do not often put Jerry Brown in the same category as Reagan, but Brown can also be regarded as moving within the same family of myths. Whatever else Brown is known for, he is known for his romance with the pessimistic futurists and the environmentalists. He has repeatedly borrowed from their vernacular of "spaceship earth," "small is beautiful," and spoken of the need for collective sacrifice in the face of the exhaustion of world resources. While we may question the ultimate political effectiveness of these messages, it is worth observing that his theme is fundamentally Calvinist: our California myth of plenty is a sinful, corrupting nightmare, and the only answer is renunciation. We must turn the California myth into its negation, and we should celebrate that negation: salvation through denial.

A Concluding Note

At the end of his famous essay on Protestantism and capitalism, Weber remarked that capitalism, while originating in the heartless discipline of Calvinism, had by the twentieth century established itself as an autonomous system, no longer dependent on that particular theological impulse. Industrial capitalism, he argued, now resting on its own institutional foundations, feeds itself and constitutes a sort of iron cage for us all; but "the spirit of religious asceticism . . . has escaped from the cage" (Weber, 1958:181). Weber may have been right about industrial capitalism, but I hope I have demonstrated that we have not escaped from the cage of salvation through asceticism and its family of related myths. In many respects, that complex of myths dictates our internal and interpersonal discourses as well as our internal and interpersonal conflicts. At the same time, it constitutes a set of limits. Whether stressing cold asceticism and recognition of worldly accumulation as an incidental by-product of salvation, whether worshipping individual success, or whether revelling in some version of a myth of plenty, these possibilities—all of which end with economic mastery of the world and materialism—seem to be growing increasingly inappropriate to the changing economic and historical circumstances of the world. There is something stale about all of them, and I think that staleness stems from our own realization of inappropriateness; new solutions do not seem to be forthcoming or even suggested by that family of myths. We keep running around the same sets of mythological tracks. It would be foolish to envision a radical break with the dualism of a mythical past that has been a part of our psychic structure for so many centuries. But given its apparently increasing irrelevance, I would, personally, hope that we might expand our horizons for some more appropriate mythical alternatives in the decades to come.

Biographical Note

Neil J. Smelser was born in Kahoka, Missouri and grew up in Phoenix, Arizona. He went to Harvard and majored in Social Relations. After college, he did graduate work in the same field. Professor Smelser teaches at University of California, Berkeley, where he offers courses in theory, methods, and collective behavior. His research interests in the past few years have been in comparative education and the future of psychiatry. His major published works are: (1) Economy and Society, with Talcott Parsons; (2) Social Change in the Industrial revolution; and (3) Personality and Social Systems, co-edited with W.T. Smelser.

REFERENCES

ALGER, H., JR.
   1879 Preface to the Young Miner; or Tom Nelson in California. Philadelphia: Coates.
FREUD, S.
   1959a "Preface to Sandor Ferenczi's Psychoanalysis: Essays in the Field of Psychoanalysis." Vol. IX in The Standard Edition of the Complete Psychological Works of Sigmund Freud. London: Hogarth Press.
   1959b "Writers and Day-Dreaming." Vol. IX in The Standard Edition. London: Hogarth Press
   1959c The Psychopathology of Everyday Life. Vol. VI in The Standard Edition. London: Hogarth Press
GUDDE, E. G.
   1969 California Place Named: The Origin and Etymology of Current Geographical Place Namer. Berkeley and Los Angeles: University of California Press.
HUGHES, J.
   1980 "California's Frontier Ethos in Post-Industria: A Literary Interpretation." Paper presented at the meetings of the American Association for the Advancement of Science. San Francisco, January.
JUERGENSMEYER, M.
   1980 "California as Religion." Paper delivered at the meetings of the American Association for the Advancement of Science. San Francisco, January 7.
LOS ANGELES TIMES
   1966a October 1.
   1966b October 16, p. 6–6.
   1966c October 6.
MALINOWSKI, B.
   1971 Myth of Primitive Psychology. Westport, Conn.: Negro Universities Press.
SEELYE, J.
   1965 "Horatio Alger Out West: A Marriage of Myths." Introduction to Horatio Alger, The Young Miner: or, Tom Nelson in California. The Book Club of California.
SOROKIN, P.
   1937 Social and Cultural Dynamics II: 500, 504. New York: American Books Co.
STEWART, G. R.
   1960 Donner Pass: And Those Who Crossed It, pp. 17–23. San Francisco: The California Historical Society.
WEBER, M.
   1958 The Protestant Ethic and the Spirit of Capitalism. Trans. T. Parsons. New York: Charles Scribner & Sons.
   1968 Economy and Society. Guenther Roth and Claus Wittich (eds.), Vol. II. New York: Bedminster Press.

Psychoanalysis and Sociology

INTRODUCTION

THE repeated assertion that a combined psychoanalytic and sociological framework would provide a comprehensive model of human behavior has met with a variety of resistances. Because so few sociologists are interested in psychoanalysis (Wallerstein & Smelser 1969; Rabow & Zucker 1980; Endleman 1981; Rabow 1979, 1981), views differ widely on what a combined framework should include and on what problems merit study.[1] Indeed, while authorities from various disciplines have argued that psychoanalysis adds to the social sciences by providing a comprehensive and useful model of human behavior (Ruitenbeck 1962; Goodman 1977; Fine 1977; Levine 1978; Gabriel 1982), receptiveness to this argument varies with the discipline (Levine 1978; Rabow 1983).

In this paper I review and evaluate selected efforts, past and present, to integrate psychoanalysis and sociology. I do not try to convince my sociological audience that psychoanalysis has something to offer sociology. A number of sociologists have found psychoanalytic concepts useful and have made this argument. I do not introduce or evaluate the considerable efforts to translate Freud into a positivist framework (Hook 1959; Wollheim 1971; Wollheim 1974). The controversy over the scientific validity of psychoanalysis continues and little would be gained from assessing the arguments (see Sulloway 1979 and Breger 1981 for the latest psychological-biological debate). I generally ignore the work of social scientists from disciplines other than sociology who have used psychoanalysis, even anthropological work in culture and socialization.[2] An evaluation of the different theories of classical psychoanalysis is also beyond the scope of this paper. Psychoanalytic theory comprises many different theories. Some address thought processes such as memory, perception, attention, and consciousness; others focus on development; still others deal with psychopathology. Such theories are usually stated as models that function by analogy and comparison, and not as precise sets of functional relations between variables.

This article was previously published in the Annual Review of Sociology.
Ann. Rev. Sociol. 1983. 9:555–78
Copyright © 1983 by Annual Reviews Inc. All rights reserved

I use the materials and assumptions I believe are fundamental to psychoanalysis. These have been stated by Loevinger (1966), Klein (1976), and further restated by Breger (1981). I find Freud's statement adequate: "The assumption that there are unconscious mental processes, the recognition of the theory of resistance and repression, the appreciation of the importance of sexuality and of the Oedipus complex—these constitute the principal subject matter of psychoanalysis and the foundation of its theory. No one who cannot accept them all should count himself a psycho-analyst" (Freud 1923: 247). The entire body of neo-Freudian work is ignored in this essay, as it is not built upon these core assumptions (Jacoby 1975).

Finally, it is beyond the scope of this chapter to introduce and evaluate all of the early efforts to integrate psychoanalysis and sociology. Fortunately these works are treated in sociological reviews by Burgess (1939), Berger (1965), Platt (1976), and Levine (1978),[3] and in two books (Weinstein & Platt 1973; Endleman 1981).[4]

In this review I discuss five ways in which sociologists have used psychoanalytic ideas. First, some sociologists have done little beyond acknowledging the real or potential contribution of Freud's work or of particular psychoanalytic concepts to sociology. I call this the *acknowledging perspective*. A second body of work in sociology has used minor aspects or concepts of psychoanalysis, found them useless, and then rejected the major corpus of psychoanalytic works. I call this the *gauntlet approach*. A third body of work is characterized by a more faithful use of psychoanalytic theory in conjunction with sociological theory to extend the latter and downplay the former. I call this the *suggestive approach*. Fourth, some have used psychoanalytic theory faithfully in studying sociological phenomena and have enriched our understanding without denigrating either discipline. This approach, which I call the *integrative approach*, goes beyond extending ideas to develop new information and theory. A fifth approach has been to treat psychoanalysis itself as a human enterprise. I call sociological analyses of the origin and development of psychoanalysis the *sociology of knowledge* approach.

THE ACKNOWLEDGING PERSPECTIVE

While the uses of psychoanalysis by sociologists have varied enormously in the last 80 years, during the 1920s the acceptance and appreciation of Freud were extensive. The major text by Park & Burgess, *An Introduction to the Science of Sociology* (1921), contained many laudatory references to Freud. Furthermore, after Freud's death in 1939 the *American Journal of Sociology* devoted an entire issue assessing his contributions. Scholars from a wide range of disciplines, including such nonsociologists as A. Brill, M.D., Howard Laswell, Ph.D., Gregory Ziborg, M.D., and Karen Horney, M.D., were represented. Ernest Burgess (1939) wrote a major article arguing that Freud's work was important to the future of sociology. He noted the usefulness of Freud's concept of the role of the unconscious, his emphasis up on the role of wish fulfillment, and his analysis of dynamic patterns in personality that are independent of cultural influence. Moreover, while discussing the initial reluctance of sociologists to accept the monistic theories of Freud as opposed to the pluralistic concepts of William James, Burgess called attention to the similar foci of symbolic interactionism and psychoanalysis and the similar efforts of Freud and Thomas and Znaniecki to interpret social life. Burgess described five ways in which sociologists had interfaced with psychoanalysis and argued for further links in the future. He cited Dollard's use of psychoanalytic concepts in *Caste and Class in a Southern Town* (1937) and *Criteria of the Life History* (1935). However, while these works indicate sensitivity and appreciation for psychoanalytic theory, they do not heed Burgess's warning about sociologists who use psychoanalytic concepts but who transform the original meanings. "The value of a conceptual system as demonstrated by Freud's own experience in developing psychoanalysis is that it is in intimate contact, interaction, and revision with the reality of behavior. Without this vital relationship, concepts are or become formal and meaningless" (Burgess 1939: 368).

The book on homicide and suicide by Henry & Short (1954) illustrates an integration of the two disciplines. The authors demonstrate that when personal frustration interacts with strong external restraints (subordinate social status or intense social involvement) to cause an individual to blame others, homicide is more likely than suicide. When external restraints are weak and frustration occurs, the self must bear responsibility and suicide is more likely. Henry & Short find strong evidence for the influence of sociological or external factors. They use a psychoanalytic variable—superego strength—to help account for differences in the incidence of suicide and homicide that are not accounted for by sociological variables. However, Henry & Short use this psychoanalytic variable in an ad hoc manner. They make no independent analysis of the concept. Instead they cite five studies (p. 104–5) that show how variability in the strength of the superego is associated with self- or other-oriented aggression.

This kind of integration is also apparent in *Small Town in Mass Society* (1958), in which Vidich & Bensman discuss the defense mechanisms used by small town residents who feel dominated and controlled by new impersonal forces from the surrounding metropolitan region. The urbanized segment of society, the mass media, and state and national political systems all operate to limit and constrain local decision-makers. The destruction of the idea that success is available to all who possess ability and determination creates havoc and tension among townspeople. People distort, deny, and repress. These defense mechanisms, however, are not studied extensively nor is their use analyzed in this monograph. Incidental use of psychoanalytic concepts is also made by Inkeles (1959) on socialization and Inkeles & Levinson (1954) on national character. Smelser uses psychoanalysis more extensively in *Theory of Collective Behavior* (1962). Applying a psychoanalytic concept of anxiety to collective behavior, he shows how different modes of socially induced stress create anxiety and differing beliefs—hysterical, wish-fulfillment, and hostile beliefs correlating with panics, crazes, and antagonistic riots. However, Smelser does not suggest that anxiety should be examined empirically.

A social historian, Christopher Lasch, thinks that narcissism is the key to understanding certain perplexities in American life. In two books (1977, 1979) Lasch uses psychoanalytic ideas to explain family and cultural patterns of the 1970s. In order to understand changes in our culture we must see narcissism as the psychic disorder of our time. In my opinion this work is only suggestive, and one sociologist contends that Lasch misuses narcissism as a psychoanalytic concept (Satow 1981).

Research on student rebellion also exemplifies the acknowledging perspective of the psychoanalytic paradigm. In *The Conflict of Generations* (1969), Feuer argues that rebellions have a generational battle as a common psychological core. His work is based on a simplified version of the father-son relationship. Feuer argues that generational struggle, not specifically oedipal struggle, was the essential element, since the typical student rebel did not have an authoritarian, patriarchal father. Such an interpretation is challenged by Endleman, who uses Keniston's *Young Radicals* (1968) to develop the Oedipal theme apropos boys who become radicals. Endleman (1970) notes that such boys experience a strong tie to their mothers. Fathers who are highly ethical and intellectually strong are also subservient to a domineering mother. An intense ambivalence results. This intense and close relationship to mothers and the mothers' pressure for academic accomplishment seem to lead radical youth to a certain identification of academic pressure with maternal pressure. While all male youth may experience ambivalence toward the father, with these radical youth the ambivalence is particularly intense because of the split image of the father held by male students. On the one hand, the father is highly ethical, intellectually strong, politically involved, and idealistic; on the other hand, this same father is weak and unsuccessful. Rage at the academic (read mother and her role in castrating father) and at the father for allowing the castration is one factor that played a role among committed youth (Keniston 1968). Endleman argues that Oedipal patterns were evident in the male rebels.

Another acknowledging work by a sociologist interested in cultural changes is *Freud: The Mind of the Moralist* (1961), where Phillip Rieff interpreted Freud as a designer of moral values. Rieff argues that Freud saw the demands of society as devoid of inherent good. Individuals need not conform to society's demands but should instead strive for freedom. The possibility of freedom is increased with psychoanalysis, and thus a new character type emerges in society. Not the conformist that Riesman and Whyte described, this character is above moral, religious, and economic concerns. He is guided only by one point of knowing, one psychological validity: the self. This egoist is, according to Rieff, becoming a predominant human type.

Rieff continues his focus on moral issues in his later book, *The Triumph of the Therapeutic: Uses of Faith After Freud* (1966), where he describes the shift in the moral demand system of our culture. This shift in culture emphasizes the movement from a culture that valued control, where wants and needs were differentiated and unequal, to a culture where wants are elevated to needs. This has resulted in the emergence of the "psychological" man, who pursues primarily his own well-being. Because he has lost many of his communal obligations and has developed a psychoanalytic attitude, each person lives experimentally; each is lost and tense. With all faiths being possible, no faith can be forceful, compelling or dominant. The goals of psychological man are to keep going and to seek well-being. Rieff believes that this was how Freud saw modern man. One religionist criticizes this view as a misinterpretation of Freud, deriving from Rieff's disproportionate emphasis upon the weakening of superego controls (Browning 1975). Both Sennett's and Lasch's analyses of the social psychology of capitalism (Sennett 1977) echo Rieff's evaluation. None of these three authors deals empirically with the issues of narcissism, the destruction of intimacy, or the uncivilized community. Although these terms have been ignored by mainstream sociologists because of their romantic simplicity, the issues they raise are profound. When they are discussed in more sociological terms, as in Turner's "The Themes of Contemporary Social Movements" (1969), they are more acceptable to most sociologists. But denial, repressions, and the psychoanalytic base of affects are lost in the translation.

THE GAUNTLET APPROACH

In a second body of work by sociologists and social psychologists, certain aspects of psychoanalytic theory are tested empirically and found wanting. Such results have occasionally resulted in rejection of the entire corpus of psychoanalytic work.

From the beginning American academics have tended to view psychoanalysis as a strange beast imported from a far-off land. As LeVine has noted, every academic evaluation of psychoanalysis, including Sears's (1943) important survey, has proceeded from the notion that psychoanalysis is a "valuable theory attached to a scientifically worthless method" (LeVine 1973: 185). On the other hand, it has been argued that most academics have little knowledge of psychoanalysis. This has led Holzman to conclude that academics "with their shallow acquaintance with primary source materials will be unable to make compelling translations of psychoanalytic theories or assertions into research proposals" (Holzman 1970: 6-7).

Some social scientists become attached to a single psychoanalytic model. Thus Jahoda (1977) and T. Parsons (1964) both stress a functionalist approach to mind. This approach stresses ego's need for synthesis and dominance in assuming integrative and adaptive functions. These authors miss the centrality of conflict in Freud's thinking, which is stressed more in libido theory and in the economic perspective than in the structural orientation. Wrong expressed it first in 1961 but it is worth restating in 1982, this time in Gabriel's words: "What we get from most functionalist readings of Freud, including Parsons's own, is a harmonious picture of nature and culture, an individual nicely integrated within him/herself" (Gabriel 1982: 259).

Holzman's description of academics' ineptness in translating psychoanalytic theory into research proposals may reflect nothing more than disagreement about what Freud thought. That interpretations of Freud diverge widely may account for the impact of certain research by experimental sociologists and social psychologists. For example, two major research efforts (Sewell 1961; Orlansky 1949) concluded there was little overall value in integrations of psychoanalysis with sociology. These efforts are part of a larger body of work that has led to a rejection of psychoanalysis altogether. In his original and instructive analysis, Platt (1976) summarized and organized the psychoanalytic and social-cultural integrations in question. His review described three basic models: (*a*) of the psychobiographies of elites; (*b*) of the shared socialization and shared personality; and (*c*) of the psychoanalytic theory in culture and personality studies.

The first model, sometimes called ontogenetic, assumed that an inference about a single elite figure might allow valid inferences about the masses, an idea unacceptable to sociologists (Bellah 1970). The model failed to gain acceptance since it invariably stressed the regressive and neurotic components of personality in persons who were accomplished, talented, and had achieved a high degree of success. The ontogenetic model stressed childhood experiences at the expense of ego processes that are relatively free of neurotic or sexually determined energies.

A second model, that of shared socialization and shared personality, tried to establish how social patterns of adult behavior could be derived from personality dispositions developed from the child-rearing practices considered critical in the Freudian paradigm. Of special importance to this literature is the work of the sociologist William Sewell. He was incensed by Green's (1946) indictment of the middle class and set out to test whether infant and childhood caretaking were related to adult personality. Sewell argued that Green's work was impressionistic and provided no evidence either for socialization patterns or for neurotic behavior. Sewell (1961) also challenged the articles of Havighurst & Davis (1955) and M. Ericson (1949), members of the Committee on Human Development at the University of Chicago who had reported systematic differences in the child-rearing practices of the middle and lower classes. Sewell disputed the interpretation that these differences produced neurotic middle class children. Sewell studied the infant-training practices of feeding, weaning, bowel and bladder training, and punishment for toilet accidents. In all, 18 of 460 relationships tested correlated significantly at the .05 level; of these, 7 were negative correlations. Sewell concluded that these early experiences were not related to personality characteristics. Work by Maccoby & Gibbs (1954), the book *Patterns of Child Rearing* (Sears, Maccoby & Levin 1957), and a study by Miller & Swanson (1958) confirmed Sewell's work. Sewell's summary in 1961 was emphatic: Study of disciplinary practices during child rearing had "found very little or no relationship between these experiences and childhood personality traits and adjustment patterns" (Sewell 1961: 350). The differences in emphasis between Green and others were moved to a new level of argument by Bronfenbrenner (1958). In a major review essay, Bronfenbrenner argued that middle-class parents, while more lenient in their discipline techniques, use methods that are more compelling. Part of the compelling power in the withdrawal of love, engaged in by middle-class parents, derives from the greater permissiveness accorded middle-class children in their earlier years of life. Middle-class children exhibit greater dependency and stronger internal controls. Whether they are more neurotic or not seems to have gotten lost in the debate.

Sewell's work, however, convinced many sociologists that they had little to gain by using psychoanalytic variables or concepts.

The third model of integration, involving psychoanalytic theory in culture and personality studies, is anthropological. This hypothesis posits that discipline during infancy shapes adult dispositions and group patterns, an idea similar to that of the shared socialization model. What Sewell did for sociologists who had adopted the shared socialization model, Harold Orlansky did for social psychologists (1949) who had embraced the culture and personality models. After reviewing literature devoted to empirical work and an extensive bibliography based on Freudian work, Orlansky delivered a scathing critique of the thesis that specific disciplines during infancy have a specific and invariant impact on children and adults. "In short," Orlansky concluded, "it is contended that personality is not the resultant of instinctual, infantile, libidinal drives mechanically channeled by parental disciplines, but rather that it is a dynamic product of the interaction of a unique organism undergoing maturation and a unique physical and social environment." Orlansky's well-accepted and popular review did not go unchallenged. Twelve years later a sociologist, better informed and sympathetic to psychoanalysis, noted Orlansky's frequent misquoting and negligence (Axelrad 1962). Point by point, Axelrad refuted Orlansky's work. The Orlansky-Axelrad debate is instructive. In it, each author sought to preserve his own disciplinary perspectives rather than establish ideas that could have resolved some of their differences. Integrative work, however, would soon be resurrected in a new form in the work of Talcott Parsons.

The Suggestive Approach

The reader should recognize a certain arbitrariness in the grouping of examples for this section and the next. When a specialist denies the validity of alternative specialties, he does little to contribute to the advancement of knowledge (Coser 1975). Nevertheless, disciplinary chauvinism continues to be a barrier to the integration or mutual appreciation of psychoanalysis and sociology. Such chauvinism is often elicited when other substantive fields are introduced into sociology. Certainly in the area of delinquency, Gibbons's (1976) comments on the uselessness of psychoanalysis for comprehending the origins of delinquency stand in sharp contrast to the early work of the psychoanalyst Aichorn (1931) and the sociologist Axelrad (1965), who attempted to integrate psychoanalytic work with that of Merton, Cohen, and Parsons on the causes of delinquency. I will use the subfield of delinquency to illustrate the problem of chauvinism. Further, I suggest that delinquency research is a promising arena for application of psychoanalytic concepts.

The classic work of Merton (1938, 1957), which has influenced the field of deviance for several decades, may be used to illustrate the failure of sociology and psychoanalysis to integrate for mutual benefit. Merton's model, described by many as a structural model par excellence for its stress upon cultural goals and structural means, also implies a psychology of actors and raises a host of psychological and psychoanalytic questions. Merton's theory leaves unresolved questions of perceived opportunities; feelings, ideas and perceptions of blocked opportunity; frustrations; and issues of learned helplessness treated in the psychological literature on Learning theory and frustration (Maier 1949,; Seligman 1975; Rabow et al 1983) and ego development (Axelrad 1965; Reiss 1952). Axelrad notes that anomie, as Merton describes it, results in cynicism. He further argues that cynicism is not so much a cause of behavior as it is a defense, a rationalization to ward off submissiveness and anxiety stemming from the superego. Thus Axelrad tries to describe the process by which high anomie is translated into delinquency. Axelrad and others (Empey & Rabow, 1961) reject the view that the delinquent subculture creates its norms by inverting those of the larger culture. Delinquents may steal, but they also retaliate against others who steal. The delinquent's zeal for warring upon those who use the very rules he plays by, and his inability to see that he and those he attacks behave similarly indicates the delinquent' s strong projection and severe superego (Axelrad 1965). Axelrad also questions Parsons's (1947) formulation of middle-class delinquency. Parsons's argument is that the modern middle-class boy has difficulty identifying with his father because of the father's absence from home, the abstract nature of the father's job and the child's lack of access to other males. The male child sees the mother as the major source of morality and discipline, and as the primary object of identification. Axelrad notes that while these barriers to identification with the father are much stronger in adolescence, the basic masculine identification occurs around the oedipal conflict. For empirical support, Axelrad turns to the work of the Gluecks (1950). Axelrad carefully describes how a negative Oedipal complex develops. He concludes:

The delinquent sub-culture permits both the projection and the gratification of the forbidden impulses. The world of the gang is almost exclusively masculine, at least in object relations. Not so much femininity but passivity is denied in the circular aggression and defiance of the gang. The negative Oedipus will be expressed in the form of delinquency where the family is unstable and where the boy can too early reject the culture of the parents, in latency rather than in adolescence. This rejection will occur most frequently in those classes and status groups which are anomic: where the culture demands what society withholds (p. 105).

Reiss's work in delinquency also made use of psychoanalytic concepts. Reiss compared integrated delinquents to delinquents with defective or weak superegos (1952). He found differences among the groups in residential mobility, educational status, age of delinquent involvement, quality of marital relationship between parents, birth order, and peer association. While the psychoanalytic variables clearly differentiated the three types of delinquents, no further refinement of the mechanisms of this correlation has been attempted. This suggestive and promising work, along with Henry & Short's work on the importance of psychoanalytic variables in *Suicide and Homicide,* has not yet been fully extended.

Another area of suggestive research derives from the influence of Parsons on a group of experimentally oriented social psychologists. Mills and Slater worked with Parsons and Bales and used learning groups at Harvard to develop a research program. Mills (1964a) showed that differential participation in three-person groups created different degrees and types of fantasy. The person who participated the most created more than his share of negative fantasy; the lowest participator had the highest degree of neutral fantasy; and the middle person had the most positive fantasies. In his book (1964b) about the role of boundaries, the openness of groups, and the group life cycle, Mills developed the idea that in groups individuals give up preconceived normative notions and establish a group culture with new normative arrangements. They transform conflict, anxiety, uncertainty, and fear into workable arrangements. Thus group culture arises independent of preconceived notions about personalities and Oedipal solutions. This phenomenon was corroborated by Slater's work. In *Microcosm* (1966), Slater suggested mythic interpretations of group culture, including analogies from *Totem and Taboo,* that were specifically based on the killing of the father. But the two works by Mills and Slater lacked systematic documentation of psychoanalytic variables and set a dubious precedent for subsequent work.

Slater based his analysis of the evolution of a group culture on interpretations of protocols from training groups at Harvard. The objective goals of the groups were growth and awareness of self and others through analysis by the participants of their own interaction. The official group leaders did not give instructions or directions; instead, they offered interpretations of the groups' interactions in light of their own nondirective role. The groups usually met for several months, moving from polite unease to a point where members took action against their leader. At some point they understood that they could no longer wait for the leader to act, and they disposed of him. But, the leader continued to rule in the members' minds even though he did not reign. Each group made sense of its own development by means of a vocabulary provided by assigned readings. These centered around the mythic themes of the primal hoard, the primal scene, and the horrors of rationality. The group was thus provided with a vocabulary of motives by means of which members could understand the group's birth and symbols (Swanson 1967).

Slater did not focus on the students' personal problems, nor did he describe how the subjects systematically related to features of the collectivity that in turn influenced the sequence of events. He studied the manner in which groups evolve and develop. Slater noted resemblances between a group's development and the moral development of a child (per Piaget); similar resemblances were suggested between group evolution and the cultural evolution of whole societies. Slater saw the training group as a microcosm of pervasive group processes. He argued that an actor's sense of what he is doing comes directly from his group experiences, which further prepare him for a new stage in the evolutionary process. Slater's explanation of the revolt against the leader stressed the individual's needs for autonomy and individuation. However, this work was interpreted by sociologists interested in psychoanalysis as evidence for the irrelevance of Oedipal themes. In other words, the overthrow of the leader need not be motivated at an unconscious and infantile level, but can occur at a later point in an adult's career. Thus a psychoanalytic explanation of group development need not rely on a model of individual development stressing early childhood experiences. *Microcosm* received much attention in the profession. A symposium review (ASR, 1967) gave it both good marks and bad: "excellent," judged Gouldner; "wasted talent," wrote Goode; "promising" thought Bettelheim. Its central ideas remain fertile leads for integrative work.

Such work has been done by Gibbard & Hartman (1973). In their study of two college groups they found strong evidence supporting both the Oedipal and pre-Oedipal paradigms. Further suggestive work applied Freud's economic perspective to collectives, which are seen to have fixed quantities of libido and defense. Accordingly, hostility may be expressed by, or depression may be lifted from, one member of the collective or one part of a subsystem only to be absorbed by another. This idea stresses the variables of energies, libido, affects, and defenses. Slater's work (1963) and Marks's work (1977) are along these lines, as is the work of Vogel & Bell (1960) on the family scapegoat. Slater's work on libidinal diffusion and contraction is, as Levine says, an ingenious translation of eros and thanatos into associative and disassociative processes (Levine 1978). Collective life is, according to Slater, ultimately dependent upon libidinal diffusion.

Such research assumes that collectives embody varying proportions of associative and disassociative processes and they all have mechanisms that anticipate an individual's withdrawal or social regression. The control mechanisms or institutions invoked to prevent regression, discussed by Slater, are: *(a)* socialization as a mechanism to prevent narcissistic withdrawal; *(b)* marriage as a mechanism to prevent withdrawal from the dyad; and *(c)* incest as a mechanism to prevent withdrawal from the family.

Excellent sociological work on mechanisms designed to prevent withdrawal and enhance commitment (Kanter 1972) often ignores the unconscious, repression, and affects and Slater uses the classic psychoanalytic concepts to argue for a more comprehensive explanation of commitment as a social pattern.

Marks (1977) challenges one aspect of Slater's argument, although his thesis is more directly aimed at Goode (1960) and Coser (1974).

He rejects the concept that time and energy are scarce, arguing that they are flexible rather than finite. Marks notes that scarcity applies to only some types of commitments. Thus without explicit recognition, Marks rejects classic libido theory (accepted by Goode and Coser), a theory not highly esteemed in modern psychoanalytic circles (Breger 1981). Resources like love (Swanson 1965) and education (Boulding 1966) can be used to generate rather than deplete energy and commitment. Marks's suggestive work does not indicate which types of collective arrangements make for under- and over-commitment. Why, for example, do some couples with objectively demanding occupational roles experience satisfaction with their amount of time together, while others, involved in objectively less demanding roles, experience a lack of time together (Cuber & Haroff 1965)? Questions about how groups balance the forces governing the withdrawal or increased commitment of their members still need to be addressed.

A number of other suggestive and promising sociological works may be evaluated in this section. Swanson has argued for the relevance of Freud to social psychology (1961a) in much the way Parsons has detailed how Durkheim and Freud converge upon moral values and personality structure. Swanson disputes the biological Lamarckian interpretation of Freud and translates the social interactions associated with the erogenous zones into sociopsychological skills and interactional issues. While both Swanson and Parsons believe that meaning and affect are important for the organization of social action, at no point for these authors can meaning be (as it could for Freud) unconscious. Indeed, in the *Structure of Social Action* Parsons completely ignores the concept of the unconscious. For Parsons, such a concept seems to have no legitimacy or scientific status. Parsons attempted (1947, 1953, 1964, 1967) with his students (Parsons et al. 1955) to explain the unique development of personality while simultaneously accounting for social order. He maintained that all levels of the personality—id, ego, and superego—are open to the internalization of the commonly shared objects, symbols, rules, and values of society. Thus id impulses and affects are not a direct or independent expression of drives or instincts but can only be symbolically generated and adapted to a particular social order. In this view, there is no antagonism. The id does not function independently, having no demands and wishes of its own.

In an unpublished paper, R. Collins has recently addressed sociology's failure to appreciate the theoretical importance of feelings. Most sociologists working in this paradigm ignore the possible significance of the unconscious meanings related to the symbols and affects emphasized by both Swanson and Parsons. In arguing that all aspects of the personality system are adapted to the social order, sociologists relegated study of the basic autonomy of the id, or unconscious, to the domain of psychoanalysts.

Parsons (1964, 1967) made a sustained effort to integrate psychoanalysis with sociology. In "The Superego and the Theory of Social Systems" (1953), Parsons revised the structural perspective of Freud. He concluded that cognitive and expressive components of culture—not only moral aspects, as in Freud—are internalized as parts of the ego and hence are subject to intrapsychic repression. Parsons's integrative effort was supplemented by his location of the personality and social systems within a common "action" frame of reference. The by now famous four functional imperatives of adaptation, goal attainment, integration, and pattern maintenance were linked to processes of the revised Freudian structural model of personality and to parallel processes in the social system. The usefulness of this model of integration as a guide for research has not been fully explored. One reason is that in translating Freudian theory into concepts with which sociologists feel comfortable, Parsons rendered the unconscious knowable through symbols and thus no longer itself an entity that deserves sociological attention. Where id is, no sociologist shall be.

This Parsonian perspective continues to be developed by his student, Gerald Platt, and a historian collaborator, Fred Weinstein. Their work has been the most systematic and sustained integrative effort since Parsons's and requires special attention. Although their substantive concern is with social change, their integrative conceptions involve general theory (Weinstein & Platt 1969, 1973). In their earlier effort, *The Wish to be Free,* the authors assert that maintenance of the nurturance-subordination relationship provides social stability while its disruption or loss leads to collective action and change. In *Psychoanalytic Sociology,* Weinstein & Platt enlarge on their earlier work and argue that all internalized standards and expectations provide stability while their disruption or loss leads to social change.

In the course of developing their model, Weinstein & Platt criticize Adorno et al.'s (1950) model of synthesis, Erikson's psychosocial model (1950), and Loewenberg's generational model (1971) because they fail to include the psychic processes that systematically relate to society and culture. The study of object relations, recognized by the authors as implied in Freud's later work, accounts for the internalized psychosocial processes operant within individuals. This concept is probably not new to psychoanalysts, who have been influenced by Erikson, Hartmann, Jacobson, and Schafer. It does, however, open up the field for sociologists unfamiliar with recent work in object relations. The authors, as Endleman (1976) has noted, focus on propositions from psychoanalytic ego theory and theories of object relations in preference to propositions and theories about drives and psychosexual development. The Freudian concepts of libido, repression, regression, and the Oedipal pattern fall by the wayside and are replaced by those of internalization, identification, and object loss. Weinstein & Platt thus play down what classical and many contemporary psychoanalysts usually emphasize—namely, the primacy of psychosexual development in later object choices, work, and love.

Weinstein & Platt argue that earlier integrative models were not inclusive enough and were too reductionist. However, they provide no evidence on whether early stages of psychosocial development are more critical than later ones or vice versa. This is significant in light of their concerns with the later stages and societal influence. Additionally, a lack of empirical data mars this otherwise original and scholarly work. With a cavalier footnote, the authors dismiss the need for psychoanalytic training. Yet psychoanalysis offers a major explanation of the complex manner in which object choices, object losses, and psychosexual stages are related to behavior through unconscious processes of reaction formation, repression, projection, and identification. Weinstein & Platt avoid this terrain. Thus while they argue that object loss, real and/or symbolic, is involved in any process of social change and hence collective action, they ignore data from clinical psychoanalysis that suggests the critical ways in which certain object attachments, especially unconscious attachments, may prevent social actions and change. They overlook the fact that all such losses need not be potent or deemed significant by an actor.

Weinstein & Platt, like Parsons, establish the primacy of cultural and social factors in a collective action. Parsons argues that causal relationships proceed from society to id, ego, and superego (1964). Weinstein & Platt continue Parsons's argument by noting that every level of the personality (including the instincts and the unconscious) is affected by society and culture.

Influenced by Parsons's orientation, Weinstein & Platt (1973) argue for the primacy of culture and society as independent realities in shaping personality. They also give more credence than did Freud and Erikson to the reality orientations of persons (equivalent to an independent ego or conflict-free ego); and explain the heterogeneity of membership in collective movements as situationally produced. They also avoid the ontogenetic socialization model. While sociologists can applaud such efforts, we must also note their failure to clarify and validate the psychic structures that are both independent of and interrelate the two levels. Weinstein & Platt have renewed interest in psychoanalysis through their work on collective behavior. Smelser's interest in stress and anxiety, and in how people's responses to anxiety take the form of beliefs and social acts, as well as Weinstein & Platt's idea that object loss and its attendant anxiety, are suggestive leads for further development (1973). Their description of the conditions of object loss and the inability of human collectivities to act securely on the basis of prior internalized cultural mandates, and of the subsequent apathy, despair, and demands for restoration, requires empirical documentation.

Not all sociologists attracted to psychoanalysis agree with Weinstein & Platt's interpretation of Freud. Indeed, at least one of Parsons's students feels their work is neither "psychoanalytic nor sociological" (Smelser 1975). Bocock, a member of a British Sociological Association study group on sociology and psychoanalysis, argues that Weinstein & Platt deemphasize the unconscious and notes that they rarely allow that an idea in Freud might lead them to change their sociology" (1977: 469). Bocock feels that Parsons and his students have ignored repression and that to ignore repression and the unconscious is to work outside of a psychoanalytic framework. However, Platt's most recent work (1980) improves on his former efforts. While continuing integrative work, he moves towards an empirical examination of collective behavior. Platt argues that sociological studies of revolution based on traditional analytic categories of class, age, and religion do not describe actors' subjective orientations to action. Using Lipset's work on Nazism (1963) and Loewenberg's work on the Nazi youth cohort (1971) he tries to account for psychological and sociological diversity among revolutionary participants. Platt uses concepts of language, affect, cognition, and ideology to indicate the ways in which subjectivities develop and function. Ideology is a key mechanism by which diverse groups are bound together. Platt describes the relationship among social action, cognition, and emotion. While his analysis is ad hoc, it is clearly an advance, bringing us closer to the actor's subjectivities.

One important challenge by a sociologist to the usual sociological assumptions about development is the recent book by Chodorow, *The Reproduction of Mothering: Psychoanalysis and the Sociology of Gender* (1978). Chodorow finds inadequate the Parsonian idea that development and socialization are problems of differentiating role sets. Referring to the

ADVANCES IN PSYCHOANALYTIC SOCIOLOGY

psychoanalytic literature, she locates the source of differing attachments to parents in the pre-Oedipal stage. Chodorow's use of contemporary psychoanalytic literature reminds us that psychoanalysis needs not to be revised but thoroughly understood. Chodorow discards the energy-libido model so familiar and objectionable to sociologists and uses the more recent object-relations literature to discover patterns of gender difference implicit in psychoanalytic writings.

Chodorow explicates the texts and cases of psychoanalytic writers and indicates how the differentials in mother-daughter and mother-son transactions provide the basis for the differing gender dispositions. These dispositions or psychic structures lead women to mother and men not to mother. This process, she argues, occurs despite shifts in the labor force, despite political or ideological shifts in thought, and despite the obviously decreasing masculine demands upon women to mother. In arguing her thesis, Chodorow successfully deals with the psychoanalytic materials that other feminists have found objectionable—i.e. concepts of penis envy, masochism, genitality, and frigidity. She does not explain the binding patterns between mothers and daughters in terms of role-training or socialization. Mothering, she argues, requires built-in personality dispositions, not behavioral acquisitions. Her account will be appreciated by most sociologists and psychoanalysts because it is a structured view of socialization and social reproduction. The structuring process is located mainly in the family, where children become gendered members of society.

By explaining the psychodynamic considerations that psychoanalysts have introduced, Chodorow advances our knowledge of the organization of gender. By explicating the differential parental patterns undetected by psychoanalysts in their own literature, she discovers a coherent and structural object-relations pattern. Her description of differential oedipal outcomes is original and significant. Chodorow, like Parsons, once again sets the stage for genuinely interdisciplinary work in psychoanalysis and sociology and gives us an example of what needs to be done. Her work has also been discussed by sociologists, enduring the full range of evaluations (Lorber et al., 1981).

THE INTEGRATIVE EFFORTS

Finally, I cite examples of works that accept the basic premises of both sociology and psychoanalysis without reducing one to the other.

In one of the rare integrations of sociology with psychoanalysis Swanson accepts and uses the concept of the unconscious. His first work (Miller & Swanson 1960) demonstrated the conditions under which adolescents come to prefer certain defense mechanisms to others.

The work with Miller did not account for much variance in the defenses used by adolescents nor did it account for their origins. These issues were addressed by Swanson in 1961b. Swanson recognized that the earlier experiments, using the same methods by which so many others had conceptualized psychoanalysis, had chosen the wrong approach to identifying independent variables. These variables included severity of weaning and bowel training, style of reward and punishment, frequency of reward, the arbitrariness of parental demands for obedience, and the degree to which parents try to control their anger when disciplining a child. Sewell & Orlansky had used these variables in their work. Swanson's breakthrough occurred when he conceptualized the independent variables to *replicate* the defenses. By social replication, Swanson means "that the relations to oneself and others implied in the definition of a particular defense seem to be embodied in the individual's social relations; that the defense as an intrapsychic pattern of attitudes seems to be a fairly faithful copy of the subject's overt relations with other people" (1961:7). Thus defenses are not intrapsychic patterns without embodiment in social relations. According to Swanson they are ways of relating at once to oneself and to others. A defense is both an individual reaction to a social situation and an aspect of a role in a social relationship. Defenses result in an individual's *(a) achieving* of some reward or *(b) avoiding* some deprivation. Swanson uses this perspective to distinguish between an anaclitic (i.e. dependency) identification and identification with an aggressor. While some studies contrast learning motivated by reward with that motivated by deprivation, none utilizes the varieties of identification posited by Swanson.

Just as Swanson sees two varieties of identification, he identifies two commonly observed styles of defense: denial is associated with identification with the aggressor, while repression is associated with anaclitic identification. Parents who interpret the world as harsh, dangerous, and unrewarding become less warm and rewarding to children; they prepare their children to cope with a harsh world by employing denial. Repression, in contrast, should be practiced by those groups who have been promised many gains if conformity is maintained. Thus repression would be more likely to occur in members of the middle than in those of the working class, in participants in formal organizations than nonparticipants, and in families who live in an homogeneous atmosphere than in those inhabiting a cultural heterogeneous setting.

Swanson used these two dichotomies to review the various defenses that Anna Freud (1936) first proposed. While proposing that such defenses are indeed aspects of particular social arrangements, Swanson holds that they are nevertheless unconscious processes. He proposes that a behavioral process is unconscious if the person *(a)* has never been aware of it or *(b)* has ceased to be aware of it through interference from others.

Swanson shows that the defenses correspond somewhat to the problem solving skills frequently mentioned in the interactional social psychological literature (Benne & Sheats 1948; Heyns 1949; Bales 1950). He further suggests that even when parents committed to the maintenance of the family unit lack certain interpersonal skills required for success, they may inadvertently create a pattern of social relationships in which their children are required to develop such skills. A child may thus relieve overly tense parents by developing skills of compromise or abilities to sort out the components of a problem. This complements the earlier work by Vogel & Bell (1960) on scapegoating. The scapegoated child also contributes to family maintenance. Family stability is maintained by projecting potentially disruptive qualities onto one child. To the best of my knowledge, there has been no analysis of defenses as aspects of social worlds that shift with the requirements of new social situations, and which attempt to establish the person's identification with the situation and make predictions about defenses.

The work of Camic (1980) is also a theoretical integration of psychoanalytic and sociological theory. Camic turns to Weber, seeking to determine the preconditions for the attribution of charisma. The major precondition is the presence, in the attributors, of extraordinary human needs. Camic uses Weber's concept of charisma as a generic label for attributions of specialness but notes that Weber did not question whether such attributions are all of one kind. He uses the structural theory of Freud to supply what is absent in sociological discussions of the preconditions of charisma. According to Freud, when people attribute charisma to others they not only gratify their own dependency needs (Weber's concern) but also express ungratified id, superego, and ego ideal needs. All such needs, when extraordinary, are the basis for attributions of specialness. Extraordinary dependency in the attributor leads to the attributed specialness of *omnipotence;* extraordinary ego ideal needs lead to the attributed specialness of *excellence;* extraordinary superego needs lead to the attributed specialness of *sacredness;* and extraordinary id needs lead to the attributed charisma of *uncanniness.* The social preconditions for the attribution of specialness are socialization or loss experiences. Traditional sociological subjects (pimps, pushers, and intellectuals: Katz 1975; delinquent groups: Redl 1942; organizations: Shils 1965) may be classified according to these charismatic types. Camic discusses the immediate and long-range consequences of these varieties of charisma. Camic's conceptual scheme has not been tested empirically but is still one of the more successful integrations of psychoanalysis and sociology.

Robert Endleman's work, though involving no original empirical materials, is a major integrative effort because Endleman tries to give equal weight to psychoanalytic and sociological work (1981). Trained both as a sociologist and a psychoanalyst, Endleman utilizes sociological and anthropological works that employ a classical psychoanalytic paradigm. His work includes a comprehensive review of the anthropological, sociological, and psychoanalytic literatures. He applies an integrative perspective to four areas of interest to sociologists: *(a)* human evolution; *(b)* sex and gender; *(c)* homosexuality; and *(d)* normality and deviance.

Endleman shows how psychoanalysis, rooted in a perspective of "species survival" and adaptation, can be used to understand evolutionary steps. According to Endleman's creative and illuminating analysis, the evolving human body shape, the changing physiology of pregnancy, and the development of erect posture, frontal coital positions, and human sex dimorphism added new dimensions to human psychology and sexuality.

Discussing sex differences, homosexuality, and deviance, Endleman rejects cultural relativism. He thus takes issue with some of the major sociological works that celebrate total human diversity. He argues for the recognition of psychic universals in human existence and for a psychic unity of humankind. His comments on the existence of psychopathology among groups that most sociologists find normal are challenging. Endleman concludes his major work with an optimism like that of Burgess some 40 years earlier. There seems now to be more basis for believing that such integrative work will continue, although one reviewer of Endleman's work suggested that a successful integration dilutes the contribution of each of the paradigms (Meltzer 1982).

THE SOCIOLOGY OF KNOWLEDGE PERSPECTIVE

Berger (1965) has written a brilliant though abortive essay on the relationship between sociology and psychoanalysis. Using a fundamental assumption of sociology, namely that behavioral scientists' models of personality are products of social structures, Berger notes that the psychological models (or theories) are in turn used to verify and test for the personalities. Berger describes the early 20th century social-structural change in the organization of work in Western societies. When industrialization took work from the home and put men into the factories it helped to create a new sense of self. The new self now had a public and work dimension as well as a familial or private one. Thus a new empirical reality (a new personality characterized by a split self or divided mind) becomes available for discovery.

If Freud had not been born, Berger argues, we would have invented him. The theory and practice of psychoanalysis are rooted in the very structures that also create the new self, a self that needs a new institutional apparatus to repair and integrate it. A new institutional diagnostic and mending apparatus arises: testing and counseling services, mental hospitals, and the like. Sociologists who have studied this apparatus have failed for the most part to focus on the macro-structure that creates the psychoanalytic enterprise, and have instead focused on limited aspects of the enterprise such as mental hospitals and counseling. Study may reveal that recent models of the self (e.g. the "growth" self, "awareness" self, "assertive" self, "restored" self, "as if" self, "false" self, "addictive" self, "borderline" self, and "narcissistic" self) reflect further change in the organization of work and the nature of the family. Indeed, that fewer diagnoses now involve the classical neuroses—hysteria, obsessive compulsiveness, and phobia—while more refer to narcissistic and borderline personalities may result either from new facts, new lenses, or a combination of both. Certainly Turner's work on the themes of contemporary social movements (1969) has marked similarities to that on the narcissistic self discovered by psychoanalysis and the themes expressed by Rieff, Sennett, and Lasch.

Turkle (1978), too, has emphasized the relationship of psychoanalysis to its environment. Turkle's work is an account of psychoanalysis in contemporary France and is based on the author's experience in France during and after the spring revolt of 1968. The revolt increased the impact of psychoanalysis on French society and culture, where analysts work in hospitals, nurseries, and schools, in vocational training and child-rearing. Whereas in the United States academia has limited connections with psychoanalysis, in France the disciplines of anthropology, history, sociology, and the fields of poetry, politics, feminism, and mathematics are engaged in psychoanalytic discourse. How did this come about? What are the relationships among a revolutionary psychoanalytic culture, psychoanalytic training, and societal institutions? Turkle addresses these questions on the basis of intensive interviews with over 100 psychoanalysts, students, and patients, as well as analysis of documents. She finds that early French resistance to Freud was based less on scientific judgment than on moral grounds. Turkle makes careful use of work by Anne Parsons and Carol Ryser to substantiate her arguments. In particular, Freud's representative to France, Marie Bonaparte, was not an M. D., which fact lost psychoanalysis the favor of the French medical establishment.

Turkle also addresses a question central to the training of psychoanalysts—i.e. "Does a psychoanalytic organization systematically destroy the theory it believes itself to be protecting?" She alerts the reader to the complexity of the issues involved in psychoanalytic training. She also examines the relationship between psychoanalysis and the world of social action. In France, as in the United States, a strong anti-psychiatric movement exists, but in France there is also a strong psychoanalytic movement that aims to bridge the gaps between normal and mad and between politics and psychology. Turkle examines the growth of psychoanalysis into popular culture and notes how its social success may undermine its radical intent. She astutely perceives the dilemmas and tensions of a psychoanalysis that both breaks down basic assumptions and is called upon to provide direction. The unnerving truth that we are not who or what we think we are, that we do not know our centers, that we do not control our lives, is embraced time and time again by the psychoanalytic theoretical and training paradigm. According to Turkle, ego-psychologists, domesticated psychoanalysts, and training institutes rush to ignore, deny, and rationalize this view and thereby create tensions both within psychoanalytic circles and between psychoanalysts and other intellectuals. Turkle has thus discovered that the nominally revolutionary psychoanalytic culture is beset by its own "Iron Law of Oligarchy" (Michels 1966). One excellent description of the dedication and characteristics of an accomplished analyst, of the conflicts within the profession, and of its vitriolic attitudes about renegades may be found in a recent book called "Psychoanalysis: The Impossible Profession" (Malcolm 1981).

Nothing akin to Turkle's analysis has been performed in the United States. The relationship between the academic and psychoanalytic enterprises is fragile and problematic. In 1927 the A.M.A. refused to allow non-M.D.s to be trained and licensed to practice psychoanalysis, and academia has reciprocated with neglect.

An excellent modern study of mental health practitioners, including psychoanalysts, raised an issue that Freud treated early in his career. The study, done by sociologists (Henry, Sims & Spray 1971) using a sample of social workers, clinical psychologists, psychiatrists, and psychoanalysts, showed that certain backgrounds and childhood conflicts predispose a person to a mental health practitioner's role, a finding that once again suggests the crucial impact of family socialization on adult patterns of occupational choice.

SUMMARY

Sociological work that recognizes the role in human behavior of unconscious factors, defense mechanisms, and repression will continue to advance the subdiscipline of psychoanalytic sociology. Such work must perform the difficult task of operationalizing the basic concepts of psychoanalytic theory. The ontogenetic model may gain from the work of scholars familiar with the original psychoanalytic literature, who stress dynamic patterns and relationships rather than traits and variables. Such efforts will continue to require mastery of two major disciplines.

Acknowledgment

This article has benefited greatly from the colleagueship of Ralph Turner. Charlotte Safavi, Sherry L. Berkman, and Jack Katz gave this paper critical and valuable readings. Roslyn Rabow helped bring it all together.

Notes

1. I asked members of the section on psychiatric sociology of the Society for the Study of Social Problems to inform me of works they thought important and relevant to the subfield of psychoanalysis. The few articles I received were concerned with psychiatry and psychiatric control rather than with theoretical work in psychoanalysis and sociology. Along these lines, the reviews by sociologists of psychoanalysis use quite different literature.

2. I have made such a preliminary effort. See "Psychoanalysis in the social sciences" (Rabow, 1983). The works by Devereux (1967, 1978), LeVine (1973), and Anne Parsons while relevant are not discussed (1964).

3. Except for the earliest by Burgess (1939), none of these reviews appears in the highest status sociological journals. Indeed Levine's essay is an anthropology journal while Platt's work was published in an American Studies journal. Most of the reviewers can be classified as broadly ranging scholars who are not identified with a single substantive area. The reviews tend to focus on different bodies of literature and thus cover many more materials than I review here. Finally, the reviewers live and work in major urban centers where psychoanalytic institutes are located. Indeed, most of the reviewers have undergone psychoanalysis, a fact relevant to understanding why sociologists continue to work in this area.

4. The books by Endleman and Weinstein & Platt, particularly valuable here, focus on different bodies of literature.

References

Adorno, T. W., et al.
1950 The Authoritarian Personality. New York: Harper & Row

AICHORN, A.
1931 Wayward Youth. New York: Viking Press. 2d ed.
AMERICAN SOCIOLOGICAL REVIEW
1967 "Microcosm: Structural Psychological and Religious Evolution in Groups." Review
Symposium of P. E. Slater. 1966. New York: Wiley.
AXELRAD, S.
1962 "Infant Care and Personality Reconsidered: a Rejoinder to Orlansky." Psychoanalytical studies 2: 275–132.
1965 "Juvenile Delinquency. A Study in the Relationship between Psychoanalysis and
Sociology." Smith Coll. Stud. Soc. Work 25:2.
BALES, R. F.
1950 Interaction Process Analysis. Cambridge, Mass.: Addison-Wesley.
BELLAH, R.
1970 Beyond Belief: Essays on Religion in a Post-Traditional World. New York: Harper.
BENNE, K. D., AND SHEATS, P.
1948 "Functional Roles of Group Members." Journal of Social Issues 4: 41–49.
BERGER, P.
1965 "Toward a Sociological Understanding of Psychoanalysis." Soc. Res 32: 26–41.
BOCOCK, R. J.
1977 "Freud and the Centrality of Instincts in Psychoanalytic Sociology." British Journal
of Sociology 38: 467–79.
BOULDING, K.
1972 "What the First Teach-in" Taught Us," pp. 463–469 in J. Rabow (ed.), Sociology,
Students and Society. Pacific Palisades, Cal.: Goodyear.
BREGER, L.
1981 "Freud Conventionalized, a Review of Freud: Biologist of the Mind," by Frank J.
Sulloway. Journal of the American Academy of Psychoanalysis 9: 459–72.
1981 "Freud's Unfinished Journey: Conventional and Critical Perspectives in Psychoanalytic Theory. London: Routledge & Kegan Paul.
BRONFENBRENNER, U.
1958 "Socialization and Social Class Through Time and Space," pp.400–425, Readings
in Social Psychology. New York: Holt.
BROWNING, D. S.
1975 Generative Man: Psychoanalytic Perspectives. New York: Dell.
BURGESS, E. W.
1939 "The Influence of Sigmund Freud upon Sociology in the United States. American
Journal of Sociology 45 (3): 356–76.
CAMIC, C.
1980 "Charisma: Its Varieties, Preconditions, and Consequences. Sociological Inquiry
1: 5–23.
CHODOROW, N.
1978 The Reproduction of Mothering: Psychoanalysis and the Sociology of Gender.
Berkeley: University of California Press.
COSER, L.
1975 Presidential Address: "Two Methods in Search of Substance." American Sociological Review 40: 691–700.
COSER, L., AND COSER, R. L.
1974 Greedy Institutions. New York: Free Press.
CUBER, J., AND HAROFF, P.
1965 Sex and the Significant Americans. Baltimore: Penguin.

352   *ADVANCES IN PSYCHOANALYTIC SOCIOLOGY*

DEVEREUX, G:
1967 From Anxiety to Method in the Behavioral Sciences. Hague/Paris: Mouton.
1978 Ethnopsychoanalysis: Psychoanalysis and Anthropology as Complementary Frames of Reference. Berkeley: University of California Press.
DOLLARD, J.
1935 Criteria of the Life History. New Haven: Yale University Press.
1937 Caste and Class in a Southern Town. New Haven: Yale University Press.
EMPEY, L. T., AND RABOW, J.
1961 "The Provo Experiment in Delinquency Rehabilitation." American Sociological Review 26 (5): 679–95.
ENDLEMAN, R.
1970 "Oedipal Elements in Student Rebellions." Psychoanalytic Review 57: 442–71.
1976 "Review of Psychoanalytic Sociology." Contemp. Sociol. J. Rev. 4 (2): 169-69.
1981 Psyche and Society: Explorations in Psychoanalytic Sociology. New York: Columbia University Press.
ERICSON, M. C.
1946 "Child Rearing and Social Status." American Journal of Sociology 52: 190–92.
ERIKSON, E. H.
1950 Childhood and Society. New York: W. W. Norton.
FEUER, L.
1969 The Conflict of Generations. New York: Basic Books.
FINE, R.
1977 "Toward an Integration of Psychoanalysis and the Social Sciences." Psychological Reports 41: 259–65.
FREUD, A.
1936 The Ego and the Mechanisms of Defense. New York: International Universities Press. Rev. ed.
FREUD, S.
1923 Complete Psychological Works, Vol. 28, S. E. London: Hogarth Press/Inst. Psychoanal.
GABRIEL, Y.
1982 "The Fate of the Unconscious in the Human Sciences." Psychoanalytic Quarterly 51: 246–83.
GIBBARD, G. S., AND HARTMAN, J. J.
1973 "The Oedipal Paradigm in Group Development." Small Group Behavior 4: 305–54.
GIBBONS, D. C.
1976 Delinquent Behavior. Englewood Cliffs, N. J.: Prentice-Hall. 2d ed.
GLUECK, S., AND GLUECK, E.
1950 Unraveling Juvenile Delinquency. New York: The Commonwealth Fund.
GOODE, W. J.
1960 "A Theory of Role Strain." American Sociological Review 25: 483–96
GOODMAN, S.
1977 Psychoanal. Educ. Res. New York: International Universities Press.
GREEN, A. W.
1946 The Middle-class Male Child and Neurosis. American Sociological Review 11: 31–41.
HAVIGHURST, R. J., AND DAVIS, A.
1955 "A Comparison of the Chicago and Harvard Studies of Social Class Differences in Child Rearing." American Sociological Review 20: 438–42.

HENRY, A. F., AND SHORT, J. F. JR.
1954 Suicide and Homicide. Glencoe, Illinois: The Free Press.
HENRY, W. E., SIMS, J. H., AND SPRAY, S. L.
1971 The Fifth Profession. San Francisco: Jossey-Bass.
HEYNS, R. W.
1949 Effects of Variation in Leadership on Participant Behavior in Discussion Groups. Ph.D. Thesis. University of Michigan, Ann Arbor.
HOLZMAN, P. S.
1970 Psychoanalysis and Psychotherapy. New York: McGraw-Hill.
HOOK, S., ED.
1959 Psychoanalysis, Scientific Method and Philosophy. New York: International Universities Press.
INKELES, A.
1959 "Personality and Social Structure," in R. K. Merton, L. Broom, L.S. Cottrell (eds.), Sociology Today: Problems and Prospects. New York: Basic.
INKELES, A., AND LEVINSON, D.
1954 "National Character," in G. Lindzey (ed.), Handbook of Social Psychology. 2: 418–92. Reading, Mass: Addison-Wesley.
JACOBY, R.
1975 Social Amnesia. Boston: Beacon Press.
JAHODA, M.
1977 Freud and the Dilemmas of Psychology. New York: Basic Books.
KANTER, R.
1972 Commitment and Community. Cambridge: Harvard University Press.
KATZ, J.
1975 "Essences as Moral Identities." American Journal of Sociology 80: 1369–90.
KENISTON, K.
1968 Young Radicals. New York: Harcourt, Brace & World.
KLEIN, G. S.
1976 Psychoanalytic Theory: An Exploration of Essentials. New York: International Universities Press.
LASCH, C.
1977 Haven in a Heartless World. New York: Basic Books
1979 The Culture of Narcissism: American Life in an Age of Diminishing Expectations. New York: W. W. Norton.
LEVINE, D. N.
1978 "Psychoanalysis and Sociology." Ethos 6: 175–85.
LEVINE, R. A.
1973 Culture, Behavior and Personality. Chicago: Adline.
LIPSET, S. M.
1963 Political Man, the Social Bases of Politics. Garden City: Anchor Books, Doubleday.
LOEVINGER, J.
1966 "Three Principles for a Psychoanalytic Psychology." Journal of Abnormal Psychology 71 (6): 432–43.
LOEWENBERG, P.
1971 "The Psychohistorical Origins of the Nazi Youth Cohort." American Historical Review 76 (5): 1457–1502.
LORBER, J., COSER, R. L., ROSSI, A. S., AND CHODOROW, N.
1981 "On the Reproduction of Mothering: a Methodological Debate." Signs: A Journal of Women Culture and Society 6 (3): 482–514.

354   *ADVANCES IN PSYCHOANALYTIC SOCIOLOGY*

MACCOBY, E. E., AND GIBBS, P. K.
1954 "Methods of Child Rearing in Two Social Classes," pp. 380–396 in W. E. Martin, C. B. Stendler (eds.), Rearing in Child Development. New York: Harcourt, Brace.
MAIER, N. R.
1949 Frustration. New York: McGraw-Hill.
MALCOLM, J.
1981 Psychoanalysis: The Impossible Profession. New York: Knopf.
MARKS, S. R.
1977 "Multiple Roles and Role Strain: Some Notes on Human Energy, Time and Commitment." American Sociological Review 42: 921–36.
MELTZER, B. M.
1982 Review Essay. Contemporary Sociology 11: 493–95.
MERTON, R. K.
1938 "Social Theory and Anomie." American Sociological Review 3: 672–82.
1957 Social Theory and Social Structure. New York: Free Press. Rev. ed.
MICHELS, R.
1966 Political Parties. New York: Free Press.
MILLER, D. R., and SWANSON, G. E.
1958 The Changing American Parent. New York: Wiley.
1960 Inner Conflict and Defense. New York: Holt.
MILLS, T.
1964a "Authority and Group Emotion," pp. 94–108 in W. Bennis and G. Schein (eds.), Interpersonal Dynamics. Homewood, Illinois: Dorsey.
1964b Transformation: an Analysis of Learning Groups. Englewood Cliffs, N. J.: Prentice-Hall.
ORLANSKY, H.
1949 Infant Care and Personality. Psychological Bulletin 46: 1–48.
PARK, R. E., AND BURGESS, W. B.
1921 Introduction to the Science of Society. Chicago: University of Chicago Press.
PARSONS, A.
1964 "Is the Oedipus Complex Universal?", "The Jones-Malinowsky Debate Revisited," and "A South Italian Nuclear Complex," in W. Muensterberger and S. Axelrad (eds.), The Psychoanalytic Study of Society 3: 278–328. New York: International Universities Press.
PARSONS, T.
1947 "Certain Primary Sources of Aggression in the Social Structure of the Western World." Psychiatry 10: 167–81.
1953 "The Superego and the Theory of Social Systems," pp.13–19 in T. Parsons and R. F. Bales, and E. A. Shils (eds.), Working Papers in the Theory of Action. New York: Free Press.
1964 Social Structure and Personality. New York: Free Press.
1967 Sociological Theory and Modern Society. New York: Free Press.
PARSONS, T., BALES, R. F., OLDS, M. Z., AND SLATER, P.
1955 Family Socialization and Interaction process. Glencoe, Ill.: Free Press.
PLATT, G. M.
1976 "The Sociological Endeavor and Psychoanalytic Thought." American Quarterly 28 (3): 342–59.
1980 "Thoughts on a Theory of Collection Action: Language, Affect, and Ideology in Revolution," pp. 69–94 in M. Alban (ed.), & Directions in Psychohistory. Lexington, Mass.: Lexington Books.

RABOW, J.
1979 "Psychoanalytic Sociology and Thomas Szasz: Transmogrifier, Traditionalist and Translator." Small Group Behavior 10 (3): 316–22.
RABOW, J.
1981 "Psychoanalysis and Sociology: A Selective Review." Sociol. Soc. Res. 65(2): 117–28.
RABOW, J.
1983 "Psychoanalysis in the Social Sciences." J. Psychohist. 12(1): 34–41.
RABOW, J., BERKMAN, S.L., and KESSLER, R.
1983 "The Culture of Poverty and Learned Helplessness: A Social Psychological Perspective." Sociological Inquiry, Vol. 53(4): 419–34.
RABOW, J., AND ZUCKER, L. G.
1980 Whither sociology. Sociology and Social Research 65 (1): 40. Rabow, J.
1981 "Psychoanalysis and Sociology: A Selective Review." Sociology and Social Research 65 (2): 117–28.
1983 "Psychoanalysis and Social Sciences: a Review." Journal of Psychohistory Vol. 12 (1): 34–41.
REDL, R.
1942 Group Emotion and Leadership. Psychiatry 5: 573–96.
REISS, A. J., JR.
1952 Social Correlates of Psychological Types of Delinquency. American Sociological Review 17 (6): 710–18.
RIEFF, P.
1961 Freud: the Mind of the Moralist. Garden City, New York: Doubleday Anchor Books.
1966 The Triumph of the Therapeutic. New York: Harper & Row.
RUITENBECK, H. M., ED.
1962 Psychoanalysis and Social Science. New York: E. P. Dutton.
SATOW, R.
1981 "Narcissism or Individualism?" Partisan Review 2: 285–88.
SEARS, R. R.
1943 "Survey of Objective Studies of Psychoanalytic Concepts. New York: Social Science Research Council
SEARS, R. R., MACCOBY, E. E., AND LEVIN, H.
1957 .Patterns of Child Rearing. Evanston: Row, Peterson.
SELIGMAN, M.
1975 Helplessness: On Depression, Development and Death. San Francisco: W. H. Freeman.
SENNETT, R.
1977 The Fall of Public Man. New York: Knopf.
SEWELL, W. H.
1961 "Social Class and Childhood Personality." Sociometry 24: 340–56.
SHILS, E.
1965 "Charisma, Order, and Status." American Sociological Review 30: 199–213.
SLATER, P.
1963 "On Social Regression." American Sociological Review 28: 339-64.
1966 Microcosm: Structural, Psychological and Religious Evolution in Groups. New York: Wiley.
SMELSER, N. J.
1962 The Theory of Collective Behavior. New York: Free Press.
1975 Non-psychoanalytic Non-sociology?" Contemporary Psychology 20 (9): 730–31.

SULLOWAY, F. J.
  1970 Freud: Biologist of the Mind. New York: Basic Books.
SWANSON, G. E.
  1961a "Mead and Freud: Their relevance for social psychology." Sociometry 24: 319–39.
  1961b Determinants of the Individual's Defenses Against Inner Conflict: Review and Reformation, in J. C. Glidewell (ed.), Parental Attitudes and Child Behavior. Springfield, Ill.: Charles C. Thomas.
  1965 "The Routinization of Love. Structure and Process in Primary Relations," pp. 162–87 in S. Klausner (ed.), The Quest for Self Control. New York: Free Press.
  1967 "Review of P. Slater, Microcosm." American Journal of Sociology 72 (4): 423–24.
TURKLE, S.
  1978 Psychoanalytic Politics: Freud's French Revolution. New York: Basic Books.
TURNER, R. H.
  1969 The Themes of Contemporary Social Movements. British Journal of Sociology 20 (4): 390:405.
VIDICH, A. J., AND BENSMAN, J.
  1958 Small Town in Mass Society: Class, Power, and Religion in a Rural Community. Princeton: Princeton University Press.
VOGEL, E. F., AND BELL, N.
  1960 "The Emotionally Disturbed Child as the Family Scapegoat, pp. 382–397 in N. W. Bell and E. F. Vogel (eds.), A Modern Introduction to the Family. New York: Free Press.
WALLERSTEIN, R. S., AND SMELSER, N. J.
  1969 "Psychoanalysis and Sociology: Articulations and Applications." International Journal of Psychoanalysis 50: 693–710.
WEINSTEIN, F., AND PLATT, G. M.
  1969 The Wish to Be Free. Berkeley, California: University of California Press.
  1973 Psychoanalytic Sociology. Baltimore: Johns Hopkins University Press.
WOLLHEIM, R.
  1971 Freud. London: Fontana.
  1974 Freud: A Collection of Critical Essays. New York: Anchor Books.
WRONG, D.
  1961 "The Oversocialized Conception of Man in Modern Sociology." American Sociological Review 26: 183–93.

AUTHOR INDEX

SUBJECT INDEX

Gandhi, M., 40, 53, 55, 57–58, 257
Geertz, C.: thick description, 278
Gender, 101–19; development, 108; differences, 122; identity, 102, based on male leadership, 131, based on parenting, 131; oppression, 110; political organization, 207; production of, 108; reproduction of male dominance, 114; role, 107; and science, 304; and sexuality, 108; social organization, 107
Goethe, 91, 97; artist, 94; emotions, 94; emotional expressiveness, 95; hysterical personality, 96; premature ejaculation, 94; scientist, 94, sexual problem, 95
Gramsci, A., 221
Grief, 32, 73; aesthetic distance, 85–86; cycle, 74; definition, 75; effective griefwork, 86; and other emotions, 74; overdistanced, 85; pathological, 74
Guilt, 83
Gujarati, 40

Hahn, R., 92
Hall, S., 8
Hass, C., 92
Herpetology , 307
Hershey, A. D., 301
Heterosexuality, 125
Historians: rationalist, 279–80
History of science: discipline of, 279; Engels, F., 281; Geertz, C., 280; inadequacies of, 279; Marx and Engels, 281; Marx and Marxist, 280; Marx and Weber, 280; Merton, R. K., 282; role theory, 282; social history, 279–98; Turner, V., 280; Weber, M., 282
Hitler, A., 6
Homicide and suicide, 331
Horney, K., 105; penis envy, 127
Human nature: assumptions, 18
Husbands, 130
Hypnosis, 6
Hysteria, 6

Identification, 102; affectionate, 126; aggressive, 19; aggressor, 345, charisma, 263; defense mechanisms, 345; with both parents, with father, with mother, 102; anaclitic, 19; presexual choice, 19; definition, 20; forces: male and female, 20; mechanism, 22
Identity, 53–54; based on male leadership, 131; parenting, 131, in sociology, 55; in social psychology, 55
Ideology, 229

Imperial dominion, 281
Incest taboo: brother-sister, 123; father-daughter, 128; mother-son, 120, 123, 128
Incestuous families, 133; determinants; fathers; fathers and daughters; fathers and sons; mothers, 133
Institutionalization of emotions, 77
Institutionalized helplessness, 44
Integration, 31–100, 313–56; identification, 19
Intelligence: creative, 71; genius: Einstein, Boltzman, 71
Interactional perspective, 159
Iron law of oligarchy, 349

Johnson, M., 101, 139
Johnson, S., 90
Jones, E., 285, 295
Jonestown, 229
Joplin, J., 258
Jung, C. G., 285, 316

Kachin myth, 53
Kekulé, 284
Keller, E. F., 305
King Midas, 317
Klein, G., 284
Kohut, H.: Narcissistic rage, 97; psychology of the self, 97
Kuhn, T. S., 277–78, 284, 286–90

Labeling theory, 159–60, 163–64
Lacan, J., 123
Lakatos, I., 294
Lamarkian preconceptions, 284
Laughter, 89
Lemert, E.: social pathology, 173
Lenin, 221
Levels of reality, 24
Lewis, H.: dynamics of shame, 73; theory of affects, 24
Libidinal diffusion, 339
Liminality, 277, 283
Lorentz, A., 295
Love, 75
Lukacs, G., 221

Mahler, G., 90
Male dominance, 120; definition of heterosexuality, 134; end of, 134; gynocentric, 122; internalization, 128; Oedipus complex, 128; phallocentric, 122; reproduction dominance, 120–37; threatened by mother-son, 128